The Social Dynamics of Pottery Style in the Early Puebloan Southwest

OCCASIONAL PAPERS OF THE CROW CANYON ARCHAEOLOGICAL CENTER

Richard H. Wilshusen, General Editor

CROW CANYON ARCHAEOLOGICAL CENTER

Crow Canyon Archaeological Center is a private, independent, not-for-profit organization committed to excellence in sustained interdisciplinary archaeological research integrated with experiential education programs. The Center seeks to broaden public involvement in, awareness of, and support for the conservation of our cultural heritage and resources, and to increase public knowledge of prehistoric and contemporary Native American cultures.

Crow Canyon Archaeological Center
23390 County Road K
Cortez, Colorado 81321

Telephone: 970-565-8975
FAX: 970-565-4859
Bitnet: alr@csn.org

The Social Dynamics of Pottery Style in the Early Puebloan Southwest

Michelle Hegmon

With a Foreword by Stephen Plog

OCCASIONAL PAPER NO. 5
CROW CANYON ARCHAEOLOGICAL CENTER
Cortez, Colorado
1995

Copyedited by Mary C. Etzkorn
Layout and production of camera-ready copy by Louise M. Schmidlap
The graphics for Table 7.1 and Figures 4.1, 6.1– 6.3, 8.1, and 8.2 by Louise M. Schmidlap;
    Figures 4.2, 4.3, 5.1, 7.1–7.5, and 8.3 by Lisa Snider of Concepts and Images, Durango, Colorado;
    Figures 1.1 and 4.4–4.11 by Lynn L. Udick
Cover illustration by Lynn L. Udick
Printed by Thomson-Shore, Inc., Dexter, Michigan

Distributed by The University of Arizona Press, 1230 N. Park Ave., Suite 102, Tucson, Arizona 85719

An earlier version of Chapter 2 was published in *Annual Review of Anthropology*, under the title
"Archaeological Research on Style," by Michelle Hegmon. Adapted, with permission, from the
Annual Review of Anthropology, Volume 21, ©1992 by Annual Reviews, Inc.

Permission was obtained to quote or paraphrase from the following works:

    "Social Contexts of Style and Information in a Seventh-Century Basketmaker Community," by
    Kelley Ann Hays. Paper presented at the 56th Annual Meeting of the Society for American
    Archaeology. ©1991 by Kelley Ann Hays.

    Archaeological Chronometry: Radiocarbon and Tree-Ring Models and Applications from Black Mesa, by
    Francis E. Smiley and Richard V. N. Ahlstrom. Manuscript ©1994 by Francis E. Smiley and
    Richard V. N. Ahlstrom. Center for Archaeological Investigations Occasional Paper, no. 16.
    Southern Illinois University, Carbondale, in press.

Library of Congress Cataloging-in-Publication Data

Hegmon, Michelle.
      The social dynamics of pottery style in the early Puebloan
    Southwest / Michelle Hegmon ; with a foreword by Stephen Plog.
          p. cm. — (Occasional paper ; no. 5)
      Includes bibliographical references.
      ISBN 0-9624640-7-4 (pbk. : alk. paper)
        1. Pueblo pottery—Themes, motives. 2. Pueblo pottery—
    Classification. 3. Pueblo art. 4. Colorado—Antiquities.
    5. Arizona—Antiquities. I. Title. II. Series: Occasional papers
    of the Crow Canyon Archaeological Center ; no. 5.
    E99.P9H37 1995
    738.3'0979—dc20   95-322
                                                               CIP

To the memory of Irith Irmgard Hegmon,
scientist, soldier, and loving mother.

Contents

1 Introduction   1

2 Style and Its Role in Small-Scale Societies   7

3 Setting Style in its Social Context: Social Dynamics in Horticultural Societies   31

4 Setting Style in its Cultural and Historical Context: Pottery, the Ninth-Century Northern Southwest, and the Study Areas   45

Illustrations

Tables

Foreword

The pottery design of the Pueblo area provides an excellent means of "trait comparison" among the various cultural centers therein. The intricacy of the motifs and arrangements used minimizes the possibility of their independent invention, and there is enough variety in the design of the various cultural centers to allow a statistical treatment of the elements isolated. Such a study, so far almost untouched, could profitably be carried out with already excavated material. Aided by the accurate dating now available on many sites, it should be a peculiarly sensitive means of tracing cultural interchange.

—Beals et al. 1945:89

In the early years of archaeological research in the Southwest, the number of archaeologists was small and the knowledge they had gained about the prehistoric people who had inhabited the region was rudimentary at best. Developing an understanding of Southwestern prehistory and providing the spatial and temporal framework for subsequent research required those pioneering scholars to make constant comparisons of one site with another, one region with another. It was thus not unusual for an archaeologist of the time to know Rio Grande pottery as well as he or she knew Kayenta Anasazi pottery. Only through analyses of broad regions could archaeologists identify patterns of similarities and differences in the development of, and interaction between, the people of different regions.

Through the years, data produced by archaeological studies accumulated, and essential spatial and temporal divisions were established. As a result, Southwestern archaeologists almost by necessity became increasingly specialized in their focus as they tried to describe more fully and understand local sequences of culture change. *Archaeological Studies in Northeast Arizona,* the now classic monograph by Beals, Brainerd, and Smith (Beals et al. 1945) on prehistoric villages from Black Mesa, Tsegi Canyon, and Monument Valley, represents one such effort, and their analysis (primarily done by Brainerd and Smith [Beals et al. 1945:xi]) of decorative patterns on pottery still provides an exemplary model for the careful analysis of ceramic designs.

In subsequent decades, the focus on local sequences was reinforced by ecological perspectives that emphasized the importance of the prehistoric people's adaptation to their immediate environment. Studies of the ubiquitous prehistoric pottery so characteristic of the northern Southwest therefore tended to emphasize collections from individual valleys or small regions (e.g., Longacre 1964b; Tuggle 1970; Washburn 1977), if not single villages (e.g., Clemen 1976; Hill 1970; Longacre 1970), with little concern for the similarities or differences between those collections and the pottery of surrounding regions. This research opened up new possibilities for studying the dynamics of prehistoric culture change in the Southwest at the local level, but at the same time, the broader social and exchange networks in which local groups participated often were neglected. As a result, Beals, Brainerd, and Smiths' vision of detailed statistical studies of pottery designs from different areas that would help elucidate regional interchanges and dynamics remained unrealized.

Fifty years after the publication of *Archaeological Studies in Northeast Arizona*, Michelle Hegmon has fulfilled that vision in her study, *The Social Dynamics of Pottery Style in the Early Puebloan Southwest*. Not only does her examination of ninth-century decorative patterns in the Mesa Verde and Kayenta areas offer broad regional comparisons, but it is also based on the type of analysis that Beals and his colleagues recommended:

> Pottery typology . . . is a simplification of the situation, justified because it facilitates the use of sherds as dating fossils. Properly applied, it permits an objective, statistical treatment of an unwieldy mass of material. But such a system cannot adequately deal with the close analysis of ceramic material, nor with its study from the viewpoint of a historical sequence [Beals et al. 1945:87].

Although Hegmon employs the broader typological categories that have long been recognized for pottery from the Kayenta and Mesa Verde regions, she uses them as analytical categories rather than as ends in themselves. Within these categories she provides a "close analysis" by studying both the structure of design styles (layout, symmetry, and the use of elements or attributes in particular contexts) and the content of decorative patterns (the frequency and diversity of design attributes). Her analysis of both structure and content allows her to exploit all aspects of the ceramic record by considering design information on thousands of broken pieces of pottery, as well as the much smaller number of exquisite whole vessels that tend to attract our attention.

Although Hegmon's study follows and builds upon the analytical tradition defined by Brainerd and Smith, her approach to the interpretation of decorative patterns on pottery breaks new ground by focusing more closely on the social and cultural contexts of style. Over the last few decades, our understanding of the role of style has changed, and archaeologists are increasingly recognizing that "style can fill many roles and convey various meanings" and is "commonly used to mark social identities and express social differences," as Hegmon argues. In particular, style is not simply a reflection of the sociocultural context, but can actively support and modify that context.

By developing this perspective on style, Hegmon answers important questions about the dimensions of stylistic variation as they relate to social dynamics among the people of the northern Southwest during the ninth century. The social contexts of pottery production and use varied across the northern Southwest in the ninth century, and style was accordingly multidimensional, conveying different types of information in the central Mesa Verde region of southwestern Colorado compared with the Black Mesa region of northeastern Arizona. Hegmon's study reinforces and expands upon other analyses that have suggested that localized social networks and stylistic zones and increased stylistic diversity did not develop in central and northern Arizona until the tenth or eleventh centuries, whereas in southern Colorado they developed much earlier, in the ninth century. Hegmon explores how these differences might reflect broader cultural trends in the two regions. Some of the ninth-century inhabitants of the Mesa Verde region aggregated into much larger communities (Vivian 1990:136–146; Wilshusen 1991) and participated in community rituals that encompassed a much greater number of people than was the case on Black Mesa, where small farming villages of a few households, each with their own small ritual structure, were typical.

These different groups used stylistic patterns to convey different types of information, but to understand those patterns, Hegmon shows that we must examine sociocultural patterns at both local and regional scales and must recognize the multidimensional aspects of design variation. Although we still have much to learn about the nature of decorative variation and social relations in the northern Southwest, Hegmon's study makes significant advances in that direction and provides the theoretical and methodological foundation upon which we can base future studies.

STEPHEN PLOG
Professor of Anthropology
Associate Dean, College of Arts and Sciences
University of Virginia

Acknowledgments

A great many individuals and institutions contributed to this research. I gratefully acknowledge their support.

This book is a revised version of my Ph.D. dissertation (Hegmon 1990). The members of my dissertation committee—Henry Wright (chair), Dick Ford, Steve Plog, John Speth, and Bill Farrand, as well as Milford Wolpoff, who graciously sat in at the last minute—contributed to my education in general and to the dissertation in particular. And, importantly to the readers of this book, my committee's comments on the dissertation helped me to improve it for publication in this form.

Bill Lipe, David Braun, and Meg Conkey provided detailed comments on earlier versions of this manuscript. Mary Etzkorn copyedited the text; Debra Stanford and Diana Mosher helped format references; and Louise Schmidlap was in charge of layout and produced the camera-ready copy. The illustrations for the volume were computer-drafted by Louise Schmidlap, Lisa Snider, and Lynn Udick. Lynn Udick also illustrated the cover.

Most of the analyses presented in this volume involved the use of collections or analytical facilities at the Crow Canyon Archaeological Center, the Bureau of Land Management's Anasazi Heritage Center, the Center for Archaeological Investigations at Southern Illinois University (SIU), and the Conservation Analytical Laboratory at the Smithsonian Institution. This research would not have been possible without the help of these institutions and associated individuals. I am particularly grateful to Crow Canyon for providing me with a home away from home at various times during my research. Victoria Atkins, Eric Blinman, Mary Etzkorn, Steve Harmon, Tim Kohler, Ricky Lightfoot, Bill Lipe, Shela McFarlin, Angela Schwab, Margo Surovik-Bohnert, Susan Thomas, Mark Varien, Richard Wilshusen, and Dean Wilson provided advice and assistance in my work with the Crow Canyon and Dolores Archaeological Program materials. At SIU, Kim Smiley made it possible, and usually easy, for me to work with the enormous Black Mesa collections. Finally, at the Smithsonian, Ron Bishop, Jim Blackman, Bill Melson, Emlen Myers, and Hector Neff taught me analytical procedures, helped me to carry them out, and provided guidance in analyzing the results.

The background work for this research was facilitated by a number of institutions. The well-organized files at the Laboratory of Tree-Ring Research were a valuable source of information on sites and dating. I also looked at a number of high-quality collections that I did not ultimately use in the analysis. Still, examination of these collections was part of the research, and I would like to thank the institutions and individuals that facilitated this work: the Arizona State Museum, especially Mike Jacobs; the Field Museum of Natural History; the Maxwell

Museum, especially Kim Trinkaus; the Museum of New Mexico, especially Curt Schaafsma; the Museum of Northern Arizona; the Ute Mountain Ute Tribal Park, especially Art Cuthair; and the Zuni Archaeological Program, especially Roger Anyon and Andrew Fowler.

A number of other individuals contributed to this work in various ways. Mike Adler, Rick Ahlstrom, Jim Allison, Kurt Anchuetz, Lis Bacus, Alex Barker, David Braun, Patty Crown, Andy Darling, Lynn Fisher, Carol Goland, Sue Gregg, Kelley Hays-Gilpin, Karin Jones, Keith Kintigh, Bruce Mannheim, Dawn Massie, Claire McHale Milner, Preston Miracle, Susan Pollock, Alison Rautman, Mike Shott, Carla Sinopoli, Tristine Smart, Kim Smiley, and Pati Wattenmaker acted as sounding boards for my ideas, helped with computer problems, provided references, and/or shared manuscripts, analysis forms, or computer programs. Elizabeth Garrett did part of the petrographic analysis; Ricky Lightfoot and Jack Ellingson helped with the study of igneous rock temper in southwestern Colorado. Jill Morrison helped manage much of the research and accounting through the University of Michigan's Museum of Anthropology.

This research was supported by a number of sources, including the Rackham School of Graduate Studies and the Museum of Anthropology's James B. Griffin Fund at the University of Michigan, the Wenner-Gren Foundation for Anthropological Research, the Sigma Xi Foundation, the Karen S. Greiner Fund of Colorado State University, the Smithsonian Institution, and the Crow Canyon Archaeological Center. I am grateful for all of this support.

Finally, I thank my parents, Irith and Rudolph Hegmon, for everything. For encouraging always, for helping whenever they could, and for their constant faith in me. For as long as I can remember, they have tried to make my life better in many ways.

1

Introduction

For more than a thousand years, people living in the northern part of the American Southwest have been decorating their pottery with beautiful painted designs. This research is motivated by a desire to better understand this practice and to use this understanding to interpret the prehistoric record. How does decoration relate to other social and cultural practices? Why do patterns of variation—that is, the distribution of designs and the degree of design homogeneity or heterogeneity—differ over time and space? Why did people in the past devote so much effort to the elaboration of their things? And can the answers to some of these questions help us understand similar practices in other societies, including our own?

These questions presuppose a basic assumption that underlies this work. That is, I consider material culture—including its elaboration—to be meaningfully constituted and to have a role in society and social relations, a view that has been put forth and developed by numerous researchers in recent years (e.g., Appadurai 1986; Douglas and Isherwood 1979; Hodder 1982b; Miller 1985a). To explore material culture from this perspective, I draw on the concept of *style*, which I define generally as "a way of doing something." This definition of style, and the perspective it affords, draws an important link between material culture in the archaeological record (the objects of study) and the people who created the record (the ultimate subject of anthropology). Thus, a consideration of material-culture style in the archaeological record demands a consideration of the social and cultural contexts of that material. The theoretical perspective used to address these questions of style and material culture is somewhat eclectic in that it draws on concepts and methods developed from both processual and postprocessual archaeologies. Because the two approaches involve very different goals and methods of explanation (for example, prediction vs. interpretation; focus on broadly applicable laws vs. specific context), a complete theoretical synthesis is difficult to conceive (see Earle and Preucel [1987], Preucel [1991], and Watson [1986] for exploration of the two approaches). Still, it should be possible to learn from and use both approaches. In postprocessual terms, I am seeking to understand and interpret certain practices in their cultural context. But I am also concerned with cross-cultural generalizations and the explanation of similarities and differences, issues most often emphasized by processual archaeologists.

My theoretical perspective can probably best be understood by considering both theory and design style at several levels. Trigger (1989:24–25) presents a useful framework in his introduction to *A History of Archaeological Thought*. He suggests that archaeologists seek explanations at three basic levels of generalization. At the broadest level are universal laws about "relations between variables that are assumed to hold true regardless of the temporal period, region of the world, or specific cultures that are being studied" (Trigger 1989:24). Such generalizations are emphasized primarily by American archaeologists working within the positivist tradition, that is, by processual archaeologists (e.g., Binford 1989a; Wobst 1977). At the opposite end of the spectrum are generalizations "specific to an individual culture or to a single group of historically related cultures" (Trigger 1989:25). These culture-specific generalizations are traditionally of concern to classical scholars and are also of great interest to postprocessual archaeologists (e.g., Hodder 1991b; Shanks and Tilley 1987a, 1987b). Trigger (1989:25) argues that, although this second type of generalization is potentially very important regarding culture-specific patterning, "no convincing way has been found to move beyond speculation in interpreting the meaning of such patterning" with only archaeological data. The third type of generalization applies only to certain kinds of societies, such as "societies that share the same or closely related modes of production" (Trigger 1989:24). This third category is a sort of middle ground, relevant to archaeologists of various theoretical persuasions, and I find this middle ground to be the most useful in the present research. Thus, I focus primarily on understanding style in the kinds of societies present in the early Puebloan Southwest, that is, in small-scale, mostly sedentary, horticultural societies.

Perspectives on style and material culture and their interpretation parallel the three kinds of generalizations described by Trigger (1989:24–25). At the broadest level, some have attempted to develop general theories of style and stylistic variation. For example, Wobst (1977) argues that style most often will be used in visible contexts to convey information regarding social identity, in part because style is an *efficient* means of conveying such information. Although the general ideas developed by Wobst (1977) have been of great value, his specific predictions often have not been supported, as is discussed in more detail in Chapter 2. At the most specific level, other researchers have described the meanings conveyed by certain kinds of style or material culture in particular cultures, as when—for example—Hodder (1982b:Chapter 4) discusses how calabash decorations constitute a silent discourse by women, free of the scrutiny of older men. However, such detailed understandings are culture-specific and require information not usually available to archaeologists. A "middle ground" theoretical perspective regarding style has not yet been extensively developed, but it appears to hold great promise. The development of this middle ground, which is the focus of this research, involves attempting to understand style in certain kinds of social and/or cultural contexts. This kind of understanding can be generalized cross-culturally (for example, to societies with similar modes of production), although not necessarily universally.

The explanatory framework used here is similar to that described by Wylie (1982) in her examination of the "Epistemological Issues Raised by a Structuralist Archaeology." She argues that, although interpretations of meaning will be "less than logically certain, . . . [such interpretations] need not be misleading and speculative" (Wylie 1982:43). She emphasizes the importance of context: "The general methodological principle involved is simply that known contexts may be expected to provide guidelines for the reconstruction of mechanisms or conditions that would have been capable of producing a given body of data" (Wylie 1982:43). Archaeological data can be used to examine constructs and models, to select among them, possibly to revise or refine them, and even to reject them.

To understand pottery decoration and style from these perspectives, I compare two areas of the northern Southwest—portions of the Kayenta and Mesa Verde regions (Figure 1.1)—during the later part of the Pueblo I period, that is, the ninth century A.D. An understanding of this period provides the basis for developing arguments about the role of style in its social and cultural contexts. Comparisons between the areas and between different components of the data then provide the basis for evaluating and refining those arguments.

During the Pueblo I period in general, population levels rose across the northern Southwest as people became increasingly sedentary and increasingly reliant on food production. In many parts of the Southwest, the earliest above-ground habitation structures (pueblos) were constructed, and architectural units appear to have become more bounded, such that space associated with one activity or social group was clearly defined or delimited. Also, aggregated settlements, which may represent the earliest villages in the northern Southwest, were established in some areas. Although they had generally similar

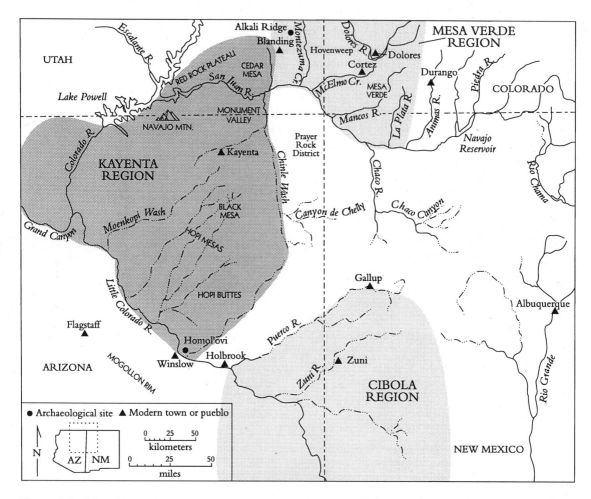

Figure 1.1. *Map of the northern Southwest, showing areas and sites discussed in the text.*

histories of occupation, the Kayenta and Mesa Verde regions had very different patterns of occupation during the ninth century. The scale and complexity of settlements and architecture increased much more dramatically in parts of the Mesa Verde region than in the Kayenta region.

Thus, it appears that during the Pueblo I period in the northern Southwest, particularly during the ninth century, social dynamics changed as people interacted more frequently with larger numbers of others. Furthermore, the changes appear to have been greater in the Mesa Verde region than in the Kayenta region. This research is concerned with understanding style and patterns of stylistic variation in the context of the changing social dynamics in the two study areas. Style can fill many roles and convey various meanings. However, style is commonly used to mark social identities and express social differences, particularly in interactions with large numbers of people.

Specific expectations for stylistic differences and changes are developed and justified in later chapters, particularly in Chapter 4. Broadly speaking, however, stylistic diversity is expected to have increased during the Pueblo I period in general but to have been greater in the Mesa Verde region than in the Kayenta region.

This research focuses on one class of artifacts, specifically, painted black-on-white pottery. This seemingly narrow focus is justified for a number of reasons, which are outlined in detail in the discussion of the database in Chapter 5. The primary reason for this focus is the apparent correlation between changes in style and changes in social dynamics. Before the ninth century, small amounts of black-on-white pottery were present and the same fairly simple designs were shared across most of the northern Southwest. The quantity and elaboration of the black-on-white pottery then increased and regional differences in designs developed during the ninth century. Regional differences are apparent in both the content of designs and the overall pattern of variation. Specifically, highly standardized Kana-a Black-on-white was common across the Kayenta region, while different and much more variable types (including Piedra Black-on-white) were present in the Mesa Verde region. It should be possible to research the similarities and differences in pottery designs—particularly the patterns of design variation—in the context of the developments in the two regions.

The research presented here proceeds from the general to the specific and is motivated by three goals. The first goal is to expand the concept and interpretation of the role of style, a goal which is addressed most directly in Chapter 2. Style is created and used by actors in a social and cultural context, and it can serve to both reinforce and change that context. Some aspects of style may incorporate general symbolic concepts about how the world is organized, and others may serve as indicators of social status. Both aspects are important to the role of style, and these are explored in terms of the various meanings that can be conveyed stylistically. Much of Chapter 2 draws on ethnographic studies, although it concludes by focusing on the dimensions of style that can be studied archaeologically.

The second goal, which builds on the first, is to understand the social and cultural context of style. Given the kinds of meanings that can be conveyed stylistically, how does the role of style relate to the social and cultural context? How and to what extent can conclusions about style be generalized cross-culturally? The context of style is explored in chapters that detail the social (Chapter 3), cultural and historical (Chapter 4), and material (Chapter 6) contexts of pottery style.

The final goal involves the archaeological study of style. The archaeological record offers time depth and comparative perspectives that are not often available in ethnographic studies. Furthermore, variation in material culture constitutes a major portion of the archaeological record, so studies of stylistic variation are broadly relevant to a wide range of inquiries ranging from the construction of time-space systematics to ceramic sociology. Thus, the third goal of this study is to develop approaches to style that can be applied archaeologically.

I argue that expectations regarding the general role of style can be derived archaeologically, given an understanding of the social and cultural context. On the one hand, specific archaeological manifestations of style, such as the kind of design used to decorate certain pots, often cannot be predicted. However, at a more general level, an understanding of the role of style can be used to make predictions about the kinds of variation that might be present and to interpret observed patterns of variation. General discussions of archaeological applications and expectations are developed in the early chapters, particularly Chapters 2, 3, and 4, in which I discuss style, its context in small-scale horticultural societies, and its context in the ninth-century northern Southwest. The database used in the study is described and justified in Chapter 5, and the material context of style with regard to pottery production and distribution is discussed in Chapter 6. The expectations set forth in the earlier chapters are evaluated in Chapters 7 and 8, which focus, respectively, on the structure and content of pottery designs. In Chapter 9, I synthesize the results of the analysis and set them in a broader context.

In summary, this research is motivated by an interest in the elaboration of material culture: Why do people devote so much time and energy to decorating their things? The problem is addressed in terms of the concept of style and its role in social dynamics, specifically in small-scale, horticultural societies. The goal of this research is to contribute to the method and theory of understanding style in general and in the ninth-century American Southwest in particular. Such an understanding will also expand the role of material-culture analysis in other archaeological investigations.

2

Style and Its Role in Small-Scale Societies

The goal of this work is to contribute to the explanation and interpretation of pottery decoration and its patterning during the early Puebloan period in the Southwest. This chapter sets the theoretical groundwork for these pursuits in several ways. I explore the concept of style, how it can be defined and understood, and why it is a useful construct for understanding pottery decoration. I then relate style to other social and cultural practices. Finally, I consider how style may best be approached archaeologically and explain how it will be approached in the case study.

Defining Style

The basic questions guiding this research are phrased in terms of pottery decoration, specifically painted designs. Decoration can be defined in a relatively straightforward manner as the product of "nonessential" operations that do not affect the serviceability of the pot (Rye 1981:3), and designs on pottery are relatively easy to identify and record. Style, on the other hand, is notoriously difficult to define and elusive to identify. So why consider style at all? Why not focus exclusively on decoration? I choose the complicated route because style, at least by some definitions, is a powerful construct that can help us bridge the gap between the material recovered in the archaeological record and the actions of the people who created the material and contributed to the record. Thus, consideration of style puts the study of material culture squarely in the realm of anthropology, that is, the study of human beings.

Although discussion of style in material culture has been a part of archaeology almost from the beginning, only in the past few decades have many archaeologists begun to question and discuss explicitly what style is and how the concept can be used in archaeological research (e.g., Conkey and Hastorf 1990; Gebauer 1987; Hegmon 1992a; S. Plog 1983). Many archaeologists and other anthropologists have recently put forth various definitions of style, have identified several kinds of style, and have developed at least as many techniques of stylistic analysis (e.g., Plog 1990b; Washburn 1983a; Weissner 1983). It sometimes seems as though we have almost as many approaches to style as we have works on the topic.

Underlying all this diversity, however, is a shared belief that style is a bridge between people and material culture. Definitions of style put forth by researchers concerned with widely different theoretical issues are surprisingly similar. For Sackett (1982:63), who primarily emphasizes style in the interpretation of time-space systematics, style is "a highly specific and characteristic *manner of doing something* which by its very nature is peculiar to a specific time and place" (emphasis added here and throughout the remainder of the paragraph). Weissner (1990:107), who is concerned with broad-ranging generalizations regarding style as a form of communication, argues that "style is a form of non-verbal communication through *doing something in a certain way* that conveys information about relative identity." Finally, Hodder (1990:45), who is concerned with interpretations in a specific cultural context, states that "style is *'a way of doing,'* where 'doing' includes the activities of thinking, feeling, being."

A second aspect of style that is emphasized in some, though by no means all, definitions is *choice* between *functionally equivalent* alternatives. In other words, style—in contrast to function—is that component of material variation not determined by technological constraints (Binford 1972:25; Sackett 1973:32). David et al. (1988:365) define style "as an aspect of form either adjunct to that required by utilitarian function or representing a choice, conscious or capable of being raised to the level of consciousness, between equally viable functional alternatives." Dunnell (1978:199) argues that style "denotes those *forms that do not have detectable selective values*"; in contrast, he argues that "*function* is manifest as those *forms that directly affect the Darwinian fitness of the populations in which they occur*" (emphasis in original).

Definitions that emphasize either aspect of style are useful in some respects and open to criticism in others. Defining style as "a way of doing" emphasizes the role of the human who created the material culture. Furthermore, because this aspect of style is part of such diverse definitions, it facilitates a broad approach that draws insights from the various perspectives. On the other hand, "a way of doing" is an extremely broad concept, and it begs the question "a way of doing *what?*" If style is simply a way of doing something, then everything can be style and the definition fails to provide any focus for research.

Definitions that contrast style with function are more restrictive, and thus they delimit, to at least some extent, a range of phenomena to be studied. Such definitions can be difficult to operationalize, however. Considering style in contrast to function is particularly problematic when the style is not adjunct (that is, added decoration) but, rather, involves a choice between functional alternatives, as the lengthy debate over style in chipped-stone artifacts demonstrates (e.g., Binford 1989b; Binford and Binford 1966; Chase 1991; Sackett 1982). A further problem with defining style in contrast to function is that it relegates style to a passive role, of interest only in time-space systematics (see Sackett 1977:369), although David et al. (1988) avoid this pitfall by contrasting style only with *technological* function and going on to explain the social and cultural significance of style.

I hope to avoid some of these problems by picking and choosing what appear to be the most useful parts of these definitions. In a more general treatment (Hegmon 1992a:517–518), I defined style as "a way of doing. . . . that involves a choice." This definition combines parts of both of the above approaches, but it is still quite broad and not easy to apply. Here, instead of relying on a universal definition, I suggest that a more restrictive definition tailored to the specific case is often more useful. Therefore, I define the style of interest in this study to be "a way of decorating pottery with painted designs." By this definition, pottery design style includes techniques of applying designs, as well as design form and variation (for example, layout, symmetry, and the use of specific elements). Although this definition does little to inform researchers concerned with style and function in chipped-stone or other undecorated material, it at least serves to focus this research and may lead to broader insights concerning style.

Defining the style of interest as "a way of decorating pottery with painted designs" delimits a certain object of study in the archaeological record—painted pottery—yet permits us to focus on the ultimate subject of research—the prehistoric people who painted the pots. Furthermore, this definition allows for various levels of focus that may correspond to both traditional and recently expressed archaeological interests. Pottery of a general style (such as the traditionally recognized Lino or Tularosa styles [Carlson 1970; Colton 1953]) may be characteristic of a given time and place and presumably was made by local residents, whether or not those residents were members of a defined social group. Within or crosscutting a general style there may be specific styles that are characteristic of certain social groups or even individuals (Friedrich 1970; Hodder 1982b). In some cases, it may be possible to recognize these specific styles archaeologically (for example, Morris's [1939:177] identification of what appears to be the style of an individual potter; see also Smith [1962]). More often, the identification of specific styles and what, if anything, they symbolize is not possible archaeologically. However, the overall patterning that results from these styles—the degree of diversity or homogeneity—as well as the components of a design style—such as design elements, configurations, and layouts—should be amenable to systematic archaeological analysis.

The overall perspective adopted in this work may help resolve some debates regarding style. On the one hand, Dunnell (1978) contrasts style and function. On the other hand, as is detailed in the following section, in the past 15 years many archaeologists have emphasized that style has a social function or that style has a role in social strategies. A middle ground is taken here. The specific form a style takes (for example, the arrangement of lines and triangles on a pot) often appears to be arbitrary and/or is not amenable to archaeological interpretation (although there are exceptions [e.g., Conkey 1982; Hodder 1982a]). The style may have meaning within a certain cultural context, but its particular form cannot be explained from either a cross-cultural or evolutionary perspective. However, at a broader level, the existence of style, whatever its particular form, can have significance from both evolutionary (Boyd and Richerson 1985, 1987; Braun 1991b, 1995; Meltzer 1981:314) and social (e.g., Binford 1965; Shanks and Tilley 1987b; Weissner 1984, 1989) perspectives. The emphasis here on patterns of stylistic variation is intended to address style at this broader, though not necessarily universal, level.

An Active Approach to Style

In past decades, including during the early years of the "new archaeology," style was believed to have served a passive role in cultural processes and social interaction and was studied primarily as a diagnostic code for *us* to interpret (Shapiro 1953:287; see also Conkey 1990:9). The distribution of styles was analyzed to define time-space systematics and to gain information about prehistoric social groups identified on the basis of those styles (e.g., Colton 1939, 1953; Kidder 1924:343). This approach to style was continued in the early "ceramic sociology" studies, for example, those reported by Hill (1970) and Longacre (1970) (see also Flannery 1976; Lipe and Hegmon 1989:26; S. Plog 1983:126). Although these studies of style resulted in important advances and insights, they continued to treat style in a traditional manner. That is, style was viewed as perhaps *reflecting* subjects of interest, but style itself was not a subject of research.

More recently, archaeologists have attempted to understand style from a more active perspective. Much of the impetus for this perspective, at least in American archaeology, derives from Wobst's (1977) exposition of what has come to be known as the "information-exchange" theory of style. Wobst argued that style functions in cultural systems as an avenue of communication and a means of exchanging information. Although the general idea of style as communication was not previously unknown (Binford 1972:25; Shapiro 1953:304), stylistic communication had rarely been discussed explicitly in archaeology. However, since 1977, treatment of style has changed profoundly, and discussion of information and/or communication has become almost de rigueur in research on style, whether or not Wobst is cited explicitly.

An active perspective on style is obviously attractive in view of current anthropological interest in the concept of practice (Ortner 1984). Unfortunately, an active perspective is often difficult to operationalize archaeologically. Wobst (1977:321) originally defined style as "that part of the formal variability in material culture that can be related to the participation of artifacts in processes of information exchange." The problem with such an approach is identifying *which* parts of formal variability convey information. As a result, all variation in material culture (or at least those aspects analyzed by the archaeologist) is sometimes treated *as if* it were a part of stylistic communication (Conkey 1990:10–11). As Hantman (1983:37) noted, information exchange can easily become a post hoc explanation for all patterns of variation. Too often there is no well-defined link between the subject of research (style as a component of human activity) and the object of study (variation in material culture) (Hegmon 1992a). Fortunately, recent research, as discussed in the remainder of this section, is taking some steps toward resolving this analytical problem, as well as other difficulties inherent in the rigid application of information-exchange theory. At the core of the work presented here is the recognition that there are different perspectives on style and variation, different kinds of style, and various social correlates of style and material-culture variation.

When the information-exchange theory of style was first proposed, it was contrasted with previous approaches that emphasized learning and tradition—what have been dubbed the "learning-interaction" and "normative" theories (Binford 1965; Plog 1980a:115–117). Many researchers, including this author (Hegmon 1986), embraced the information-exchange approach and rejected all other perspectives. As a result, we emphasized only the *use* of style-bearing objects, with little consideration of the production and perpetuation of style. The implicit assumptions behind this work were that style functioned as part of a cultural system and that the style's function somehow explained all production of, and variation in, material culture. Fortunately, recent research has examined and refined various aspects of information-exchange theory and its applications.

Wobst (1977) originally argued that because style is usually a permanent or intrinsic part of material objects, style is a relatively expensive form of communication, compared with spoken language, for example. He further argued that in order to minimize expense and maximize efficiency, style will be used primarily to communicate relatively invariant information to persons who might otherwise not already know the information. Specifically, Wobst (1977:325) predicted that style would be used primarily to communicate information regarding social identity to "socially distant" persons, that is, persons beyond one's immediate family and group of acquaintances. Although the argument makes sense theoretically, in many empirical cases it appears that human material culture is more extravagant than efficient (Weissner 1985:162). Furthermore, this extravagance, or inefficiency, can convey important information as an "index of ability and worth" (Weissner 1985:162). In some contexts, extravagant material—such as Hawaiian feather cloaks (Earle 1990), Kuba brocaded textiles (Vansina 1978:222), or Olmec iconography (Flannery 1968)—serves as an important symbol of power and status (see Jones and Hegmon 1991).

Most researchers seem to agree that the use of style is more complex than would be expected if efficiency were the only consideration. Specifically, at least two of Wobst's points have been disputed. First, although he suggested that "only simple invariate and recurrent messages will normally be transmitted stylistically" (Wobst 1977:323), in many cases it appears that style conveys fairly complex and/or ambiguous information. For example, in the Ucayali Basin of Peru, complex and highly diverse Shipibo-Conibo Quenea designs on pottery and many other media express ethnic and personal identity and also encompass symbolic meanings that are important in ritual and healing (DeBoer 1990; Gebhart-Sayer 1985). The cosmic anaconda snake is the mythic donor of the designs, and the snake combines all conceivable designs in its skin pattern (Gebhart-Sayer 1985:149). Weissner (1990:111) argues that the ambiguity of some stylistic information, rather than being inefficient, may actually be an important strategy in social relations because it leaves "room for the creation of a wide variety of relationships."

Second, Wobst (1977:322–335) suggested that stylistic messages will be most effective in communicating with socially distant people, that is, with those who are close enough that they are likely to encounter and decode a message but not so close that they would already know the message. Therefore, he argued that stylistic information will be found primarily in visible contexts (a similar point had been raised by the Prague School [cf. Bogatyrev 1936]). Although these predictions hold in some cases, a number of studies dispute the importance of visibility and argue that subtle variation may convey important information in close social relations (e.g., David et al. 1988:378; Dietler and Herbich 1989; Hodder 1982b:55; Sterner 1989; see also S. Plog 1983:130–132). In a cross-cultural comparison, Jones and I (Jones and Hegmon 1991) found that the importance of visibility and social distance varies with the kind of information being transmitted stylistically. Specifically, material visible only in private is more likely to convey messages regarding ritual or belief systems, whereas highly visible material often indicates group or ethnic boundaries.

Information-exchange theory was first proposed from a strongly functionalist, systems-theory perspective. Style was considered to be "active" in the sense that it functioned in a cultural system, but little consideration was given to the active role of the people who created and used the style (see Hodder 1991b:64). Recent work, however, explicitly considers the active use of style in individuals' social strategies (e.g., Weissner 1983, 1984, 1989) or considers material culture to be social production that is created and manipulated by social actors (e.g., Miller 1985a; Shanks and Tilley 1987b:98). Thus, the active perspective of style, developed as part of Wobst's (1977) information-exchange theory, has now been broadened to include participating human actors. In this sense, archaeologists' interpretations of style and material culture have paralleled more general anthropological developments with regard to practice and agency (Ortner 1984).

Finally, an important advance in the application of information-exchange theory and the development of an active concept of style is that researchers are increasingly recognizing that information exchange does not explain all aspects of style or variation in material culture. Instead, debates about which theory of style is correct are now commonly replaced by the conclusion that many theories may be applicable, depending on the problem at hand. Kintigh (1985) and J. Hill (1985) explicitly apply both the learning-interaction and information-exchange theories. Kintigh (1985:372), in an analysis of designs on Cibola pottery from northwestern New Mexico, suggests that subtle aspects of design are more likely to be a product of learning, whereas more visually distinct attributes are more likely to have been used in information exchange (see also Voss 1980). J. Hill (1985) proposes an evolutionary framework that combines the two theories in a different way. He argues that a pool of stylistic variation is maintained primarily through processes of learning and interaction. Cultural selection then perpetuates those aspects of style that are useful for information exchange or other purposes. Braun (1995) takes an evolutionary approach similar to Hill's, although

Braun focuses on understanding why certain stylistic practices persist through many generations. At the opposite end of the theoretical spectrum, Hodder (1982c), in what he calls a "reactionary view," reconsiders what might be called a normative view of material culture and emphasizes interpretations within a historical context (see also Hodder 1991b:Chapter 5). Other researchers have recently focused on how style is learned and how material culture is produced (e.g., DeBoer 1990; Gosselain 1992; Dietler and Herbich 1989; Herbich 1987). Very importantly, although many of these researchers do not explicitly draw on information-exchange theory, and some (e.g., Hodder 1982c) specifically eschew the functionalism inherent in the approach, all employ an active view of style and consider its cultural role and/or function (see Miller 1985a:55).

As researchers have increasingly recognized that a single theory may not be sufficient to explain all aspects of style or all facets of material-culture variation, they have also recognized that style is not a unidimensional phenomenon. As a result, in the past few years, a number of scholars have identified various kinds of style, with the understanding that they may co-occur on the same object or at the same event and that they may be applicable in different situations. Important advances recognizing the multidimensional nature of style have been made as a result of the exchange between Sackett (1982, 1985, 1986, 1990; cf. Binford 1989b) and Weissner (1983, 1985, 1990) and have been developed in recent studies by other researchers (e.g., Macdonald 1990; Plog 1990b). Sackett argues that style resides in the choices made by artisans, particularly choices that result in the same functional end. He calls these choices isochrestic variation, *isochrestic* meaning "equivalent in use" (Sackett 1982:72–73, 1990:33). He notes that those choices are learned or socially transmitted, and therefore variation may reflect both social interaction and historical context. Sackett contrasts his isochrestic approach with what he calls the *iconological* approach (used by Weissner and others), which, he says, holds that style, by definition, has as its "primary function the symbolic expression of social information" (Sackett 1985:82).

Weissner views style as being multifaceted. Drawing on Wobst (1977), as well as on a number of social theorists (e.g., Tajfel 1978), she argues that style transmits information about personal and social identity and that identity is developed through comparison of oneself with others (Weissner 1983:256–257). She describes two kinds of style, which convey different kinds of information; both of these would be iconological in Sackett's terms. *Emblemic* style has a distinct referent, that is, it refers to some clearly definable entity or concept such as a social group or status. *Assertive* style lacks such a distinct referent and often carries information about vaguer (or less easily verbalized) notions, often relating to individual identity and expression.

Very significantly, in a series of exchanges and later statements, Sackett (1985, 1986, 1990) and Weissner (1985, 1990) both asserted that several different kinds of style and/or variation may coexist and can be subject to separate analysis. Although he emphasizes isochrestic variation, which bears only a tenuous relationship to active social processes, Sackett does not reject the iconological approach out of hand. Instead, he considers the possibility that, although isochrestic variation is not *necessarily* imbued with social information, it may, under certain circumstances, take on iconographic cultural meanings (Sackett 1985:158). This could occur, for example, when an "unconscious" tradition becomes ethnically significant in times of conflict. Weissner emphasizes iconographic style, although she also recognizes that some components of material culture are best explained as isochrestic variation.

Others have expanded these perspectives and developed archaeological applications. Macdonald (1990) relates Weissner's two kinds of style directly to social behaviors that he calls *protocol* and *panache*. Specifically, he argues that protocol—a "set of social processes . . . aimed at the promotion of group identity" (Macdonald 1990:53)—results in emblemic style, whereas panache—social processes that emphasize the individual—results in assertive style. Franklin (1986, 1989) also considers emblemic style in contrast to what she calls *stochastic* style, which she says varies independently of ethnographic boundaries (Franklin 1986:122).

Plog (1990b), in an elegant application of these recent developments, interprets different patterns of pottery design variation manifested by different traditional Southwestern pottery types as evidence of different kinds of style. He argues that strongly covarying designs on Kana-a Black-on-white are a product of isochrestic variation, whereas increasingly variable designs on later types (Black Mesa and Sosi black-on-white) are probably symbolic—that is, assertive or emblemic style. In addition, Plog suggests that Dogoszhi Black-on-white, which tends to be associated with ceremonial structures and the Chaco regional system and which has strongly covarying designs, may involve a special iconographic style, indicative of some kind of special status.

The delineation and consideration of multiple theories and kinds of style represent an important advance in the development of an active concept of style. Style can be interpreted in terms of its general function or in terms of its role in social strategies. Style can have many roles, including—in the case of isochrestic variation—relatively inactive ones. At one level, style is produced as part of the production of material culture, and style's production can thus be influenced by social interaction. At another level, style can be said to function as part of a social system, that is, as part of a strategy employed by social actors. Our understanding of style is growing, although archaeological applications seem to have lagged behind the development of terminology and general concepts. Much of this work is concerned with developing such applications.

Interpreting Style in its Cultural Context

Central to the operationalization of the concept of style is an understanding of the relationship between material culture and society and/or culture. A tremendous amount of study has been devoted to understanding this relationship, including everything from ethnologists and art historians exploring the aesthetic and cultural principles of art (e.g., Faris 1972:44; Kubler 1962; Jopling 1971; Thompson 1974), to ethnoarchaeologists attempting to discern the material correlates of social groups (e.g., Graves 1985; Stark and Longacre 1993; see also review in Kramer 1985), to studies of modern material culture (e.g., Appadurai 1986; Hodder 1982b; Miller 1985a). This issue is considered here in order to explore how style and patterns of stylistic variation can be interpreted archaeologically.

Production Context: Learning and Interaction

The burgeoning archaeological interest in style in the last several decades was inspired, at least in part, by the ceramic sociology studies of the 1960s (e.g., Deetz 1965; Hill 1970; Longacre 1970; Whallon 1968). A basic premise of these studies was that material similarity is directly related to social interaction and shared production and/or learning contexts, and therefore stylistic similarity can be interpreted as an indication of interaction intensity. Although many of the methods and specific results of these studies have been criticized (e.g., Plog 1978; Stanislawski 1973), the studies inspired a vast amount of profitable research regarding sources of variation in material culture. One topic that has received considerable attention (including work by one of the original "ceramic sociologists" and his students [Longacre, ed. 1991; Graves 1981, 1985]) is the effect of learning and production context on material-culture variation.

Results of various studies suggest that the association between learning and/or production locale and stylistic similarity is variable and dependent on context. In analyses of Kalinga pottery (from the Philippines), Graves (1981, 1985) found only a weak association between work groups and design similarity. Similarly, Friedrich (1970) found that, in most cases, Tarascan pottery design styles (from

Michoacán, Mexico) do not parallel work groups. Among the Shipibo-Conibo, DeBoer (1990:103) found that "learning may lead to similarity or difference depending on the context." That is, a woman generally learns from her mother and adopts some aspects of her mother's style, although she may also develop a very different style either because of differences in talent or because of a deliberate attempt tò distance herself from her mother. At Zuni Pueblo, in western New Mexico, where pottery making is taught in a fairly formal setting (associated with the high school), different styles of design are strongly associated with different teachers (Hardin 1991:55). Finally, Luo potting communities in Kenya have distinctive decorative "microstyles" that appear to be perpetuated by a patrilocal residence system and postmarital socialization of women potters (Dietler and Herbich 1989; Herbich 1987).

The association between learning/production context and stylistic similarity is far from absolute, but important insights can be gained by examining these data from a comparative perspective. Longacre (1991a:8) suggests that the link between learning and material similarity is strong in cases in which instruction is more formalized, as at Zuni. The link between learning context and material similarity also appears to be stronger in cases (including Zuni and the Shipibo-Conibo) in which designs have more specific symbolic content. In addition, the learning/production context may be expressed at one level but not at another. That is, in several cases, including the Luo and the Zuni, producer-groups have distinctive "microstyles," although they conform to a broader stylistic (possibly ethnic) tradition (this possibility was considered by Kintigh [1985]). Finally, in a number of cases, including the Luo, Tarascans, and Kalinga, stylistic distinctions may be understood only by the producers or a limited subset of society (Dietler and Herbich 1989; Friedrich 1970; Longacre 1991b).

Although specific findings of these studies vary, some general conclusions can be drawn. On the one hand, it is clear that style does not simply reflect learning or production context: there is no one-to-one correspondence between style and social interaction. At the same time, there are some cross-cultural regularities, such as Longacre's (1991a) conclusion that formal instruction results in stylistic similarities in the products of potters instructed together. Thus, it appears that, although a simple association between style and social organization is lacking, style can be related to social processes and to the context and the nature of those processes. In other words, a style is not necessarily isomorphic with a social and/or production group; however, in certain social contexts—for example, when learning is formalized—groups of people and sometimes social units are distinguished stylistically.

The Meaning of Style

Anthropologists, as well as art historians and other researchers, have long noted and investigated the meanings of art and material-culture style (Boas 1955; Geertz 1983:94–120; Levi-Strauss 1963:245–273). As can style itself, the meanings conveyed by style can be understood at multiple levels.

In some cases, art and material-culture style convey highly specific meanings, what Boas (1955:12–16) called "significance." Numerous examples are cited in the anthropological literature. Munn (1986) and Gebhart-Sayer (1985) explore the symbolic significance of design iconography among the Walbiri of the Australian desert and the Shipibo-Conibo. Feather designs on Pueblo pottery are equated with prayers or with the placing of prayer sticks, and a gap in a line along the rim of a vessel (also called a life line) is a sign that one's life is not yet complete (Bunzel 1972; Hardin 1983a). In many complex societies, style serves as a symbol of rank or status (Earle 1990; Helms 1987).

In many other cases, however, material-culture style does not appear to convey such highly specific meanings, and what meanings are present cannot be easily verbalized. Many contemporary artists cannot state specifically what their art means; instead, they argue that art is an alternative form of expression:

> *If I could tell you what it means, there would be no point in dancing it.*
>
> —Isadora Duncan (quoted in Bateson [1972:137])

> *If you can talk about it, why paint it?*
>
> —Francis Bacon (quoted in Kimmelman [1989:42])

At one level, this kind of artistic expression can be explained in terms of aesthetics and thus has traditionally been contrasted with art that conveys highly specific meaning (Boas 1955). However, aesthetic and other less specific expression has significance in its cultural context. Such expression is a unique form of communication that provides an alternative to more straightforward verbal media (see McCracken 1988:Chapter 4). Messages conveyed stylistically may be advantageous specifically because of their ambiguity (Weissner 1985:162, 1990:111). Conversely, in the case of status or power symbols, messages may be reinforced by their material expression, such as patina as a verification of long-held status (McCracken 1988:Chapter 2) or the use of precious metals as an indication of wealth.

Miller (1985a) argues that variability in contemporary pottery from central India, including variability in style, is often best interpreted from the perspective of pragmatics, which emphasizes context, rather than semantics, which emphasizes specific meaning.

Following Goffman (1974) and Gombrich (1979), Miller uses the concept of *framing* in his interpretations of pottery. In Goffman's (1974:10) sense, a frame comprises the basic assumptions and structures that allow one to make sense of an event. As a frame, pottery is on the margins of perception; it does not serve as a central focus. This is not to say that pottery is unimportant but, rather, that it is appropriate to, and takes meaning from, its context. Furthermore, as a frame, pottery has an important role in establishing a setting (for example, for ritual) and thus cues people to appropriate behavior.

In many cases, the meaning inherent in art and material-culture style concerns relationships rather than individual concepts. Bateson (1972) describes how a Balinese picture is great, not because it symbolizes one thing, but because it can represent many things and the relationships between them (see also Forge 1973; Layton 1981). The organization and structure of style is essential to conveying such meanings about relationships (Conkey 1982; Washburn 1983b), and style can sometimes be interpreted as a structured sign system (Shanks and Tilley 1987b:98). The meaning of particular attributes can change depending on the relationships between attributes and the context in which the attributes are used. For example, white can symbolize both health and mourning in Mount Hagen (New Guinea) body decoration (Strathern and Strathern 1971). Furthermore, a style may gain meaning only in relation to other styles, such as an ethnic marker that denotes one group *in contrast* to another.

A number of studies demonstrate how the structure of style and/or artistic expression parallels basic societal values and organizational principles. Aesthetics are thus defined in terms of these principles. In west and central Africa, a beautiful figure is one that stands well, relaxed but proud, and thus embodies virtues including respect for the ancestors and links with the divine (Thompson 1974). Anthropologists have noted parallels between social organization and design layout in everything from Indonesian cloth (Adams 1973) to South American face painting (Levi-Strauss 1963). Arnold (1983:71) argues that designs on pottery in Quinua, Peru, "are organized by the same structural principles that organize the environmental and social space in the community."

Although the structure of style may, in some cases, parallel the structure of society, style should not be interpreted merely as a *reflection* of society. Instead, the meaning expressed in material culture often has an active role in social relations. Hodder (1991a) considers how calabash containers and their decorations—which are made and used by women—symbolize structural contrasts between milk and blood, or women and young men. Furthermore, he links these contrasts to the structure of social relations, particularly to dominance by older men, and suggests (see also Hodder 1982b:58–86) that calabash

and spear styles may function as a sort of silent discourse by which
women and young men maintain solidarity and possibly disrupt the
dominance of older men. David et al. (1988) interpret Mafa and
Bulahay pottery decoration in terms of the symbolic parallels between
pots and people, and the basic conclusion of their essay, entitled
"Why Pots are Decorated," is that pots are decorated because pots
are like people. They argue that pottery helps to reinforce social
values: "Designs on pottery, far from being 'mere decoration,' art for
art's sake, or messages consciously emblemic of ethnicity, are low-
technology channels through which society implants its values in
the individual—every day at mealtimes" (David et al. 1988:379).
Braithwaite (1982) argues that decoration on pottery is a form of
symbolic and ritual discourse used primarily in stressful interactions
between men and women.

Style and material culture often convey meanings regarding social
distinctions. Weissner (1983, 1984, 1985, 1989) explores the use of
style for establishing one's identity through comparison. At one level,
social distinctions involve meanings in and of themselves; at another
level, they may incorporate other kinds of meanings. For example,
styles that distinguish ethnic groups also express differences in societal
values. Amish dress (Hostetler 1964) is a case in point. Specifically,
Amish rejection of items (such as buttons and belts) that are reminiscent of military uniforms is clearly linked to their pacifist philosophy,
and it also serves to distinguish them from non-Amish groups. Styles
that have no clear-cut symbolic meaning can also serve to mark
social distinctions if two groups employ or make two different styles;
in such cases, the styles can probably be classified as isochrestic
variation in Sackett's (1982) terms. Stylistic distinctions are particularly important for archaeological application because such distinctions
will be visible archaeologically as some form of stylistic difference,
whether or not more specific meanings can be interpreted.

Weissner (1983, 1984, 1989, 1990) and others (Macdonald 1990;
DeBoer 1990) have discussed the use of style for establishing one's
individual identity, sometimes through artistic expression. At a slightly
broader, though still intrasocietal level, numerous ethnographic studies have documented the association of certain styles with various
social groups, including Maasai (west Africa) age grades (Larick 1985),
Hopi Pueblo political factions (Wyckoff 1990), and Kalinga age cohorts (Graves 1981, 1985). In some cases, the styles appear to be a
conscious expression of identity. Spears carried by young Maasai
men serve as an emblem of their grade and promote solidarity in
their competition with older men (Larick 1985). On Third Mesa,
Hopi conservatives and progressives use different design styles on
their pottery; the conservative style is used in all ritual contexts,
whereas the progressive style is similar to that used on items made

for sale to tourists on First Mesa (Wyckoff 1990). In contrast, among the Kalinga, the association of pottery styles (specifically, the number of bands of decoration) and age cohorts appears to be a product of gradually changing style and conveys no culturally recognized meaning (Graves 1981, 1985).

In many cases, material-culture differences are associated with ethnic differences. The shape or profile of a Kalinga vessel seems "to be actively employed as a marker of important social boundaries . . . at the regional level" (Longacre 1991b:105). In the Baringo district of Kenya, some forms of material culture (including dress and, to some extent, pots and stools) clearly distinguish ethnic and tribal groups, although other forms crosscut ethnic boundaries (Hodder 1979, 1982b). Ethnic groups (including the Shipibo-Conibo) in the Ucayali Basin of Peru have distinct styles that "almost certainly constitute a form of iconologic signaling in which adjacent and competing riverine groups distinguish themselves in a stylistically indelible manner" through tattooing and head-flattening (DeBoer 1990:86). In Guatemala, Reina and Hill (1978) found a link between ceramic and linguistic differences. Washburn (1989; see also Washburn 1983a, 1983b) argues that certain aspects of material culture—what she calls "basic-level features," such as design symmetry—are most likely to display ethnic identity, and she documents these kinds of ethnic distinctions in a number of cases, including among Laotian refugee weavers in New York and Bakuba weavers from Zaire. An important component of many of these studies that associate material culture and ethnicity is the understanding that the association is not automatic, a result of some kind of mental template. Rather, the authors of these studies recognize that style—that is, a way of making or decorating material culture—is an active component of group definition. Furthermore, in several cases researchers have found that differences in material culture are associated with competition and tend to increase as tensions increase (DeBoer 1990; Hodder 1979, 1982b; Longacre 1991b; Osborn 1989; Wobst 1977).

Although this association between material-culture differences and ethnic differences offers encouraging prospects for archaeological application, the association clearly cannot be taken for granted. An entire book (Shennan 1989), as well as other recent research (e.g., Boyd and Richerson 1987; Larick 1991; Mead 1990), has been devoted to understanding the material expression of cultural differences, and the process is complex. Cultural identity and ethnicity are not clear-cut concepts; they are often difficult to define even with ethnographic data (see, for example, Eriksen 1991). A number of authors point to cases in which perceived cultural differences have no material component (DeCorse 1989; Miller 1985a:48) or in which some material distinctions parallel ethnic distinctions while others crosscut them

(Hodder 1982b). In still other cases, material expression of ethnic distinctions, although present, is considered to be a somewhat passive epiphenomenon of other kinds of expression (Larick 1991; see also Sackett 1982).

Despite the potential pitfalls, archaeologists have been quite successful at identifying what appear to be spatially distinct social units in the archaeological record (e.g., Hantman 1983; Hodder 1979; Plog 1980a; Sampson 1988; Wright 1986). Although the absence of archaeologically observable stylistic boundaries is difficult to interpret, the presence of such boundaries can be interpreted, with some confidence, as an indication of social distinctions. Furthermore, change in the distribution of boundaries or the development of style zones can be interpreted in terms of changes in the architectural and symbolic "boundedness" of social units (Hantman 1983; Plog 1980a).

The Role of Style

To this point, in discussing style in material culture, I have compartmentalized many issues (for example, function, meaning, and production) in order to explore each in some depth. But in each case it is clear that an understanding of style must go beyond these issues. Style does have function in society. It conveys information, it promotes solidarity, it creates boundaries, it reinforces cultural values. However, style cannot be explained from a purely functional perspective, nor can its function be understood independent of its meanings. Style does bear some relationship to production, but that relationship is strongly dependent on context and the intentions of the producers, such as rebellion or conformity. Style conveys all sorts of meanings, ranging from aesthetics and cultural values to expressions of individual identity, but the meanings are not necessarily inherent in the style, and they are not independent of context. Instead, meanings—in particular, expressions of social difference—are often created by use and context.

An understanding of the dynamic and multifaceted role of style in society provides a perspective that can begin to integrate these various issues pertaining to function and meaning or society and the individual. Style can fill a functional role, as a means of maintaining social boundaries or expressing social solidarity. At the same time, style can play a role in the social strategies of individual actors, and as such it may reinforce or disrupt social boundaries or expressions of solidarity. The style may be created by those actors, but it is used and given meaning in the larger cultural context, and that meaning becomes a part of its role. Finally, once created, material culture (unlike speech and other forms of nonliterate communication) can exist independent of its maker (see Fletcher 1989; Hodder 1989:70) and its original social context. Thus, stylistic meanings can change as material moves over space (and becomes an import) or persists over time (and becomes an heirloom).

This discussion of the role of style draws to some extent on the terminology of postprocessual archaeology (for example, social production, actors, and context). In this sense, a consideration of the role of style can provide insights on how style, as a form of social production set in a specific historical and cultural context, takes on meanings within that context and is manipulated as part of the social strategy used by conscious actors. However, this perspective does not necessitate the highly specific, somewhat particularistic, approach advocated by some postprocessual archaeologists (e.g., Tilley 1982:32; but see Hodder 1987:516). The perspective can also provide insights into the general kinds of meanings that might be conveyed in certain kinds of cultural contexts (such as elaborate goods and elite symbolism in a ranked society), even if information about the specific meanings conveyed is lacking. Furthermore, the role of style need not be an active one, and that role may change, as when isochrestic variation takes on conscious ethnic significance.

The perspective provided by this understanding of the dynamic role of style can be illustrated with two examples. The first concerns the role of style in maintaining boundaries. Style is produced within a specific historic and cultural context. On a general level, the overall style may be learned as part of the process of socialization and explained simply as "the way we do things." Thus, the practical consciousness (the things actors know about social life [Giddens 1984:xxiii])—including any structures or values expressed through style—is reinforced and reproduced (see also Bourdieu's [1977] concept of habitus). Simultaneously, the producers also create minor variations, and they may use those variations as a form of individual expression or a means of identifying oneself with a subgroup. For example, modern Zuni pottery is a form of individual and learning-group expression, as well as a marker of ethnic identity (Hardin 1983a, 1991).

These roles of style will change, however, if social conditions change and two social groups with distinctive styles come into competition. Style that was produced for no apparent reason or that seemingly expressed only intrasocietal values can come to symbolize the larger group distinctions, and new stylistic production will emphasize those distinctions. Weissner (1985) discusses how isochrestic variation can come to be used actively in social strategies (see also Hodder 1979; Sackett 1985:158). Furthermore, the style not only marks that distinction, but it can come to integrate the groups internally and thus reinforce and perpetuate social distinctions. In this manner, style contributes to social change.

The second example concerns the role of style in the process of emulation, a concept formulated by Veblen (1953) and recently applied in archaeological analyses of hierarchical societies by Miller (1982, 1985b) and Pollock (1983b). In emulation, actors manipulate style or other aspects of material culture as a strategy to gain or maintain their prestige, and these manipulations contribute to the changing meaning of style. Elite individuals acquire a marker (sometimes a new style) that comes to be a symbol of their status. If nonelites obtain the marker, they may gain status. If too many non-elites obtain the marker, it becomes commonplace and loses its value as an elite symbol. Elites then obtain a new status marker, and the process of emulation begins anew. Thus, emulation involves markers, including style, that take on meanings, fulfill roles, and change roles through the manipulation of individual actors, although without changing the basic structure of society.

Archaeological Approaches to Style

This chapter outlines a great many things that style can mean or do. Style is a matter of taste and aesthetics, and style conveys meanings about ethnic identity. Style can play a role in reproducing or changing the existing structure of society. Style is created and manipulated by actors as part of social strategies, and it is also created and given meaning within a cultural and historic context. Style is used to establish group or individual identity, and one stylistic meaning or boundary can crosscut another. The concept of style has a great deal of potential, including the potential to be everything and nothing in archaeological research. One of the goals of this work is to help bring the potential that I believe to be inherent in the concept of style into the practice of archaeological investigation.

I began this book, as is traditional in archaeology and many academic disciplines, by stating my general theoretical perspectives. I attempt to draw from both processual and postprocessual archaeologies and occupy something of a middle ground theoretically. Specifically, I am interested in many of the issues of concern to postprocessualists, such as the interpretation of meaning, an understanding of cultural context, and practice theory (sensu Ortner 1984), which emphasizes the interaction between the individual and society. At the same time, I am interested in making cross-cultural generalizations and developing a method that is as rigorous as possible and/or reasonable.

In part, of course, my theoretical perspective is a matter of personal taste, training, and politics. However, in this case, I have found that my perspective has developed in response to my work with style. In a sense, the nature of my data has strongly influenced my theory. In the remainder of this chapter, I explain this influence as I develop my arguments about how style can be approached from an archaeological viewpoint.

A functional processualist perspective, which emphasizes the generation of universally applicable laws of cultural process and from which Wobst's (1977) information-exchange theory was developed, contributes to an understanding of style. Specifically, this perspective helps archaeologists to understand that style conveys information that can be used in the negotiation of social relationships. However, although functionalism contributes to our general understanding of why style exists in material culture or why it developed in the course of human evolution, it does little to help us understand or predict particular styles or even particular patterns of variation (see Braun 1991b; Hodder 1982b). A consideration of the role (rather than the function) of style leads to an understanding at this more specific level. That is, style can be understood, not only from the perspective of how the society as a whole functions (or fails to function), but also from the perspective of the strategies of individuals or groups who create and manipulate style for their own ends (see Hodder 1982b; Miller 1985a; Shanks and Tilley 1987a, 1987b).

This kind of interpretation implies that the meanings conveyed by style are central to its role. Clearly, an understanding of specific meanings can contribute to an interpretation of the role of style. However, not all style or material culture necessarily incorporates such specific (or easily verbalized) meanings, and our ability to discern highly specific meanings with only archaeological data is limited at best. For a few examples, see Fritz (1987), Gibbs (1987), and Hays (1989).

The absence of highly specific information about the meaning of style does not preclude an understanding of the role of style at a slightly more general level. That is, even though archaeologists cannot determine precisely what everything means, it is often possible to interpret the general range of meanings conveyed by a class of artifacts (Earle 1990:74; Pollock 1983a:359–360). For example, Crown (1990) argues that standardized representational designs on Salado polychrome pottery, prevalent across much of the Southwest in the late prehistoric period, constitute some form of ritual symbolism, and she interprets the role of that symbolism in relatively egalitarian religious practices (possibly associated with the Kachina religion) by considering the contexts in which the pottery is found. Pollock (1983a) interprets redundancy in ceramic designs from the Susiana Plain in Mesopotamia in the context of the development of social complexity and stratification, and she argues that the redundancy relates to vertical social differentiation. Hodder (1982a) suggests that banded designs on Neolithic ceramics and battle axes parallel social divisions (see also Conkey 1982). Braun (1991b) interprets increases and decreases in the amount and diversity of pottery decoration in terms of the role of that decoration in making social distinctions. Trigger (1990b) argues that conspicuous consumption is a universally recognized symbol of power and authority.

These kinds of interpretations of the general range of meanings conveyed by style and material culture and the role of the material in social relations depend on the analysis of various dimensions of material variation. In the studies cited above, analyses of the dimensions of redundancy, material differences, and structural boundaries provide important insights. Focusing on such dimensions of variation facilitates an understanding of style as "a way of doing" and thus emphasizes the human actors who created and used the style. At the same time, these dimensions provide a means of studying style archaeologically. Dimensions of variation can be quantified and/or analyzed systematically and therefore provide a basis for comparison and generalization. That is, although similar patterns of variation do not necessarily involve similar cultural processes, it is possible to compare dimensions of variation in different contexts. When do stylistic differences, or boundaries, coincide with social and/or ethnic differences? Does redundancy consistently play a role in status differentiation?

In almost all cases, an understanding of context is necessary to interpret style—its role and meaning. Even when a style is obviously representational, interpretation of that style does not necessarily follow. For example, interpretation of Venus figurines as symbols of fertility or motherhood or female empowerment demands an understanding of the figurines' context: Who made and used them? Interpretation also seems to be influenced by the gender and political views of archaeologists (see Nelson 1990). Although interpretations of style can be highly particularistic—applicable only to a given cultural-historical setting—a broader, more archaeologically applicable perspective is also possible if context is considered in terms of general social dynamics, such as the negotiation of boundaries or competition for status. Such an understanding of context fits with the analysis of dimensions of stylistic variation and consideration of the general range of meanings (for example, meanings regarding social boundaries or status relations) that are expressed stylistically.

Recent comparative and cross-cultural work enhances prospects for archaeological studies of style. Given similar contexts, style appears to convey similar meanings and/or vary along similar dimensions.

For example, as was discussed earlier in this chapter, when designs convey important symbolic meanings, design traditions appear to remain relatively strong, and members of a learning and production group are likely to produce similar designs. In a cross-cultural study, Jones and I (Jones and Hegmon 1991) found fairly strong correlations between dimensions of material-culture variation, context, and meaning, including an association between highly visible material and messages pertaining to group or ethnic identity and an association between costly or elaborate material and messages pertaining to status.

The perspective afforded by approaches and concepts such as dimensions of style and general social context makes feasible a variety of archaeological applications. It should be possible to make predictions about style in the archaeological record, to interpret archaeologically observable style in a systematic manner, and to support those interpretations with a variety of arguments (e.g., Crown 1990; Hodder 1982a; Pollock 1983a). Unfortunately, because whole classes of style-bearing objects are not preserved archaeologically, in most cases archaeologists are not able to rigorously test or falsify predictions about style. For example, it may be possible to predict that stylistic boundaries will be present in a certain context, then, if boundaries are found, to tentatively support the model used to generate that prediction, although not without acknowledging that the boundaries could have resulted from other processes. However, if boundaries are not found, it is not possible to know whether they were absent prehistorically or whether they were marked by perishable materials that did not survive in the archaeological record. Clearly, preservation and negative evidence are always potential problems in archaeological research, but in the case of style, these problems appear to be particularly acute because predictions may apply only to classes of material that do not preserve.

Despite this conclusion, neither the potential for understanding style archaeologically nor the possibility of developing testable predictions should be rejected outright. Given an understanding of the social and cultural context—derived from various ethnographic and archaeological data—it should be possible to develop expectations regarding the role of style and the kinds of meanings it might convey. Furthermore, given the information that style is manifested on a certain class of well-preserved material (such as painted pottery) and given some understanding of how that material was made and used, it should be possible to develop more specific expectations regarding style and dimensions of stylistic variation. Although such expectations about style cannot be rigorously evaluated in all respects, they can be used to guide the interpretation of style in its various contexts. This kind of approach, combining prediction and interpretation, is used in this research.

Developing the Case Study

I have argued that an interpretation of style requires that the social and cultural context be understood and/or controlled for and that style be considered in terms of various dimensions. To conclude this chapter, I discuss how these needs are met in this research.

Context is considered from several angles and at several levels. First, the analysis involves a comparison of pottery decoration in two regions of the Southwest—the Kayenta and the Mesa Verde—that share many stylistic traditions, in architecture as well as in pottery. During the Basketmaker III period, which preceded the time period of interest here, pottery decoration in the two regions was almost identical and therefore probably carried the same meanings. If this is true, subsequent regional differences in pottery decoration can be interpreted in terms of changing social contexts.

The context of style can also be interpreted in terms of the social and environmental setting of the particular group being studied. An understanding of the social organization and adaptational strategies of the group, as well as an understanding of how the style-bearing objects were made and used, is essential to any interpretation of style. The following chapter considers the social dynamics of early Puebloan societies and provides insights into the kinds of roles that style might have filled. The specific context of pottery production and use is also explored in general in Chapter 4 and in more detail in Chapter 6.

The stylistic analysis considers multiple levels of stylistic variation and stylistic meaning, including information gleaned from traditional typologies (Chapters 4, 5, and 7), analyses of design structure and symmetry (Chapter 7), and analyses of a hierarchy of design elements (Chapter 8). Recent archaeological research has developed this kind of multilevel approach to style (see Hegmon 1992a:530–531).

Analyses of dimensions of stylistic variation and the range of meanings that may be conveyed by that variation also have been developed in previous research, although there has been relatively little explicit discussion of these approaches. The focus here is on two sets of dimensions—dimensions of difference and dimensions of structure—that are particularly applicable to social processes in fairly small scale societies. Both structure and difference relate to the content of a design. *Structure* involves the organization of that content (how the design elements are arranged), whereas *difference* is concerned with variation in the presence and use of various components of designs.

Difference is basic to the existence of style as a way of doing that involves choice, the basis of the general definition used in this research. A choice among alternatives (in this case, alternative ways to decorate a pot) is a matter of style. Difference is also critical to a whole range of stylistic meanings that involves making and marking social distinctions at the individual, group, or ethnic level. Regardless of other meanings that might be conveyed stylistically, the existence of difference is significant and can fill a role in and of itself.

Structure is a system of organization and, like difference, it is essential to the role of style. To define style as a way of doing something—a way of decorating a pot, for example—implies that there is some consistency in that process; a random act does not constitute style. In this sense, structure involves specific rules for how something (a design, a society) is organized. In some cases, the specific structures of designs have been interpreted in relation to the larger social structure (e.g., Conkey 1982; Hodder 1982a), although this kind of relationship does not necessarily hold in all cases. Structure can also be interpreted more generally in terms of how rules are used, and a style can be described as more or less rule-bound (Dondis 1973:128). This aspect of structure—the use of rules—is emphasized in this research. Thus, design structure is considered in terms of more general concepts of social and stylistic constraints.

The dimensions of structure and difference emphasize and encompass different aspects of design variation, but they also overlap in some respects. On the one hand, difference can include differences in structure (for example, banded vs. "all-over" designs). Conversely, stylistic differences (for example, the presence of two kinds of designs) may be part of the overall structure of style. Miller (1985a:36), in his study of contemporary Indian pottery, also focuses on structure and difference, although from a slightly different perspective: "Each stage in the manufacturing process . . . [contributes] its measure of differentiation, by creating a dimension upon which variability, as style, may be structured."

Structure and difference are interesting aspects of style, but they are also important to this research because they are highly amenable to archaeological analysis. Almost all methods of classification involve judgments regarding similarity and difference—in design elements, color, form, and so on. Furthermore, measures of difference such as similarity and diversity coefficients can be used to systematize the analysis of difference and compare various contexts. Various methods have been developed to describe structure (Faris 1972; Glassie 1975; Hodder 1982a, 1982b; Holm 1965; Miller 1985a; Washburn and Crowe 1987; Wright 1981), and many type descriptions include general discussions of design structure (e.g., Beals et al. 1945; Morris 1939). Thus, analyses of structure and difference should provide a means to operationalize some of the general concepts developed in this chapter in archaeological application.

3

Setting Style in its Social Context: Social Dynamics in Horticultural Societies

The basic premise of this work is that the patterning of pottery design style seen in the prehistoric record can be understood in terms of the role of that style in its social and cultural context. This chapter begins to set style in its context in early Puebloan societies by considering the kinds of social dynamics that would have been present in these societies and the possible role of pottery design style in those social dynamics. The focus here is on general social processes. Specific consideration of the archaeological evidence for these processes in the prehistoric northern Southwest is undertaken in the following chapter.

Pueblo I occupations across the northern Southwest were highly diverse, but they shared some characteristics, including dependence on horticulture, above-ground rooms with associated pit structures, and relatively large quantities of black-on-white painted pottery. However, social organization during Pueblo I times is not well understood, and evidence that can be related to social organization is highly variable. In some areas, Pueblo I settlements consist of aggregated villages that may have housed more than 500 people and that have what are interpreted as elaborate ceremonial structures and possible evidence of hierarchical organization (Wilshusen 1991). In other areas, the settlements are much smaller and less elaborate.

In this chapter, I attempt to set style in the general context of Pueblo I societies and to establish a basis for understanding variation in the social forms. To establish the basic social context, I focus on characterizing the mode of production and associated social dynamics of sedentary horticultural societies, and I consider factors that are expected to result in variation in those social dynamics. Finally, I discuss the possible role of style in these contexts.

The Mode of Production

A broad range of social forms—including tribes (Middleton and Tait 1958; Sahlins 1968; Service 1971; Braun and Plog 1982), local groups (Johnson and Earle 1987:101),[1] and other nonstate sedentary or mostly sedentary societies (Feinman and Neitzel 1984; Gregg 1991)—is based on a horticultural mode of production. As are most anthropological efforts at categorization, descriptions of these societies have been strongly contested in the anthropological literature (e.g., Fried 1975a, 1975b; Godelier 1978:70–96). At the same time, classification, as well as critical evaluation of classificatory schemes, is essential to the pursuit of explanations in anthropology (Wolf 1990:587). The goal here is to build on an understanding of the social processes involved in a horticultural mode of production, as well as on descriptions of specific organizational forms, to better understand the general range of social dynamics that might have been present in the early periods of the Puebloan Southwest.

A mode of production includes both the means for making a living (that is, subsistence technologies) and the relationships involved: "Who owns these means, how is production organized, who controls the product and how is it distributed, and who consumes what part of it?" (Leacock and Lee 1982:7; see Ingold [1988:273–276] for further discussion of mode of production in anthropological applications; see also Harris [1983] and Himmelweit [1983] for stricter Marxist definitions). Many textbook accounts of various subsistence strategies (for example, foraging, horticulture, and intensive agriculture) are, in a general sense, descriptions of different modes of production, since these accounts consider social relations, as well as the technologies of hunting, gathering, farming, or herding. Consideration of the mode of production focuses attention on the social relations involved in economic strategies and therefore is especially useful for developing links between archaeological data on subsistence and economic systems, on the one hand, and interpretations of prehistoric social dynamics, on the other. This kind of approach also directs attention toward process rather than static organization and provides a useful focus for understanding culture change.

---

1. Johnson and Earle (1987:101) define local groups as "groups of several hundred people with strong ties of economic and sociopolitical cooperation and exchange."

Here I develop an understanding of a horticultural mode of production primarily by contrasting horticulturalists with foragers (that is, gatherer-hunters with a high degree of residential mobility [Binford 1980]). This approach provides insights into links between food production and social relations. It also allows me to draw on a large body of literature (e.g., Ingold 1983, 1986, 1988; Kelly 1991; Meillassoux 1972, 1973; Woodburn 1982) that includes comparative analyses of certain social forms, as well as discussions of the origins of agriculture, particularly accounts that emphasize the social implications of increasing reliance on food production and sedentism rather than the origins of domestication per se (e.g., Bogucki 1988; Brandt and Clark 1984; Flannery 1972, 1986; Gebauer and Price 1992; Plog 1990a; Stark 1981; see also Eder [1984], Kelly [1992], and Rafferty [1985] for specific discussions of sedentism and its definition).

Egalitarianism and Property Ownership

Most researchers seem to agree that forager, or band-level, societies are strongly egalitarian (Leacock and Lee, eds. 1982; Lee 1988; Woodburn 1982; but see Bender 1990). That is, these societies fit Leacock's (1983:394) definition of primitive communism, which involves "the collective right to basic resources, the absence of hereditary status or authoritarian rule, and the egalitarian relationships that preceded exploitation and economic stratification in human history." Woodburn (1982) argues that equality is asserted in these societies through various social mechanisms that level any emergent differences in wealth or status. For example, successful hunters who share the bounty of a large kill are expected to act with proper humility so that they do not gain status, and the recipients do not lose status, as a result of the sharing (Lee 1969).

Many horticultural societies are classified as "egalitarian" because leadership and status are achieved rather than ascribed (Service 1971). However, egalitarianism in these societies is often much less absolute than in foraging societies because certain individuals can emerge as leaders, have power or authority over others, and may have access to more resources (but see Poyer 1991). In some cases, such as Melanesian big-man societies, relations involve what Woodburn (1982) calls "competitive egalitarianism," in that social institutions—such as ceremonial exchange—involve competitions in which one group or individual gains prestige at the expense of another.

The presence and form of property ownership is a basic difference between foragers and food producers, as well as between foragers and other kinds of gatherer-hunters. Among foragers, the means of production (the wild resources and the land on which the people gather and hunt) are not owned by either individuals or corporate groups, although loosely defined groups may maintain some level of control over certain territories or resources such as water holes. Bender (1990:253; see also Bender 1978) suggests that, for foragers, land is not a means of production but, rather, an object of production (see also Ingold 1983; Meillassoux 1973).

In contrast, private or corporate-group ownership and control of land and/or resources are prevalent among food producers and some sedentary gatherer-hunters (for example, the Yanomamo [Johnson and Earle 1987:114], Western Pueblo societies [Eggan 1950; Forde 1931; but see Whiteley 1985a, 1985b[2]], and the Nata River Basarwa [Hitchcock 1982]). In some cases, clear definition and closure of group membership limit access to resources (Milner 1991; Davenport 1959; Eggan 1955). In cross-cultural research in which he considered 25 sedentary, non-stratified societies (most of which were horticultural), Adler (1990) found that community organization creates and perpetuates land-tenure rights for the community members. People who live in the same place year after year or even generation after generation lay claim to the land. Crop production demands that a patch of land and the labor to work it be controlled, at least through the course of a growing season (see Ingold 1983; Meillassoux 1972, 1973).

Such emphasis on private or corporate-group ownership is not restricted to land. Instead, ownership of produce and material culture is also more prevalent among food producers, as well as among recently settled foragers (Hitchcock 1982:228; Kelly 1991). Sedentary people can and do accumulate and own more things, including everything from the harvest that must last through the winter and provide seed for the next planting, to paraphernalia necessary for fertility rituals, to body ornaments. For the most part, this kind of ownership does not result in permanent wealth inequalities or the use of coercive power, but relations are much less egalitarian than those of foragers. For example, skilled individuals are expected to share the benefits of their skill, but they gain prestige and possibly special privileges for doing so (Johnson and Earle 1987:102; see also Trigger 1990a).

Storage practices also are very different among foragers and horti-culturalists. Some foragers store very little, whereas others accumulate fairly large quantities of goods, although foragers' stores are collective and, from a social perspective, are treated much like wild resources (Ingold 1983). Horticulturalists often accumulate large stores

---

2. Whiteley (1985a, 1985b) has strongly contested classic interpretations of Hopi clans as permanent, corporate, landowning groups. He argues instead that descent groups can be ambiguously defined and open to reinterpretation. However, it appears that some Hopi social groups—primarily lineages, as well as other variously defined units—do establish control over land.

of food; people in many ethnographically known Pueblo societies have stored more than one and sometimes two years' worth of food (Burns 1983; Hough 1897; Cushing 1974). Furthermore, among food producers, storage involves appropriation, such that a single individual or social group establishes control over the distribution of food or other goods (Ingold 1983, 1988). This kind of appropriation—what Ingold calls "social storage"[3]—is often associated with indications of private property, such as marked containers or special storage places.

These basic differences between foragers and food producers concerning the control of property are also important in a growing number of studies regarding the origins of food production (e.g., Bender 1975, 1978, 1990; Hayden 1990, 1992; Kabo 1985). The sharing ethic among foragers appears to preclude the kind of organization—that is, control of land and seed—necessary for food production. For food production to be viable, at least some members of society must break free from these sharing obligations and develop social strategies for generating a surplus and social inequalities. Hayden (1990) argues that competitive feasting or other forms of economic competition could have provided such a strategy by giving ambitious individuals justification for controlling others' labor and resources. Furthermore, he presents convincing archaeological evidence from various areas of the world that supports his model. This kind of perspective on the origins of food production emphasizes the fundamental nature of appropriation and control of property in horticultural economies.

Sharing and Exchange

The difference in ownership and communality involved in the different modes of production is highlighted by considering patterns of sharing and exchange among foragers and horticulturalists. Foragers widely practice generalized reciprocity, which is based on social relationships rather than on expectations of return. Food is given, and the favor may or may not be returned at some time in the future (Sahlins 1972:193–194). A forager who kills a large animal shares the meat with others in camp; however, return obligations are not prescribed, and the hunter can only expect that the next big kill by someone else will also be shared. Foragers' social relations, including

---

3. Ingold's (1983, 1988) use of the term social storage is very different than O'Shea's (1981). By social storage, O'Shea (1981:169) refers to the exchange of food "for some non-food token with at least the implicit understanding that such tokens can later be re-exchanged for food." I adopt Ingold's usage here.

sharing and exchange, are structured; !Kung *hxaro* exchange partners are expected to share information and access to resources (Weissner 1982b). However, foragers do not keep accounts of food sharing (Leacock and Lee 1982:8). Their relationships "stress sharing and mutuality but do not involve long-term binding commitments and dependencies" (Woodburn 1982:434). Generalized reciprocity is also practiced among more sedentary peoples, including food producers, but to a more limited extent. Among the more permanent Nunamiut hunter-gatherer local groups, sharing is obligatory within a hamlet, but the ownership of food is carefully noted (Johnson and Earle 1987:135). In sedentary societies, sharing with people other than close relatives entails obligations to return, and failure to meet those obligations may result in social stigma or "rubbish-man" status (Burridge 1975, cited in Woodburn 1982:448).

The extent of sharing, or the sharing radius, takes on different scales in foraging and sedentary societies, as Kelly (1991) demonstrates. Foragers practice "total sharing" with whoever is in camp; that is, not everything is put into a common pot, but "no one goes hungry if there is food in camp" (Leacock and Lee 1982:8). In more long-term settlements, which are often much larger than foragers' camps, there are "more definite sectoral breaks in the social structure" (Sahlins 1972:228), and sharing is restricted. In sedentary societies, spheres of social relationships determine spheres of sharing: Generalized reciprocity may be practiced with close kin; other social relationships entail more defined and balanced sharing obligations; and beyond a certain point sharing is not obligatory (Connelly 1979).

Two explanations may be offered for these differences in sharing practices. First, general materialist considerations provide some insights. Because it is practical for them to own more than they can carry, sedentary people can accumulate more things, including stores of produce. Different patterns of resource acquisition also help to explain the differences in sharing, storage, and consumption. Foragers get an almost immediate return on their labor because a hunting or gathering trip lasts a few hours or a few days, and foragers often do not invest heavily in elaborate facilities or processing (Meillassoux 1972, 1973; Woodburn 1982; cf. Ingold 1983). For sedentary horticulturalists, the return on labor is both more delayed (at least for the length of a growing season) and more concentrated (often in a short harvest season). Thus, very generally, foragers obtain relatively small quantities of resources almost every few days and consume them almost immediately. Sedentary horticulturalists harvest large quantities once or a few times a year and store their resources for gradual use until the next harvest. Therefore, a horticulturalist has much more to lose and can be expected to define sharing obligations and their extent very carefully (see Cohen 1989:23).

Second, recent analyses of subsistence risk in various kinds of small-scale economies indicate that, although foragers may be able to reduce risk by pooling their resources and/or sharing widely, such a strategy is less beneficial for food producers or other kinds of gatherer-hunters. In simulation studies of a horticultural economy, I used data on Hopi crop production to study the effects of various strategies of food distribution (Hegmon 1989a, 1991b, 1992b). I found that independent households, which stored their surplus and did not share with other households, had a 45 percent chance of surviving over a 20-year period. Surprisingly, chances of survival decreased when households pooled their resources; the survival rate among groups composed of five pooling households was only about 12 percent. In many cases, households that failed to produce apparently pulled down entire groups and caused them to fail. Survival rates increased only when households restricted their sharing, that is, when they first consumed what they needed and then shared (rather than stored) any surplus. More than 90 percent of groups consisting of 10 or more households that followed this strategy of restricted sharing survived for 20 years. These results indicate that, although sharing may reduce risk, it can also be a substantial source of risk in a horticultural economy.

Other researchers have reached similar conclusions regarding risk and food production. Winterhalder (1990), in an examination of risk-reduction mechanisms among foragers and food producers, concludes that sharing is much more effective for foragers, whereas farmers can best reduce risk with storage and/or scattered fields. Kohler and Van West (1992) also conclude that sharing is not always the best strategy for food producers. In a study based on models that assess the utility of various strategies of storage and sharing, they found that sharing is beneficial only when productivity is relatively high (and when spatial and temporal variability are also high). In addition, a number of researchers concerned primarily with gatherer-hunters argue that pooling, although beneficial to foragers, is probably not a good strategy for other kinds of gatherer-hunters or for food producers (e.g., Weissner 1982a; Cashdan 1985). In contrast, Braun and Plog (1982) argue that regional tribal social networks may develop in response to the risks associated with food production, although they do not emphasize sharing as a major component of those networks.

Social Organization and Scale

Many classic accounts of tribes, including those that describe horticultural tribes, emphasize the relatively formal social groupings and ties that are characteristic of such societies (cf. Service 1971;

Sahlins 1968). The all-encompassing bands-tribes-chiefdoms-states typology and the explanatory or predictive framework it implies are no longer widely accepted and will not be used here. However, the descriptive material, especially that emphasizing the segmentary nature of what are classified as tribal societies, continues to receive at least some degree of both theoretical and empirical support (e.g., Braun 1991a; Braun and Plog 1982; Feinman and Neitzel 1984; Johnson and Earle 1987; Johnson 1982).

The segmentary nature of society and the presence of relatively formalized social groups among food producers can be understood by considering the social demands involved in their subsistence strategies, the basis of the mode of production in this type of society. Meillassoux (1972, 1973), in comparisons of foraging and farming economies, argues that farming involves more time and more continuity and thus requires more long-term and stable social bonds (see also Ingold 1983). In particular, farmers are dependent on the production, and therefore the farmers, of the past to provide seed for planting and to sustain them between planting and harvest times. "The duration of the productive process and the delayed acquisition of the product lead to a prolonged and continuous cooperation in carrying out productive activities" (Meillassoux 1973:198). As a result, in food-producing societies, kinship bonds, including descent groups and ties to the ancestors, are particularly important.

This understanding of economic relations highlights the importance of the control of property—whether land or produce or ritual paraphernalia—in horticultural economies. Such control does not necessarily imply individual ownership or permanent economic inequality, since control may be in the hands of a corporate and/or descent group and real economic differences may be equalized over time, as well as by leveling mechanisms. However, the control of property still has important implications for understanding the dynamics of early Puebloan societies. Specifically, such control implies social segmentation at many levels, including among individuals who no longer share freely with all others and among corporate groups that control different resources. The social segmentation noted in descriptions of tribal societies can be understood from this perspective.

Finally, social segmentation can also be understood through consideration of decision making and integration. In sedentary communities, regardless of their subsistence strategy, people live and work together or in proximity over extended periods. Therefore, the effective scale of these communities is generally greater than that of foragers. Whereas foragers can sometimes resolve disagreements simply by moving away (Lee and DeVore 1968:9; although see Silberbauer [1982:33] for a discussion of the serious implications of this strategy), such fission is a much more drastic step for members of sedentary communities with investments in architecture, fields, and other facilities (see Whiteley 1988).

The organizational complexity of horticulturalists or other sedentary societies can be related to the increased scale and permanence of such communities, as social scientists have long noted (e.g., Berreman 1978; Carneiro 1967; Naroll 1956). However, the measurement of scale and its relationship to social organization is highly complex. For example, in their cross-cultural study, Feinman and Neitzel (1984) found a strong correlation between total population size and number of administrative levels but only a weak relationship between population size and degree of status differentiation (see summary in Drennan 1987:310–311). Upham (1987), using different analytical procedures to manipulate Feinman and Neitzel's (1984) data, found stronger relationships between variables of scale and social organization, although he also found that not all measures of scale are directly related to measures of social complexity.

Despite the absence of consistent correlations between population size and different measures of social complexity, studies of the relationship between scale and complexity have identified some important thresholds. Kosse (1992) found that complex, regionally organized polities are present when polity population size is greater than 2,500 to 3,000. She notes that in only a few instances (for example, Casas Grandes and the Chaco regional system, including outliers) did the size of organizations in the prehistoric Southwest exceed this level.[4] Upham (1987, 1990) argues, on the basis of his analyses of Feinman and Neitzel's (1984) data, that political complexity is statistically more likely to occur when the total regional population is greater than 10,500. He also argues that population density, not simply total size, is important in understanding complexity. In other studies (Naroll 1956:690; Foster 1960:178), researchers have observed that some form of coercion or strong authority is associated with settlements that have populations greater than 1,500.

Johnson's (1982) discussion of scalar stress is particularly useful for understanding the apparent link between scale and organizational complexity among horticulturalists and in other relatively small scale societies. He notes that in groups consisting of more than six individuals or units, the group experiences scalar stress, which he

---

4. Kosse (1992) does not discuss any Pueblo I cases, although it is doubtful that any social group reached her 3,000-person threshold during the Pueblo I period. The peak population for the Dolores River valley in the ninth century A.D. is estimated by Wilshusen (1991:496) to have been 2,778 and by Schlanger (1987:601) to have been 1,613, but there is no evidence to suggest that there was a unified polity in the valley.

relates to humans' limited ability to process information. Groups experiencing scalar stress evidence "decreasing consensus in decision making and decreasing member satisfaction with group performance" (Johnson 1982:393). The development of some sort of hierarchical organization, in which the number of decision-making units is reduced, is thus seen as a response to scalar stress. However, hierarchical organization need not involve vertical differentiation. Instead, Johnson (1982) suggests that scalar stress can also be reduced with what he calls "sequential hierarchies," in which the size of the basal decision-making unit is increased. He considers the !Kung San and demonstrates how variation in the size of their organizational units (for example, individual adults, nuclear families, or extended families) can be related to scale (that is, camp size).

The segmentary organization present in many horticultural societies can therefore be understood as a means of increasing the size of decision-making units and decreasing scalar stress. Johnson (1982:403–404) suggests that New Guinea clans represent a kind of sequential hierarchy, and he notes that the number of clans per political unit shows little variability. Braun (1991a:435–436) argues that sequential hierarchies constitute a well-explained cross-cultural regularity in tribal societies:

> [A sequential hierarchy] consists of a nesting of patterns of interaction and decision making, so that people interact as members of nested categories of social identity . . . [or] of culturally defined groups. . . . Above the household level, these groups consist of descent groups, sodalities, totemic societies, ritual societies, barrios, entire settlements, clusters of settlements, and so forth [Braun 1991a:435].

Group Ritual

Most humans practice some form of ritual, which can be defined as a relatively invariant and formal sequence of actions that is established by tradition (Rappaport 1979). However, group ritual, often called ceremonialism, appears to be associated primarily with certain kinds of societies, including societies with a horticultural mode of production. Johnson and Earle (1987) argue that ceremonialism is "pervasive" among local groups (a category that includes sedentary, fairly large scale, horticultural societies such as the Tsembaga Maring and the Central Enga of the New Guinea highlands), whereas smaller-scale, family-level groups have fewer public ceremonies (see also Drennan 1976, 1983). Among more mobile societies, group ritual appears to be associated primarily with times of fairly large scale aggregation (Gross 1979; Lee 1979). Furthermore, among small-scale, nonstratified ("tribal") societies, the presence of structures used primarily or exclusively for ritual is associated with larger communities, that is, those with an average of about 250 members or more (Adler and Wilshusen 1990).

A vast literature makes clear that ritual can be understood or interpreted from a variety of perspectives in anthropology, ranging from the symbolic and structural (e.g., Turner 1969; Ortner 1978) to the functional (e.g., Rappaport 1984). The emphasis here is on understanding ritual—primarily group ritual, or ceremonialism—in the context of the social dynamics of horticultural societies.

At least since the work of Durkheim (1968), anthropologists and other social scientists have understood that ritual can serve to integrate social groups (e.g., Turner 1969; Wallace 1966). Ritual involves shared transcendent or numinous experiences and therefore can reinforce cultural norms, promote social solidarity, and generally reduce social conflict. More specifically, in societies with some sort of segmental organization, ritual can reinforce the definition of social groups and social obligations. "The cultural assertion that the world is shaped in this way and not in some other has to be repeated and enacted [ritually] lest it be questioned and denied" (Wolf 1990:593). Among the Tsembaga Maring, land rights are defined in terms of multifamily units—including clans and residential local groups—and ceremonies serve to "symbolize and unite these larger groups" (Johnson and Earle 1987:139; see Rappaport 1984).

Recent research has considered more specifically how and why ritual fills the role of uniting and defining social groups. Rappaport (1971a, 1971b, 1979, 1984) argues that ritual is, among other things, a form of communication. Thus, religious rituals endow the messages communicated with a degree of sanctity, which in turn increases the likelihood that the information will be imparted truthfully and acted upon in a predictable and orderly fashion (Rappaport 1971a:72). In this manner, ritual serves to sanctify and promote the acceptance of important decisions (such as the establishment of an alliance).

Ceremonial activity is often dependent on scale, and for a number of reasons it can be interpreted as a means of reducing scalar stress (Johnson 1982:405–406). By uniting an aggregate of people or defining social groups, the integrative aspects of ritual facilitate an organization with large basal units. Ritual can also reduce the scalar stress associated with decision making because it communicates and sanctifies relevant information and reinforces decisions.

Finally, ritual is also a means of regulating sharing, which, as discussed above, can be problematic in horticultural societies. Ritual both reinforces the social relationships that structure sharing and provides a context for the sharing itself. Rituals often involve the distribution or redistribution of food (e.g., Heinen and Ruddle 1974), and among many gatherer-hunters, the distribution of large game is ritually, or at least formally, prescribed (Gould 1967). Specially valued foods—such as pigs in the New Guinea Highlands or cattle among the Nuer—are eaten primarily on ritual occasions (Evans-Pritchard 1940; Rappaport 1984). In his study of the Eastern Pueblos, Ford (1972) found that periodic rituals tend to occur during the relatively lean months and thus promote sharing at particularly critical times.

The Social Dynamics of Style

Style has an important role in the social dynamics of small-scale, horticultural societies in a number of ways. The role of style can be understood in terms of the social strategies of individuals who use style to establish and maintain their identities. Both dimensions of style—structure and difference—are relevant in this respect. Style as difference can have a particularly important role in making and marking social distinctions. Weissner (1983, 1984, 1985, 1989) argues that style is universally used to establish social identity through comparison. Probably the most pervasive use of style, particularly stylistic differences, is the definition of social relationships. By expressing individuals' characteristics—including taste, status, and group affiliation—style may identify them as being like or unlike other individuals and thereby can unite or distinguish social groups.

The role of the structural dimension of style is less straightforward and more difficult to predict, although some general expectations can be developed. A relationship between the structure of designs and social or cultural concepts has been demonstrated in a number of cases (e.g., Adams 1973; Arnold 1983; David et al. 1988), but such specific interpretations are often not possible archaeologically. Instead, the structure of style can be considered, from a less specific perspective, in terms of the rules that compose the structure. Conformity, or lack of conformity, to the structural rules can then be interpreted in relation to the social setting. That is, in cases in which group definition or signification of group membership is particularly important, the structural rules might be emphasized and followed relatively closely. Similarly, in formalized ritual contexts, design style might also be more formalized.

Style in material culture conveys information in a relatively expensive and permanent medium (see Wobst 1977). Thus, style adds significance to the information it conveys and helps to maintain social relationships. People do not simply claim to be members of a group—their membership is demonstrated materially by the style they display and by their conformity to stylistic rules. Differences between groups are reinforced and perpetuated because they are given material expression through style. Furthermore, as a nonverbal medium, style is able to convey meanings, both subtle and obvious, that cannot readily be conveyed with words.

Style is an important means of conveying messages to those who already know the information, as well as to those for whom the information is new. For those who already know the information, style serves as a constant reminder: This person is no longer a boy, he is now a man (see David et al. 1988). But when larger numbers of people are involved, relevant social information cannot be known by everyone, and stylistic communication becomes particularly important. Both theoretical arguments (Wobst 1977) and empirical evidence (Jones and Hegmon 1991) suggest that the use of style to express one's social identity will be most important in interactions with relative strangers and that such style will tend to be conveyed on visible objects. Thus, style plays an important role in large-scale interactions involving many socially distant people. Style can express information about social relations strongly, silently, and often immediately. As a visible but nonverbal medium, style can define individuals, groups, and their intentions before any words are spoken or other actions taken, and thus it sets the stage for further interaction. Also, because of its permanence, style in material culture adds emphasis to these definitions and declarations of intent. As a result, style serves to make these interactions more predictable and therefore to ease some social tensions in the interactions of large numbers of people (Schortman 1989); this is part of style's role as a frame for social contexts (Goffman 1974; Miller 1985a).

Style is important, not only in the interaction of large numbers of people, but also in the integration of those people into cooperating social groups. Certain aspects of style may symbolize and thus reinforce the values of a group (David et al. 1988). Stylistic differences can promote group unity through contrasts with other groups. And style can simply be a shared way of doing things and a shared set of rules that reinforces unity without conveying any more specific meanings.

Among San foragers in the Kalahari desert of southern Africa, Weissner (1983) found that group membership was expressed stylistically only at the level of the language group. The language group is the level at which the San pool risk, since access to resources is generally shared within this group. In this case, style is important as an expression of intragroup cooperation, regardless of relations with other groups. In other cases, primarily involving more sedentary societies, the role of style in distinguishing groups seems to gain importance. Hodder (1979, 1982b) found that stylistic distinctions between groups became more pronounced in times of economic stress, and Braun and Plog (1982) argue that the development of relatively bounded zones of style is associated with increases in risk (see also Sampson

1988; Wobst 1977). In these cases, style as a shared way of doing things may come to emphasize differences and competition between groups.

The relationship between stylistic distinctions and resource stress or competition suggests that style plays a role in defining access to resources, a particularly important matter among some sedentary horticulturalists. Although sharing is more restricted among horticulturalists than among the San, the principle of pooled risk may apply at a different level. That is, style zones may define an area over which a farmer may travel to collect resources or perhaps relocate (see Hantman 1983). Style can also help to establish and reinforce exchange relationships and thus contribute to another means of controlling resources. For example, in the New Guinea Highlands, clans and big-man groups, which are stylistically distinct in at least some contexts, have direct control over land and other facilities (Layton 1981; Strathern and Strathern 1971).

Ritual is an important strategy in sedentary horticultural societies, and style can play a role in ritual in several ways. In many cases, styles associated with ritual are somehow distinctive (made of special materials, noticeably fancy, or starkly plain). Ritual styles also sometimes include particular motifs that convey meanings relevant to the content of the ritual, such as the water motifs on Zuni ceremonial bowls (Bunzel 1972; Hardin 1983a). In this manner, style helps to create the ritual context and contributes to the ritual itself.

Finally, the structure of style may have important parallels to the structure of ritual. Rituals involve formalized and invariant actions—they "tend to be stylized, repetitive, stereotyped" (Rappaport 1979:175). These properties apply to paraphernalia involved in the ritual, as well as to the ritual actions themselves. For style to fit into and contribute to this context, it may also need to be formalized, with a strongly rule-bound structure.

Thus, style can fill various roles in the dynamics of small-scale, horticultural societies, particularly in the definition of social groups. Furthermore, the use of style is expected to vary as the social dynamics of these societies vary. At this general level, the role of style is predictable, at least to some extent. In the analyses that form the core of this work, I compare the remains of prehistoric societies that appear to have had different social dynamics. At a general level, the roles of style in those societies can be predicted, and observed patterns of stylistic variation are interpreted from this perspective.

4

Setting Style in its Cultural and Historical Context: Pottery, the Ninth–Century Northern Southwest, and the Study Areas

Decorated artifacts, including painted pottery, were present in the northern Southwest long before the ninth century A.D. (the late Pueblo I period). However, during the ninth century, as the size and complexity of settlements increased in some areas, pottery decoration became more elaborate and, for the first time, exhibited regional variation. The co-occurrence of changes in settlement and architecture and changes in pottery style suggests that style took on new roles during the ninth century. Furthermore, the regional variation suggests that style may have filled different roles in different areas. This work is concerned with interpreting pottery design style from this perspective.

The previous chapter examined the kinds of social dynamics that are associated with horticultural societies and thus set style in a general social context. This chapter establishes a more specific context for style in the prehistoric northern Southwest by reviewing general cultural developments, including those related to pottery manufacture, before and during the early Puebloan period. The study areas and time frame considered in this research are then described in detail. The chapter concludes with a discussion of the kinds of patterns of stylistic variation that are expected to be associated with these areas.

The Development of Early Pueblos in the Northern Southwest

Early Puebloan occupations in the northern Southwest, and the painted pottery associated with those occupations, can in part be understood through comparisons with what came before, that is, with Basketmaker III settlements. The Basketmaker III period dates from about A.D. 500 to 700 (Figure 4.1), and an important hallmark of this period is the first widespread appearance of pottery in the northern Southwest (Kidder and Guernsey 1919; Eddy 1966). Thus, it is appropriate to begin a review of culture history with this early pottery-making period.

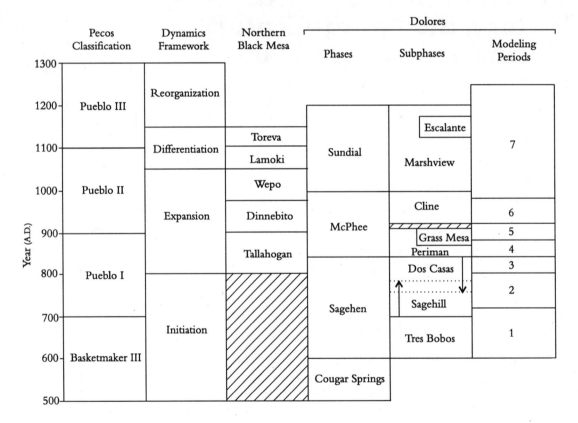

Figure 4.1. *Chronological classifications used in the northern Southwest. The Pecos Classification is after Lipe (1978:345); the Dynamics Framework is after Cordell and Gumerman (1989); the Northern Black Mesa sequence is after Nichols and Smiley (1984); the Dolores phases and subphases are after Kane (1986a:363–398); and the Dolores modeling periods are after Breternitz et al. (1986:16, Figure 2.1). The chronological subdivisions that are most relevant to this study are the Tallahogan phase (A.D. 800–900) of the Northern Black Mesa sequence; the Dos Casas (A.D. 760–840), Periman (A.D. 840–910), and Grass Mesa (A.D. 870–910) subphases defined by Dolores researchers; and Modeling Periods 3 (A.D. 800–840), 4 (A.D. 840–880), and 5 (A.D. 880–920), also used at Dolores. Shaded cells indicate occupational hiatuses.*

Basketmaker III sites generally consist of clusters of substantial sub-terranean pithouses with external storage structures. Both the location of Basketmaker III sites—near deep, well-watered soils—and the types of plant remains recovered archaeologically indicate that Basketmaker III subsistence was based on the cultivation of corn, beans, and squash, as well as on the gathering and hunting of wild foods.

The site of Shabik'eshchee in Chaco Canyon (Roberts 1929), which was occupied between about A.D. 500 and 750, is one of the best known Basketmaker III sites. It has at least 18 Basketmaker III pithouses, a large structure interpreted as a great kiva, and numerous other structures and features, including storage cists and pits. In a recent reanalysis, Wills and Windes (1989; see also Wills 1991, 1992) argue convincingly that the many Basketmaker III structures are the result of periodic reuse of the site, and they believe that some structures may have been dismantled to obtain construction materials for new houses. The number of structures in use at any one time cannot be determined precisely, but it is clear from both Roberts's (1929) original work and Wills and Windes' (1989) reanalysis that not all structures were used simultaneously and the site does not represent a single large village community. Wills and Windes (1989) argue that Shabik'eshchee was formed by the episodic aggregation of local groups who may not have lived at the site year round. Furthermore, they argue that the external storage facilities were used for caching food and possibly other materials in a relatively "public" space and thus suggest some degree of communal storage and sharing (in addition to private storage in pits inside the pithouses). Wills (1991, 1992) argues that the architecture at Shabik'eshchee is consistent with a communal mode of production in which sharing is emphasized and surplus production discouraged.

Although a well-known case, Shabik'eshchee is fairly atypical of Basketmaker III sites across the northern Southwest. Some similarly large clusters of Basketmaker III pithouses and other features, including possible great kivas, are known (for example, Broken Flute Cave, in the Prayer Rock district of northeastern Arizona [Morris 1980]; Juniper Cove, in the Kayenta region [Vivian and Reiter 1965]; Sambrito Village, in the Navajo Reservoir area [Eddy 1966]; the Cerro Colorado site, in west-central New Mexico [Bullard 1962]; and the Yellow Jacket site, in southwestern Colorado [Wheat 1955]). However, most Basketmaker III sites are small, consisting of one or two pithouses and associated features. At least 163 Basketmaker III habitation sites (including Shabik'eshchee) are known in Chaco Canyon and the surrounding area, and, if estimates made primarily on the basis of surface remains are correct, these sites have an average of only three pithouses (Hayes et al. 1981; Wills and Windes 1989:349). In the

Mesa Verde region, Step House Cave (on Mesa Verde), which has six contemporaneous pithouses, is considered to be relatively aggregated compared with contemporaneous sites (Orcutt et al. 1990).

Other descriptions of Basketmaker III architecture suggest that the relationship between habitation and storage structures was different from that described by Wills and Windes (1989). In their summary of the western Anasazi (ancestral Pueblo) area, including the Kayenta region, Gumerman and Dean (1989:114) describe standardized Basketmaker III units that comprise a pithouse and one to three slab-lined storage pits. Similarly, Basketmaker III sites in the Mesa Verde region consist of one or two pithouses, each with an arc of surface features and structures, including beehive-shaped storage structures (Kane 1986a; Hayes and Lancaster 1975). Kane argues that these sites represent a relatively mobile population (Kane 1986a). In the Dolores River valley, this pattern is associated with what researchers at the Dolores Archaeological Program (DAP) called the Tres Bobos and Sagehill subphases (see Figure 4.1).

Gumerman and Dean (1989) offer a different interpretation of Basketmaker III settlement, at least for the western Anasazi area. They argue that the "pithouse-cist units were organized into 'villages' that ranged from fewer than five to scores of such units" (Gumerman and Dean 1989:114), and they consider these villages to represent permanent, year-round habitations. However, the absence of Kana-a Black-on-white pottery leads them to believe that the Basketmaker III period lasted until A.D. 825, approximately 125 years later than the end of the Basketmaker III period in the Mesa Verde region. It may be that the pattern they are describing for Basketmaker III in the Kayenta region includes sites that are contemporaneous with sites classified as Pueblo I in the Mesa Verde region.

The contrast between Wills and Windes' (1989) emphasis on the nonprivate nature of Basketmaker III storage and others' descriptions of the spatial association of pithouses and storage structures is difficult to interpret. The differences could be due to differences in archaeological data, differences in interpretations and theoretical perspectives, differences in the definition of periods, or a combination of factors. In general, although Basketmaker III storage may not always have been public or communal, storage units most often were external to, and separate from, the habitation structures. As a result, information about what and how much was stored, if not the goods themselves, would have been available to many members of the community.

Beginning in the early to mid-eighth century, sites appeared that were more complex, differently organized, and sometimes larger than the earlier Basketmaker sites. These sites are generally considered to be characteristic of the Pueblo I period, although settlements dating to the late eighth century are often described as Basketmaker III/Pueblo I (Bannister et al. 1969:38). Aggregated sites dating to the late eighth century are found across the Mesa Verde region, including Site 2 at Ackmen-Lowry, near Cahone, Colorado (Martin 1939:360–385), Site 13 at Alkali Ridge, in southeastern Utah (Brew 1946), and Grass Mesa Village, in the Dolores area (Lipe et al. 1988). These sites have numerous pit structures associated with long, above-ground room-blocks consisting of double rows of habitation and storage structures. At least one great kiva (at Grass Mesa Village) and possibly others (for example, at Badger House community on Mesa Verde [Hayes and Lancaster 1975]) are associated with these late-eighth-century settlements.

Across the Colorado Plateau and much of the northern Southwest, climatic conditions generally worsened from the mid– to late A.D. 700s through the 800s. Specifically, the alluvial record indicates a change from aggregation to degradation at this time, which is argued to have been associated with a decrease in effective moisture (Karlstrom 1988). The dendroclimatic record indicates a definite increase in variability over time and some increase in the amplitude of variability (Dean 1988). In general, there was an increase in the frequency of climatic variations that lasted less than 25 years—what are called "high-frequency processes" (Dean et al. 1985; Gumerman 1988a). However, the details and effects of these climatic conditions vary widely, depending on the specific topographic conditions of an area.

In much of the northern Southwest, the transition between the Basketmaker III and Pueblo I (A.D. 700–900) periods is marked by the pithouse-to-pueblo transition (see Gilman 1987; Hegmon 1992b; Lipe and Breternitz 1980; Plog 1974; Wilshusen 1988a). Typical Pueblo I sites, consisting of a surface roomblock, a pit structure, and a midden, are early examples of what Prudden (1903, 1918) calls the "unit-type" pueblo (see also Gorman and Childs 1981). Prudden notes that such units occur by themselves and also form the basic building blocks for many larger pueblos in the Mesa Verde region (although his focus is on Pueblo II and later sites). Roberts (1939) shows how this pattern developed during the Pueblo I period (see Lipe 1989:54; Bullard 1962). In the Mesa Verde region, the ratio of surface rooms to pit structures is roughly eight to one (Lipe 1989:56), which suggests that the residents of several suites of surface rooms shared a pit structure, probably for both domestic and ritual use (Kane 1986a; but see Lightfoot 1992a). In many cases, one or two storage rooms are attached to each habitation room, an arrangement that would have afforded more privacy and possibly more restricted access than the Basketmaker III practice of storing materials in cists or other structures not connected to habitation structures.

Pueblo I architecture, which includes both subterranean and above-ground habitation structures and continuously accessible storage, suggests that many sites were occupied year round by sedentary farmers who also gathered wild plants and hunted. Other sites, however, may represent seasonal occupations (Powell 1983; but see Matson 1991). Most Pueblo I sites were probably occupied for fairly short periods (10 to 20 years), as were many pre–A.D. 1300 Pueblo sites in the northern Southwest (Schlanger and Wilshusen 1993; Ahlstrom 1985:598–602).

Pueblo I sites are highly variable across the northern Southwest. In the Mesa Verde region, the basic unit-type pueblo was well established by the late eighth century. Almost all known Pueblo I habitation sites have a pit structure and a substantial surface roomblock consisting of adjoining rows of habitation and storage rooms. By the late eighth century, some sites, such as Grass Mesa Village and Site 13 at Alkali Ridge, had become aggregated villages, and some great kivas were present. By the mid-ninth century, aggregated villages were established across the Mesa Verde region. These villages include Badger House community on Mesa Verde (Hayes and Lancaster 1975); Site 33 (5MT2831) and perhaps other sites in the La Plata district (Morris 1939; Wilshusen and Blinman 1992; Wilshusen 1991); and McPhee community (Kane 1988), May Canyon Ruin (Blinman 1986a:Figure 2.12), Cline Crest Ruin (Kane 1986b:Table 14.1), and Grass Mesa Village (Lipe et al. 1988) at Dolores. On the basis of a sample of 35 villages in the Mesa Verde region, Wilshusen (1991:211–212) estimates that the average population of a Pueblo I village was 215 persons; the range was 44 to 1,084. Many of these sites, especially the largest villages, have large, elaborate pit structures (known as "oversize" pit structures) that appear to have been used for fairly large scale ritual gatherings (Blinman 1989; Kane 1988; Wilshusen 1988b, 1989). Great kivas, which are significantly larger than "oversize" pit structures, are not consistently associated with large sites, and although dating is often tentative, many great kivas probably date to the late eighth and early ninth centuries (Orcutt et al. 1990:200). Wilshusen (1991:229–230) argues that great kivas served dispersed communities rather than large, aggregated villages.

An aggregated village that was to become Pueblo Bonito apparently was established by the early tenth century A.D. in Chaco Canyon, New Mexico (Lekson 1986). Other than in Chaco, however, most Pueblo I settlements south of the Mesa Verde region were small and dispersed, and no Pueblo I great kivas are known in either the Cibola or Kayenta regions (Gumerman and Dean 1989:116; LeBlanc 1989:340–341). Furthermore, although surface habitation and storage rooms are often present at Pueblo I sites in the Kayenta and Cibola regions, the arrangement of the surface rooms is not as strongly patterned as the double rows of habitation and storage rooms in the Mesa Verde region. In addition, what is called the Pueblo I period begins later (about A.D. 825) in the Kayenta region (Gumerman and Dean 1989) than in the Mesa Verde region. The presence of aggregated Pueblo I villages with public architecture in the ninth century A.D. in the Mesa Verde region, but not in the Kayenta region, provides an important basis of comparison because different kinds of social dynamics are likely associated with aggregated and dispersed settlements.

Early Pottery in the Northern Southwest

Small amounts of pottery may have been present in the northern Southwest during the first few centuries A.D. (Dittert et al. 1963). However, pottery did not become widespread in this area until about A.D. 500, the beginning of the Basketmaker III period. Most of this early pottery consisted of plain gray ware in various forms, although jars were more common than bowls. Within a few centuries, pottery became much more elaborate, as different wares, painted decoration, and surface manipulation were developed.

Pottery Manufacture

Interpretations of prehistoric Puebloan pottery-making procedures generally draw from a combination of accounts of traditional procedures used by Puebloan peoples historically (e.g., Colton 1953:14–27; Gifford 1928; Guthe 1925; Stevenson 1904:373–377), more recent general studies of ceramic ecology (e.g., Arnold 1985), technological analyses (e.g., Carr 1990; Schiffer and Skibo 1987), and archaeological evidence (see Blinman 1988a; D. Hill 1985). Production begins with the collection and preparation of pottery clay and nonplastic temper. Once cleaned, the clay may be used immediately, although it often requires additional processing to increase its plasticity. One common means of processing involves soaking the clay in water and then allowing it to dry to a manageable consistency. Another form of processing involves drying the clay completely, then grinding it to a powder and adding water. Temper—that is, nonplastic particles such as sand, crushed rock, or crushed pot sherds—is added to the clay in either its wet or powdered state. The resulting paste is kneaded to form a workable mass. Once prepared, the clay can be formed into vessels or stored for future use.

Ancestral Puebloan peoples generally made their pottery using the coil-and-scrape method. That is, vessels were constructed by stacking coils of clay and then scraping and sometimes pinching the coils together to bond them. Manufacturing techniques can be discerned through examination of scrape marks and breakage patterns and possibly through X-ray examination of clay and temper particles (Carr 1990; Shepard 1965:183–186).

After the vessel is constructed by coiling and scraping, gray, or utility, wares are ready to dry and fire. However, vessels that are to be decorated are dried only to a "leather-hard" state and then are slipped and/or polished and/or painted. Slip is a fine, liquid clay that is spread on the surface of a pot, often to give it a finer finish. Most slips on white wares in the northern Southwest are either the same color as the clay used in the body of the vessel or only slightly whiter; it is possible that the vessel body and slip were made from the same clay.

Decorated pottery is painted with pigments made of organic and/or mineral substances. Organic paint is generally made of processed plant or animal material; tansymustard and beeweed, boiled for many hours into a thick, sticky syrup, have been used for paint in historic times (Guthe 1925). Organic paints are absorbed into the vessel, and they carbonize during firing. Mineral paint consists of finely ground ferric or magnesium minerals, usually mixed with an organic binder. Mineral paint is not absorbed into the clay but, rather, remains on the surface and thus can often be distinguished macroscopically from organic paint. In historic times, paint has been applied with small brushes made of yucca leaves (Colton 1953).

Many decorated vessels are polished before and/or after slipping and before and/or after painting. The vessel is polished with a very smooth stone, which is rubbed over the leather-hard surface (Guthe 1925). Polishing forces the temper particles below the surface and aligns the clay particles, which results in a lustrous surface finish (Shepard 1965:66–67). Individual streaks left by the polishing stone may be clearly evident, especially on poorly polished vessels.

After a pot is made and decorated, it is dried completely to remove all free (that is, not chemically bonded) water and then fired. Firing to temperatures above approximately 600° C chemically bonds the clay together and ideally produces a durable, impermeable vessel. In the prehistoric northern Southwest, pottery was probably fired on the surface of the ground or in shallow pits; wood and brush were used as fuel. The atmosphere of the fire is important in determining the color of the pot. An oxidizing atmosphere (in which free oxygen is available) turns most pottery a buff, brown, or reddish color, in part because the oxygen bonds with iron in the clay, producing FeO_2. A fully oxidizing atmosphere will also burn off any organic paint. A reducing atmosphere (which "pulls" oxygen from the clay) generally produces a dark vessel because it turns iron into FeO. Dark vessels can also be produced by smudging, a process that results in carbon being deposited on the surface of the vessel. Finally, a neutral atmosphere, in which oxygen is neither added to, nor taken from, the clay, ideally will produce a light-colored or white vessel. The specific techniques used by ancestral Pueblo peoples are not known, although it is likely that they achieved desired pottery colors both by controlling the firing atmosphere and by carefully selecting their clay (Swink 1993). Experiments have shown that the same firing can produce both brown and gray pottery if different clays are used (Wilson 1993).

Pottery Forms and Wares

A number of vessel forms were made and used during the Basketmaker III and Pueblo I periods. Detailed definitions of the forms analyzed in this study are presented in Chapter 6. Brief general descriptions are offered here as background. Bowls are open vessels thought to have been used for serving and eating. Ladles and scoops are open vessels with handles; they are well suited for scooping up food or other material. Jars have restricted openings, often with necks. Seed jars are small, neckless vessels with small openings; they are well suited for storing small quantities of dry goods such as seeds. Pitchers are jars, sometimes shaped like gourds, with unopposed handles. Ollas are large jars, often with long, narrow necks, that frequently are found in storage rooms; their shapes and the contexts in which they are found suggest that they were probably used for storage. Finally, cooking pots are jars with wide mouths and rounded bases; they are often sooted from having been used over fires.

Pottery made during the Basketmaker III through Pueblo I periods in the northern Southwest includes white, gray, and red wares. By the definition used here, gray ware vessels are not polished, painted, or slipped. They generally have gray or grayish white paste and fairly coarse temper. Almost all cooking pots are gray ware, although other gray ware vessel forms are also seen. Beginning in the ninth century, the necks of many gray ware jars displayed the coils used to construct the pot; "neckbanded" is the term used to refer to such vessels. After about A.D. 1000, most gray ware jars were corrugated, that is, the coils were left exposed over most or all of the exterior of the vessel and were textured, sometimes with elaborate patterns of indentations.

White ware vessels are polished and/or slipped and/or painted. Many white wares, especially those made during the Pueblo I period and later, have a whiter and finer paste than do gray ware vessels. However, according to the definition used here (which is also used by analysts at the Crow Canyon Archaeological Center), any decorated vessel fired in a neutral to reducing atmosphere (in other words, not a red ware) is a white ware. Thus, a gray pot with a few painted decorations is considered a white ware. White ware vessels were made in a variety of forms, including bowls, ollas, seed jars, and pitchers.

Gray and white wares apparently were made in various locations across the northern Southwest (see analyses of temper reported by Morris [1980:55], Wilson and Blinman [1991b], and Blinman and Wilson [1992]). A number of specific ware categories have been defined on the basis of location (the area in which they are most commonly found) and differences in technology (primarily temper and paint type). Tusayan White Ware and Tsegi Gray Ware, associated with the Kayenta region, generally have sand temper, and the paint, if present, is usually pure organic (Colton and Hargrave 1937). Cibola wares, associated with east-central New Mexico and west-central Arizona, generally have sand temper and mineral paint (Gladwin 1945; Sullivan and Hantman 1984). Mesa Verde white and gray wares are associated with the Mesa Verde region (Breternitz et al. 1974). If made before A.D. 1000, they generally are tempered with crushed igneous rock, although other types of temper, particularly sand or crushed sandstone, are not uncommon. Paint, if present, is usually mineral in an organic binder.

Red ware vessels have a reddish orange paste, a result of the vessels having been fired in an oxygen-rich atmosphere. Early red ware vessels are often polished and/or painted, and later ones are also often slipped. Most are bowls, although seed jars and pitchers are also found. Only San Juan Red Ware (Breternitz et al. 1974) was common in the northern Southwest before A.D. 1000. It is most common in southeastern Utah, although fairly large quantities are found across the Mesa Verde region, and it is not uncommon in the Kayenta and Cibola regions. A growing body of evidence suggests that San Juan Red Ware was made primarily in southeastern Utah and exported across the northern Southwest (Blinman and Wilson 1992; Hegmon et al. 1994; Hurst 1983; Lucius and Breternitz 1981; Reed 1958).

Changes in Pottery over Time

The earliest Basketmaker III pottery in the northern Southwest was plain gray. Toward the end of the period (by about A.D. 700), painted decorations became more common (Figure 4.2), although decorated pieces still constituted only a small fraction of pottery assemblages. Regional traditions of white and gray ware pottery production are recognized on the basis of temper and paint characteristics. Decorated white ware types dating to the Basketmaker III period include Lino Black-on-white (often called Lino Black-on-gray) in the Kayenta

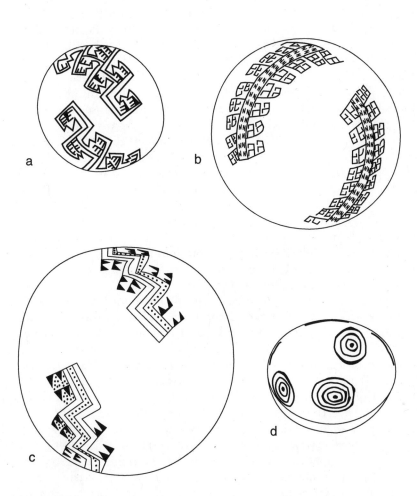

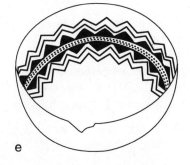

a

b

c

d

e

f

g

Figure 4.2. *Basketmaker III painted pottery:* a–c, *La Plata Black-on-white bowls from the Prayer Rock district, northeastern Arizona (after Morris 1980:Figure 31a, f, m);* d–e, *Chapin Black-on-white bowls from the La Plata district (after Lister and Lister 1978:Figure 8);* f, *Chapin Black-on-white bowl from Mesa Verde (after Lister and Lister 1978:Figure 8);* g, *Chapin Black-on-white bowl from House Creek Village at Dolores. Scale is 1:4. Lister and Lister (1978) call d–f La Plata Black-on-white, probably following Hawley (1936), who includes all mineral-painted pottery, regardless of temper type, in the La Plata Black-on-white category. However, Abel (1955) splits this broad category into rock-tempered Chapin Black-on-white and sand-tempered La Plata Black-on-white. Although the illustrations of these vessels do not provide information on temper, given the vessels' proveniences and Shepard's (1939) identification of crushed-rock temper in most Basketmaker III vessels from the La Plata valley, it is likely that d–f should be classified as Chapin Black-on-white.*

region, La Plata Black-on-white in the Cibola region (Figure 4.2*a–c*), and Chapin Black-on-white in the Mesa Verde region (Figure 4.2*d–g*), as well as several varieties with more limited distributions (Abel 1955; Breternitz et al. 1974:25–27; Colton and Hargrave 1937:194; Hawley 1936; Roberts 1929:118–124; Wilson and Blinman 1991a). These white ware types are differentiated only on the basis of technological characteristics, that is, temper and paint. Most researchers agree that the same style of design was used across most of the northern Southwest (Abel 1955; Breternitz et al. 1974:26; Reed 1958:75; Wasley 1959:245).[1] Furthermore, although detailed design analyses are limited, at least one study suggests that intraregional design variation was also minimal (Hays 1991).

Designs on Basketmaker III white wares are very similar to those found on basketry and other woven materials (including tump bands, aprons, and sandals) from sites dating to the same and earlier periods (Morris 1927; Hays 1991). Some of the motifs (including anthropomorphic figures) found on pottery are also found on rock art (Roberts 1929:122), although Hays (1991) argues that different styles are applied to portable (including pottery) and nonportable (including rock art) media at Broken Flute Cave, a Basketmaker III site in the Prayer Rock district of northeastern Arizona. Designs on plate- or bowl-shaped baskets tend to radiate out from the center of the basket, probably as a result of the weaving technique. Many Basketmaker III pottery designs have a similar central focus, as well as a textural quality—resulting from lines of Z-figures, sometimes called "basketstitch" (Breternitz et al. 1974:26)—reminiscent of basketry (see Figures 4.2*b* and 5.1*a–b*). Gumerman and Dean (1989:115) suggest that the widespread Basketmaker III design style "could be due more to the application of technologically determined basketry designs to pottery than to the direct sharing of ceramic design principles." Regardless of the reason, the homogeneity of Basketmaker III designs on black-on-white pottery provides an important contrast to the variability seen in later designs.

San Juan Red Ware was first produced in the mid- to late eighth century and is associated with the Basketmaker III and Pueblo I periods. The earliest (Basketmaker III/Pueblo I) type, Abajo Red-on-orange, has centrally focused designs reminiscent of basketry, but the design elements are different than those used on contemporaneous white wares. Bluff Black-on-red, which is associated primarily with

---

1. One exception is White Mound Black-on-white (Gladwin 1945:22–23), which is associated with late Basketmaker III–early Pueblo I occupations in the Cibola region and has designs similar to those seen on the later Cibola white wares.

Pueblo I occupations, does not have basketlike designs. Although Breternitz et al. (1974:58) state that Bluff resembles contemporaneous Piedra Black-on-white, in many ways the designs on the two types are quite different. Bluff Black-on-red generally has much thicker lines and cruder line work and lacks the elaborate ticking and rows of triangles seen on Piedra Black-on-white, which is described in detail below.

Pottery across the northern Southwest became more elaborate and more regionally differentiated during the Pueblo I period. Neckbanded gray wares became common. In the Kayenta region, these included Kana-a Gray, then Coconino or Medicine gray; in the Mesa Verde region, these included Moccasin Gray, then Mancos Gray. Vessels of these types have concentric bands around their necks, the result of the coils being left exposed during manufacture. Kana-a and Moccasin gray vessels have fairly wide, flat bands around their necks, and these two types are morphologically indistinguishable (although they *are* distinguishable on the basis of temper). Mancos and Coconino/Medicine gray, which became more common in the late ninth and tenth centuries, have narrower, rounder neckbands. Whereas early gray wares assumed a variety of vessel forms, almost all Pueblo I gray wares are jars, including cooking pots and large storage jars.

White wares, which were distinguished only on the basis of temper and paint type in the Basketmaker III period, have regionally distinct design styles in the Pueblo I period. Specific types include Kana-a Black-on-white in the Kayenta region, White Mound and Kiatuthlanna black-on-white in the Cibola region, and Piedra Black-on-white in the eastern portion of the Mesa Verde region, that is, in southwestern Colorado (Breternitz et al. 1974; Colton and Hargrave 1937; Gladwin 1945; Roberts 1931; Wilson and Blinman 1991a). In addition, a type called White Mesa Black-on-white has recently been recognized in southeastern Utah, in the western portion of the Mesa Verde region (Hurst et al. 1985).[2] Pueblo I white ware designs are illustrated in Figure 4.3. The distributions of the white ware types are fairly restricted; that is, few are found outside the region with which they are associated.

Painted designs on white wares made during the Pueblo I period, particularly after A.D. 800, are both more common and more varied than those on pottery made during earlier times. The quantity of

---

2. Although originally defined as a variety of Piedra Black-on-white (Hurst et al. 1985), White Mesa Black-on-white is distinguished from Piedra on the basis of paste and finish, as well as design characteristics. Therefore, most researchers seem to agree that White Mesa Black-on-white should be considered a separate type (Wilson and Blinman 1991a).

Figure 4.3. *Pueblo I painted pottery:* a, *Case 22, a Kana-a Black-on-white pitcher from D:7:134 on Black Mesa;* b, *Case 128, a Kana-a Black-on-white bowl from D:11:2027 on Black Mesa;* c, *a Piedra Black-on-white gourd jar fragment from Golondrinas Oriental at Dolores (the neck design is Case 207, the shoulder design is Case 208);* d, *Case 317, a Piedra Black-on-white bowl fragment reworked as a scoop from the Duckfoot site;* e–f, *White Mesa Black-on-white bowl and bowl fragment from Edge of the Cedars Pueblo near Blanding, Utah. Scale is 1:2 for d, 1:3 for all others. Case numbers here and in other figure captions refer to the case-by-case design-structure data detailed in Hegmon (1990:Appendix B). In Kuckelman (1988:Figure 7.45), specimen c is described as Cortez Black-on-white. However, in the Dolores Archaeological Program computer database, the vessel is classified as Piedra Black-on-white.*

a

b

c

d

e

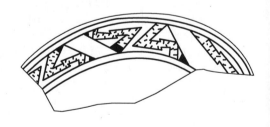

f

decorated pottery (measured in terms of both absolute counts and proportions of assemblages) increases. Whereas Basketmaker III decorations tend to occur mostly on bowls and to be small relative to the overall field of decoration, Pueblo I decorations occur on more vessel forms, including ollas, pitchers, ladles, scoops, and seed jars, and the designs tend to fill the field more completely. Finally, whereas Basketmaker III "white wares" are essentially gray wares with some painted designs, Pueblo I white wares are often more finely made than contemporaneous gray wares. The white wares typically have a finer, whiter paste and are often polished and sometimes slipped.

Some researchers have emphasized the general uniformity of Pueblo I black-on-white pottery designs across the northern Southwest; however, in a number of more specific studies, regional differences have been noted (see Figure 4.3). Roberts (1931:133–134) states that "in the early period of the Pueblos the black-on-white decorative patterns were widespread" (see also Plog 1980a:126–128, and references cited therein). Wasley (1959:250) considers the Kana-a style, which he characterizes as having a profusion of pendant dots and ticks, to be characteristic of Pueblo I pottery in general, although he also suggests that there were two major centers of development of the style—one in the Kayenta region and one in west-central New Mexico. He also states that Piedra Black-on-white is "in part" characterized by the Kana-a style (Wasley 1959:246), although he does not explain the basis for his reasoning. According to Hantman et al. (1984), the Kana-a style—which they define as having thin lines of uniform width, secondary forms, and no hatching—is found on both Cibola and Kayenta Pueblo I black-on-white types, including Kana-a Black-on-white, Kiatuthlanna Black-on-white, and White Mound Black-on-white (however, apparently not on Piedra Black-on-white). Descriptions of Pueblo I types from the different regions note both similarities and differences in the designs (see Jernigan and Wreden 1982:44). For example, wavy hatching is considered to be a distinguishing characteristic of Kiatuthlanna Black-on-white (Gladwin 1945:41), but it is rare or absent on Kana-a and Piedra black-on-white.

Furthermore, two detailed analyses of patterns of stylistic variation in Pueblo I pottery designs in different regions reached very different conclusions. Morris (1939:177) argues that the painted designs on Piedra Black-on-white are "markedly fluid and variable"; although he identified "certain trends," he argues that "these had not become sufficiently crystallized to herd the pot painters into any definite or particularly restricted path." In contrast, Plog (1990b) states that Kana-a Black-on-white, from the Kayenta region, has design attributes (including parallel and zigzag lines, acute triangles, and flags) that covary strongly in comparison with later types. He suggests, therefore, that the regular designs might represent isochrestic variation, that is, they might have resulted from behavior "acquired by rote learning and imitation and . . . employed automatically" (Weissner 1985:160–161). The different conclusions reached by Morris and Plog may be a product of their analytical techniques. Morris developed a general description—a sort of grammar—of designs on whole vessels; Plog employed a quantitative study of attributes on sherds. However, the differences may also be more fundamental, and they suggest that designs differed not only in content but also in terms of broader dimensions of variation such as structure and diversity. Furthermore, the opposite conclusions reached by Morris (1939) and Plog (1990b) strongly suggest that a comparison based on comparable analytical techniques is needed.

The Study Areas: Setting and History of Research

Black Mesa and the Kayenta Region

Black Mesa, in northeastern Arizona, lies in the heart of the Kayenta region (Gladwin and Gladwin 1934) (Figure 4.4). The mesa, part of the Colorado Plateau, rises from the Little Colorado River, which flows in a northwesterly direction approximately 60 km to the southwest. Black Mesa ranges in elevation from about 1800 m at the southern end (around the Hopi Mesas) to over 2400 m at the northeastern escarpment. The area is part of the Upper Sonoran life zone; ephemeral washes cross the mesa, and estimates of annual precipitation range from 50 cm at the northeastern rim, to 25 cm near the center of the mesa, to 30 cm at the Hopi Mesas. A 120-day frost-free period, necessary for growing corn, occurs in most years. Modern environmental conditions are summarized in Christenson and Parry (1985), and detailed studies of the paleoclimatic record, including geologic, hydrologic, botanical, and dendrochronological data, are available in Gumerman (1988a). In addition, a series of specialists' reports have been published or are in preparation (e.g., Green [1985] on chipped-stone raw material; Klesert [1983] on settlement patterns; Leonard [1989] on faunal remains; Parry and Christenson [1987] on chipped stone).

As is the case throughout the Southwest, Black Mesa and the entire Kayenta region are subject to a great deal of microtopographic and climatic variability. Although there was an increase in high-frequency processes across the northern Southwest in general in the late eighth century A.D., the paleoclimatic record indicates that the degree of variability was less on Black Mesa than in areas farther

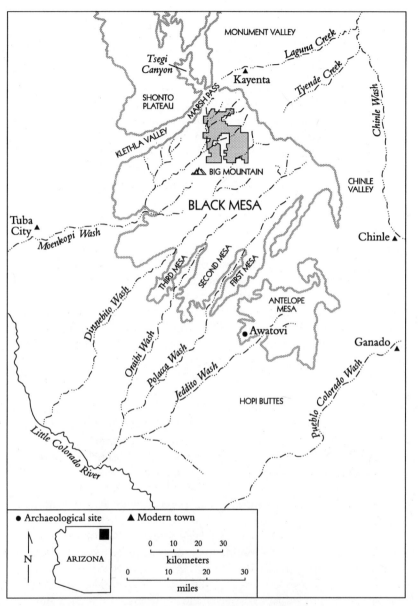

Figure 4.4. *Map of a portion of the Kayenta region, in northeastern Arizona, showing the location of the Black Mesa Archaeological Project study area (shaded) (after Smiley et al. 1983:Figure 1).*

north, including Tsegi Canyon, immediately north of Black Mesa, and Navajo Mountain, on the Arizona-Utah border (Gumerman and Dean 1989:107–108).

In general, Black Mesa provides a marginal environment for farming, although arable land is available near the major washes. Areas just north of Black Mesa (for example, the Klethla Valley) are better watered, and probably were the destinations of many of the people who abandoned northern Black Mesa by A.D. 1150. Many areas in northernmost Arizona and southern Utah—including Long House Valley (Dean et al. 1978), the area around Navajo Mountain (Lindsay et al. 1968), and Glen Canyon (Jennings 1966)—have evidence of small-scale water-control features beginning in the twelfth century A.D.

Agricultural conditions are better in the Hopi Mesas area because numerous (although mostly intermittent) drainages, productive springs, and broad arable areas that contain the water are found there (see Hack 1942). Farther to the south and east, in the arid Hopi Buttes area, agricultural conditions are again marginal. Well-watered agricultural land is available along the Little Colorado River, south of the Kayenta region. When most of the Colorado Plateau was abandoned at the end of the thirteenth century, many people aggregated on the Hopi Mesas and in the Little Colorado River valley (see Adams 1989).

The Kayenta Anasazi region (or the Kayenta branch within the western Anasazi region [Gumerman 1991; Gumerman and Dean 1989]) includes part of southeastern Utah and the northeastern corner of Arizona north of the Little Colorado River and east of the Grand Canyon, although the boundaries change depending on the researcher and the time period in question. What are sometimes called the Winslow and Tusayan branches, particularly after A.D. 900, are included in the Kayenta region as discussed here; the Virgin branch (in northwestern Arizona and southwestern Utah) is not included (Gumerman and Dean 1989:104–105; Gumerman and Skinner 1968). Pottery wares in the Kayenta region include Tsegi Gray and Tusayan White; both have quartz sand temper, and the latter has organic paint (Colton and Hargrave 1937:190–217). Before the Black Mesa Archaeological Project (BMAP) began in 1967, little systematic archaeological research had been done on Black Mesa itself. However, the areas surrounding the mesa, particularly to the north, have a long history of research.

Researchers with the Awatovi expedition of 1939 conducted extensive studies in the Hopi Mesas area. Although most of the work centered on the Pueblo IV site of Awatovi, expedition researchers also conducted intensive excavations at the Basketmaker III/Pueblo I site of Jeddito 264 (Daifuku 1961) and undertook important environmental studies (e.g., Hack 1942). More recent work on the Hopi Mesas includes the Turquoise Trail Project, which involved excavation of a multicomponent Basketmaker III and Pueblo II site (Sebastian 1985). South of the mesas, Gumerman (1988b) conducted research in the Hopi Buttes area. Upham's (1982) research on fourteenth-century regional settlement and exchange included examination of some large pueblos in the Hopi Mesas area and along the Little Colorado River. The thirteenth- and fourteenth-century Homol'ovi

Villages along the Little Colorado were investigated by Fewkes (1898, 1904) and have recently been the subject of extensive work conducted as part of the Homol'ovi Research Project (Adams 1989; Adams and Hays 1991).

On other parts of Black Mesa, BMAP archaeologists conducted extensive surveys and excavations in the northern part of the mesa between 1967 and 1983 (see Powell et al. [1983] for a history of this research). Research by the Navajo Nation (Linford 1983) and Northern Arizona University (Ambler 1987, as cited in Kojo 1989) provides information on areas of Black Mesa south of the BMAP area.

The canyon and mesa country north of Black Mesa has been studied since the early part of the century (Guernsey 1931; Guernsey and Kidder 1921; Hargrave 1935; Kidder and Guernsey 1919). During the Rainbow Bridge–Monument Valley Expedition in the 1930s, detailed surveys and excavations were conducted in the better-watered Marsh Pass–Tsegi Canyon area immediately north of Black Mesa. These projects focused on occupations dated to Pueblo II and later times (Beals et al. 1945). Researchers working on this project also ably described the development of pottery designs, and some pottery and other materials have recently been reanalyzed (Crotty 1983). More recent work immediately north of Black Mesa includes detailed studies of the Pueblo III cliff dwellings (Dean 1970) and a survey of Long House Valley (Dean et al. 1978) that focused primarily on the post–A.D. 1000 period. Haas and Creamer (1993) recently conducted research north of Black Mesa focusing in part on evidence of conflict and warfare in the twelfth and thirteenth centuries A.D. Farther to the north, but still in the Kayenta region, ancestral Puebloan sites have been studied in the Rainbow Plateau and Navajo Mountain areas (Lindsay et al. 1968) and in Glen Canyon (Jennings 1966), although these areas were sparsely occupied or abandoned between A.D. 700/800 and 1000/1050. Researchers working in southern Utah on Cedar Mesa (Matson et al. 1988) and the Red Rock Plateau (Lipe 1970) documented both Kayenta and Mesa Verde occupations, although both areas also were sparsely populated during the Pueblo I and early Pueblo II periods.

The Central Mesa Verde Region

The Mesa Verde, or northern San Juan, region includes the San Juan drainage north of the San Juan River in southwestern Colorado, southeastern Utah, and northernmost New Mexico, as well as parts of the Dolores River drainage in southwestern Colorado and parts of the Colorado River drainage in southeastern Utah (Figure 1.1; Eddy et al. 1984). Although Mesa Verde itself is the region's most famous feature, the focus in this volume is on the area north and west of Mesa Verde, along the Dolores River and McElmo Creek (Figure 4.5); I refer to this area as the central Mesa Verde region. The Mesa Verde region in general sustained large Puebloan populations during the thirteenth century A.D. (Rohn 1989).

Agricultural conditions vary across the Mesa Verde region (Petersen et al. 1986; Petersen 1988; Van West 1990), although, overall, the conditions for agriculture are more favorable than on Black Mesa or in other parts of the Kayenta region. In the Dolores River drainage (elevation = 2320 m at the rim of the Dolores River canyon), the annual rainfall (46 cm) is sufficient for agriculture, but the growing season is close to the minimum (110–130 days) for aboriginal corn.

Figure 4.5. *Map of a portion of the Mesa Verde region, in southwestern Colorado, showing the location of the Dolores Archaeological Program study area (shaded), the Duckfoot site, and other features discussed in the text.*

Modern dry-farming of crops, including beans and corn, is successful in portions of the area, although the Dolores River valley is on the edge of the modern dry-farming belt (Petersen 1988:111). Farther to the west, on Mockingbird Mesa, the growing season is more than adequate (145 days), but rainfall is marginal (28 cm). Schlanger (1988) provides an excellent synthesis of how paleoclimatic changes might improve the conditions for dry farming in one area, while making it

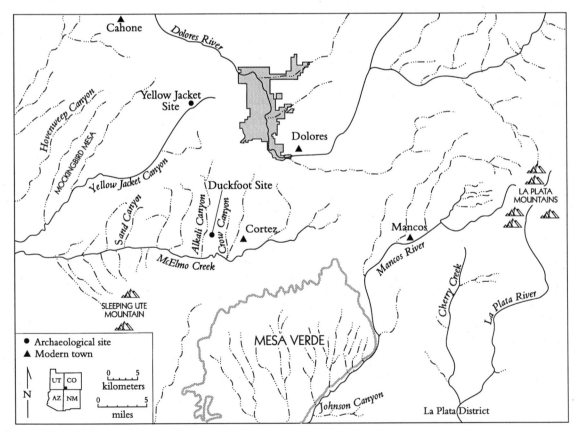

difficult or impossible to farm in another. Detailed modern and paleoenvironmental studies are available in Petersen et al. (1986), Petersen and Orcutt (1987), and Petersen (1988). Van West (1990; see also Van West and Lipe 1992; Kohler and Van West 1992) has recently made detailed calculations of yearly agricultural potential for areas in the central Mesa Verde region using Geographic Information System technology, although her focus is on the tenth through thirteenth centuries A.D.

Overall, agricultural conditions in the central Mesa Verde region are relatively good compared with conditions in other portions of the Mesa Verde region, especially drier areas in southeastern Utah. However, the relative attractiveness of a particular area depends on the current rainfall regime and the elevation of the area. During the ninth century, the area was drier than it is today, with relatively little winter precipitation and relatively high summer precipitation. As a result, higher-elevation areas (such as the Dolores River valley), which benefit more from summer moisture, were relatively attractive at this time (Petersen 1988; Schlanger 1988).

Thus, the central Mesa Verde region provides an interesting contrast to northern Black Mesa. Both areas are subject to a high degree of microtopographic and climatic variability, but the central Mesa Verde region is generally more favorable for agriculture. Furthermore, whereas Black Mesa was relatively marginal in comparison with the surrounding areas, the central Mesa Verde region was relatively favorable compared with the surrounding region, at least during the ninth century.

The Mesa Verde region also has a long history of research, dating back at least to the Hayden survey in the 1870s (Holmes 1878) and Prudden's (1903) work during the early twentieth century. On Mesa Verde itself, archaeological research has been ongoing for nearly a century, from the early work of Nordenskiöld (1979) and Wetherill (McNitt 1957) to more recent projects conducted by the National Park Service (e.g., Hayes 1964; Hayes and Lancaster 1975; Rohn 1971). Much of this work has focused on the spectacular late (Pueblo III) cliff dwellings, although some sites dating to earlier periods were also excavated. The most extensive excavations of pre–Pueblo III sites were those conducted at Badger House community (Hayes and Lancaster 1975). Hayes and Lancaster's descriptions of pottery types, particularly Cortez Black-on-white, are among the most extensive in the literature. Surveys on both Chapin and Wetherill mesas (Hayes 1964; Rohn 1977) also provide a general picture of cultural development over time.

Along the Piedra River, east of Mesa Verde, Roberts (1930) excavated a series of Basketmaker III and Pueblo I sites. Southeast of Mesa Verde, in the La Plata district, E. H. Morris conducted extensive work on sites ranging from Basketmaker III to Pueblo III in age, and his report (Morris 1939) includes detailed descriptions of the pottery. In addition, Shepard (1939) conducted detailed technological studies of pottery recovered from the La Plata district, including petrographic examination of the temper. Some of the sites reported by Morris have recently been subject to additional excavation (Reed et al. 1985), mapping, and analysis (Wilshusen 1991; Wilshusen and Blinman 1992). In Mancos Canyon, south of Mesa Verde, the University of Colorado conducted a series of excavations that documented, among other things, the Pueblo I–Pueblo II transition from pithouse, or protokiva, to kiva (Gillespie 1976; see also Reed 1958).

A large amount of research, much of it recent, has been done in the area north of McElmo Creek. Researchers at the Crow Canyon Archaeological Center have recently completed their investigation of the Duckfoot site, a late Pueblo I habitation that was occupied from the mid– to late A.D. 850s to about 880 (Lightfoot and Etzkorn 1993). Crow Canyon archaeologists are currently conducting extensive multidisciplinary studies in the area around and including Sand Canyon, including survey, small-site testing, environmental studies, and partial excavation of Sand Canyon Pueblo, a large, late Pueblo III site (Lipe 1992; Bradley 1992). Another extensive survey in the area was completed by Fetterman and Honeycutt (1986) on Mockingbird Mesa. University of Colorado researchers have undertaken extensive excavations at a number of sites (primarily Basketmaker III and Pueblo II in age) near the enormous Yellow Jacket site (Lange et al. 1986). Researchers from the Field Museum of Natural History investigated numerous sites, ranging from Basketmaker to Pueblo III in age, in the Ackmen-Lowry area, near Cahone, Colorado (Martin 1936, 1938), and crews from Fort Lewis College, under the direction of W. James Judge, are currently investigating the Pigg site, located in the same area. Numerous smaller sites of all periods have been investigated in conjunction with various cultural resource management and other research programs (e.g., Fuller 1984; Gould 1982; Kent 1991; Morris 1986).

The largest single archaeological project conducted in the Mesa Verde region was the Dolores Archaeological Program, or DAP (Breternitz et al. 1986). Between 1978 and 1983, Dolores researchers surveyed and excavated over 100 sites just north of the town of Dolores, Colorado. Most of this work focused on the late Basketmaker III and Pueblo I periods because the area was only sparsely occupied after A.D. 900. Overlooking the reservoir that now covers most DAP sites is a Chacoan outlier called the Escalante Ruin, which, along with the nearby Dominguez Ruin, was excavated and stabilized in the 1970s (Hallasi 1979; Reed 1979).

Research in the Mesa Verde region extends across the Colorado-Utah border. In Hovenweep National Monument, the primary focus has been on the later Pueblo II and Pueblo III periods (Winter 1977; Neily 1983). Recent survey and excavation (Morris 1991) has been conducted at a number of sites ranging from Basketmaker III to Pueblo III in age near the Colorado-Utah border north of McElmo Creek. Brew (1946) excavated a series of sites on Alkali Ridge, in southeastern Utah, that ranged from Basketmaker III to Pueblo III in age, although late Pueblo I occupations were scarce or absent. Other recent projects in southeastern Utah include Brigham Young University's excavation at the Nancy Patterson site, in Montezuma Canyon (Thompson et al. 1988), and Davis's (1985) investigations on White Mesa, near the town of Blanding.

The Study Areas in the Ninth Century

Black Mesa and the Kayenta Region

In the Kayenta region as a whole, adaptations that developed during the Basketmaker III period continued and intensified during the ninth century A.D. (the late Pueblo I period) (Gumerman and Dean 1989:116). Basketmaker III sites, consisting of pithouses and associated surface storage structures, were established along the margins of the floodplains. Into the Pueblo I period, many sites continued to be located in the lowlands and were built on the floodplains, as well as on their margins. Because many of these sites were later buried by alluvium, relatively little is known about them. However, Gumerman and Dean (1989:116) report that some "sizeable communities" were present, although no great kivas or other large ceremonial structures are known from this period.

During the ninth century A.D., the population of the Kayenta region expanded into the uplands, including moving onto northern Black Mesa (Figure 4.4). Although Basketmaker III sites are known from the southern part of Black Mesa and along the escarpments and surrounding valleys, no pre–A.D. 800 sites with pottery are known from the BMAP study area on northern Black Mesa. Earlier Basketmaker II and Archaic sites have been identified, however. Thus, the mid-ninth century (the Tallahogan phase in BMAP systematics) was a time of reoccupation of an area that had been inhabited much earlier but had been unoccupied or used only sporadically during the immediately preceding centuries. This reoccupation generally coincided with a period of relatively unfavorable climatic conditions, including a decrease in effective moisture and an increase in climatic variability (that is, high-frequency processes). People may have moved onto Black Mesa because the climatic variability was less extreme there than in the areas to the north (Dean 1982, cited in Nichols and Smiley 1984:101; see also Gumerman and Dean 1989:116).

Subsistence on northern Black Mesa and across the Kayenta region during the ninth century was based on the cultivation of corn, beans, and squash, the hunting of animals, and the gathering of wild foods. Several factors suggest that reliance on cultivated foods increased during the ninth century (Nichols and Smiley 1984:101; see also Gumerman and Dean 1989:116). Intensification of cultivation is indicated by the possible addition of new varieties of beans, changes in ground-stone and chipped-stone technology, and the increased use of masonry and stone-lined storage structures well suited for long-term storage of corn.

All the excavated ninth-century habitation sites in the BMAP project area (Figure 4.6) are located near relatively favorable agricultural land along major washes. Thus, as farmers moved onto the upland of Black Mesa, they first settled in the most arable areas, often the lowest areas. However, the overall settlement pattern is not well known, because sites of this period have relatively few painted white wares and therefore are difficult to date on the basis of surface remains (Plog 1986:79). Most of the settlement and other studies reported in a recent synthetic volume (Plog 1986) are based on survey data and do not include the period before about A.D. 870. The settlement pattern for the late A.D. 800s was characterized by habitation sites along the major washes and other sites more distant from the washes (Catlin 1986; Plog 1986:Chapter 9). The population density in the BMAP study area during the late ninth century A.D., calculated on the basis of estimated number of rooms, was very low—under one person per square kilometer (Plog 1986:Chapter 10).

Excavated ninth-century sites on northern Black Mesa—well dated with clusters of tree-ring dates ranging from A.D. 813 to 874 (Nichols and Smiley 1984:99)—contain fairly consistent suites of structures and features. Deep pit structures have characteristics common to both domestic pithouses (many pits and other features; radial walls or wing walls[3]) and ritual kivas (benches and sipapus). Shallow pit structures and roomblocks consisting of rows of semisubterranean rooms generally lack features and are interpreted as storage areas, as are extramural slab-lined cists. Surface rooms made of jacal and

---

3. Radial walls in Black Mesa pit structures are low ridges made of clay and sometimes other materials that extend from the hearth and divide the pit structure. Similar constructions, although not necessarily attached to hearths, are called wing walls in the Mesa Verde region. Wing walls often incorporate large slabs and appear to be more substantial than radial walls.

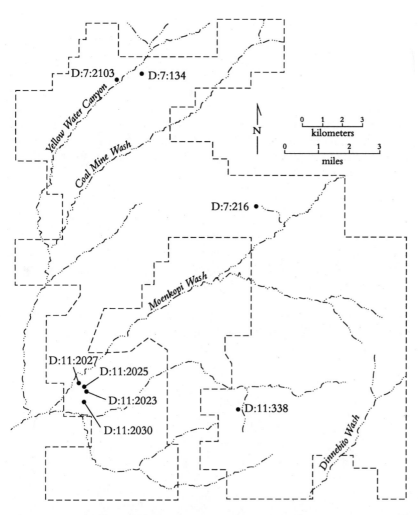

Figure 4.6. *Map of the Black Mesa Archaeological Project (BMAP) study area, showing the sites included in the analyses (after Nichols and Smiley 1984:Figure 1.2). The dashed line indicates the boundaries of the lease area studied by BMAP researchers. The location of the lease area is shown (shaded) in Figure 4.4.*

containing hearths are interpreted as dwelling areas. Pit structures have also been interpreted as indicating winter residence, whereas surface jacal rooms and/or exterior hearths have been interpreted as evidence of summer residence (Powell 1983; see also Lightfoot 1992a).

The ninth-century sites excavated by BMAP archaeologists can be divided into three general categories (following Nichols and Smiley 1984:101): seasonal-occupation sites, small habitation sites occupied for short periods, and larger habitation sites occupied for longer periods. Seasonal-occupation sites are small and consist of shallow pit structures and extramural features. Small habitation sites that were occupied for short periods have one or very few deep pit structures, roomblocks, diffuse middens, extramural activity areas, and sometimes jacal rooms that may or may not be attached to the roomblocks.

One such site, D:11:2025, is shown in Figure 4.7, *top*. Three very similar small habitation sites (D:11:2023 [Olszewski 1984], D:11:2025 [Stone 1984], and D:11:2027 [Olszewski et al. 1984]) located within half a kilometer of each other yielded tree-ring dates that suggest that they were occupied sequentially over roughly a 30-year period, possibly by the same group of people. Larger habitation sites that were occupied for longer periods of time contain the same kinds of structures and features as do sites in the second category, but the structures are more numerous and are more formally arranged. A good example of a larger habitation site is D:11:2030 (Green et al. 1985), which has five deep pit structures, three masonry roomblocks, and several jacal structures, some of which are attached to the roomblock (Figure 4.7, *bottom*). D:11:2030 has well-dated evidence of construction in every decade from the A.D. 840s through the 870s, and it appears to have three roomblock–jacal–pit structure components (Smiley and Ahlstrom 1994; Nichols and Powell 1987). Thus, although the site was occupied over the course of at least 40 years, the entire site may not have been in use at any one time.

As is the case across the northern Southwest, no formal cemeteries were found on Black Mesa, although some burials were found at both small (for example, D:11:2025) and large (D:11:2030) habitation sites. Thus, known burial locations on Black Mesa do not con-

Figure 4.7. *Black Mesa habitation sites:* top, D:11:2025, *a small habitation site (after Stone 1984:Figure 3.22); bottom, D:11:2030, the largest ninth-century site known in the BMAP study area (after Green et al. 1985:Figure 3.13).*

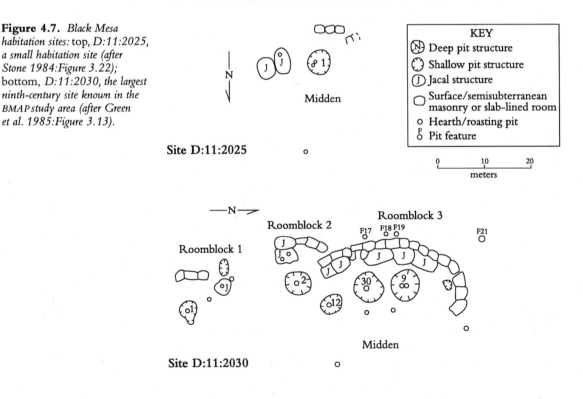

form to the pattern common among intensive agriculturalists (burial in formal cemeteries) or to that common among swidden horticulturalists (burial in separate locations away from settlements) (Chapman 1981; Schlanger 1992). Most or all known ninth-century burials on northern Black Mesa were found in middens; in other parts of the northern Southwest, burials are often found on or under structure floors (Schlanger 1992). The practice of burying the dead in middens—which appear to be associated with whole sites rather than with individual roomblocks—may indicate an emphasis on group, rather than private or household, affiliation, or it may indicate a weak attachment to residential structures.

Only three kinds of pottery were common on northern Black Mesa during the ninth century A.D.: Kana-a Black-on-white, Kana-a Gray, and San Juan Red ware. Kana-a Black-on-white and Kana-a Gray are ubiquitous and dominate the pottery assemblages. San Juan Red Ware (primarily Bluff Black-on-red) was found at all excavated sites, but in much smaller quantities than the white and gray wares. Small amounts of two other decorated white ware types were also present, specifically, Lino Black-on-white, which is associated with the Basketmaker III period, and Wepo Black-on-white (Gumerman et al. 1972), which is a late variant of Kana-a Black-on-white.

Analysis of various categories of artifacts has revealed some evidence relating to the movement of goods. Noting the homogeneity of early white ware designs in the Kayenta region, Cordell and Plog (1979:416) argue that this pottery was produced at a few manufacturing centers and exchanged across the region. However, no sites with evidence of large-scale production are known. Recent analyses of white ware pottery (Hegmon 1991a) indicate that there was considerable compositional heterogeneity, which in turn suggests that white wares were produced at a fairly small scale, probably at many locations throughout the region (see also Hantman and Plog 1982). However, evidence of localized, small-scale production by no means precludes the possibility that Kana-a Black-on-white was moved and/or exchanged across the Kayenta region. San Juan Red Ware, present in small quantities in most pottery assemblages, was imported to Black Mesa, probably from southeastern Utah. Pottery production and exchange are discussed in more detail in Chapter 6.

Analyses of chipped-stone material have produced conflicting results regarding exchange. Green (1986) found that chipped-stone assemblages from sites dating to after the introduction of pottery contain a much higher percentage of nonlocal materials than do earlier, "preceramic" Basketmaker II assemblages (over 50 percent vs. 6 percent). Plog (1986:Chapter 12) argues that this change indicates intensification of exchange, and Leonard et al. (1989) suggest that the changes are a result of a shift from embedding lithic procurement in the subsistence system to obtaining lithic material through exchange. However, recent analyses (Parry and Christenson 1987:210) suggest that, although the proportion of imported chipped stone increased over time, the amounts did not change significantly. Parry and Christenson (1987) argue that, whereas reliance on local lithic material—primarily baked siltstone—decreased over time, there was little change in the access to, or use of, imported materials.

In some respects, ninth-century settlement on Black Mesa was characterized by relatively high mobility (see Eder 1984; Kelly 1992). The short occupation spans at the small habitation sites indicate a relatively low degree of permanence—the sites appear to have been occupied for less than a generation. Seasonally occupied upland sites suggest high mobility for resource procurement. However, the presence of larger sites with longer occupation spans (such as D:11:2030 and D:7:134 [Layhe et al. 1976; Layhe 1984]) indicates that more permanent settlements were also present. Furthermore, the burials in the middens of both the small and large habitation sites may symbolize some form of permanent attachment to a site, even if the occupation was fairly brief.

Powell (1983) suggests that before A.D. 1050 northern Black Mesa was occupied only seasonally. Primarily on the basis of ethnographic analogy and studies of the Navajo use of Black Mesa, she argues that pit structures and internal hearths indicate winter occupation and external hearths indicate summer occupation. However, she also acknowledges that some of the large sites are "problematic" because they have characteristics of both summer and winter occupation (Powell 1983:126). She describes one particularly problematic site, D:7:134, which yielded tree-ring dates indicating construction in the mid–A.D. 800s and early 900s: "D:7:134 has multiple storage rooms, a kiva [pit structure], and jacal structures, although no trash middens were present. This suggests that some sites were beginning to be occupied year-round prior to . . . A.D. 1050" (Powell 1983:136). After the completion of Powell's research (she included only sites excavated before 1979), excavation at a number of ninth-century sites revealed that this combination of summer- and winter-occupation characteristics was common, both on large sites, such as D:11:2030, and on smaller sites, such as D:11:2027. These new data confirm Powell's suggestion of problems in her hypothesis; that is, there is good evidence that at least some Black Mesa sites were occupied year round before A.D. 1050, including during the ninth century (see also Plog 1982, 1986:Chapter 9).

Evidence suggests that ninth-century social organization on Black Mesa, and possibly across the Kayenta region, consisted of fairly small units with flexible but broad integrative mechanisms. The apparently high degree of residential and logistic mobility suggests that social ties were extensive rather than intensive. Extensive social relations involve broad and generally flexible social networks in which many interactions are based on individuals; in contrast, intensive social relations involve a more inward focus with an emphasis on the definition of groups. Intensive social relations do not preclude far-reaching or long-distance interactions, but such interactions are generally perceived as interactions among groups rather than among autonomous individuals (see Kelly 1991). Long-distance movement of pottery and possibly chipped stone also points to the importance of extensive contacts. The scale of architecture is fairly small, and although the same basic units are used repeatedly, their patterning—especially the association of jacal dwellings with storage rooms—is not highly consistent, particularly at the small habitation sites (Nichols and Smiley's [1984] second category, as described above). Even at the larger sites, which consistently include double rows of habitation and storage rooms, there is no evidence of an overarching organization or a larger-scale integrative structure such as an oversized pit structure or great kiva.

These architectural and settlement patterns continued into the tenth century in the Kayenta region. Habitation sites continued to be located in the lowlands or, on Black Mesa, along the major washes, with seasonal procurement sites in other areas. The population in the BMAP study area appears to have fluctuated greatly during the tenth century, and for several short time spans there is no evidence of construction or occupation (Plog 1986:236).[4] The same basic settlement pattern continued until about A.D. 950.

The Central Mesa Verde Region

Many characteristics of Pueblo I settlement in the Kayenta region are also present in the Mesa Verde region, including year-round habitation sites consisting of pit structures and pueblos. However, in the Dolores area and other parts of the central Mesa Verde region, these characteristics were present earlier, by the mid-eighth century. Furthermore, by the late eighth century and especially during the ninth century, the scale and apparent complexity of settlements in the Mesa Verde region in general—and in the central part of the region in particular—increased dramatically, with the construction of

---

4. Plog's (1986:Chapter 10) population estimates are based on the assumption, reasonable for Black Mesa, that structures were occupied for 15 years. Estimates that assume a longer structure use life or that use different methods (e.g., Layhe 1981; Swedlund and Sessions 1976) produce much smoother population curves.

large-scale architectural facilities, aggregation into large sites, and the development of a settlement hierarchy.

The DAP project area was located along the Dolores River, north of the town of Dolores (Figure 4.8). Most sites were in an area with elevations ranging from 2105 to 2285 m (Petersen 1987), which is greater than the elevation in much of the rest of the central Mesa Verde region. Relatively favorable agricultural conditions were present in the Dolores area in the early two-thirds of the ninth century (before about A.D. 860/880) (Petersen et al. 1986; Petersen 1988). During this period, subsistence was based on corn, bean, and squash horticulture, as well as on gathering and hunting. Changes in stone tool assemblages and ethnobotanical remains suggest an increase in dependence on cultivation in contrast to earlier periods (Kane

Figure 4.8. *Map of the Dolores Archaeological Program (DAP) study area, showing the sites included in the analyses (after Robinson et al. 1986:Figure 1.5). The dashed line indicates the "takeline," that is, the land purchased by the government and intensively studied by DAP researchers. The location of the takeline area is shown (shaded) in Figure 4.5. See Figure 4.11 for the names and locations of the individual sites in McPhee Village. Site numbers are provided in Chapter 5 text, under individual site descriptions.*

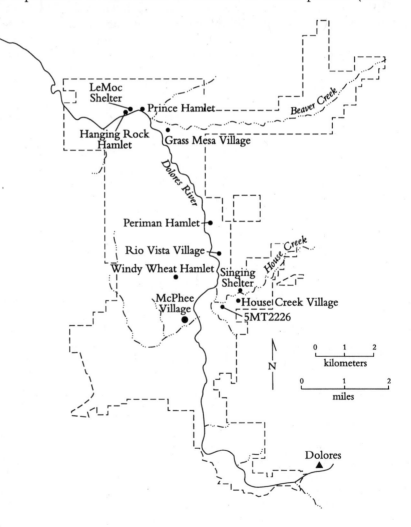

1986a:366–368; see also Orcutt et al. 1990). The Dolores population also grew during the early 800s, probably as the result of migration as well as of in situ growth, and reached a peak between A.D. 860 and 880 (Schlanger 1986, 1988).

The Pueblo I style of architecture was well established by the late eighth century across the Mesa Verde region. Common architectural components include deep pit structures that, like those on Black Mesa, have features (for example, storage pits and wing walls) indicative of domestic use and others (for example, sipapus and benches) indicative of ritual use. Because of their mixed characteristics, such structures were labeled "protokivas" by Morris (1939). Jacal and masonry roomblocks consist of double rows of rooms. Rooms in the back row usually have no features and therefore are interpreted as storage rooms; rooms in the front row generally have hearths and therefore are interpreted as dwellings. Middens, ramadas, and extramural features are also present at Pueblo I sites in the central Mesa Verde region.

The basic unit of Pueblo I architecture is made up of a pit structure and a suite of surface rooms, usually with two to four front dwelling rooms and two or more back storage rooms per dwelling room. In the Dolores area, Kane (1986a) labels this configuration an "interhousehold unit" and suggests that one surface dwelling room and its associated storage rooms would have been occupied by a single nuclear family household; two or three such households would have shared the pit structure (Figure 4.9). An interhousehold unit is a form of Prudden's (1903, 1918) unit-type pueblo, although unit-type pueblos are not necessarily made up of double rows of surface rooms (Gorman and Childs 1981). Lightfoot (1992a) has recently challenged the standard interpretation of a suite of rooms and associated pit structure as an interhousehold unit. He suggests that, rather than having been shared by two or three nuclear families, the unit was occupied by a single extended family that used the pit structure for ritual and for winter residence and used the front rooms for summer residence.

Most Basketmaker III sites in the Dolores area are very small, generally consisting of only one pit structure and an arc of surface structures. These were probably occupied by single family units (for example, Aldea Sierritas [Kuckelman 1986]; see also summary in Kane [1986a:404]). Site complexity and size increased with the development of pueblo architecture in the eighth century. Some early Pueblo (Dos Casas subphase) sites are characterized as small hamlets (for example, Windy Wheat Hamlet [Brisbin 1986]); these consist of one or a few interhousehold units and a midden. Other early Pueblo settlements are quite large. At Grass Mesa Village, the portion of the site that dates to the late eighth century (Dos Casas

Figure 4.9. *Household and interhousehold units, as defined by Dolores Archaeological Program researchers (after Kane 1986a:Figure 5.2). A household unit consists of a suite of surface rooms, typically one front habitation room and two rear storage rooms. An interhousehold unit typically includes two or more suites of surface rooms and a pit structure.*

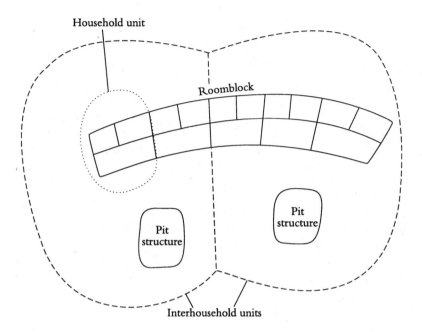

subphase) includes at least 12 pit structures, many surface rooms, and a great kiva, which makes it one of the largest known early Pueblo sites in the Southwest (Lipe et al. 1988).

Although not all early Pueblo sites are large, their occupational histories may be more complex than those of pithouse sites. Kane (1986a:365–366) suggests that early Pueblo hamlets, which often appear to have been remodeled, were occupied for longer than one generation (30 to 50 years) and thus represent an increase in site use life compared with site use life during earlier periods. Schlanger and Wilshusen (1993) have recently argued that the occupation at Dolores was less continuous than Kane suggests. Using tree-ring data, as well as analyses of abandonment assemblages, they argue that the Dolores area was residentially occupied for four distinct periods: the A.D. 680s–690s, the 730s–740s, the 760s–790s, and the 830s–870s. Although Schlanger and Wilshusen (1993) present a convincing challenge to assumptions of long-term, continuous occupation, their analyses also lend some support to Kane's argument of an increase in settlement longevity. That is, their last two (Puebloan) occupational periods last approximately 40 and 50 years, respectively, in contrast to their earlier 20-year periods. Furthermore, although residential use may have been discontinuous, Grass Mesa Village was occupied, on and off, for over a century, from the mid-eighth century (possibly as early as the A.D. 720s) to the late ninth or early tenth centuries (possibly as late as A.D. 910) (Lipe et al. 1988).

Evidence suggests that across much of the Mesa Verde region there was a hiatus in construction in the first two or three decades of the ninth century, followed by fairly large scale construction that continued until the A.D. 870s (Orcutt et al. 1990; Schlanger and Wilshusen 1993). At Dolores, major construction at McPhee Village (Kane and Robinson 1988) and House Creek Village (Robinson and Brisbin 1986) began after this hiatus. Elsewhere in the region, major new construction was begun in Mancos Canyon (Gillespie 1976), the Ackmen-Lowry area (Martin 1938, 1939), and the La Plata district, including the great kiva at Site 33 (5MT2831) (Ahlstrom 1985:234; Morris 1939; Reed et al. 1985; Wilshusen and Blinman 1992).

Many demographic, settlement, and environmental trends peaked during the ninth century in the Dolores area. From the late eighth century until around A.D. 875, conditions for agriculture were relatively favorable in the Dolores area in comparison with those in the surrounding lower-elevation areas. However, drought and a shortened growing season made the Dolores area much less attractive after A.D. 875 (Petersen 1988:124). The population increased in the eighth century, probably as a result of migration and in situ growth, and reached a peak between about A.D. 860 and 880 (Schlanger 1986, 1988). Finally, the trend toward large, substantial, and complex settlements continued until about A.D. 880, when less substantial and less architecturally complex habitations again became common. Dolores researchers divided this period into two partly contemporaneous subphases: the Periman subphase (A.D. 840–910) includes the complex settlements, and the Grass Mesa subphase (A.D. 870–910) includes the later ephemeral habitations.

Many small habitation sites, each consisting of a roomblock, several pit structures, and a midden, are known from the Periman subphase, and these sites are often clustered, sometimes around one larger site. The Duckfoot site (Lightfoot and Etzkorn 1993), described in Chapter 5, is one such habitation (Figure 4.10). It consists of a roomblock with four pit structures securely dated to the A.D. 850s through the 870s. Approximately 3 km east of the Duckfoot site is the Cirque site, another Periman subphase settlement, which appears to have multiple roomblocks and at least one very large pit structure that may have served multiple roomblocks and/or sites. This site, with roomblocks that housed perhaps hundreds of residents, is a village, a type of settlement that first appears during Pueblo I times (Wilshusen 1991). The Cirque site might have been the focal point of a village-centered community that included surrounding smaller sites such as Duckfoot. Earlier villages are known elsewhere in the region. Brew's (1946) Site 13 on Alkali Ridge in southeastern Utah dates to the late eighth century, and large villages in the La Plata district (such as Morris's Site 33) date to the early ninth century. The Dos Casas

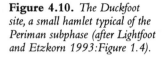

Figure 4.10. *The Duckfoot site, a small hamlet typical of the Periman subphase (after Lightfoot and Etzkorn 1993:Figure 1.4).*

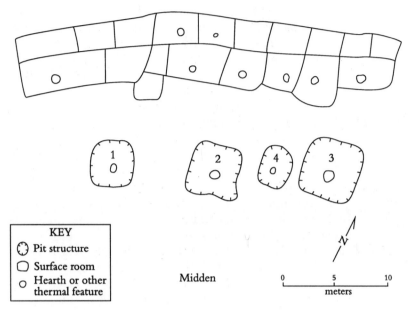

subphase occupation of Grass Mesa Village may also represent a small village. However, at Dolores and possibly in the nearby area, it was not until the later part of the ninth century that a number of large villages were established. These villages are considered to be part of the Periman subphase.

At Dolores, villages comprise aggregations of roomblocks and other structures. Some roomblocks in the Dolores area have as many as 70 to 75 rooms and eight or nine associated pit structures (for example, Rabbitbrush Pueblo [Kuckelman and Harriman 1988]). In addition to roomblocks and small pit structures, a variety of larger "integrative structures" (Adler 1989b; Hegmon 1989b) are present. These include community pit structures, possible plaza areas inside large U-shaped roomblocks, and perhaps great kivas, although at Dolores the great kiva at Grass Mesa Village was no longer in use by the mid-ninth century and the great kiva at Singing Shelter is poorly dated. Community pit structures have rectangular vaults interpreted as specialized ritual features (see Wilshusen 1985, 1986b, 1988b, 1989), and they are often larger than regular pit structures or kivas, although they are smaller than great kivas. Furthermore, community pit structures are generally associated with entire roomblocks rather than with only a few rooms, and they tend to be associated with larger villages (Kane 1986a, 1988; Orcutt and Blinman 1987). An architectural hierarchy can be discerned among the roomblocks and community pit structures at McPhee Village, one of the largest settlements at Dolores (Figure 4.11). Two roomblocks (McPhee Pueblo and Pueblo de las Golondrinas) are U-shaped and have very large community pit structures; other roomblocks have smaller community pit structures; and still others have only regular pit structures (Kane 1988; Wilshusen 1985, 1991).

Periman subphase settlements are located in several places in the DAP study area (Figure 4.8). One cluster of sites in the northern part of the area includes Grass Mesa Village, which has at least seven roomblocks and 28 pit structures. In the central part of the area, McPhee Village (Figure 4.11) consists of 21 habitation units (most of which were assigned individual site numbers), each including surface rooms arranged in roomblocks and associated pit structures. Also in the central part of the area but across the river from McPhee is a cluster of sites that includes House Creek Village (Robinson and Brisbin 1986)

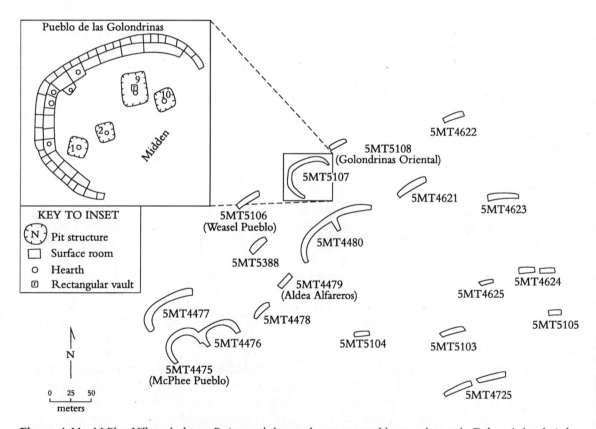

Figure 4.11. *McPhee Village, the largest Periman subphase settlement excavated by researchers at the Dolores Archaeological Program. Shown are the outlines of individual roomblocks; the pit structures associated with the roomblocks are not illustrated. The inset in the upper left corner shows Pueblo de las Golondrinas in more detail; of the 10 pit structures identified at this site, only the four used during the A.D. 840–920 period are shown. The largest, Pit Structure 9, is a community pit structure. All the hearths revealed by excavation at Pueblo de las Golondrinas are shown; however, because not all the rooms were completely excavated, more hearths may have been present prehistorically. After Brisbin (1988:Figure 6.2) and Kane (1988:Figure 1.1).*

and an isolated great kiva at Singing Shelter (Nelson and Kane 1986). It is clear that the habitation sites were occupied during the Periman subphase, but the great kiva at Singing Shelter is very poorly dated and only tentatively associated with the Periman occupation.

The first part of the Periman subphase (from about A.D. 840 to 880) was probably a time of subsistence intensification at Dolores. The subsistence (plant and animal) remains from Dolores-area sites are difficult to interpret partly because incompatible temporal units were used in the analysis (Kane 1986a:371). However, several lines of evidence can be considered. Using information on soil quality, estimated length of the growing season, and settlement size, Kohler et al. (1986) concluded that the "cost" of agriculture (specifically, the effort involved in traveling to and from fields and carrying produce from fields) would have increased around A.D. 840. Populations at larger sites would have been particularly susceptible to those increased costs. The proportion of two-hand manos (in relation to all ground-stone tools) increased during the Periman and Grass Mesa subphases (Phagan 1986:579), which suggests an increase in the grinding of corn. Agricultural field houses (small, one- or two-room sites thought to have been used by people tending fields far from their residences) were most common in the decades from A.D. 840 to 880 (Kohler 1992). The increase in the number of field houses suggests that greater use was being made of lands located at some distance from residences; it may also reflect an increased need to watch or mark fields. The ratio of cooking-jar sherds (argued to be associated with the boiling of cultigens) to animal bones increased after A.D. 850 and again after A.D. 880, which suggests an increased reliance on cultigens relative to game, possibly because game became less available (Blinman 1986c; see also Petersen 1986). The development of increasingly substantial, above-ground, contiguous storage rooms during the eighth century may indicate an increased reliance on cultivation and stored cultigens at that time. Storage rooms again became larger in the mid-ninth century (Gross 1986b), possibly indicating an increase in reliance on stored foods (although Gross's [1986b:622] calculations suggest that adequate storage space was available during all periods). Evidence of subsistence intensification is not clear-cut, however. Petersen (1986) found that the ubiquity of both cultigens and wild plants increased beginning in the eighth century and peaked during the A.D. 840–880 period, contrary to his expectation that wild and cultivated plants would be alternative resources. On the other hand, he found that the ubiquity of corn pollen decreased in the mid-ninth century. Petersen (1986:488) suggests that the apparently conflicting results are due to a false dichotomy between wild and cultivated resources; that is, many plants classified as "wild" colonize disturbed areas and thus are often encouraged by cultivation. Overall, however, these many lines of evidence suggest that residents of the Dolores area intensified their subsistence strategies, including cultivation and possibly the gathering of plants, in the mid-ninth century A.D.

Social integration and ritual also intensified during the ninth century. The repeated architectural unit (consisting of a suite of surface rooms and a pit structure) suggests that the basic social unit and ritual context were well established by the beginning of the century. This social unit may have been an extended family (see Lightfoot's [1992a] interpretation of the Duckfoot site) or a group of smaller households that shared an interhousehold unit, including a pit structure. Integration of multiple extended-household or inter-household units in aggregated communities is inferred from the presence of larger-scale integrative and ritual structures (Wilshusen 1991). On the basis of spatial organization and propinquity (see Lipe 1989), researchers believe that community pit structures were associated with entire roomblocks (in contrast to regular pit structures, which were associated with only a small suite of rooms) and that community pit structures were associated primarily with larger villages (Kane 1986a, 1988; Orcutt and Blinman 1987). Furthermore, community pit structures are distinguished, not only by their larger size, but also by the presence of special ritual features (Wilshusen 1985, 1986b, 1988b, 1989). These pit structures would have contributed to the integration of groups larger than those who shared regular pit structures. Although residents of more than one roomblock or community might have used the community pit structures, the association of these pit structures with particular roomblocks suggests that the facilities were controlled by a particular social group (much the way big-man groups control dance grounds in New Guinea [Strathern 1971]). Great kivas may have been used and shared at the site or intersite level, but their association with mid-ninth-century occupations at Dolores is not well established. Furthermore, because great kivas are not consistently associated with residential sites or particular habitation units (for example, the great kiva at Singing Shelter), they may have been less strongly associated with, or controlled by, localized social groups.

Several lines of evidence suggest that the definition of social units may have become increasingly important as the population grew and subsistence strategies intensified during the mid-ninth century. Access to arable land would have been limited (Orcutt 1986:550-551), and Kane (1986a:369) suggests that corporate-group organization would have helped to maintain access to land through land-tenure systems (see also Adler 1989a; Hayden and Cannon 1982). Preucel (1988:236), cited in Kohler (1992), states that field houses "may have developed as a means of laying claim to especially good agricultural land." The possible shift from great kivas to community pit structures might signal a change from more expansive, area-wide rituals to more community- and/or site-centered practices.

Ninth-century burials in the central Mesa Verde region are found primarily in structures and middens at habitation sites. In some cases, burials are located in the fill layers of abandoned structures; in other cases, entire pit structures apparently were used as graves and were collapsed or burned over bodies that had been placed on the floors (Schlanger 1992; Wilshusen 1986b). Floor burials are primarily associated with the late-ninth-century abandonment of the area. Burials in structure fill were found in many Pueblo I contexts at Dolores and are more common than burials in the midden areas. At the Duckfoot site, which was occupied fairly late in the Pueblo I period, seven burials were found in the midden and seven were found on the floors of pit structures (Lightfoot 1992a). Floor burials, which are often associated with the destruction of a pit structure (see Wilshusen 1986b), may indicate disruption and/or impending abandonment (Schlanger 1992). Burials in midden areas and in the fills of rooms more likely indicate attachment to a site, and the burials in rooms perhaps suggest an association of individuals with particular structures.

The scale of the occupation in the Dolores area increased during the mid-ninth century. Population increased to the highest known prehistoric levels. Schlanger (1986:509) estimates the momentary population for the DAP study area during the A.D. 840–880 period at 1,250 persons, that is, 19 persons per square kilometer or 37 persons per productive square kilometer. Wilshusen (1991:211) argues that the peak Dolores population was 2,860 persons. I use Schlanger's more conservative figures here. A hierarchy of pit structure types—including large and smaller community pit structures, as well as regular pit structures—is evident (Kane 1986a, 1988; Orcutt and Blinman 1987). At least seven aggregated villages were present. Furthermore, settlement data show a three-tiered site-size hierarchy in the Dolores area (Kane 1989).

Interpretations of this increase in scale vary considerably. Orcutt et al. (1990) note that there is no evidence of high-status leaders or elites in architectural patterning, mortuary data, or the distribution of artifacts. Instead they suggest that aggregation during the ninth century was a response to density-dependent competition for productive land. They argue that the aggregates were organized through relatively egalitarian formulations such as consensual leadership or coordination by a leader who lacked economic control (following Johnson and Earle 1987:159). Furthermore, they suggest that the aggregates were unstable, which caused them to dissolve, possibly violently, when environmental conditions worsened.

In contrast, Kane (1989) argues that the settlement hierarchy at Dolores is evidence of some degree of hierarchical social organiza-

tion. He believes that economic factors, specifically, catchment productivity, do not explain the settlement pattern; instead, a social
model in which leaders in the various villages were differentially
successful at attracting followers better explains the settlement hierarchy. However, Kane admits that architectural data are equivocal
regarding the presence of elites. That is, larger sites are associated
with higher-order ritual facilities (large community pit structures),
although the larger sites lack larger storage facilities and elite residences. Furthermore, mortuary evidence gives no indication of elites
at Dolores; one possible "high-status" burial was identified at Dolores,
but it was at House Creek Village, not associated with the largest
sites (Robinson and Brisbin 1986; Stodder 1987). Kane (1989:358)
suggests that "covert leadership groups at Dolores were on the threshold of achieving sanctioned power, but were not able to lift the
traditional checks of ritual and conformity." In addition, he suggests
that the dissolution of local communities and the eventual abandonment of the Dolores area can be viewed as a result of leadership
failure.

On the basis of a detailed comparison of McPhee and Grass Mesa
villages, Wilshusen (1991) offers yet a third interpretation with regard to social complexity. He estimates that McPhee had a population of 560 to 770 persons, whereas Grass Mesa had between 230 and
490 persons. McPhee also had a much more pronounced hierarchy
of ritual structures than did Grass Mesa, and McPhee would have
had a larger ratio of people per community pit structure. Thus,
Wilshusen (1991) argues that, although the community at Grass
Mesa Village may have been organized in terms of a sequential
hierarchy (Johnson 1982), there is evidence of social ranking and a
simultaneous hierarchy at McPhee. Furthermore, he suggests that
differences in social organization may be related to the agricultural
potential around each site. The area around Grass Mesa Village has a
lower risk of cold-air drainage but also has less highly productive
land. In contrast, the area around McPhee Village has more productive potential but also is at greater risk from cold-air drainage.

Taken together, these arguments suggest that evidence of social
hierarchy, even at the peak of the Dolores occupation, is limited at
best. If elites were present, they had few material trappings of their
status and limited economic control, and they did not last long.
Furthermore, the contrasts between McPhee and Grass Mesa villages
noted by Wilshusen (1991) suggest that, even if elites were present,
they were not associated with all the large villages. Thus, evidence of
a valley-wide hierarchy is lacking. Finally, although the population at
Dolores peaked in the mid-ninth century, the various estimates of
population size are below those generally associated with social
complexity. That is, Kosse (1992) found that complex, regionally

organized polities are present when polity population size is greater than 2,500–3,000. Wilshusen's (1991:211) estimate for peak population (2,860) is within this range, but Schlanger's estimate for the momentary population during the A.D. 840–880 period (1,250) is much smaller.

In the final part of the ninth century (after about A.D. 880), population declined across the Dolores area, with the exception of the northern cluster of sites, including Grass Mesa Village. This decline is associated with drought and a shortened growing season and thus with a decrease in agricultural productivity (Petersen 1988:124). In many cases, the Periman subphase villages appear to have been abruptly abandoned (Schlanger and Wilshusen 1993). A number of pit structures were burned, with large numbers of artifacts and sometimes bodies on the floors. Wilshusen (1986b) argues convincingly that the burning was not the result of accident or violence. Instead, the burning appears to have been part of a ritual abandonment. Furthermore, the apparent ritual abandonment was associated primarily with community pit structures, and it was more common at McPhee Village than at Grass Mesa Village. A number of authors (Kane 1989; Orcutt et al. 1990; Wilshusen 1991) interpret this abandonment as a failure of the Dolores population and/or leadership to cope with social and environmental conditions.

Although the aggregated settlement pattern associated with the Periman subphase continued—albeit with a declining population—in a few locations, the settlement pattern changed dramatically in the northern portion of the Dolores area. Researchers at the DAP labeled the new pattern the Grass Mesa subphase (A.D. 870–910). At Grass Mesa Village, and possibly at other sites, including Rio Vista Village (Figure 4.8), some use of surface roomblocks continued, but many interhousehold units were replaced by small pit structures that were often isolated or only loosely associated with surface rooms (Lipe et al. 1988; Wilshusen, comp. 1986). One such pit structure was also present at the Duckfoot site (Lightfoot and Etzkorn 1993).

Pit structures associated with the Grass Mesa subphase are approximately the same size as surface habitation rooms associated with the Periman subphase and therefore are interpreted as single-family dwellings (Kane 1986a:374). These pit structures also have less evidence of ritual (for example, sipapus and benches) than do Periman pit structures. An exception is Pit Structure 32 at Grass Mesa Village, which, because it is large and apparently lacks what are considered to be domestic features (for example, storage pits), has been interpreted as a communally used ritual facility (Lipe et al. 1988:1245–1246).

The Grass Mesa subphase represents a reversal of many of the trends seen in the earlier part of the ninth century. A decrease in settlement permanence and community organization and an increase in mobility are suggested by several lines of evidence (see Kane 1986a:372–373). Architectural variability was much greater, and people seem to have invested less time and energy in constructing permanent facilities. Specially constructed storage facilities were uncommon, which suggests that people also relied less heavily on multi-year storage of resources (Gross 1986b). There is some suggestion that subsistence intensification decreased and that people relied increasingly on wild resources (Lipe et al. 1988:1251–1261; Blinman 1986c).

By about A.D. 910, many of the sites and areas occupied through the ninth century were abandoned, including those areas that saw both Periman and Grass Mesa subphase occupations. With the possible exception of a small population at McPhee Village and the surrounding community, the Dolores area was abandoned (Schlanger 1986). Farther south, there is no evidence of construction or repair at the Duckfoot site after A.D. 876 (Lightfoot 1992b). Elsewhere in the region, the occupation at Badger House on Mesa Verde may have continued into the tenth century (Hayes and Lancaster 1975), but few other sites are securely dated to this period. A major shift in settlement apparently occurred but is poorly understood.

Pottery made in the Mesa Verde region during the ninth century includes Mesa Verde Gray Ware, Mesa Verde White Ware, and San Juan Red Ware. Chapin Black-on-white (Figure 4.2d–g), considered a Basketmaker III/Pueblo I type, was made and used throughout the century, although it was most common in the first few decades. In the central and eastern parts of the region, Piedra Black-on-white (Figure 4.3c–d), considered a Pueblo I type, was common throughout the A.D. 800s, and Cortez Black-on-white, considered an early Pueblo II type, is present, although in fairly small quantities, after about A.D. 880. In the western part of the region (that is, in southeastern Utah), White Mesa Black-on-white (Figure 4.3e–f) appears to be roughly contemporaneous with Piedra Black-on-white. There is some evidence of both local production and intraregional exchange of gray and white wares (Blinman 1986b; Blinman and Wilson 1992). Most San Juan Red Ware, represented primarily by Bluff Black-on-red during the ninth century, was produced in southeastern Utah and imported into the rest of the Mesa Verde region. Pottery imported from outside the Mesa Verde region is present in many assemblages but in very small amounts. Pottery production and exchange are discussed in greater detail in Chapter 6.

The ninth century in the central Mesa Verde region, particularly as it is known from the Dolores area, was a period of short-term economic and social intensification, at least until the A.D. 870s. Some multigeneration aggregated settlements were present by the end of the eighth century. Then, following a hiatus in construction and possibly in the occupation of the area, aggregated and complex settlements became the norm by the middle of the ninth century. Population density and possibly reliance on food production increased. Then, when the climate worsened in the latter part of the century, the population may have been confronted with both subsistence and social stress. One apparent result was a reversal of the intensification trend and a switch to more mobile strategies, as indicated by the settlement patterns during the Grass Mesa subphase (but cf. Orcutt 1986).

Comparing the Study Areas: Implications for Pottery Style

On northern Black Mesa and in the central Mesa Verde region, population levels increased as people moved into the areas during the ninth century A.D., but the processes and apparent consequences were very different in the two areas. On northern Black Mesa, during the early ninth century, people moved into an area that had been at most sparsely inhabited for centuries. Even with this influx, population levels remained low; the population density on northern Black Mesa during the ninth century is estimated to have been less than one person per square kilometer (Plog 1986:Chapter 10). Population levels fluctuated, increased slightly, and the occupation of northern Black Mesa continued into the tenth century.

In the central Mesa Verde region, the Dolores River valley was occupied fairly intensively during the eighth century. Then, following what was possibly a brief hiatus in permanent occupation in the early A.D. 800s, population increased dramatically and peaked between A.D. 860 and 880, for a maximum of about 19 persons per square kilometer (Schlanger 1986, 1988). In the latter part of the century, people began to leave the valley, and it was virtually abandoned by the early tenth century. A similar, though less dramatic, pattern of growth and decline took place across much of the central Mesa Verde region. That is, although some areas (such as Mockingbird Mesa [see Schlanger 1988]) experienced some population growth in the tenth century, sites dating to this period are relatively rare in the region.

These ninth-century developments on northern Black Mesa and in the central Mesa Verde region occurred at a time of climatic deterioration across the northern Southwest. Both the northern Black Mesa and Dolores areas may have experienced relatively favorable conditions in comparison with surrounding areas. However, overall, Dolores offered a much more favorable environment for food production and possibly also for gathering and hunting. Perhaps as a consequence, many more people moved into the Dolores area, which experienced a sort of boom-and-bust cycle in the ninth century, in contrast to much more gradual changes on northern Black Mesa.

Unit-type pueblo architecture was established across the northern Southwest, including in the Kayenta and Mesa Verde regions, during the Pueblo I period. F. Plog (1983) has suggested that this widespread pattern symbolized alliances during the Pueblo I period. Although such alliances may have been present, the architecture also provides more concrete information about the social units that occupied it. Numerous studies have documented links between architecture and other aspects of society; such studies have considered everything from sleeping space to the structural organization of the universe (Bourdieu 1973; Glassie 1975; see also Hegmon 1989b; Rapoport 1982). Architecture is often constructed with a social unit and/or activity in mind, and once constructed, it helps to maintain and reproduce that unit or activity. Thus, differences in the architecture in different regions can provide information about different social practices.

In the Mesa Verde region, a very consistent unit-pueblo architectural pattern was established by the beginning of the ninth century. Each unit consisted of a double row of surface rooms (with smaller storage rooms in back and usually two to four larger dwelling rooms in front), a pit structure, and a midden area (see Figures 4.9 and 4.10). This unit was present on sites of all sizes—from Hamlet de la Olla (Area 2), with nine surface rooms and one pit structure (Etzkorn 1986), to Rabbitbrush Pueblo, with 70 to 75 rooms and eight or nine pit structures (Kuckelman and Harriman 1988). The pattern persisted throughout the century, until the dramatic change in settlement that occurred during the Grass Mesa subphase.

Unit-pueblo architecture was also present, although less formally organized, in the Kayenta region. The basic unit of small roomblock–pit structure–midden was well established by the ninth century and may have been present during the Basketmaker III period. However, the relationship between surface storage rooms and habitation rooms was not consistent, at least at the known Black Mesa sites. Roomblocks generally consist of rows of storage rooms; habitation rooms may or may not be attached, and even when attached, the rooms do not always form a double line. The units were more formally organized on large sites such as D:11:2030 (Figure 4.7, *bottom*) and D:7:134 and were more variable on small sites such as D:11:2023, D:11:2025 (Figure 4.7, *top*), and D:11:2027.

The more formal and consistent unit-pueblo architecture in the Mesa Verde area suggests that the basic social unit was also more formally defined in this area. That is, in the Mesa Verde region, small social units were clearly defined architecturally, even on small sites. In contrast, on Black Mesa, the architectural definition of social units was less clear at small sites and appears to have been well established only at larger settlements.

The differences in architectural units also involve different means of organizing storage. In the Mesa Verde region, storage rooms were consistently attached to dwelling rooms, and the occupants of those rooms would have had exclusive or private access to the stored goods. Again, this pattern is seen even at the smallest sites. The organization of storage is less clear on Black Mesa, where storage and habitation rooms were not consistently attached. It may be that the small sites were occupied by only one family and the entire site was therefore "private," but it is still the case that the architectural definition of an individual household's storage was less well established on Black Mesa than in the Mesa Verde region.

Mobility was greater and settlements less permanent on Black Mesa as compared with Dolores, with the exception of the later Grass Mesa subphase occupation at Dolores. Small habitation sites on Black Mesa appear to have been occupied for only 10 to 15 years. In contrast, many small Dolores sites show evidence of remodeling or reoccupation, suggesting longer-term, if not continuous, use. At least one large site at Dolores, Grass Mesa Village, appears to have been occupied—on and off—for at least 100 years, from the mid- to late eighth century to the late ninth century. On Black Mesa, numerous small, ninth-century sites that lack evidence of year-round occupation occur in the uplands, at some distance from year-round habitation sites, which suggests a high degree of logistic mobility.

Sites and communities were much larger in the Dolores area than on Black Mesa during the ninth century. The smallest Black Mesa habitation sites had only one pit structure and possibly only one surface dwelling room. The small Dolores sites also had only one pit structure, but this structure was generally associated with several substantial surface habitation rooms. Furthermore, large aggregated settlements became common by the mid-ninth century at Dolores. The largest known ninth-century site in the BMAP study area is D:11:2030 (Figure 4.7, *bottom*), which has three roomblocks and five deep pit structures; in contrast, McPhee Village at Dolores comprises 21 roomblock units (Figure 4.11), each with one or more pit structures (however, in neither case were all the units occupied simultaneously). The larger community size in the Mesa Verde region can probably be related to the greater population density in that area.

Only the Mesa Verde region had evidence of large-scale, formalized integrative architecture. Pit structures with ritual features that may have been shared by small groups of households were present in both the Mesa Verde and Kayenta regions; however, community pit structures, great kivas, and more elaborate ritual features were found only in the former.

Finally, these many contrasts between the Pueblo I occupations in the Mesa Verde and Kayenta regions suggest important differences in social organization. Social organization appears to have been more formalized, and social groups more bounded, in the Mesa Verde region. Specifically, the presence of well-defined unit-type pueblos suggests that the basic social unit was more clearly defined in the Mesa Verde region, and larger social units may have been defined in terms of the larger integrative structures. The larger, more permanent settlements probably would have required more predictable means of social integration, which may have centered on these structures. The scale of social integration may have increased at Dolores during the A.D. 840–880 period, when population reached a maximum and there is some evidence of subsistence intensification.

The contrasting interpretations of social relations on northern Black Mesa and in the central Mesa Verde region, as well as the overall differences between the two regions, have a number of implications for the role of style. I conclude this chapter by discussing these implications and relating them to what is known about pottery style at a general level and thus set the stage for the subsequent analysis.

The Mesa Verde region in general had a greater population density, more settlement aggregation, and more evidence of large-scale group activities (in community pit structures) than did Black Mesa and the Kayenta region. Residents of the Mesa Verde region would have interacted more with people to whom they were not closely related. In these contexts, it is likely that it would have been important for people to publicly establish and/or display their social identities. Such display could have taken the form of group presentations (similar to big-man groups in New Guinea [Strathern and Strathern 1971]), or it could have simply involved individuals displaying themselves in the best possible light. In either case, the context is one of relatively high visibility, and Wobst (1977) predicted that, in such contexts, highly visible objects will be most appropriate for carrying stylistic messages. Wobst's prediction has not gone unchallenged; it is clear that objects with low visibility often convey important messages, whereas some highly visible objects are very plain and appear to have little stylistic content (Dietler and Herbich 1989). However, cross-cultural research (Jones and Hegmon 1991) suggests that publicly visible media often do convey stylistic messages regarding group or individual identity. Thus, although the use of style to express personal or social identity may be important in various situations, this role is expected to be particularly important in public contexts involving larger groups of people. Therefore, this role of style is expected to have been more developed in the Mesa Verde region than in the Kayenta region.

Architectural and settlement data suggest that social groups and units were more clearly distinguished at Dolores, in the Mesa Verde region, than on Black Mesa, in the Kayenta region. Larger sites (including some aggregated settlements), consistent patterning of unit-type architecture, and large-scale integrative facilities were all more prevalent in the Mesa Verde region. At Dolores these differences were most pronounced during the A.D. 840–880 period, when there might have been some competition for good agricultural land, as suggested by an increase in field houses and agricultural costs (Kohler et al. 1986; Kohler 1992). Style is expected to play a role in defining and distinguishing social groups, particularly when there is competition between them (Hodder 1979; Wobst 1977). Overall, this role of style would have been more important in the Mesa Verde area than in the Kayenta region, and at Dolores it would have been particularly important during the A.D. 840–880 period.

Style is an important means of establishing one's social identity, but it can express identity in terms of similarity as well as difference. That is, stylistic similarity can be a means of symbolizing solidarity or maintaining social networks, as has been reported for the San (Weissner 1983). The ninth-century inhabitants of Black Mesa were not mobile foragers, but evidence of briefly occupied habitations and extensive use of the uplands suggests that they were fairly mobile. Thus, *extensive* social networks might have been particularly important on northern Black Mesa and possibly across the Kayenta region, in contrast to the more *intensive* social relations in the Mesa Verde region. Style can play an important role in expressing solidarity and maintaining links within such an extensive network. Thus, stylistic similarity, rather than differentiation, is expected to be more prevalent in the Kayenta region.

Finally, in both regions, certain contexts may have been associated with ritual activities. Various lines of evidence, including the presence of ritual features, burials on and under the floors of pit structures, and elaborate—sometimes fiery—abandonments, suggest that pit structures were used for ritual, as well as nonritual, activities. Larger community pit structures may have been particularly important for large-scale ritual. Because ritual involves formalized activities, the style associated with ritual contexts is expected to be relatively formalized (that is, rule-bound). Thus, pottery associated with burials and pit structures is expected to have more formalized designs than pottery found in other contexts.

The expected style differences between the two regions are supported by two general lines of evidence. First, the analyses by Plog (1990b) and Morris (1939) suggest that there are differences in the structure of pottery style in the two regions. Plog found the designs on Kana-a Black-on-white to be relatively invariant, whereas Morris characterized the designs on Piedra Black-on-white as fluid and variable. Second, pottery types provide some information about stylistic diversity and the rate of stylistic change. Both areas had types considered characteristic of the Basketmaker III and Pueblo I periods (Lino Black-on-white and Kana-a Black-on-white in the Kayenta region; Chapin Black-on-white and Piedra Black-on-white in the Mesa Verde region). However, there was more temporal overlap of the types in the Mesa Verde region, which resulted in greater stylistic diversity at any given time. Furthermore, Cortez Black-on-white, considered an early Pueblo II type, appeared in the Mesa Verde region in the last two decades of the ninth century. Although Cortez shows some stylistic continuity with Piedra, it is distinctive in many ways, including technology, layout, and the addition of new design forms such as scrolls. In the Kayenta region, some researchers have distinguished a late Pueblo I/early Pueblo II type called Wepo Black-on-white (Gumerman et al. 1972). However, the distinction between Wepo and Kana-a black-on-white is quite subtle (based on line width and the use of dots rather than ticks). Therefore, the addition of Wepo Black-on-white increases the stylistic diversity much less than does the addition of Cortez Black-on-white. Obviously, pottery types reflect archaeological conventions, but assuming that the types also reflect real similarities and differences in the pottery designs, there appears to have been a greater diversity of designs and a faster rate of change in the Mesa Verde region.

Clearly, the comparison of Plog's (1990b) and Morris's (1939) analyses and the discussion of the types present in the two regions do not provide absolute support for the expectations developed here regarding differences in the roles of style in the two regions. Plog's and Morris's analyses are not easily comparable, because they are based on different sets of criteria and variously defined types. Furthermore, types, the basis of Plog's and Morris's analyses and the basis of the above discussion regarding typological diversity, are archaeological constructs, defined by various researchers in the two regions. They do not necessarily represent prehistoric categories, nor do they necessarily encompass the same kinds of variability (see Plog 1990b). However, taken together, the apparent contrast between Kana-a Black-on-white and Piedra Black-on-white and the discussion of typological diversity at least suggest that the expectations developed here may be valid. More detailed evaluations of these expectations are provided by the analyses reported in Chapter 7, which focuses on style structure, and Chapter 8, which focuses on stylistic similarity and diversity.

5

Background for Analysis:
The Database and the Sites

The Database: Preview and Justification

The Pueblo I period in the northern Southwest provides an excellent context for stylistic analysis for at least two reasons. First, the contrast between the small, dispersed settlements in the Kayenta region and the larger, more aggregated settlements in the Mesa Verde region provides a good basis for comparison. That is, similarities and differences in patterns of stylistic variation can be compared with similarities and differences in the broader cultural contexts. Second, excellent comparative databases are available as a result of recent large-scale projects in both regions—specifically, the Black Mesa Archaeological Project (BMAP), the Dolores Archaeological Program (DAP), and the Crow Canyon Archaeological Center's research at the Duckfoot site. Both regions also have long histories of research that provide important background data. In addition, vegetation and environmental conditions in both regions facilitate detailed chronological control through tree-ring dating. Thus, this case study involves a comparison of pottery styles from the Kayenta and Mesa Verde regions in general and from the northern Black Mesa area and central Mesa Verde region in particular.

The choice of areas and time periods is fairly straightforward. Decisions regarding what kinds of material to include in a study of style are more complex, and many researchers have emphasized the need to include a broad variety of materials (e.g., Hays 1992; Hodder 1982b; Shanks and Tilley 1987b). I chose to focus almost exclusively on designs on black-on-white pottery for both practical and theoretical reasons. Clearly, pottery constitutes a large and well-preserved class of artifacts, although just as clearly, the fact that pottery is conveniently available does not mean that it necessarily can be used to build a meaningful database. However, a number of factors justify the focus.

The presence of painted designs on the pottery implies that a considerable degree of extra effort was spent on decoration. To paint even simple designs on their pots, the early potters would have had to (1) obtain and prepare pigments, (2) obtain and prepare brushes, (3) plan and apply the designs, and (4) control the firing. Although evidence of effort clearly cannot be taken as proof that the early pottery designs conveyed specific stylistic information, the amount of effort involved suggests that, at the very least, the designs were meaningful in some sense (Wylie 1982).

The correlation between changes in pottery design and changes in architecture and settlement during the early Pueblo I period further suggests that pottery style is somehow related to social dynamics. Most significant are changes, not in the content of the designs, but in various dimensions of the designs and in their application. Some of these changes include the following: (1) indications of regional differentiation in design style, (2) increases in the amount of painted area, and (3) application of designs to more vessel forms. The increase in the quantity of decoration (suggested by an increase in the decorated area on a vessel), the greater variety of decorated forms, and the increased fineness of white wares suggest that the amount of effort invested in the production of white wares increased between Basketmaker III and Pueblo I times. Thus, if effort can be linked to cultural meaning in at least a general sense, the argument that the pottery designs were culturally meaningful is even stronger for the Pueblo I period than for the Basketmaker III period.

Several authors have noted that similar designs were applied to various Basketmaker III media, including pottery, basketry, and clothing (Hays 1991; Morris 1927); that is, the style was pervasive (DeBoer 1991). Cross-culturally, such pervasive styles tend to be associated with complex and culturally important messages (for example, Northwest Coast art [Holm and Reid 1975] and the Quenea designs of the Shipibo-Conibo [DeBoer 1991; Gebhart-Sayer 1985]; see discussion in Jones and Hegmon [1991]). Comparable multimedia analyses are not available for Pueblo I material, probably because perishable design-bearing materials are rarely found in Pueblo I sites. Still, if the pervasive Basketmaker III designs were associated with complex and important messages, it is likely that later and more elaborate designs on one of the same media (pottery) might also convey such messages.

Differences and similarities between the Kayenta and Mesa Verde regions and the specific study areas within those regions also provide an important basis for comparison. Differences include the content of black-on-white designs (that is, the specific attributes) and the dimensions of stylistic variation (suggested by the analyses of Plog [1990b] and Morris [1939]), as well as site structure and settlement patterns. The contrasts suggest that style may have had different roles in the two regions. However, despite these differences, both regions are also part of the same general Puebloan cultural tradition, which includes pit structures and pueblos, black-on-white pottery, and pottery designs developed from similar Basketmaker III antecedents. Although "cultural tradition" is a vague and somewhat archaic concept, its importance to contextual interpretations has recently been reestablished (Hodder 1982c). Because the Kayenta and Mesa Verde regions share the same general tradition, differences between them cannot be dismissed simply as a result of different cultural trajectories; instead, explanation or interpretation of those differences emerges as an analytical goal.

For style to have a role in social or cultural dynamics, it must be seen or used in certain contexts, whether in private domestic settings, in esoteric rituals, or in highly visible public displays. Pottery, because it is used to store, cook, serve, and eat food, is used in various contexts, and ethnographic studies suggest that such food-related contexts—and the pottery used in these contexts—often have particular cultural significance (e.g., David et al. 1988; Douglas and Isherwood 1979:66; Goody 1982; Miller 1982; Welbourn 1984; see also Sinopoli 1991:122–124). Archaeologically, the context of pottery use can often be determined by considering both the recovery context and the vessel form, and this kind of information is often available even for small pot sherds. Thus, pottery analysis facilitates the comparison of style in different contexts and at different analytical levels, including within and between sites and regions.

Finally, the focus on white ware pottery is justified because it is the only medium that meets many of the above criteria. That is, different kinds, or types, of white ware with different designs are associated with the different regions. A number of vessel forms are made of white ware, whereas the forms of red and gray ware vessels are more limited (primarily bowls and jars, respectively). Thus, only with white wares can a variety of comparisons (across vessel forms, between contexts, between sites, and between regions) be made.

In the analysis that forms the core of this research, I used two sets of data from the Kayenta and Mesa Verde regions. The *primary database* consists of observations recorded for black-on-white sherds and vessels recovered from well-controlled (that is, relatively undisturbed and well-excavated) archaeological contexts on northern Black Mesa and in the central Mesa Verde region. The materials were analyzed directly as a part of this research; the analyses are discussed in part in Chapter 6 and primarily in Chapter 8. The *secondary database* consists of observations recorded for vessels and large vessel fragments of

Kana-a Black-on-white and Piedra Black-on-white, the dominant Pueblo I white ware types in the Kayenta and Mesa Verde regions, respectively. Some of these pieces were analyzed directly as part of this research; others were analyzed on the basis of published descriptions. These analyses are described in Chapter 7. Chapter 6 also reports some analyses based on published counts of the total pottery assemblages recovered from individual sites or contexts. The contexts are described as part of the analyses, but the database is not discussed separately here.

The Primary Database

The primary database was selected to maximize chronological control. It was derived from the analysis of 1,518 black-on-white sherds and vessels from excavated contexts for which absolute dates, or at least temporal placement based on criteria other than black-on-white design style, are available. Case-by-case data are listed in Hegmon (1990:Appendix D), with the exception of data for D:7:134 on Black Mesa, as is explained in more detail in the discussion of the Black Mesa data. Pottery from 16 sites was analyzed and the results were included in the primary database. Some sites had multiple or lengthy occupations, and the collections from these sites were divided into chronologically distinct assemblages. Otherwise, I treated all the material from one time period at one site as a single assemblage; no intrasite comparisons were made.

Only data on bowls and jars were included in the primary database. Eccentric forms, miniatures, ladles, and scoops often have unusual or irregular painted designs and therefore should not be combined with regular bowls and jars in a stylistic analysis. However, the samples of these other forms are far too small (often with only one or two sherds per site) to allow separate analysis. Sherds were classified as bowls if they had designs on their concave surfaces; a small number of bowls also had designs on their convex surfaces. Some small fragments of scoops or ladles were probably included in the bowl category, but they undoubtedly make up a very small fraction of the assemblage, not enough to have a statistical effect.[1]

---

1. Blinman (1988a) analyzed 376 whole and partial pottery vessels from Dolores sites. Of these, only one was a white ware dipper or ladle, whereas 29 were white ware bowls. Assuming that the ratio of bowl to ladle/dipper sherds is roughly proportional to the ratio of whole vessels, and assuming that bowls are roughly twice the size of ladles and dippers, it is likely that only about 1/60 of the specimens classified as bowl sherds in the stylistic analysis actually were parts of dippers or ladles.

Sherds were classified as jars if they had designs only on their convex surfaces.

All black-on-white bowls and jars, regardless of traditional archaeological type, were considered for inclusion in the analysis. Before the stylistic and technological analyses, the sherds were checked for refits, with most of the effort being devoted to examining sherds from the same or proximate proveniences. Systematic refitting was not done with entire site assemblages, because the samples from many sites included no more than a few hundred white ware sherds. However, in most cases, sherds that were part of the same vessel were identified and the vessel was counted only once. Although site-formation processes were not fully accounted for in all cases, this cursory refitting procedure at least reduced the chances that clusters of similar designs would reflect clusters of sherds from a single vessel (see Schiffer 1989). The results of Lightfoot's (1994) comprehensive refitting of pottery from the Duckfoot site suggest that the abbreviated procedure used here was sufficient preparation for the stylistic analysis. As a result of Lightfoot's (1994:137) research, 125 vessels were reconstructed and over 500 "sherd refits" (sherds that fit together but do not constitute a large proportion of a vessel) were identified. Of these, only eight vessels and two sherd refits, none of which were white wares, included numerous sherds from more than one structure (Lightfoot 1992a).[2]

Only pottery for which at least minimal design attribute information could be judged were included in the analysis. That is, a sherd was included if a primary and/or secondary form or a filled area with a discernible shape or composition was present (these forms are defined in Chapter 8, Table 8.4). For example, a sherd with a large area that was painted solid or filled with hatch was included, even if the form of the filled area could not be determined. However, sherds that had only small solid areas of paint that could have been part of a number of design attributes (for example, the corners of intersecting lines, portions of broad line designs, or portions of solid designs) were excluded from the analysis. In addition, sherds with only a small portion of a line were excluded from the analysis if the shape of the line (straight, curved, etc.) could not be determined. In general, roughly one-third to one-half of the white ware sherds that were considered were included in the analysis. The technological

---

2. Two other vessels and two other sherd refits (including one white ware ladle) also included sherds from more than one structure. However, all but one of the pieces of each of these vessels were found in a single location, and the sherd refits combined only two or three sherds from two or three proveniences.

characteristics (for example, temper, paint type, and surface finish) and design attributes of all pottery analyzed for inclusion in the primary database were analyzed according to the procedures described in Chapter 8.

The primary database includes information on material from sites excavated as part of three different projects: the Black Mesa Archaeological Project, the Dolores Archaeological Program, and the Crow Canyon Archaeological Center's excavation of the Duckfoot site. Because the sites and the strategies used to excavate the sites differed from one project to another, different criteria were used to select the pottery samples from each set of excavations. In general, all black-on-white sherds from sites with fairly small samples of pottery collected from well-controlled contexts were considered for analysis; the maximum sample size for these cases was 139 (from D:11:2023). A few sites produced very large collections of black-on-white pottery from well-dated, unmixed contexts. Analysis of these large collections was limited because of time constraints and because it was necessary to collect samples of roughly similar sizes from all sites: a comparison of samples of widely varying sizes (for example, 100 sherds and 2,000 sherds) would have been of limited utility. Therefore, for sites with very large collections of black-on-white pottery (D:11:2027, D:11:2030, and Duckfoot), all the pottery associated with the structures and a 10 or 20 percent sample of pottery from the midden areas was included in the analysis. The exception was D:7:134, which was added to the study for comparative purposes after the initial analysis had been completed. Very little material could be definitively associated with any particular structure, feature, or occupation at D:7:134, so the materials for analysis were taken from a random 20 percent sample of the site (by area). The pottery samples are explained and brief descriptions of the sites are presented below, by project.

The Black Mesa Archaeological Project

Archaeologists conducted research on northern Black Mesa from 1967 to 1983 (Figure 4.6). Pottery from five sites occupied during the ninth century was included in this analysis. These sites are particularly well-dated with tree-ring samples, and they provide a range of variation in site size, location, and architecture that is important to the analysis. Three of the sites (D:11:2023, D:11:2025, and D:11:2027) are small habitation sites located within half a kilometer of each other on a ridge near Moenkopi Wash in the southern part of the BMAP study area. These three sites are very similar architecturally, and they have buildings whose construction and repair has been dated to approximately A.D. 852–861 (D:11:2023), A.D. 862–863

(D:11:2025), and A.D. 873–877 (D:11:2027). The proximity of the sites, their structural similarities, and the sequence of consecutive dates all suggest that they were occupied sequentially, possibly by the same group of people. Although these three sites are quite small (each has only one pit structure and a small number of surface rooms), each has characteristics indicative of both summer and winter habitation (surface rooms with hearths, external hearths, and substantial pit structures). Furthermore, at least three burials are associated with the occupations of the sites. Thus, it is likely that they were year-round, albeit short-term, habitation sites. The assemblages from these sites provide an opportunity to consider changes in pottery style that occurred over a limited period of time, perhaps across just one generation.

The two other sites, D:11:2030 and D:7:134, are much larger, with five deep pit structures and two or three roomblocks each. D:11:2030 is the largest ninth-century site excavated by BMAP researchers. Other contemporaneous sites in the lowland valleys adjacent to Black Mesa may be larger than D:11:2030, but most are covered with alluvium and none is well known. D:11:2030 is located near the three small sites and, on the basis of tree-ring dates, its occupation is believed to have preceded and overlapped that of the small sites. Comparing D:11:2030 with the three small sites provides an opportunity to assess the effects of site size and occupation length on the pottery assemblages. D:7:134 is located in the northern part of the study area, approximately 16 km from the other sites. It is roughly similar to D:11:2030 in size, and it was occupied during the late ninth century and part of the tenth. Materials from D:7:134 were not included in the initial analysis (reported in Hegmon 1990) but were added later to provide a spatially broader sample of Black Mesa sites. Whereas in the initial analysis I considered a large number of attributes, I recorded only selected attributes for the D:7:134 material; these attributes are used in the analyses discussed in Chapter 8.

Similar excavation strategies were used for all the Black Mesa sites. The four southern sites (excavated in 1982 and 1983) were each divided into four or five sampling strata. Sampling Stratum I on each site included the primary structural remains, and all or a substantial portion of this stratum was excavated. Sampling Stratum II included the midden area. This stratum was extensively tested using both stratified, systematic, unaligned sampling and nonrandom sampling. The remaining strata covered other areas of the sites, and excavation in these areas revealed only isolated features and light scatters of artifacts. Excavations at D:7:134 also involved both random and nonrandom sampling, but a slightly different procedure was used to select areas for excavation. The site was divided into eight approximately equal and arbitrary strata. Excavation focused on structures and features but also included a 5 percent sample of each stratum.

Site D:11:2023

Site D:11:2023 was excavated in 1982 (Olszewski 1984). It consists of a deep, ovoid pit structure, a small roomblock, a midden, and three activity areas. The pit structure has a bench, a sipapu, radial walls, and two connected, adobe-collared hearths. The body of an adult had been formally laid out in the middle of the floor. The roomblock consists of three slab-lined, semisubterranean rooms. Because no hearths were found in any of these rooms, they are interpreted as storage rooms. No jacal structures were found. The activity areas consist of three possible cooking areas inferred from the presence of a roasting pit and two hearths.

The presence of only one pit structure and no definite surface habitation rooms suggests that D:11:2023 was occupied by only a single household, that is, a nuclear family or small extended family. Following Wilshusen (1991:143), who draws on a variety of information about household size in the Southwest and cross-culturally, a household is assumed to include five or six (an average of 5.5) persons.

Tree-ring samples from the pit structure at D:11:2023 yielded a series of cutting dates, with a cluster at A.D. 852–855 interpreted as initial construction and a cluster at A.D. 858–861 interpreted as repair (Smiley and Ahlstrom 1994). Some of the features in the pit structure had been remodeled, but the low artifact density and the small range of dates suggest that the occupation was brief, lasting perhaps 10 years or so. There is no evidence of a later occupation.

The sample considered for analysis consisted of all pottery recovered from excavated contexts in the midden and in and around the structures (Sampling Strata I and II). The sample actually analyzed—after refitting and excluding sherds for which even minimal design information was lacking—consisted of 139 sherds. The results of this analysis were included in the primary database.

Site D:11:2025

Site D:11:2025 was excavated in 1982 (Stone 1984). It consists of a deep, ovoid pit structure, a small roomblock, jacal rooms, a midden, and a possible roasting pit (Figure 4.7, *top*). The pit structure, like that at D:11:2023, has a bench, radial walls, and two connected, adobe-collared hearths. Unlike its counterpart at D:11:2023, the pit structure at D:11:2025 does not have a sipapu. The roomblock consists of a discontinuous arc of three slab-lined storage rooms and two poorly preserved masonry rooms. None has a hearth, but possible pottery manufacturing equipment (a polishing stone and two worked sherds) was found on the floor of two of the rooms. Two jacal structures (which may be the remains of more than two rooms), one with an internal hearth, are located at the side of the site opposite the room-block. One burial was found in the midden, a second was found next to one of the jacal structures, and a third, thought to be intrusive and associated with a brief later occupation (Stone 1984:203), was found on the floor of one of the slab-lined storage rooms. The presence of only one pit structure and one surface habitation room (the jacal room with the hearth) suggests that the site was occupied by only one or two households, that is, between five and 11 persons.

A series of cutting dates indicates that the pit structure at D:11:2025 was constructed in A.D. 862 or 863 (Smiley and Ahlstrom 1994). Single pieces of wood dating to A.D. 848, 851, 858, and 860 were also recovered from the pit structure; these are interpreted as wood that was reused, possibly after being scavenged from D:11:2023 (Stone 1984:197). The pit structure showed some signs of remodeling; how-ever, the low artifact density and the limited range of dates also indicate a brief occupation (roughly 10 to 15 years). The intrusive burial in the roomblock and a concentration of corrugated gray ware sherds around the jacal structures suggest limited later reuse of the site.

The sample from D:11:2025 analyzed for inclusion in the pri-mary database consisted of all pottery recovered from excavated contexts in the midden and in and around the structures (Sampling Strata I and II). The area around the jacal structures (which may have been subject to later reuse) was included so as to not bias the sample against a certain kind of structure. Only one sherd (a piece of Dogoszhi Black-on-white) that may have been associated with the reuse of the site was identified in the sample. The total sample analyzed for the primary database consisted of 104 sherds.

Site D:11:2027

Site D:11:2027 was excavated in 1982 (Olszewski et al. 1984). It consists of a deep, ovoid pit structure; a roomblock; 30 features, including 11 external hearths; and a midden overlying some of the features. No burials were found. The pit structure has a sipapu, radial walls, and two contiguous, adobe-collared hearths. A number of arti-facts were found on or near the floor, including polishing stones and two black-on-white vessels. The roomblock consists of four semisubterranean, slab-lined storage rooms that were probably con-structed in two episodes, a centrally located surface room, and a poorly preserved jacal structure. Polishing stones and a shallow, clay-lined basin were discovered in the central room, which suggests that it may have been used for pottery production. This site, like D:11:2023 and D:11:2025, is estimated to have housed only one or two house-holds, that is, between five and 11 persons.

The pit structure at D:11:2027 yielded a cluster of tree-ring cutting dates that indicates construction in A.D. 873–874; single dates of A.D. 875 and 877 are evidence of later repair (Smiley and Ahlstrom 1994). The substantial midden, the presence of features that predate the midden, and the indication of separate episodes of construction for the roomblock all suggest that D:11:2027 was occupied for a longer period (more than 10 years) than were the other two small sites. However, there is no evidence of a later (post–A.D. 870s) reoccupation.

The sample analyzed for the primary database consisted of all pottery recovered from excavated contexts in and around the structures (Sampling Stratum I) and the midden features (part of Sampling Stratum II) and a portion of the pottery in the remainder of the midden. The midden sample included pottery from excavated units that covered 20 percent of Sampling Stratum II.[3] The total pottery sample analyzed for inclusion in the primary database consisted of 161 sherds and vessels.

Site D:11:2030

Site D:11:2030 was excavated in 1982 and 1983 (Green et al. 1985). It consists of three roomblocks, five deep pit structures, other features and small structures, and a large midden, from which seven burials were recovered (Figure 4.7, *bottom*).

Roomblocks 1 and 2 are each associated with one deep pit structure, and the configurations of surface rooms and pit structures are similar to those seen at the three small sites. Each roomblock consists of three slab-lined, semisubterranean storage rooms. One or two jacal rooms (some with hearths) adjoin or are adjacent to the storage rooms. The pit structures each have one hearth (they lack the distinctive double-collared hearths of the small sites) and radial walls, but no sipapus.

Roomblock 3 consists of a double row of rooms, a configuration that is not common at the other ninth-century Black Mesa sites but is ubiquitous in the Mesa Verde region. The roomblock was not completely excavated, but it appears to include at least 23 rooms, with smaller storage rooms in the rear fronted in many places by

---

3. Sampling Stratum II, as defined by BMAP researchers, includes 45 2-x-2-m squares. Twelve of these squares were excavated as part of the random sample, and 12 were excavated as part of the judgmental sample. I included pottery from a 20 percent random sample of these 45 units, which resulted in the inclusion of materials from nine units.

larger jacal structures. The jacal rooms may have been habitation areas, although the partial excavation did not reveal any internal hearths. Three deep pit structures are associated with Roomblock 3. They were not completely excavated, but hearths were found in all three.

Pit Structure 9 is centrally located in relation to the length of the roomblock and, with a floor area of 30.17 m^2, is the largest pit structure at the site. Its size led Green et al. (1985:241) to suggest that it may have been used as a ceremonial gathering place. This structure also has the distinctive double-collared hearth found in the pit structures at the small sites but not present in the other pit structures at D:11:2030. Furthermore, it was not filled with trash and therefore may have been in use throughout the occupation of the site. Pit Structure 9 is within the size range of community pit structures at Dolores (that is, larger than 24 m^2 [Kane 1988:49]), although it lacks the distinctive ritual features found in the Dolores community pit structures. The interpretation of Pit Structure 9 as a community gathering or ceremonial location is plausible, though far from clear-cut. No other possible ninth-century community pit structures or integrative structures have been identified on Black Mesa or in the Kayenta region, although few sites dating to this period have been investigated.

Behind the roomblock are four clay-lined basins (Features 17, 18, 19, and 21) that may have been used for mixing clay, possibly for pottery manufacture. The largest (Feature 21) is 1.56 m long and 1.22 m wide. Tree-ring dates indicate that the site was occupied from at least the A.D. 840s through the 870s. Pit Structure 9 yielded five cutting dates ranging from A.D. 840 to 842, which indicate construction in the early 840s, the earliest well-dated construction event at the site. The other two pit structures associated with the large roomblock did not yield any dates. They apparently were robbed of their beams and then were filled with trash, which suggests that they were built and used early in the site's occupation and abandoned before the site as a whole was abandoned.

Pit Structure 2 (associated with Roomblock 2) yielded two clusters of cutting dates, one in the A.D. 840s and one in the 860s and 870s. These dates could indicate two construction episodes for Pit Structure 2, although it is more likely that the earlier (A.D. 840s) cluster dates beams that were taken from one of the pit structures associated with Roomblock 3 and reused in Pit Structure 2 (Smiley and Ahlstrom 1994). If this is the case, Pit Structure 2 was constructed fairly late in the occupation of the site. Roomblock 1 and Pit Structure 1 are not well dated.

Although the sequence of occupation of the various units cannot be absolutely determined, it is clear that all the structures were not occupied at the same time (see Nichols and Powell 1987). Smiley and Ahlstrom (1994) argue that only two of the four pit structures associated with Roomblocks 2 and 3 were occupied at the same time.

Eight jacal rooms are present on D:11:2030. The number of rooms suggests that if the entire site had been used simultaneously, it would have been occupied by roughly eight households, or 44 persons. However, tree-ring dates from the pit structures suggest that only about half of them (two or three of five) were occupied simultaneously. Therefore, it is likely that the maximum momentary occupation of the site included only about four households, or 22 persons.

To limit the sample size and consider a sample roughly equal in size to samples from the smaller sites, only a portion of the pottery recovered from D:11:2030 was considered for analysis as part of the primary database. Because the site is so large, only pottery from the unit consisting of Roomblock 3 and its associated pit structures was selected for the analysis. Occupation and use of the unit, including the discarding of trash in two of the pit structures, probably spanned most of the site's use life (about 40 years). Pottery recovered from the floor and fill of Roomblock 3 and its associated pit structures was considered for analysis. The sample also included material recovered from 10 percent of the excavated midden area[4] and whole vessels recovered from other areas of the site. The total sample analyzed for inclusion in the primary database consisted of 299 sherds and vessels.

Site D:7:134

Site D:7:134 was excavated in 1975 (Klesert 1977; Layhe et al. 1976:1–14; Powell 1984:121–130). It consists of one large, centrally located pit structure, four smaller pit structures, two roomblocks, several jacal structures, and numerous features, including burials outside the structures. One roomblock comprises seven rear masonry rooms fronted by jacal structures; the other consists of three masonry rooms with attached jacal structures. The large pit structure was excavated into the bedrock and has features (including post holes indicative of a cribbed roof and a full bench) more typical of later kivas. Two of the smaller pit structures have hearths and/or ventilator shafts and may have been habitation areas (that is, pithouses); the others have no identifiable features but are associated with a grinding area.

---

4. A 25 percent unaligned sample of 2-x-2-m units in the midden was excavated in addition to the burials. I divided this sample into two strata (north and south) and took a random sample from each stratum, including a total of 10 percent of the excavated units.

On the basis of wall bonding and abutment, fill sequences, and construction style, the long roomblock appears to have been built in several stages (Layhe et al. 1976:12,14). The large pit structure is believed to have been constructed after some parts of the site had been abandoned, because bedrock debris (apparently removed during the construction of the pit structure) was found in the fill of one of the surface rooms. Tree-ring dates indicate that there were episodes of construction between about A.D. 850 and 870 and again around A.D. 940 (Smiley and Ahlstrom 1994). It is not clear if the site was continuously occupied through the mid-ninth and early tenth centuries or if there were two distinct occupations.

Most of the pottery found on D:7:134 cannot be associated with any particular construction episode and can be dated only generally to the A.D. 850–950 period. Therefore, this material was not initially analyzed for the primary database, which consisted only of data from tightly controlled contexts from the four clustered sites (D:11:2023, D:11:2025, D:11:2027, and D:11:2030). The material from D:7:134 was added later to provide a sample that was different—and spatially distant—from samples representing the other BMAP sites. All the pottery from excavated contexts across 20 percent of the site (randomly selected) was considered for analysis in developing the primary database. The total sample analyzed for the primary database consisted of 217 sherds and vessels.

The Dolores Archaeological Program

Archaeologists with the Dolores Archaeological Program conducted research in the Dolores River valley from 1978 through 1985 (Figure 4.8). Pottery from 10 sites occupied during the ninth century was included in this analysis. The sites were selected to provide a range of sizes, architectural components, and time periods.

Many sites are quite large and most were not completely excavated. Instead, a combination of judgmental and random sampling techniques was used to select structures and units in surrounding areas for excavation. Much of the excavation focused on understanding occupational sequences and architectural details.

Temporal control of pottery recovered from the Dolores sites is problematic for at least two reasons. First, much of the wood used in construction could not be dated through tree-ring dating. Absolute dating of Dolores sites was limited to a scattering of tree-ring dates, as well as a few archaeomagnetic and radiocarbon dates. Second, many of the Dolores sites were occupied for more than 50 years (though not always continuously), and it was not unusual for a site to have had multiple construction episodes.

Researchers at the DAP were able to obtain fairly good chronological control by taking into account all possible information, including architectural characteristics, the content of the pottery assemblage, and the few absolute dates that were available. Fortunately for this analysis, pottery dating at the DAP focused primarily on the presence of various wares and technological characteristics. White ware design style was not considered in the dating scheme, except that the presence of Cortez Black-on-white, which is distinguished on the basis of both technology and design style, was one of the criteria used to distinguish assemblages dating to after A.D. 880 (Blinman 1988c).

For each excavation unit, DAP researchers assessed the context and assemblage content. For each assemblage, they determined the following: (1) its integrity (whether and to what extent it was mixed), (2) its association with a particular structure or occupation, and (3) its temporal placement in terms of modeling periods (abbreviated "MP" throughout the remainder of this volume). They also assigned a confidence level to the temporal placement.

This research relied heavily on the assessments of DAP researchers. All pottery from relatively unmixed contexts (element integrity in the DAP database = 3 or 4) that could be dated with a relatively high degree of certainty (modeling period confidence = 3 or 4) was considered for analysis as part of the database. These same criteria were used by many DAP researchers in other pottery analyses (e.g., Blinman 1988b). The resulting pottery sample is fairly small, especially considering the massive scale of excavations, but it is well controlled. These assemblages include pottery from both the judgmental and random samples from various areas of the sites, and they are divided according to date ranges that correspond to DAP modeling periods: A.D. 800–840 (MP 3), A.D. 840–880 (MP 4), and A.D. 880–920 (MP 5). For some purposes, the sample was divided by subphase on the basis of the presence or absence of a community pit structure.

The DAP sites used in the analysis are described briefly below, grouped by community affiliation or area. Because the assessments used to select the samples analyzed as part of the database were made by DAP researchers, the distribution of particular samples or specific chronological evidence is not discussed here. Information on site chronology is available in the site reports (cited below, in the individual site descriptions), as well as in the synthetic studies produced by the DAP (including Blinman 1988c; Hathaway 1988; and Kane 1986a).

Grass Mesa Community

Grass Mesa Village. Grass Mesa Village (Site 5MT23 [Lipe et al. 1988]) is one of the largest sites excavated by DAP researchers. Throughout the ninth century, the occupations at Grass Mesa Village differed in many ways from those at most other Dolores sites.

Aggregated settlement of Grass Mesa Village began in the late eighth century, and the site at this time was one of the only aggregated settlements of the Dos Casas subphase (A.D. 760–840). Unfortunately, evidence of the Dos Casas occupation was severely disturbed by later construction; the architectural configuration is poorly known, and few artifacts can be securely associated with it. The occupation is represented by at least 12 pit structures, most or all with associated surface rooms, and a very large great kiva with a floor area of approximately 401 m^2. One of the other pit structures is also very large (49 m^2), although it was poorly preserved. On the basis of his analysis of materials recovered from a random sample of excavation units, Kohler (1988) estimates that Grass Mesa Village was occupied by 17 households (roughly 94 persons) in the early ninth century (MP 3).

There is no evidence of construction between roughly A.D. 830 and 850, and Grass Mesa Village may not have been occupied during that time. Following this interval, there was a period of major construction during which several large roomblocks and pit structures characteristic of the Periman subphase were built. The Periman occupation is represented by one extremely large roomblock and six other smaller roomblocks, all with associated pit structures. Roomblocks that were investigated were found to consist of double rows of small rear rooms and larger front rooms. The largest roomblock is approximately 130 m long and includes approximately 80 rooms (this estimate is based on the 20 outlined rooms revealed in Area 3 [not including Rooms 1 and 137], which constitute approximately one-fourth of the total roomblock). Kohler (1988) estimates that Grass Mesa Village was occupied by an average of 92 households, or 506 persons, between A.D. 840 and 880 (MP 4).

At least five fairly large (over 35 m^2) pit structures are known to have been part of the A.D. 840–880 architecture at Grass Mesa Village. Those that were excavated sufficiently to allow observation have rectangular floor vaults, which are thought to have served as elaborate ritual features (Wilshusen 1989). A number of smaller pit structures also have rectangular vault features. However, neither the large pit structures nor the vault features tend to be associated with the larger roomblocks; one of the large pit structures is associated with one of the smallest roomblocks. On the basis of the ratio of rooms to pit structures, Wilshusen (1985, 1991) argues that at Grass Mesa Village there were only four or five households for each pit structure with a rectangular vault feature, in contrast to 13 or 14 households per community pit structure at McPhee Village. Therefore, the pit structures at Grass Mesa Village that are large and/or have rectangular vaults do not appear to have functioned as community integrative facilities, and they are not classified as community pit structures.

In the last part of the ninth century, Grass Mesa Village was again reorganized. Many of the Periman structures were abandoned and replaced by a scattering of small pit structures (49 are known). These pit structures are highly variable in size and construction details, they often lack wing walls and ritual features, and they are interpreted as primarily habitation units (that is, pithouses). Some surface rooms, including portions of the Periman roomblocks, were also used during this time, although some of the rear storage rooms appear to have been converted to habitation areas. Overall, there was a decrease in storage space and architectural investment during the Grass Mesa subphase. One Grass Mesa subphase pit structure (Pit Structure 32) is quite large (42.5 m^2) and may have been a community facility. This large pit structure does not have wing walls, a sipapu, or a vault, and it is not associated with a large roomblock; therefore, it probably served a different function than did the Periman community pit structures. Kohler (1988) estimates that an average of 124 households, or 682 persons, occupied Grass Mesa Village during the A.D. 880–920 period (MP 5).

The pottery sample from Grass Mesa Village analyzed for the primary database consisted of 81 sherds and vessels: two from contexts dating to A.D. 800–840 (MP 3), 32 from contexts dating to A.D. 840–880 (MP 4), and 47 from contexts dating to A.D. 880–920 (MP 5). The MP 4 sample is associated with the Periman subphase (with no community pit structure), and the MP 5 sample is associated with the Grass Mesa subphase.

Prince Hamlet. Prince Hamlet (Site 5MT2161 [Sebastian 1986]) is a small site in the northern part of the DAP study area, just over a kilometer from Grass Mesa Village. On the basis of the clustered settlement pattern throughout the Dolores River valley and the proximity of Prince Hamlet and Grass Mesa Village, Prince Hamlet is considered to be part of Grass Mesa community. Structures from two occupations are present at the site. The earlier occupation is represented by one isolated storage room and the lowest layers of the midden. Part of this occupation is dated to A.D. 800–840 (MP 3). The A.D. 840–920 (MP 4 and MP 5) occupation includes a roomblock with a double row of 19 rooms and two pit structures. Both pit structures have hearths and wing walls but no sipapus; neither is interpreted as a community pit structure. Prince Hamlet was probably originally occupied by only a single household. The second occupation involved the use of what appear to be five surface habitation rooms, which suggests that the site was occupied by roughly five households, or 27 persons (see Sebastian 1986:437).

The pottery sample from Prince Hamlet analyzed for the primary database consisted of 26 sherds: 19 dating to A.D. 800–840 (MP 3), two dating to A.D. 840–880 (MP 4), and five dating to A.D. 880–920 (MP 5). The MP 4 and MP 5 samples are both associated with the Periman subphase, with no community pit structure.

Central DAP area

As used here, the central DAP area encompasses the area north of McPhee Village and south of the Grass Mesa community; it includes the area designated by DAP researchers as the Middle Canyon area (Kane and Robinson 1986).

House Creek Village. House Creek Village (Site 5MT2320 [Robinson and Brisbin 1986]) is a large site located across the Dolores River from, and slightly north of, McPhee Village (described below). The site includes an extensive arc of rubble mounds indicative of perhaps four roomblocks. Only one small mound and a portion of a larger one were excavated. Both areas have evidence of an occupation dating to the Periman subphase, and the larger complex also has evidence of an occupation dating to the Dos Casas subphase. The only Dos Casas structure excavated is a small, subrectangular pit structure with a hearth, a sipapu, and a burial on the floor. The small complex consists of a double row of eight rooms, as well as one pit structure, which has a hearth and a sipapu, but no wing wall. Only small portions of the large rubble mound and associated Periman subphase pit structures were excavated. One pit structure is subrectangular and has a hearth and a sipapu. A community pit structure was not identified. Given the limited excavation at House Creek Village, overall population estimates cannot be derived, although Robinson and Brisbin (1986:753) suggest estimates for at least one area of the site.

The pottery sample from House Creek Village analyzed for the primary database consisted of 28 sherds and vessels, 17 associated with the A.D. 800–840 period (MP 3) and 11 with the A.D. 840–880 period (MP 4). The MP 4 assemblage is associated with the Periman subphase, with no community pit structure.

Windy Wheat Hamlet. Windy Wheat Hamlet (Site 5MT4644 [Brisbin 1986]) is a small site in the center of the DAP study area, west of the river canyon, and about 1.5 km north of McPhee Village. The hamlet consists of a small row of surface rooms and three pit structures. There is evidence of three occupations at Windy Wheat. Only the latest occupation dates to the ninth century, and it is confined to the A.D. 800–840 period (Dos Casas subphase). One pit structure was constructed about A.D. 800, and a second pit structure, constructed in the A.D. 770s, may still have been in use in the early 800s. Both pit structures are subrectangular, and both contain hearths and wing walls, as well as sipapus surrounded by possible prayer stick holes. Using various estimation methods, including calculations based on roofed space and consideration of household clusters, Brisbin (1986:726) estimates that an average of 15 to 25 individuals occupied Windy Wheat Hamlet in the early ninth century. At least two, and possibly as many as four, habitation rooms were associated with this occupation (Brisbin 1986:727). If each of the four rooms had been occupied by a household of 5.5 persons, the site population would have been 22 persons.

The pottery sample from Windy Wheat Hamlet analyzed for the primary database consisted of 11 sherds dated to A.D. 800–840 (MP 3).

Periman Hamlet. Periman Hamlet (Site 5MT4671 [Wilshusen 1986a]) is a small site on the Dolores River floodplain in the northern part of the Middle Canyon area. The site consists of a double row of 14 rooms with one pit structure and a midden. The occupation is dated to the A.D. 800–840 period. The pit structure has a hearth, a wing wall, and an elaborate ritual feature known as a complex sipapu (Wilshusen 1986b). If the four surface rooms that have hearths are assumed to have been household habitation rooms, then the population of Periman Hamlet is estimated to have been 22 persons (see Wilshusen 1986a:165).

The pottery sample from Periman Hamlet analyzed for the primary database consisted of 12 sherds recovered from contexts that date to the A.D. 800–840 period (MP 3).

Rio Vista Village. Rio Vista Village (Site 5MT2182 [Wilshusen, comp. 1986]) is a large site in the Middle Canyon area. It is located on a bench east of the Dolores River and is surrounded by a cluster of smaller sites. Rio Vista was occupied before the ninth century and probably during the A.D. 800–840 period, but evidence of the early occupation was severely disturbed by later construction. The site consists of four roomblock units, three of which were investigated.

The largest occupation of Rio Vista was during the second half of the ninth century and is characteristic of the Periman subphase. The three roomblocks that were investigated were associated with this occupation. All three consist of double rows of rooms. The smallest has eight rooms and one associated pit structure. The next largest consists of at least 17 rooms and two pit structures. One of these pit structures (Pit Structure 201) is classified as a community pit structure; it has a rectangular vault feature and is fairly large (33.2 m²). The largest roomblock has at least 30 rooms, possibly including a third row, and three associated pit structures. One of these pit structures (Pit Structure 107) is also classified as a community pit structure; although it is not particularly large (26.6 m^2), the structure does have a rectangular vault. Because of the site's complex occupational history, it is difficult to estimate population, but the presence of approximately 22 front (that is, possible household habitation) rooms associated with the Periman subphase occupation (Wilshusen, comp. 1986:Figure 3.150) suggests a maximum momentary population of roughly 121 persons.

The occupation of the site in the late ninth century is poorly understood. The large roomblocks were abandoned, leaving only three small pit structures and possibly two surface rooms in use during this late period. None of the pit structures were extensively excavated, although the limited excavations revealed hearths. Two pit structures are quite small—one has an area of 12.3 m^2, and another has an estimated diameter of 4 m. The third pit structure is larger, with an area of 26.1 m^2. This occupation is considered part of the Grass Mesa subphase.

The pottery sample from Rio Vista analyzed for the primary database consisted of 17 sherds and vessels, 16 dated to the A.D. 840–880 period (MP 4) and one to the A.D. 880–920 period (MP 5). The A.D. 840–880 assemblage is associated with the Periman subphase occupation (including a community pit structure), and the post–A.D. 880 assemblage is associated with the Grass Mesa subphase occupation.

McPhee Village

McPhee Village is a large, aggregated settlement in the central portion of the Dolores valley (Kane and Robinson 1988) (Figure 4.11). It comprises at least 21 roomblock units, including two U-shaped roomblocks that enclose plazas and have very large community pit structures (Pueblo de las Golondrinas and McPhee Pueblo). Several other roomblocks also have community pit structures. Many of the roomblock units were designated as separate sites. Pottery from four of these sites—Aldea Alfareros, Pueblo de las Golondrinas, Golondrinas Oriental, and Weasel Pueblo—was included in the analysis.

The large, aggregated occupation of McPhee Village dates primarily to the later part of the ninth century (after A.D. 840), although an early occupation probably dates to the late seventh century, and two of the roomblocks were constructed during the A.D. 800–840 period. The village was abandoned between approximately A.D. 900 and 920. Later, in the tenth century, a small population returned and reinhabited some of the roomblocks. The focus here is on the aggregated occupation that dates to the post–A.D. 840 period. Using estimates based on roomblock length and assuming that there was a

75 percent occupancy rate, Kane (1988:38) estimates the momentary population of McPhee Village to have been 328 at around A.D. 840, 640 at around A.D. 870–880, 481 in the A.D. 880s, and 94 in the last decade of the ninth century.

Aldea Alfareros. Aldea Alfareros (5MT4479 [Kleidon 1988]) is the smallest of the four McPhee sites included in this analysis. It consists of a roomblock with three front and two rear rooms, two deep pit structures, features, and a midden. Both pit structures have hearths and wing walls; one pit structure has a sipapu, and the other has a series of small holes interpreted as prayer stick holes (see Brisbin 1986:668–669). More than half a kilogram of unfired clay and 12 unfired sherds were found in Pit Structure 2, which suggests that pottery was made in the structure.

The pottery sample from Aldea Alfareros analyzed for the primary database consisted of 82 sherds and vessels dated to the A.D. 840–880 period (MP 4). In the analyses, the occupation is classified as part of the Periman subphase, with no community pit structure.

Pueblo de las Golondrinas. Pueblo de las Golondrinas is the largest of the McPhee sites included in the study. It is flanked by two smaller sites, Golondrinas Oriental and Weasel Pueblo, and together these three sites constitute a cluster within the village.

Pueblo de las Golondrinas (5MT5107) consists of a U-shaped roomblock with 48 rooms, 10 pit structures (some of which were superimposed), and a large midden (Brisbin 1988; see inset, Figure 4.11). The roomblock and at least four of the pit structures were used during the second half of the ninth century. One of these pit structures (Pit Structure 9) is very large (64 m^2) and has a rectangular vault feature. These characteristics, as well as the location of the structure in the plaza of a U-shaped roomblock, indicate that it was a community pit structure. The pottery sample from Pueblo de las Golondrinas analyzed for the primary database consisted of 47 sherds and vessels, seven dated to the A.D. 840–880 period (MP 4) and 40 dated to the A.D. 880–920 period (MP 5). The occupation in both periods is classified as Periman subphase, with a community pit structure.

Golondrinas Oriental. Golondrinas Oriental (5MT5108 [Kuckelman 1988]) has a suite of structures similar to that at Aldea Alfareros, although Golondrinas Oriental is slightly larger. The site was occupied primarily in the second half of the ninth century. It has two pit structures and a double row of 14 rooms. Both pit structures have hearths, wing walls, and burials interred on the floors; a sipapu surrounded by possible prayer stick holes was identified in one pit structure. Several sherd scrapers, possibly used in pottery manufacture, were found at the site. The pottery sample from Golondrinas Oriental analyzed as part of the database for this research consisted of only 20 sherds and vessels, all dated to the A.D. 880–920 period (MP 5). The occupation is classified as Periman subphase, with no community pit structure.

Weasel Pueblo. Weasel Pueblo (5MT5106 [Morris 1988]) is only slightly larger than Golondrinas Oriental, but it has one community pit structure. The primary occupation, which dates to the late ninth century, is represented by three pit structures, a double row of 18 rooms, features, and a midden. All three pit structures have hearths and wing walls. Pit Structure 2 has a floor area of 24.3 m^2 and a rectangular vault feature. Although not especially large, Pit Structure 2 is centrally located and therefore is classified as a community pit structure. Pit Structure 3 has a complex sipapu surrounded by prayer stick holes, and four burials surrounded by 40 gaming pieces were interred on the floor. The only ritual features found in the third pit structure were a number of prayer stick holes. The pottery sample from Weasel Pueblo analyzed for the primary database consisted of 41 sherds dated to the A.D. 880–920 period (MP 5). The occupation is classified as Periman subphase, with a community pit structure.

The Crow Canyon Archaeological Center

The Duckfoot site (5MT3868) was excavated by the Crow Canyon Archaeological Center between 1983 and 1987 (Lightfoot and Etzkorn 1993). Although Duckfoot is approximately 24 km from the Dolores River valley, pottery from the site was included in the analysis in part to provide a contrast to the Dolores assemblage in terms of site size and location. The site consists of a roomblock, four pit structures, and a large midden area. Its location is shown in Figure 4.5, and its plan is illustrated in Figure 4.10. The site was very well preserved and thoroughly investigated. All the structures, the entire courtyard, and most of the midden were excavated, and areas beyond the apparent extent of the site were tested.

The roomblock consists of a double row of rooms, with larger habitation rooms (many with hearths) in front and smaller storage rooms in the rear. Pit Structures 1, 2, and 3 appear to be "typical" Periman subphase pit structures. They are subrectangular and range in size from 14.9 to 23.9 m^2. All three have hearths, sipapus, and burials on the floor, and two of the three have wing walls. Pit Structure 4 has the same features as the others (including burials and a wing wall), but it is ovoid and much smaller (8.9 m^2) and therefore more closely resembles the pit structures associated with the Grass Mesa subphase at Dolores.

The early part of the occupation of Duckfoot was associated with the three large pit structures (Pit Structures 1, 2, and 3) and the roomblock. Cutting dates suggest that initial construction or collecting of construction wood began in the A.D. 850s; strong clusters of dates indicate continued construction or remodeling during the 860s; and scattered dates suggest even later remodeling during the A.D. 870s. Pit Structure 4 was built in the early A.D. 870s, and at some point during the occupation, the functions of several of the surface rooms changed from storage to habitation or vice versa. There is no evidence of construction or remodeling after A.D. 876. Features excavated into the fill of Pit Structure 3 and one of the surface rooms indicate later reuse of the site. If each large front room at the Duckfoot site had been occupied by one household, an assumption commonly made in interpretations of DAP sites, approximately 38 people would have occupied the site. Lightfoot (1994) offers an alternative interpretation. He argues that each architectural suite (that is, a pit structure and associated surface rooms) was occupied by one household and that only between 14 and 25 people occupied Duckfoot at any one time (Lightfoot 1994:149).

All the pottery from tightly controlled excavated contexts in the pit structures and rooms and from 20 percent of the midden[5] were considered for analysis in developing the primary database. The total sample from Duckfoot actually analyzed as part of the primary database consisted of 223 sherds and vessels. This sample is considered to be contemporaneous with the samples from the A.D. 840–880 occupation at Dolores. In the analyses, Duckfoot is classified as a Periman subphase occupation, with no community pit structure, and for some analyses, it is grouped with the Dolores sites.

The Secondary Database

The secondary database was compiled to provide the largest possible sample of black-on-white designs for the structural analysis. Data derived from the analysis of 305 vessels and large sherds recovered from Pueblo I sites across the Kayenta and Mesa Verde regions was included. The sites are listed in Table 5.1; case-by-case data are presented in Hegmon (1990:Appendix B). To obtain an adequate sample, I included pottery from less-than-ideal contexts—for example, contexts

---

5. Almost all of the midden was excavated in 2-×-2-m units. To limit the sample size, I divided the excavated area into four strata and took a 20 percent random sample of each.

Table 5.1. Origins of Pottery Analyzed for Inclusion in the Secondary Database

Site or Area	Source[a]	Kana-a Black-on-white		Piedra Black-on-white	
		Bowls	Jars	Bowls	Jars
Rainbow Bridge/Monument Valley sites (northeastern Arizona and southeastern Utah)	Beals et al. 1945:Figures 18–25	60	1		
D:7:134	Black Mesa Archaeological Project	3	5 vessels, 6 cases		
D:7:216	Black Mesa Archaeological Project		2		
D:11:2023	Black Mesa Archaeological Project		2		
D:11:2025	Black Mesa Archaeological Project	3	2		
D:11:2027	Black Mesa Archaeological Project	17	7 vessels, 8 cases		
D:11:2030	Black Mesa Archaeological Project	23	15		
D:7:2103	Black Mesa Archaeological Project	1			
Unknown	Colton 1953:Figure 17	1	1		
Northeastern Arizona	Kidder and Guernsey 1919:Plate 63	1	3		
Navajo Reservoir, New Mexico	Lister and Lister 1969:Figure 18		2 vessels, 3 cases		
Lowry Ruin, Colorado	Martin 1936:Plate CVI	1			
ca. Blue Canyon (Moenkopi Wash, north of Hopi)	Martin and Willis 1940:Plates 2–4		2 vessels, 3 cases		
North of Holbrook, Arizona	Martin and Willis 1940:Plates 2–4		2		
Bidahochi (Hopi Buttes)	Martin and Willis 1940:Plates 2–4	1			
Hopi	Martin and Willis 1940:Plates 2–4	1	5 vessels, 6 cases		
Unknown	Dittert and Plog 1987:Figure 90		1 vessel, 2 cases		
Tse-Ta'at (Canyon de Chelly)	Steen 1966:35	1			
Duckfoot	Crow Canyon Archaeological Center			7	5 vessels, 6 cases
Aldea Alfareros	Dolores Archaeological Program			9	2
Golondrinas Oriental	Dolores Archaeological Program			3	3 vessels, 4 cases
Grass Mesa Village	Dolores Archaeological Program			5	2 vessels, 3 cases
House Creek Village	Dolores Archaeological Program			1	
Pueblo de las Golondrinas	Dolores Archaeological Program			3	3 vessels, 4 cases
Rio Vista Village	Dolores Archaeological Program			4	
Weasel Pueblo	Dolores Archaeological Program			5	3
Badger House (Mesa Verde)	Hayes and Lancaster 1975:Figure 115				1 vessel, 2 cases
Site 875 (Mesa Verde)	Lister 1965:79			1	
La Plata district, Colorado	Morris 1939:Figures 43–49, Plates 222–249			64	21 vessels, 28 cases

NOTE: The numbers in the bowl and jar columns are counts. A "case" is an example of a design or design element on a vessel. A single vessel may provide multiple cases for analysis.

[a] The collections of the Black Mesa Archaeological Project are housed at Southern Illinois University, Carbondale; the collections of the Crow Canyon Archaeological Center and the Dolores Archaeological Program are housed at the Anasazi Heritage Center, Dolores, Colorado.

for which there were no absolute dates and/or only limited control of archaeological context. However, some degree of control was maintained by selecting the sample according to four criteria.

First, most of the pottery analyzed for inclusion in the secondary database is from sites that either are dated to the ninth century or at least have architecture characteristic of the Pueblo I period. Specifically, such architecture includes both surface rooms (including storage and/or habitation rooms, often arranged in a row or roomblock) and pit structures. When excavation data are available, the pit structures are found to have domestic features (for example, storage pits and radial or wing walls), as well as possible ritual features (for example, sipapus). These general criteria can be used to separate Pueblo I sites from Basketmaker III sites, which generally consist of pithouses with few or no surface rooms. To a certain extent, the features present in pit structures make it possible to distinguish Pueblo I and Pueblo II sites—Pueblo II pit structures have fewer domestic features than do their Pueblo I counterparts and are traditionally considered to be kivas.

Pottery recovered from these sites is only generally attributable to the Pueblo I period, for several reasons. Architectural criteria provide only a limited degree of temporal control. Complete provenience information is not available for all of the pottery. Also, many whole vessels were recovered with burials in middens, and there is often little clearcut association between the midden burials and architecture.

A greater degree of temporal control than is possible with only architectural information was achieved by applying a second set of criteria. Specifically, only pottery types associated with the Pueblo I period in the Kayenta and Mesa Verde regions (Kana-a and Piedra black-on-white) were analyzed for inclusion in the database. The samples of each type were selected on the basis of attributes—primarily technology and details of design form (such as the presence of certain elements)—that were not considered in the analysis of design structure. The criteria for selecting samples of each type are described later in this section. The use of typological criteria also allowed a small number of specimens with almost no provenience information to be included.

Third, the areas included were selected specifically to maintain some geographic separation between the regions. Thus, the Kana-a Black-on-white sample includes only material from northeastern Arizona, with the exception of one bowl from Lowry Ruin in southwestern Colorado. The Piedra Black-on-white sample includes primarily material from southwestern Colorado, although material from the La Plata district, which extends into northern New Mexico, is also included. A few specimens from southeastern Utah (where the line between the Kayenta and Mesa Verde traditions is indistinct) and northwestern New Mexico (where the boundaries of the Cibola tradition are indistinct) were excluded.

Finally, control of vessel form was achieved by including only bowls and jars. As was the case with analyses that provided data for the primary database, other vessel forms were excluded.

Material analyzed for the secondary database was obtained from two general sources. The first source consisted of collections, including those analyzed as part of the primary database, that I examined directly; some specimens were analyzed as part of both the primary and secondary databases. The second source consisted of published descriptive material, primarily photographs and drawings of pottery and its painted designs.

From these sources, pieces that displayed large portions of designs were considered for analysis. These were judged according to the typological criteria listed below. Those determined to be Kana-a or Piedra black-on-white were selected. Examples of Kana-a and Piedra black-on-white are shown in Figure 4.3.

The criteria used to determine pottery type are based on traditional type descriptions (Beals et al. 1945; Breternitz et al. 1974; Colton and Hargrave 1937; and Morris 1939). The criteria emphasized here are those used to distinguish the Pueblo I types (Kana-a Black-on-white and Piedra Black-on-white) from earlier and later types. That is, how can Pueblo I pottery be distinguished in collections that include not only Pueblo I pottery, but possibly pottery from the preceding and following periods as well? Distinctions between types are not always obvious or clear-cut. These criteria are intended to be conservative, and therefore they exclude pottery that has some attributes of Basketmaker III or Pueblo II types, even if the pottery does not completely fit the definitions of the earlier or later types.

- Pottery was excluded from the Pueblo I sample if it had the following designs or characteristics typical of Basketmaker III types (Lino Black-on-white and Chapin Black-on-white): (1) thick (5 mm wide or wider) lines with very rough brushwork; (2) step, Z-motif, or basketstitch designs (Figure 5.1a–b); (3) framed-cross designs (Figure 5.1c).
- Kana-a Black-on-white is often easily distinguished by line brushwork. The lines are very thin (less than 2 mm wide) and discontinuous. Individual brush strokes with tapered ends can often be discerned (Figure 5.1d). Presence of such brushwork was one criterion used to include pottery in the Kana-a Black-on-white sample. However, absence of such brushwork was not used to exclude pottery, because not all Kana-a Black-on-white pottery necessarily has such brushwork.

Figure 5.1. *Design criteria used in type distinctions:* a–b, *steps and* Z-*motifs—both are sometimes called basketstitch and are typical of Basketmaker III types;* c, *framed cross, typical of Basketmaker III types;* d, *Kana-a Black-on-white brushwork;* e, *Kana-a Black-on-white design consisting of multiple narrow lines and one wide line;* f, *scrolls, typical of Cortez Black-on-white.*

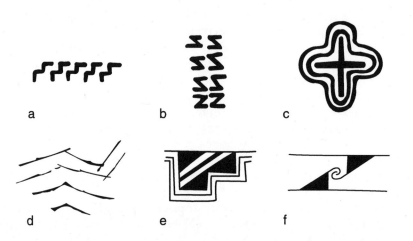

- Kana-a Black-on-white is distinguished from later types (Black Mesa Black-on-white and Sosi Black-on-white) on the basis of line width. The two later types typically have designs dominated by broad lines (over 5 mm wide), and in some cases, the broad lines appear to have been constructed by painting the edges and filling in the center. Pottery was not excluded from the Kana-a Black-on-white sample if such broad lines constituted only a fraction of the design (Figure 5.1*e*).
- Hatched designs are typical of Dogoszhi Black-on-white, a Pueblo II type in the Kayenta region. However, in at least one type description (Beals et al. 1945:Figure 19*Q*), hatched bands are considered to be present, although not necessarily common, on Kana-a Black-on-white. Therefore, pottery with designs that otherwise fit the Kana-a Black-on-white criteria but also had some hatched forms were included in the Kana-a Black-on-white sample, although the hatched designs were not included in the structural analysis.
- Piedra Black-on-white can sometimes be distinguished from Cortez Black-on-white and later types according to technological criteria. Piedra Black-on-white typically has mineral paint, little or no slip, and crushed-rock temper. Some Cortez Black-on-white has an even, white slip that distinguishes it from Piedra. Later types (Mancos, McElmo, and Mesa Verde black-on-white) are distinguished by crushed-sherd temper, and McElmo and Mesa Verde black-on-white often have organic paint.
- Piedra Black-on-white is also distinguished from later types on the basis of certain design forms. Specifically, scrolls (Figure 5.1*f*) and any kind of hatching (squiggle or straight-line) is distinctive of the later types.

Summary

The primary database was selected to maximize temporal control. It consists of data on black-on-white sherds and vessels recovered from well-documented, fairly well dated contexts in the northern Black Mesa and central Mesa Verde areas. Collections are never large enough and there are never enough tree-ring dates. However, the collections analyzed for the primary database provided a relatively good sample of pottery that could be used to examine variation over time and space in ninth-century pottery designs. Criteria for selecting the primary database should be generally acceptable by the standards of archaeology in the 1990s.

The secondary database may be more problematic. It was selected to provide a sample of pottery, made and used in the Kayenta and Mesa Verde regions during the Pueblo I period, that could be used in the structural analysis. To amass a sufficiently large sample, I had to include whole vessels and large sherds from contexts that were not necessarily well documented or well dated. Criteria for inclusion included traditional type descriptions and normative architectural patterns, criteria which have been criticized in recent decades (e.g., Cordell and Plog 1979; Fish 1978). The criteria used to select the secondary database are, admittedly, somewhat outdated and perhaps now unorthodox. However, the use of such criteria was necessary if the large collections established by researchers early in this century were to be included, and these collections were essential to creating a database sufficiently large to permit examination of variation in the structure of Pueblo I pottery designs.

In using traditional typologies to select a sample of pottery for stylistic analysis, I recognize that types are archaeological constructs that do not necessarily parallel the classificatory systems of the people who made the pottery. Types have been shown to encompass different kinds of variation, to be defined differently by different analysts, and to be subject to various definitions. Still, in many situations, types are also useful chronological indicators, and what archaeologists call Kana-a and Piedra black-on-white pottery has consistently been found in contexts securely dated to the late eighth and ninth centuries A.D. Furthermore, these types are the predominant white ware types known to have been made in the Kayenta and eastern Mesa Verde regions during the Pueblo I period; therefore, selection of these types is not likely to result in the exclusion of other material that should potentially be included. In summary, I argue that use of these typological categories is legitimate and necessary for my purposes, in that the categories provide a means of selecting materials associated with the time period of interest. The analytical limitations of the secondary database are discussed in the structural analysis presented in Chapter 7.

6

Setting Style in its Material Context: Pottery Production, Distribution, and Use

The meaning of many symbols, including stylistic symbols, is dependent on their context in relation to other symbols and to the world at large. Thus, the role of pottery design style depends in part on how the pottery is produced, distributed, and used. Did people make the pottery they used, or did they obtain all or some in trade or as gifts? If they obtained it from others, what kinds of social relations did they have with the producers? What was the scale of pottery production, and to what extent might the making and decorating of a pot have been a personal matter? How was the pottery used, and how did its use affect who saw the design style? The various information and analyses reviewed in this chapter provide the contextual background necessary for understanding design style of Pueblo I white wares.

The Organization of Pottery Production

An understanding of pottery production is essential to interpretations of the role of pottery and pottery design style in various social processes. Information about production is a necessary baseline for analyses of pottery distribution and exchange as both social and economic strategies. The distribution of pottery also affects the distribution of pottery styles and must be taken into account in stylistic analyses. Furthermore, the scale of production affects the degree of control individuals have over the styles they use. The focus here is on the organization of the production.

For many years, despite evidence to the contrary (e.g., Kidder and Shepard 1936; Shepard 1942), many archaeologists assumed that pottery had been made by nearly every household across the Southwest (e.g., Haury 1962, 1976; see discussion in Plog 1989b). Thus, pottery was interpreted under the assumptions that it had been made at the site where it was found and that the people who used the pottery were also the makers of that pottery (e.g., Hill 1970; Longacre 1970). Since the late 1970s, growing interest in exchange has resulted in numerous studies that clearly demonstrate the widespread distribution and exchange of at least some kinds of pottery in the prehistoric Southwest (e.g., Deutchman 1980; Doyel 1991; Garrett 1986; Hantman and Plog 1982; Neff and Glascock 1992; Plog 1980b, 1989a, 1989b; Toll 1981, 1985, 1991; Toll et al. 1980; Upham 1982). However, although researchers have discussed the pottery's point of origin in general terms, relatively little attention has been devoted to studying pottery production itself. Only in the past few years have many archaeologists working in the Southwest focused specifically on studying pottery production—that is, on understanding how and where pottery was made and at what scale (e.g., Bishop et al. 1988; Blinman 1988b; Blinman and Wilson 1992; Hegmon 1991a, 1993, 1995; Hegmon and Allison 1990; Mills and Crown 1994; Sullivan 1988). Some of these recent studies are not yet published or are ongoing, but what information is available is summarized here.

The process of actually making a pot was described in Chapter 4. The focus here is on understanding the organization of this process, particularly for white ware pottery. Where were the pots made and at what scale? To answer these questions, I consider three general lines of evidence. First, I describe the geology of the study areas to determine what raw materials were available. Then I review analyses of pottery composition and relate these to the geologic information. Finally, I consider the material remains of pottery production.

This consideration of pottery production draws on Costin's (1991) recent formulation. She conceives of the organization of production in terms of four parameters: context, concentration, scale, and intensity. Her formulation considers only specialized production, but it can be expanded to include unspecialized household production as well. Because there is no evidence of elite control, state-style administrative complexity, or elaborate workshops with expensive technology (see Rice 1987:158–162), the focus here is on the portion of Costin's (1991) model that deals with less complex organization. Specifically, three basic modes of production are considered: (1) unspecialized household production, in which each household makes pottery for its own use; (2) dispersed individual specialization, in which a few individuals or households make pottery for an entire community; and (3) community specialization, in which individual specialists, aggregated in a limited number of communities, produce pottery for regional distribution. All of these modes involve relatively simple technology, but they differ in terms of the scale of production and distribution. For related discussions of various modes of pottery production, see Rice (1987:184), van der Leeuw (1977, 1984), and Peacock (1981, 1982:8–10), particularly their discussions of household production and household industry.

Raw Materials and Geologic Resources

The basic materials needed to make pottery are clay for the body and slip, temper, and sometimes pigment, as well as water and fuel. The following observations apply specifically to pottery manufacture during the Pueblo I period. In the Kayenta region, most pottery was tempered with sand. In the Mesa Verde region, most pottery was tempered with crushed igneous rock, although sand or crushed sandstone was sometimes used. In both the Kayenta and Mesa Verde regions, slip, when used, could have been made of the same clay as the vessel body. Most paint in the Kayenta region was organic with no mineral component, whereas pigment in the Mesa Verde region was usually mineral (iron or magnesium based) in an organic binder. Despite evidence of local deforestation and changes in the type of fuel wood used during the Pueblo I occupation of the Dolores River valley (Kohler and Matthews 1988), it is likely that some kind of fuel was available at most locations. Thus, neither fuel nor water can be considered to have been a limiting resource for pottery production during the Pueblo I period. In some areas of the world, humid weather conditions limit the production of pottery to certain seasons and areas (Arnold 1985:63); however, given the arid climate of the northern Southwest, it is likely that pottery could have been made during most times of the year in most areas.

Ethnographic models of pottery production provide some useful guidelines for interpreting the distribution of raw materials used in pottery making. Arnold (1985:32–51) identifies thresholds that represent the maximum distances that traditional potters will travel to obtain resources. Typically, clay and temper resources no more than 1 km distant are preferred, and few potters will go more than 7 km to obtain clay or more than 9 km to obtain temper. However, in some cases, potters have been known to obtain clay from sources as much as 50 km distant and temper from sources 25 km distant. Special resources needed in small quantities—specifically, pigments and special slip clays—are more commonly gathered or imported from more distant sources (Arnold 1985:52–53).

Black Mesa

Black Mesa is a massive highland on the Colorado Plateau composed of a series of horizontal or slightly sloping Mesozoic sedimentary (shale and sandstone) formations (Beaumont and Dixon 1965; Franczyk 1988; Haynes and Hackman 1978). These include—from youngest to oldest—the Mancos Shale Formation, a marine clay shale; the Dakota Sandstone, a sandstone with conglomerate lenses and interbedded siltstone; and the Morrison Formation, a bentonitic mudstone with lenses of sandstone (Haynes and Hackman 1978). All three formations outcrop along the edges of the mesa, and the Mancos Shale also outcrops as bedrock in various locations across the mesa top. The upper layer of Black Mesa is formed by the Mesa Verde Group, which is also the upper layer of Mesa Verde itself, in southwestern Colorado. The Wepo Formation of the Mesa Verde Group is the bedrock across much of Black Mesa, and it outcrops in many locations within the area studied by the Black Mesa Archaeological Project (BMAP) (Garrett 1986:118). The Wepo Formation consists of siltstone, sandstone, and thick beds of coal (much of the work conducted by the BMAP consisted of mitigation prior to the mining of this coal by the Peabody Coal Company). The only other formation exposed to any extent in the BMAP study area is the Toreva Formation (Garrett 1986:118), which is stratigraphically below the Wepo Formation in the Mesa Verde Group. The Toreva Formation consists of sandstone, siltstone, mudstone, and carbonaceous shale. No igneous formations are present on Black Mesa itself. In Monument Valley and the area to the northeast of the mesa, a few dikes and other small intrusives, consisting primarily of lamprophyric rocks, are present (Haynes and Hackman 1978).

Black Mesa is cut by numerous washes that begin on the mesa, flow southwest, and ultimately drain into the Little Colorado River. The Moenkopi and Dinnebito washes flow through the BMAP study area. Four of the five Black Mesa sites analyzed in this study are located near Moenkopi Wash.

Clays that can be used to make pottery are expected to occur in places where claystone deposits have weathered. Suitable deposits are present in the Morrison, Dakota Sandstone, and Mancos Shale formations, and Ambler (1983:79) reports that good-quality clays are available in the Mesa Verde Group along the edge of Black Mesa. In a small survey (Hegmon 1991a), I found good-quality clays in many arroyo cuts near the sites considered in this research. Furthermore, the massive layers of Mancos Shale exposed on the sides of Black Mesa include large deposits of high-quality clays. Thus, clay for pottery manufacture would have been readily available to the residents of Black Mesa.

The sandstones of both the Wepo and Toreva formations are described as weakly cemented (Garrett 1986:118–119), and eolian deposits are present along the washes and in many other areas across the mesa. Therefore, sand that could have been used as pottery temper is ubiquitous across Black Mesa. Because igneous rock would not have been available, San Juan Red Ware, which is tempered with igneous rock, is generally assumed to have been imported onto the mesa (Plog 1986:Chapter 12).

The Central Mesa Verde Region

Geologically, the central Mesa Verde region consists primarily of the same Mesozoic sedimentary formations that make up Black Mesa. These horizontal or slightly sloping formations are cut by streams and canyons and are intruded by a series of shallow igneous features (Haynes et al. 1972; Tweto 1979). The igneous features were formed during the late Cretaceous or early Tertiary periods (approximately 65 million years ago) and are thought to be roughly contemporaneous with each other; they are generally similar in geologic composition, although internally each is quite heterogeneous, containing numerous rock types, including diorite, granodiorite, and monzonite porphyry (Bromfield 1967; Eckel et al. 1949; Ekren and Houser 1965; Larson and Cross 1956). Of these igneous features, the Sleeping Ute, La Plata, and Wilson mountains are of particular relevance to this research because they would have been the most likely sources of igneous rocks for potters at the Duckfoot site and in the Dolores area.

All the sites investigated as part of the Dolores Archaeological Program (DAP) are located near the Dolores River. Six sedimentary formations were recognized in the project area (Leonhardy and Clay 1985). These include the Mancos Shale Formation, the Dakota Sandstone, and the Brushy Basin Member of the Morrison Formation. Although no igneous features are within easy reach of the Dolores sites, the Dolores River drains the La Plata and Wilson mountains and abundant igneous cobbles are available in the river bed and terraces.

The Duckfoot site is on a ridge between Crow and Alkali canyons, two tributaries of McElmo Creek, and the site is less than 5 km from McElmo Creek itself (see Figure 4.5). The bedrock at Duckfoot is Dakota Sandstone; the Mancos Shale and the Brushy Basin Member of the Morrison Formation are exposed in the washes and streams near the site. The watercourses near Duckfoot carry few igneous rocks, but people at the Duckfoot site could have obtained igneous rock directly from Sleeping Ute Mountain—in particular from a large, north-trending dike that is approximately 15 km from the site—or from watercourses that drain the mountain.

As is the case on Black Mesa, pottery-making clays in the central Mesa Verde region should be available in locations where claystone deposits have eroded, such as in the Dakota Sandstone and the Mancos Shale Formation and possibly in the Brushy Basin Member of the Morrison Formation (Blinman 1987; Wilson et al. 1988). Thus, clay suitable for pottery manufacture would have been available near both Duckfoot and the Dolores sites, certainly within the 7-km threshold that Arnold (1985:32–51) proposes for the exploitation of clay resources by traditional potters (see also Blinman 1988b:62). Sources of igneous rock for temper also would have been within easy reach of potters in the Dolores area. In contrast, potters at the Duckfoot site would have had to travel 15 km or more to collect igneous rock from the Sleeping Ute Mountain, a distance that exceeds the 9-km threshold that Arnold (1985:51–52) proposes for temper collection.

Refiring experiments with naturally occurring clays from the Dolores area and from Sand Canyon (approximately 15 km west of Duckfoot) suggest that these clays could have been used for the manufacture of gray and white wares (Blinman 1987, 1988b:63–64; Wilson et al. 1988). Furthermore, the naturally occurring clays found in the Dolores area and clays found in archaeological contexts at Dolores sites refired to the same range of colors (Wilson et al. 1988). However, only about 5 percent of the clays refired to red, and none of the red archaeological clays matched the color of San Juan Red Ware pottery (Blinman 1988b:64). The absence of red ware clays further supports the argument that red wares were probably made in southeastern Utah and imported to the Dolores area (Blinman 1988b:114–115; Hegmon et al. 1994; Hurst 1983; Lucius and Breternitz 1981).

Temper material would have been readily available throughout the Mesa Verde region. On the basis of the availability of various types of temper, Dolores researchers identified a number of potential pottery manufacturing tracts (Blinman 1988b:101–115; Blinman et al. 1984; Lucius 1984). The two tracts most relevant to the production of gray and white wares are the Dolores and Cahone. The Dolores tract covers a broad area north of the San Juan River from southeastern Utah to the La Plata River drainage; it includes the Dolores River valley and the area around the Duckfoot site. The Dolores tract is distinguished by the availability of igneous rock—primarily cobbles found in streams and terraces—although sedimentary rock is also available throughout the area. The Cahone tract covers a more restricted area between the Dolores River and Montezuma Creek. Igneous rock is rare in the Cahone tract, and sedimentary rock, primarily sandstone, would have been the only commonly available temper material.

In the DAP study area, iron minerals needed to make pigment, particularly hematite, are available in a few high-density concentrations in or at the mouths of drainages and in lower-density concentrations scattered throughout the area (Keane and Clay 1987:510). Although some authors have suggested that pigment was imported to the Dolores area (Blinman 1988b:64; Travis 1984), at least some materials were available locally. No information about iron minerals in the area around the Duckfoot site is available, but given that the geology is quite similar to that in the Dolores area, some iron minerals are probably present and could have been used by potters.

To summarize, the distribution of geologic resources on northern Black Mesa and in the central Mesa Verde region suggests that the white and gray ware pottery found in those areas could have been made locally. The basic materials—clay and temper—were widely available. Thus, pottery could have been made by unspecialized households or by individual or household specialists in widely dispersed locations. It is possible that the pottery found on a site was locally made at that site. However, this conclusion does not preclude the possibility that pottery was exchanged and/or produced on a larger scale.

Analysis of Pottery Composition

Three types of analyses of the chemical and mineralogical composition of Pueblo I pottery were conducted to provide information about pottery production in the Kayenta and Mesa Verde regions. These analyses consisted of (1) examination of pottery under a low-power microscope to determine the general characteristics of the temper, (2) examination of pottery thin-sections to examine temper mineralogy in more detail, and (3) chemical analysis of the elemental composition of the pottery using neutron-activation analysis.

Low-Power Microscopic Analysis

Microscope analysis involved examining the edges of freshly broken sherds under a low-power (usually 20×) microscope. Because this method is fast and inexpensive, a large number of sherds can be examined and the general class of temper present (for example, sand, crushed sandstone, or crushed igneous rock) can be determined. This method was used in DAP pottery analysis and in the current study. As part of basic pottery analysis at the DAP, temper in every sherd was identified (Blinman et al. 1984). Basic temper categories and identifications were confirmed through petrographic analysis of thin-sections from a small number of sherds (Eric Blinman, personal communication 1989; Kamilli 1983). However, some detailed distinctions between different kinds of sedimentary rocks and different kinds of igneous rocks were not supported by the results of petrographic analysis. Therefore, in this research and in my discussion of the DAP results, I use broader categories than those originally defined by the DAP.[1]

To develop the method of analysis used in this research, I worked with two DAP pottery analysts—Eric Blinman and Dean Wilson—to learn about the Dolores system. I then examined some of the pottery from Dolores-area sites and developed an abbreviated form of the system. In the analysis reported here, five kinds of pottery temper were recognized in a total of seven combinations. The temper categories are listed, along with the DAP codes, in Table 6.1. I used this system to identify the temper in approximately 20 percent of the analyzed pottery from the Duckfoot site and the four originally analyzed Black Mesa sites (D:11:2023, D:11:2025, D:11:2027, and D:11:2030). My analysis included every fifth sherd or vessel that was used in the stylistic analysis and other specimens that were unusual in any way (for example, possible imports). The systematic and judgmental samples were kept separate to facilitate statistical analysis.

Information on temper obtained through low-power microscopic examination confirms general statements regarding the temper used in Pueblo I pottery (Breternitz et al. 1974; Colton and Hargrave 1937). That is, more than 98 percent of the analyzed gray and white ware specimens from Dolores and Duckfoot have crushed andesite/diorite or sandstone temper, and all the analyzed specimens from Black Mesa have quartz sand temper. Thus, almost all the pottery was made from materials that were available locally, although because these materials were also available across most of both regions, these results cannot be used to argue that the pottery was locally made at the sites where it was found. However, results of the gross temper analysis can provide information regarding long-distance exchange, and they are presented in more detail below, in the discussion of pottery distribution and use.

---

1. For example, the DAP analysts attempted to distinguish between andesite/diorite (types of igneous rock) and what they called "San Juan temper." Andesite/diorite was considered to be local to Dolores and the surrounding area, that is, the Dolores tract. San Juan temper was described as a finely crushed andesite/diorite with slightly more dark particles than regular andesite/diorite temper. It was thought to be from an area south of Dolores, possibly along the San Juan River, although a specific source was not identified. However, the distinction between andesite/diorite and San Juan temper was not supported by the DAP's petrographic analysis (Kamilli 1983). Therefore, in my evaluation of DAP results and data, I combine the two categories and consider all andesite/diorite temper to be potentially local to the Dolores area.

Table 6.1. Temper Categories Identified Through Examination
with Low-Power Microscope

Temper Category	DAP Codes[a]
Crushed andesite/diorite	3, 12
Crushed sherd and andesite/diorite	4
Sand/quartz sand	6, 52[b]
Crushed sherd and quartz sand	9
Crushed trachyte basalt	11
Crushed sedimentary rock	13, 16, 18
Crushed andesite/diorite and sand	50

[a] This column lists the numeric codes used by Dolores Archaeological Program (DAP) researchers to record temper type (Blinman et al. 1984:Table 4). The listing of multiple codes indicates cases in which I grouped more than one DAP category into a single broader category.

[b] Code 52 is not a DAP code, but my own, used to indicate quartz sand in the Black Mesa pottery.

Gross temper characterizations provide some information about the scale of production of Pueblo I white and gray wares in the central Mesa Verde region. Sedimentary rock and sand would have been readily accessible at both Dolores and Duckfoot; andesite/diorite would also have been readily available to Dolores potters and available with moderate effort to Duckfoot potters. However, igneous rock, including andesite and diorite, is probably a better temper material than quartz-based sand and sedimentary rock for at least two reasons. First, the thermal expansion rate of igneous rock is similar to, or lower than, that of clay; therefore, igneous rock temper may help to increase thermal-shock resistance in cooking pots (Rye 1976:118; see also Blinman 1988b:63; Sinopoli 1991:14–15). Second, quartz-tempered vessels require a higher firing temperature to produce a well-fired pot (Bronitsky 1986:218). More than 95 percent of the gray and white pottery in the Dolores assemblage has igneous rock temper. However, most of the pottery found in the Cahone tract, where igneous rock is not available, is tempered with crushed sandstone (Blinman and Wilson 1992:164). The presence of locally available material in the pottery from each area suggests that much of the pottery found in a given area was actually made there. This argument does not preclude the possibility that pottery was exchanged or otherwise distributed within each area, although it does suggest that large-scale exchange of white and gray wares across the region was unlikely. The restricted distributions of White Mesa Black-on-white (found only in southeastern Utah) and Piedra Black-on-white (found only in southwestern Colorado) further suggest that Pueblo I white wares were made and used locally in various parts of the Mesa Verde region (Hegmon et al. 1994).

Thin-Section Analysis

The results of thin-section analysis of samples of white ware from Black Mesa, Dolores, and Duckfoot provide much more detailed information about the temper used in the two areas. The analysis was done by Elizabeth Garrett (1990) and by this author (Hegmon 1991a, 1995).

Analysis of 49 white ware sherds from three BMAP sites (D:11:2027, D:11:2030, and D:7:134) revealed that all were tempered with what appeared to be the same kind of coarse quartz sand (grain sizes over 1 mm were common). Very little variability in temper is apparent in either the intrasite or intersite comparisons. It is likely that the same general source of temper was used for all the pottery examined.

The homogeneity of temper is not surprising, given that the same geologic formations are present across northern Black Mesa. However, the source of the temper is not entirely clear. Sandstone of the Wepo Formation, which is ubiquitous across the area, in general is much finer-grained than the sand temper (Garrett 1990), although it is possible that Wepo outcrops of coarser sandstone are also present. Sandstone of the Toreva Formation, which underlies the Wepo, is quite similar to the temper in both size and mineralogy (Garrett 1990). Outcrops of the Toreva Formation are common across northern Black Mesa, although the Toreva is not nearly as ubiquitous as the Wepo (Garrett 1990). That is, in most places, a small investment of time would have been necessary to gather material from the Toreva formation, whereas Wepo deposits are available within a few hundred meters of almost any location. More research on source material is needed to determine if the sand temper was derived from the Toreva deposits.

Thin-section analysis of white ware from the central Mesa Verde region focused on pottery tempered with igneous rock, including andesite/diorite (Hegmon 1995). Fifteen samples from the Duckfoot site and 46 samples from seven DAP sites were analyzed, as were 10 samples of igneous rock from the central Mesa Verde region. The temper in the pottery samples appears to be very heterogeneous, including a suite of igneous rocks and minerals of various textures and states (Hegmon 1995). For example, some temper is made of rocks characterized as groundmass with porphyry, some is made of coarse diorite, some consists of rock described as cryptocrystalline with quartz, and some is composed primarily of individual (but various) pieces of minerals. The characteristics of the feldspars (a major component of igneous rock) and the presence of other minerals, such as hornblende, biotite, and pyroxene, vary widely. The quantity of silt-size particles, thought to be a property of the clay rather than of the temper that was actually added to the clay, is also variable.

The variability in the temper composition reveals some important patterns when samples from different sites are compared and when the temper is compared with possible source materials. The pottery from McPhee Village has a larger proportion of silt-size particles than does the pottery from other Dolores sites or Duckfoot. Specifically, 18 of 25 specimens from McPhee Village are characterized as having abundant silt-size particles, whereas only two of the 21 specimens from other Dolores sites and two of the 15 specimens from Duckfoot have abundant silt-size particles. Several characteristics distinguish the temper in the Duckfoot specimens from the temper in the Dolores specimens. Feldspars in the Duckfoot pottery show more twinning (characteristic of plagioclase feldspars), more zoning, and less clouding than do those in the Dolores pottery. In addition, temper with a texture described as "cryptocrystalline with quartz" is fairly common in the Duckfoot sample but not at all common in the sample from Dolores.

These differences in temper between areas are viewed as tendencies in the overall sample rather than as absolute distinctions. Thus, at least with these data, it is not possible to determine the point of production of an individual piece of pottery on the basis of the characteristics of its igneous rock temper. However, the analyses provide important information about patterns of white ware production. It appears that different temper sources were used in the pottery found at Duckfoot and Dolores, and different clays may have been used in the pottery found in different parts of the Dolores area. These data suggest that Pueblo I white ware was made at various locations across the central Mesa Verde region and that at least some of the pottery found on each site was locally made at or near that site.

Igneous sources across the Mesa Verde region are both similar to each other and internally heterogeneous. Thus, isolation of a specific temper source is unlikely. However, to better understand the variability in the temper, possible temper sources, including rocks collected from the Dolores River and from various locations around the Sleeping Ute Mountain, were analyzed in thin-section. Both macroscopically and in thin-section, these rocks are very heterogeneous and are much more variable than the igneous temper. Furthermore, many rocks are more heavily altered—through chemical weathering—than the rock that was used as temper. Kamilli (1983) reached similar conclusions in her analyses of igneous cobbles from various watercourses in southwestern Colorado and southeastern Utah. These results suggest that, although igneous temper appears to be quite variable, only a small proportion of the available rock types were used as temper. Thus, it appears that potters in both the central Mesa Verde region and on northern Black Mesa were highly selective in choosing rocks to use as temper. Furthermore, in both areas, the selection criteria were widely applied.

Neutron–Activation Analysis

Neutron-activation analysis (NAA) was used to determine the bulk (that is, paste and temper) chemical and elemental composition of pottery from both northern Black Mesa and the central Mesa Verde region. NAA is a highly sensitive technique that can detect trace-element concentrations (elements present as only a few parts per million). NAA is often used to identify minor differences in raw material, particularly clay, and it is an important tool in research on pottery production and exchange (e.g., Bishop et al. 1988; Neff 1989, 1992; Perlman and Asaro 1969; Wilson 1978). Research generally involves identifying groups of chemically similar pottery specimens that could have been made from the same raw materials and thus may have been made at the same place. These groups are usually identified by multivariate pattern recognition and statistical techniques.

Samples of Kana-a Black-on-white from four ninth-century BMAP sites (D:7:134, D:11:2027, and D:11:2030, plus D:11:338, a very small site located on a tributary of the Moenkopi Wash south and east of D:11:2023, 2025, 2027, and 2030 [Anderson 1978]) were subjected to NAA. Although 134 samples were analyzed, only a few very small and poorly defined chemical composition groups, including only a small fraction of the samples, could be identified. The distributions of two groups according to the concentrations of iron and scandium are shown in Figure 6.1. Each chemical composition group includes only specimens from a single site; however, in no case do most or all specimens from a site belong to the same group.

Sixteen samples of clay from northern Black Mesa were also subjected to NAA (Hegmon 1991a). These samples were from the Wepo and Mancos formations, as well as from alluvial deposits. Clays from proximate sources (for example, several samples from around one collection site) tend to group together, suggesting that pottery made from those sources should have a distinctive chemical signature. None of the clays is a close match for the chemical composition groups of the Black Mesa pottery. However, some clays from the Wepo formation are quite similar to some pottery samples, which suggests that at least some of the pottery was made from locally available clays.

These results suggest that, during the ninth century, white ware on Black Mesa was made and used at a number of locations. The presence of site-specific chemical composition groups and the similarity of some pottery and some clay suggest that at least some pottery was made locally, at the sites where it was found. However, because not all the pottery from each site or location is a member of the same compositional group, it is likely that a number of production events, either at a single site or at various sites across the area,

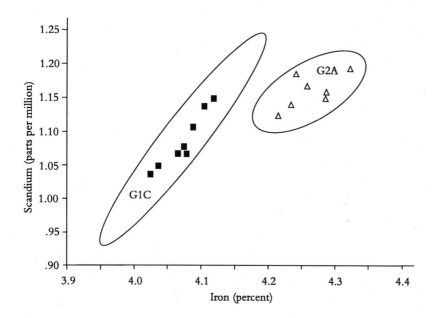

Figure 6.1. *Distribution of groups of Kana-a Black-on-white pottery from northern Black Mesa based on the concentrations of iron and scandium. Group G1C includes samples from Site D:11:338. Group G2A includes samples from two sites (D:11:2027 and D:11:2030) located approximately 8 km from Site D:11:338. The ellipses are 95 percent confidence intervals, calculated assuming a very large sample size.*

contributed to an assemblage found at a single site. These multiple production events suggest that pottery was produced at a small scale at many sites and that exchange across the area contributed to the chemically diverse assemblages.

In a comparative study of Pueblo I white and red wares from across the Mesa Verde region, samples of white and red ware from both the central and western portions of the Mesa Verde region were subjected to NAA. The samples consisted of 17 pieces of White Mesa Black-on-white from southeastern Utah, 11 pieces of Piedra Black-on-white (10 from Duckfoot and one from Dolores), and 19 pieces of Bluff Black-on-red, a San Juan Red Ware (18 from southeastern Utah and one from Black Mesa). The individual specimens, plotted according to the concentrations of iron and scandium, are shown in Figure 6.2. The Bluff Black-on-red and White Mesa Black-on-white specimens form fairly tight chemical compositional groups, whereas the Piedra Black-on-white specimens are broadly scattered and do not form a distinguishable chemical group. These results suggest that White Mesa Black-on-white and Bluff Black-on-red were probably made from one or a group of closely related sources, whereas the Piedra Black-on-white probably was made with material from a number of different sources. Thus, it appears that a number of production events contributed to a single assemblage of Piedra Black-on-white. These multiple events could reflect small-scale household production of pottery, intraregional exchange, or both.

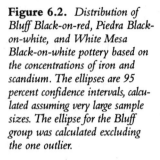

Figure 6.2. *Distribution of Bluff Black-on-red, Piedra Black-on-white, and White Mesa Black-on-white pottery based on the concentrations of iron and scandium. The ellipses are 95 percent confidence intervals, calculated assuming very large sample sizes. The ellipse for the Bluff group was calculated excluding the one outlier.*

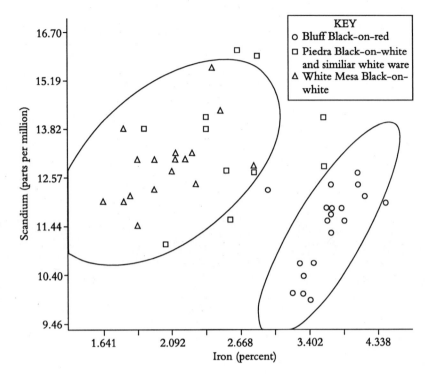

Pottery-Making Remains

The distribution of the remains of pottery manufacture can provide information on the distribution, and possibly the scale, of white ware production. Unfortunately, however, if pottery was made at a small scale, the remains of pottery production may be difficult to detect archaeologically because tools were likely curated and production features may have been small. Stark (1985) cites a case in Mesoamerica in which one ideally preserved site (buried by a volcanic eruption) provided evidence of household-level pottery production. Such small-scale production probably occurred at many sites in the area, but evidence of such production is lacking from other, less perfectly preserved, sites.

Firing features, such as kilns or piles of wasters (misfired sherds), provide unequivocal evidence that pottery was manufactured in situ. Although a few stone-lined firing pits are known from later periods in the northern Southwest (e.g., Fuller 1984; Helm 1973; see also Sullivan 1988), none have been found dating to the ninth century. Most of the firing features that have been found or tentatively identified (Adler and Metcalf 1991) are isolated features or clusters of features, which suggests that pottery was not fired at habitation sites, perhaps to reduce fire danger and/or to locate the firing nearer to fuel sources. During the Pueblo I period, white ware may have been fired on the surface of the ground, a practice that would have left few archaeological traces. In the course of the DAP investigations, extensive areas were cleared around some sites, but no pottery-firing features were found (Blinman 1988b:72). If surface firings were done in areas distant from habitation sites, the probability of detecting small firing features is extremely remote.

Other features possibly associated with pottery making include basins and slabs where clay was mixed and ground. Possible mixing basins were identified at Site D:11:2030, on Black Mesa (Green et al. 1985:234). Unfortunately, it is not possible to determine whether the material mixed in these basins was pottery-making clay or some other substance, such as adobe. If such features were used for mixing pottery clay, their small sizes (none has a volume greater than .1 m^3) suggest that pottery was produced at a fairly small scale. Clay stains on a slab and on a room floor were noted at two Dolores sites, Dos Casas Hamlet and Kin Tl'iish (see Blinman 1988b:70), which suggests that clay for pottery making was mixed in these locations.

The distribution of portable items also provides evidence of pottery manufacture. Such items include raw materials (clay and temper), unfired vessels, and pottery-making tools such as scrapers and polishing stones. These materials have been found on northern Black Mesa and in the central Mesa Verde region, although the evidence can be difficult to interpret, especially with regard to white ware production. Scrapers, clay, and temper may all be associated with the production of gray ware, as well as white ware. Only the presence of polishing stones or the unlikely preservation of an unfired decorated vessel provides clear evidence of white ware production.

Microwear analysis of worked sherds and chipped-stone tools strongly suggests that at least some of these materials were used for scraping pottery (Neusius 1988; Waterworth and Blinman 1986). Traces of clay and possibly the results of microwear analysis may allow the identification of prehistoric polishing stones (Gieb and Callahan 1988), although in many cases, the use of a smooth stone cannot be determined. Furthermore, Stark (1985:173) notes that such pottery-making tools are often curated and therefore will be underrepresented in the archaeological record. If prehistoric potters cared for their polishing stones as conscientiously as do modern potters, it is likely that few polishing stones were deposited in the archaeological record. Pottery scrapers were probably more easily made and therefore may have been less carefully curated, but some scrapers may have been made of perishable materials, such as shell or gourd, and therefore would have been less likely to preserve archaeologically.

At all four Black Mesa sites, as well as at Duckfoot, tools were found that could have been used for pottery manufacture. Scrapers, polishing stones, and raw clay were all found at Duckfoot (Etzkorn 1993a, 1993c). All the Black Mesa sites had worked (modified) sherds, including some, at each site, that had microwear indicative of pottery scraping (Hegmon 1991a; Waterworth and Blinman 1986). Unfired clay was also found at D:11:2030 (Green et al. 1985). Smooth stones that *may* have been used to polish white wares were found at D:11:2025, D:11:2027, and D:11:2030 (Stone 1984; Olszewski et al. 1984; Green et al. 1985). Furthermore, at D:11:2027, one room contained several polishing stones, which led the excavators (Olszewski et al. 1984:211) to suggest that the room may have been used for pottery production.

Possible remains of pottery production were found at many, though not all, DAP sites (for example, see the descriptions of Aldea Alfareros and Golondrinas Oriental in Chapter 5). However, the sites were not completely excavated, and some were only tested. Therefore, the absence of such remains does not necessarily indicate that pottery was not made at the sites. DAP researchers (Blinman 1988b:76–95; Blinman and Wilson 1988b, 1992) used models that related the presence or absence of production evidence to the size of the sample recovered from a particular context in order to determine the cases for which the absence of production evidence was significant. They included only two types of production evidence—pottery scrapers with distinctive microwear (see Waterworth and Blinman 1986) and unfired clay.

For the A.D. 800–840 period, Blinman and Wilson (1992) concluded that only two interhousehold units (a pit structure and an associated room suite) *lacked* evidence of production. No households or interhouseholds after A.D. 840 lacked evidence of production. The manufacture of all kinds of pottery was considered in these analyses. Data on polishing stones are not sufficient to evaluate evidence of white ware production at the DAP sites with these models (Blinman 1988b:96–97). However, the presence of some polishing stones, as well as an unfired white ware jar, suggests that some white ware was produced at Dolores.

Taken alone, pottery-making remains provide evidence that at least some pottery was produced locally. Combined with the compositional and geologic data, the pottery-making remains further support the interpretation that pottery was produced at a small scale. The distribution of pottery-making remains suggests that many or most households made gray ware pottery. However, the technical demands of handling pigment and firing suggest that white ware production may have been slightly more specialized; Blinman and

Wilson (1988b:1312, 1992) suggest that white ware was produced by specialists on a small scale (see also Blinman 1988b:117).

One production area that operated on a slightly larger scale is known from Building II at Site 33 in the La Plata district, southeast of Mesa Verde. Most of the building appeared to have been used for habitation and storage, but two rooms, in different parts of the roomblock, had abundant pottery and pottery-production remains. In Room 2, Morris (1939:8) found 17 whole vessels and additional fragments, raw clay, scrapers, molds, pigment trays, and seven polishing stones. Nearby, in Room 13, were rows of pottery vessels (26 whole or reconstructed and many more fragmentary). Most of the vessels were gray ware, but some were black-on-white and at least one was black-on-red. Morris notes that two vessels appeared to be unused, although others, including the black-on-red jar, had been used for food storage; therefore, the abundance of vessels cannot necessarily be interpreted as finished products awaiting distribution. The abundance of pottery-making remains suggests that production was concentrated and probably done at a larger scale at Site 33 than at many other contemporaneous sites. However, it is unlikely that the scale of production exceeded what could be expected of a household industry (van der Leeuw 1977) with part-time specialists.

One final line of evidence, although primarily negative, suggests that pottery production was not highly specialized. Although abundant grave goods are rare in the prehistoric northern Southwest, a few post–A.D. 900 burials of women contain numerous pottery-making materials including pukis (molds for vessel bases), polishing stones, and scrapers (Beals et al. 1945:138; Crotty 1983:30; Guernsey 1931:110–111). The presence of the grave goods may indicate that these women were specialized producers of pottery (Ambler 1983), although other interpretations are also possible (Crotty 1983:30). No such graves are known from the Pueblo I period, which may suggest that such specialization did not exist at that time; however, the small number of Pueblo I burials makes the absence of such cases difficult to interpret.

Summary

The results of much research, ranging from geologic studies to analyses of pottery-making tools, provide information on pottery production. Analyses of the temper and chemical composition of white wares from northern Black Mesa and the central Mesa Verde region reveal that the pottery is homogeneous in some respects but heterogeneous in others. The pottery is homogeneous in that it is tempered with material that is far less variable than the raw materials available locally. Black Mesa potters apparently did not use fine sand from the ubiquitous Wepo sandstone but instead selected coarser and less readily available material, possibly from the Toreva Formation. Potters in the central Mesa Verde region apparently selected only certain kinds of igneous rocks, ignoring others that were abundantly available.

On the other hand, detailed analysis of temper, as well as analysis of the pottery's chemical composition, reveals a high degree of heterogeneity, including some site- and area-specific differences. Neutron-activation analysis of white ware from four Black Mesa sites and from the Duckfoot site shows that, chemically, the pottery is very heterogeneous, which suggests that the analyzed assemblages were not all made from the same source or by the same producers. Two small, site-specific groups of chemically similar pottery can be identified in the Black Mesa material, which suggests that at least some of the production was site specific. Similarly, detailed analysis of temper and clay inclusions in pottery from Duckfoot and Dolores reveal some site-specific patterns, also suggesting local production.

Both the presence and absence of pottery-making remains suggest that pottery was made in many locations in both regions during the Pueblo I period. Other than evidence of one fairly small pottery-making workshop, and despite extensive excavation and research, there is no indication that white or gray ware pottery was produced at a large scale during the Pueblo I period in either the Kayenta or Mesa Verde regions. Instead, at almost all sites that have been excavated extensively, a few remains of pottery production, usually pottery scrapers and unfired clay, have been found. This distribution of pottery-making evidence suggests that pottery was produced at a small scale in many locations. Although the pottery-making remains that were recovered could have been associated with the production of gray wares, the compositional analyses of the white ware suggest that it, too, was made at a small scale in many locations.

Overall, these multiple lines of evidence suggest that the Pueblo I pottery found in the Kayenta and Mesa Verde regions was made in numerous, probably small-scale, production events. The pottery may have been made on a small scale by unspecialized households or individual or household specialists. Both local production and exchange are likely, but there is no evidence of large-scale production. There is, however, evidence of a widespread technological tradition, indicated by the overall homogeneity in temper selection. Thus, although production was small scale, the technique was widely shared.

Pottery Distribution and Use

My research is predicated on the assumption that style plays some role in social and cultural processes. If that assumption is correct, an understanding of the use and distribution of style-bearing objects is essential to understanding style. In this section, various sets of data relating to pottery distribution and use on northern Black Mesa and in the central Mesa Verde region are presented. I begin at a general level and consider the distribution of various wares in the total site assemblages to determine how pottery was distributed and what kinds of pottery were used at the different sites. Then I consider pottery use more specifically and examine the white ware assemblages in more detail.

Tracking the Distribution of Pottery

The analyses described in the preceding section suggest that gray and white ware pottery was probably produced at most Pueblo I habitation sites in the study areas and possibly throughout the northern Southwest. Such widespread production in no way precludes the possibility of the movement of pottery, however. Pottery, empty or filled with food or other materials, may have been transported to, or exchanged among, sites within a region or between regions. Small amounts of pottery may have been moved as a result of migration (Wilson 1988). Pottery could have been moved to a site in conjunction with some kind of gathering or ceremonial activity (Blinman 1989; Toll 1985). Pottery may have been distributed as part of a ceremonial exchange (Strathern 1971). Finally, large amounts of pottery could have been distributed over long distances as a result of regional exchange networks (Irwin 1978).

Researchers have long argued that San Juan Red Ware was made in southeastern Utah and exported to other areas of the northern Southwest (e.g., Hegmon et al. 1994; Hurst 1983; Lucius and Breternitz 1981; Reed 1958), and evidence in support of this argument was summarized above. It is unlikely that red ware tempered with igneous rock was produced on Black Mesa, because no igneous formations are present on the mesa. It is possible that some red ware was produced in the central Mesa Verde region, although the results of chemical analysis suggest that most red ware was made from a single source or group of sources in southeastern Utah (Neff and Glascock 1992). Therefore, San Juan Red Ware is considered to have been imported to northern Black Mesa (a distance of approximately 75 km) and to the central Mesa Verde region (roughly 50 km away). Allison, Hurst, and I have argued (Hegmon et al. 1994) that red ware production in southeastern Utah can be characterized as a form of community specialization (Costin 1991) and that the red ware was exchanged or otherwise distributed throughout the northern Southwest.

Assessment of the distribution of white and gray wares on Black Mesa is less clear-cut. No extraregional imports were identified at any of the sites included in this study. However, identification of imported white and gray wares requires a high level of analytic detail; specifically, pottery from the Mesa Verde region should be distinguishable on the basis of its crushed-rock temper, whereas sand-tempered imports from the Cibola region can be identified on the basis of their painted designs. Because not all the pottery in the Black Mesa collections was examined microscopically, it is possible that a small number of imports were present but not identified during analysis. A study by Hantman and Plog (1982) provides information on the movement of white wares across their apparent zones of production. Hantman and Plog (1982) compared samples of Kana-a and Lino Black-on-white pottery from Black Mesa with samples from the Apache-Sitgreaves area (more than 120 miles south of the BMAP study area); they found that the samples from the two areas were compositionally distinct in some respects, but compositionally similar in others. Thus, there is evidence for both local production and exchange of the pottery across the region. To summarize, interregional movement of white and gray wares to Black Mesa during the Pueblo I period may have occurred, but only at a small scale, since it was not detected in the basic pottery analysis. Hantman and Plog's (1982) study suggests that intraregional movement of pottery occurred, but in the absence of extensive compositional analysis, this movement is difficult to detect and cannot be quantified on the basis of available data.

Movement of white and gray wares, both inter- and intraregionally, is more clearly evident at Duckfoot and the Dolores sites than it is on Black Mesa. A few pieces of pottery were identified as extraregional imports. Some are tempered with materials (such as trachyte basalt or sandstone with a pink chalcedonic cement) that are not available in the Mesa Verde region. Many others have sand temper, which is widely available, but rarely used, in Mesa Verde pottery. In general, imports were identified according to a suite of technological and stylistic attributes (see Wilson and Blinman 1988).

Assessing the intraregional distribution of white and gray wares in the Mesa Verde region is more complicated. The manufacturing-tracts model, developed by DAP researchers, provides a method of evaluating general trends. According to this model, pottery that has igneous rock temper is assigned to the Dolores tract, which includes Duckfoot and the Dolores area. Pottery that has crushed sedimentary rock temper is assigned to the Cahone tract. The manufacturing-tracts model is not without its problems. Because the Dolores tract includes a large portion of the Mesa Verde region, pottery assigned to this tract is not necessarily local to the Dolores or Duckfoot sites. Furthermore, although igneous rock is rare in the Cahone tract, sedimentary rock is abundant throughout the Dolores tract; therefore, pottery assigned to the Cahone tract could have been made in the Dolores tract. In fact, a sample of unfired clay at Grass Mesa Village was probably tempered with a degraded or crushed sandstone (Blinman 1988b:110), which indicates that some pottery tempered with sedimentary rock was made in the Dolores area.

Despite these problems, the concept of the manufacturing tract can be applied to obtain a tentative picture of interaction between the Duckfoot-Dolores area and the Cahone area. Every sherd that has sandstone temper cannot be assumed to have been made in the Cahone tract. However, changes in the proportion of pottery that has sandstone temper can be taken as a tentative indicator of exchange with the Cahone tract (see Blinman 1987, 1988b; Blinman and Wilson 1988a).

Pottery Wares in the Total Assemblages

Black-on-white pottery, the focus of this research, constitutes only a fraction of the total pottery assemblages at most Pueblo I sites. The majority of the pottery is gray ware; decorated red ware is usually present in smaller amounts. White and gray wares were made both on Black Mesa and in the central Mesa Verde region, but red wares in both areas are assumed to have been imported. Some gray and white wares were also imported to the central Mesa Verde region.

Data on the total pottery assemblages are presented in order to make comparisons between areas and between different kinds of sites. These data include type and ware counts made by BMAP and DAP analysts, and they include much larger samples than were analyzed for either the primary or secondary databases described in Chapter 5 and used in the stylistic analyses. The four Black Mesa sites are examined separately and as a group (Table 6.2). The data from the Dolores sites and Duckfoot are presented according to the spatial distribution of the sites and the presence of possible integrative facilities (great kivas or community pit structures) (Table 6.3). Grass Mesa community consists of Grass Mesa Village and a cluster of nearby small sites, although data from Grass Mesa Village and the other sites in the same community are separated in Table 6.3. The counts and percentages given for Grass Mesa community in Table 6.3 include data from three small sites: Prince Hamlet (also considered in the primary database and described in Chapter 5), LeMoc Shelter (5MT2151 [Hogan 1986]), and Hanging Rock Hamlet (5MT4650 [Gross 1986a]). McPhee Village consists of a large cluster of roomblocks (many designated as separate sites) with many community pit structures that were used between A.D. 840 and the early tenth century. Data from all excavated McPhee Village sites reported in Kane and Robinson (1988) are included in Table 6.3. The Middle Canyon area consists of a number of scattered sites and smaller

Table 6.2. Pottery Ware Percentages, Black Mesa, Total Site Assemblages

Site Number	Gray Ware		White Ware[a]		Red Ware		Total	
	N	%	N	%	N	%	N	%
D:11:2023	3,244	76.22	980	23.03	32	.75	4,256	100.00
D:11:2025	2,228	44.64	2,738	54.86	25	.50	4,991	100.00
D:11:2027	3,709	57.67	2,629	40.88	93	1.45	6,431	100.00
D:11:2030	31,131	70.65	12,566	28.52	364	.83	44,061	100.00
TOTAL	40,312	67.48	18,913	31.66	514	.86	59,739	100.00

SOURCES: Christenson and Parry (1985:Table H.2); Nichols and Smiley (1984:Table H.2).
[a] The white ware category includes what some analysts call Lino Black-on-gray.

Table 6.3. Pottery Ware Percentages, Central Mesa Verde Region, Total Site Assemblages

Time Period	Site or Site Group	Gray Ware		White Ware		Red Ware		Total	
		N	%	N	%	N	%	N	%
A.D. 800–840	Grass Mesa Village*	4,772	88.96	166	3.09	426	7.94	5,364	100.00
	Grass Mesa community	3,832	89.12	253	5.88	215	5.00	4,300	100.00
	Middle Canyon area	20,107	87.01	738	3.19	2,264	9.80	23,109	100.00
	TOTAL	28,711	87.61	1,157	3.53	2,905	8.86	32,773	100.00
A.D. 840–880	McPhee Village*	17,449	89.49	923	4.73	1,126	5.77	19,498	100.00
	Grass Mesa Village	5,795	91.13	308	4.84	256	4.03	6,359	100.00
	Grass Mesa community	1,185	91.44	53	4.09	58	4.48	1,296	100.00
	Middle Canyon area*	17,411	92.56	595	3.16	805	4.28	18,811	100.00
	Duckfoot	100,768	89.82	5,621	5.01	5,795	5.17	112,184	100.00
	TOTAL	142,608	90.17	7,500	4.74	8,040	5.08	158,148	100.00
A.D. 880–920	McPhee Village*	45,296	88.76	3,556	6.97	2,181	4.27	51,033	100.00
	Grass Mesa Village	10,254	88.84	657	5.69	631	5.47	11,542	100.00
	Grass Mesa community	456	85.23	51	9.53	28	5.23	535	100.00
	Middle Canyon area	19,145	92.83	633	3.07	846	4.10	20,624	100.00
	TOTAL	75,151	89.75	4,897	5.85	3,686	4.40	83,734	100.00

SOURCES: Data on McPhee Village from Blinman and Wilson (1988b:Table 14.7); data on Grass Mesa Village from Blinman and Wilson (1988a:Table 13.9); data on Grass Mesa community from Blinman and Wilson (1988a:Table 13.12); data on Middle Canyon area from Blinman and Wilson (1986:Table 7.6); data on Duckfoot from Etzkorn (1993b:Table 3.1).
*Sites or groups of sites with great kivas or community pit structures.

communities east of the Dolores River. The Middle Canyon data are from House Creek Village, Rio Vista Village, Periman Hamlet (used in the primary database), Singing Shelter (5MT4683 [Nelson and Kane 1986]), and a small hamlet called 5MT2226 (included in the Middle Canyon area summary analyses [e.g., Blinman and Wilson 1986], but not reported separately in Kane and Robinson [1986]). The great kiva at Singing Shelter, although poorly dated, was probably in use at some point during the earlier part of the eighth century; in addition, Rio Vista Village had a community pit structure that was used during the A.D. 840–880 period.

Counts and percentages of the wares present in the different assemblages are listed in Tables 6.2 and 6.3. Ideally, comparisons of assemblages should take into account the relative proportions of different categories, as well as the quantities of each category independent of the other categories. The latter is sometimes achieved with density measures. However, density measurements require detailed information about excavation volumes and the availability of comparable contexts from the different sites. Comparable information is not available here, in part because the sites under consideration were excavated as part of three different projects. Therefore, I rely only on relative proportions.

The assemblages from northern Black Mesa and the central Mesa Verde region differ in several ways. Decorated pottery, white and red wares combined, makes up a much larger proportion of the Black Mesa assemblages than of the Dolores and Duckfoot assemblages. Over 30 percent of the Black Mesa pottery assemblage is decorated, compared with only approximately 10 percent of the Dolores-Duckfoot pottery assemblage. The vast majority of decorated pottery on Black Mesa is white ware.

Overall, red wares are slightly more common than white wares in the assemblages from the central Mesa Verde region, although white wares outnumber red wares in the latest period (A.D. 880–920). Red wares were imported to both study areas, and they constitute between 4 and 10 percent of the Dolores and Duckfoot assemblages but never more than 1.5 percent of the Black Mesa assemblages (Tables 6.2 and 6.3). However, the difference in the proportion of red wares can be accounted for by the different distances to the source. That is, the distance from the red ware source to Duckfoot and Dolores is roughly two-thirds the distance from the source to Black Mesa. A simple gravity model of interaction and distribution (Haggett 1965; Olsson 1970; see summary in Plog 1976) shows that the frequency of contact is expected to diminish with the inverse-square of the distance. According to this model, the sites on northern Black Mesa are expected to have between one-quarter and one-ninth as many red wares as the sites in the central Mesa Verde region, and the observed data fit these expectations almost exactly.

The four Black Mesa sites do not show any consistent patterning in the relative distributions of different pottery wares. The largest site, D:11:2030, has an intermediate proportion of decorated pottery. The site with the highest percentage of white ware (D:11:2025) has the lowest percentage of red ware, and the site with the highest percentage of red ware (D:11:2027) has an intermediate proportion of white ware.

Analysis of McPhee Village suggests that decorated pottery, especially red ware, was particularly important at the roomblocks with community pit structures. Blinman (1989) found that pottery assemblages associated with very large and elaborate community pit structures had the highest proportions of red wares, primarily bowls. Furthermore, the roomblocks associated with these pit structures tended to have relatively fewer cooking jar sherds and smaller cooking jars than did other roomblocks. Blinman (1989) argues that food may have been prepared elsewhere and brought to the elaborate community pit structures for "potluck-style" gatherings, a form of redistribution. The concentration of red wares may be a result of more serving and consuming at these pit structures, or it may indicate that residents of the associated roomblocks had increased access to imported goods, or both.

Comparisons among the four groups of Dolores sites (Grass Mesa Village, Grass Mesa community, Middle Canyon area, and McPhee Village [Table 6.3]) provide only tentative support for the association of either red or white wares with community pit structures or great kivas. Grass Mesa Village during the A.D. 800–840 period, McPhee Village during the A.D. 840–920 period, and Rio Vista Village in the Middle Canyon area during the A.D. 840–880 period had great kivas or community pit structures that are interpreted as possible evidence of large-scale integrative activities. However, the assemblages associated with these sites and periods do not stand out consistently in terms of the percentage of decorated pottery. McPhee Village has a higher percentage of decorated pottery than does any other site during the A.D. 840–880 period, but the differences are slight and the pattern does not continue into the later part of the ninth century.

The discrepancies between the intra- and intercommunity comparisons involving McPhee Village may be a result of the different scales of analysis. That is, Blinman (1989) suggests that the roomblocks with the most elaborate pit structures at McPhee Village had a higher percentage of red wares, and other roomblocks had a higher percentage of gray ware cooking jars. When the assemblages from these roomblocks are combined, the extreme red ware and gray ware percentages should average to moderate levels. Thus, when McPhee Village as a whole is compared with other communities, differences in the percentages of red wares are slight.

In the Dolores area, there is also evidence, summarized in the previous section on distribution and use, that both white and gray wares were exchanged or otherwise distributed across the central Mesa Verde region and imported from other regions, including the Kayenta region. Evidence suggesting the movement of gray and white wares is much more limited in the Black Mesa assemblages. Some intraregional distribution was indicated by Hantman and Plog's (1982) analysis, discussed in the preceding section, although such distribution is difficult to quantify without a substantial investment in petrographic analysis. Interregional movement of pottery also may be difficult to detect on Black Mesa because sand temper is so widely available outside the region as well as within it. However, imported painted white ware should be identifiable because of differences in design and paint technology, and no such differences were found in the pottery from the Black Mesa sites. Thus, there is no evidence that pottery was moved long distances to northern Black Mesa during the ninth century.

Evidence of the intraregional and extraregional distribution of gray and white wares at Dolores is summarized in Table 6.4 (similar data are not available for the Duckfoot site). There is strong evidence of intraregional movement of pottery associated with the occupation of Grass Mesa Village during the A.D. 800–840 period, the time when the great kiva was apparently in use (see also Blinman and Wilson 1988a:1013, 1018). A far higher percentage of pottery from the Cahone tract, especially white ware, is present in the A.D. 800–840 assemblage from Grass Mesa Village than in any other assemblage. The percentage of Cahone tract pottery drops off after A.D. 840, and no other assemblage has exceptionally high percentages. The decrease in pottery from the Cahone tract may be associated with deteriorating climatic conditions and possibly a population decline in the Cahone area after about A.D. 840 (Blinman and Wilson 1988a:1013; Schlanger 1988). The social mechanism that resulted in this movement of pottery is difficult to determine. The presence of Cahone tract pottery at Grass Mesa Village and other sites in the Dolores area could be the result of exchange with residents of the Cahone tract, or it could be the result of residents of the Cahone area coming to Dolores and bringing pottery, perhaps with food for a ceremony. In either case, the distribution of pottery indicates that there was interaction between the Dolores and Cahone areas.

An unequal distribution of pottery from outside the Mesa Verde region is also indicated at the Dolores sites. Grass Mesa Village has the highest percentage of imports during the A.D. 800–840 period, the Middle Canyon area has the highest percentage of imports during the A.D. 840–880 period, and McPhee Village has the highest percentage of imports during the A.D. 880–920 period. Thus, imported pottery appears to be more common at sites with great kivas and community pit structures, although it is also present at sites that do not have large-scale integrative architecture. At the Duckfoot site, only 13 sherds (less than .01 percent of the total assemblage) were classified as nonlocal or "other" (Lightfoot 1992a:Table 3.2).

These data on pottery distribution provide evidence of limited interaction between the two study areas. The presence of San Juan

Table 6.4. Origin of Total Assemblage of Gray and White Wares, Dolores Sites

Time Period	Site or Site Group	Ware	Intraregional				Extraregional		Indeterminate		Total	
			Dolores Tract		Cahone Tract							
			N	%	N	%	N	%	N	%	N	%
A.D. 800–840	Grass Mesa Village*	gray	4,363	91.43	383	8.03	12	.25	14	.29	4,772	100.00
		white	125	75.76	19	11.52	19	11.52	2	1.21	165	100.00
		TOTAL	4,488	90.91	402	8.14	31	.63	16	.32	4,937	100.00
	Grass Mesa community	gray	3,799	99.14	23	.60	8	.21	2	.05	3,832	100.00
		white	252	99.60	1	.40	0	.00	0	.00	253	100.00
		TOTAL	4,051	99.17	24	.59	8	.20	2	.05	4,085	100.00
	Middle Canyon area	gray	15,649	98.29	202	1.27	69	.43	1	.01	15,921	100.00
		white	646	97.29	2	.30	14	2.11	2	.30	664	100.00
		TOTAL	16,295	98.25	204	1.23	83	.50	3	.02	16,585	100.00
	All sites	gray	23,811	97.09	608	2.48	89	.36	17	.07	24,525	100.00
		white	1,023	94.55	22	2.03	33	3.05	4	.37	1,082	100.00
		TOTAL	24,834	96.98	630	2.46	122	.48	21	.08	25,607	100.00
A.D. 840–880	McPhee Village*	gray	17,310	99.20	87	.50	30	.17	22	.13	17,449	100.00
		white	877	95.02	36	3.90	9	.98	1	.11	923	100.00
		TOTAL	18,187	98.99	123	.67	39	.21	23	.13	18,372	100.00
	Grass Mesa Village	gray	5,757	99.34	31	.53	5	.09	2	.03	5,795	100.00
		white	296	96.10	1	.32	11	3.57	0	.00	308	100.00
		TOTAL	6,053	99.18	32	.52	16	.26	2	.03	6,103	100.00
	Grass Mesa community	gray	1,173	98.99	10	.84	2	.17	0	.00	1,185	100.00
		white	53	100.00	0	.00	0	.00	0	.00	53	100.00
		TOTAL	1,226	99.03	10	.81	2	.16	0	.00	1,238	100.00
	Middle Canyon area*	gray	17,143	98.49	146	.84	94	.54	23	.13	17,406	100.00
		white	579	97.31	6	1.01	8	1.34	2	.34	595	100.00
		TOTAL	17,722	98.45	152	.84	102	.57	25	.14	18,001	100.00
	All sites	gray	41,383	98.92	274	.65	131	.31	47	.11	41,835	100.00
		white	1,805	96.06	43	2.29	28	1.49	3	.16	1,879	100.00
		TOTAL	43,188	98.80	317	.73	159	.36	50	.11	43,714	100.00
A.D. 880–920	McPhee Village*	gray	44,830	98.98	324	.72	95	.21	44	.10	45,293	100.00
		white	3,352	94.26	43	1.21	123	3.46	38	1.07	3,556	100.00
		TOTAL	48,182	98.63	367	.75	218	.45	82	.17	48,849	100.00
	Grass Mesa Village	gray	10,110	98.60	109	1.06	15	.15	20	.20	10,254	100.00
		white	640	97.41	9	1.37	8	1.22	0	.00	657	100.00
		TOTAL	10,750	98.52	118	1.08	23	.21	20	.18	10,911	100.00
	Grass Mesa community	gray	453	99.34	3	.66	0	.00	0	.00	456	100.00
		white	51	100.00	0	.00	0	.00	0	.00	51	100.00
		TOTAL	504	99.41	3	.59	0	.00	0	.00	507	100.00
	Middle Canyon area	gray	18,944	98.96	100	.52	14	.07	85	.44	19,143	100.00
		white	617	97.47	8	1.26	4	.63	4	.63	633	100.00
		TOTAL	19,561	98.91	108	.55	18	.09	89	.45	19,776	100.00
	All sites	gray	74,337	98.92	536	.71	124	.17	149	.20	75,146	100.00
		white	4,660	95.16	60	1.23	135	2.76	42	.86	4,897	100.00
		TOTAL	78,997	98.69	596	.74	259	.32	191	.24	80,043	100.00

SOURCE: Blinman and Wilson (1988a:Tables 13.9, 13.12, and 13.13).
*Sites or groups of sites with great kivas or community pit structures.

Red Ware in both the Black Mesa and the Dolores and Duckfoot assemblages suggests that there was interaction between both areas and southeastern Utah, although not necessarily between the two study areas themselves. No Mesa Verde white or gray wares were found on the Black Mesa sites. A small fraction (.36 percent) of the white and gray wares from the Dolores sites were probably imported from other regions. The specific source of most imports could not be determined, but 64 sherds (from all sites and time periods in Table 6.4) were from the Kayenta region, although not necessarily from Black Mesa. The small quantity of Kayenta imports suggests that interaction between the two areas was limited. The pottery could easily have been transported by individuals who migrated from the Kayenta region to the Mesa Verde region or by individuals from the Mesa Verde region who traveled to the Kayenta region. There is no indication, at least from the distribution of pottery, of any large-scale or formalized interaction between the areas. Furthermore, the presence of imports in one area but not in the other suggests either that interactions between the two areas were nonequivalent (that is, pots were not exchanged for pots) or that the residents of Dolores and Duckfoot were interacting with people from elsewhere in the Kayenta region.

Vessel Form and Use

Pottery manufacture involves the use of a highly flexible medium—clay. Human creators can produce a wide variety of forms according to their needs and desires. The form of a pottery vessel is often closely related to the use of that vessel, as has been documented by a long history of research (e.g., Holmes 1903; Henrickson and McDonald 1983; Smith 1985; Hally 1986). Vessel form is also related to the painted designs on pottery because the form of the vessel determines the field that can be painted. Furthermore, vessel use, which is closely linked to form, will influence where, when, and how the painted designs will be seen. The focus here is on vessel forms and wares included in the stylistic analysis, that is, on black-on-white bowls and jars.

A bowl is a shallow, open container that, by definition, has an orifice equal to, or only slightly smaller than, its girth, that has no neck or inflection point, and that has a height less than its girth (Blinman 1988a:454, 1988b:129). The shape allows easy access to contents, and bowls are often used for serving or eating (Braun 1980; Smith 1985). A study of over 500 whole vessels from the northern Southwest showed that the volumes of what appear to be individual serving bowls (a category that excludes very large vessels) remained relatively constant (at about 700 cm^3) between A.D. 600 and 1300

(Turner and Lofgren 1966). Thus, relatively little variation in bowl size is expected in the pottery included in this research. Diameters of the bowl rim sherds analyzed as part of the primary database are compared in Figure 6.3. Few differences between the areas are evident; both histograms show broad but unimodal distributions, with one or two very large bowls but otherwise no clear breaks indicative of different size classes.

The white ware jar category includes a variety of vessel forms that have necks or other types of constricted openings. Several kinds of jars are present in the samples from both regions, although the different jar forms usually cannot be distinguished with only fragmentary sherd evidence. Generally, sherds on which decoration (including paint, slip, or polish) is present only on the convex side are classified as jars. Three general forms of white ware jars—ollas, pitchers, and seed jars—are present in the analyzed samples (see descriptions by Blinman 1988a, 1988b:131–143). Ollas are large jars with narrow mouths and often long necks. Their restricted openings suggest that manipulation of their contents would have been difficult; however, the presence of handles on many ollas suggests that the contents could have been dispensed by pouring (see also Smith 1985). A limited sample of whole and reconstructible vessels from the Dolores sites suggests that white ware ollas were rare before A.D. 880 (Blinman 1988a).

Pitchers are relatively small jars with unopposed (that is, single) handles and fairly wide orifices that sometimes have rims shaped for pouring. A gourd jar is a special form of pitcher that is shaped like a gourd and generally has a smaller orifice than do other kinds of pitchers. Blinman (1988a:459–463, 1988b:134–136) argues that, at Dolores, both pitchers and ollas were used primarily for storing fluids, with pitchers having been used for shorter-term storage. The shape of the vessels, particularly ollas, suggests that they would have been well suited to this use. Furthermore, vitrification, which decreases the permeability of pottery, is most commonly associated with ollas and pitchers (Blinman 1988b:134–136). Finally, with the exception of a few vessels that were broken and then used in a fragmentary state, ollas and pitchers were not sooted, which suggests that they were not used as cooking pots.

The final category of white ware jar considered here is the seed jar. Seed jars are small vessels that have very small orifices but no necks. They often have holes or attachments near the rim that would facilitate closure; therefore they would have been well suited to the long-term storage of dry or perishable goods (Blinman 1988a:459).

Bowls and jars differ in a number of ways with respect to their use and their deposition in the archaeological record. All three types of white ware jars were probably used primarily for storage, whereas

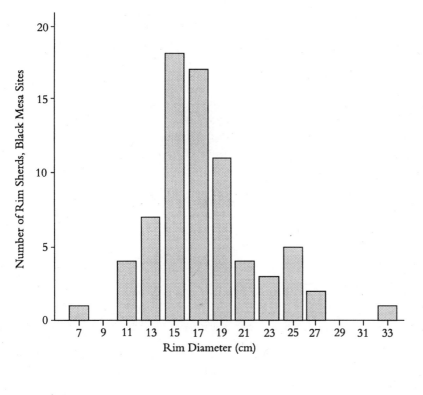

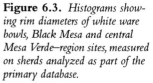

Figure 6.3. *Histograms showing rim diameters of white ware bowls, Black Mesa and central Mesa Verde–region sites, measured on sherds analyzed as part of the primary database.*

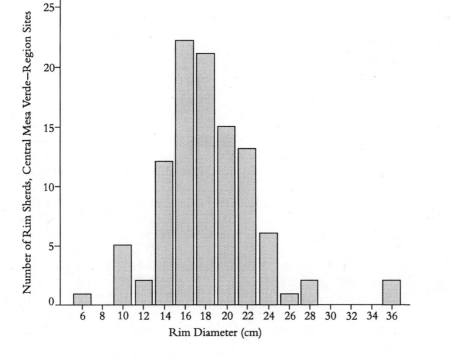

bowls were probably used for serving and eating. Thus, jars are expected to have had longer use lives than bowls. In the ethnographic cases reviewed by Mills (1989), serving vessels often had use lives of less than two years, whereas storage vessels often had use lives of greater than five years. Different breakage rates obviously will result in differential representation of vessel forms in the archaeological record. However, Mills (1989) notes that the length of time a site is occupied will affect the proportion of vessels represented. She argues that proportional representation should stabilize as the duration of the occupation exceeds the maximum expected use life of the vessels. Thus, she suggests that sites occupied for more than 10 years should, theoretically, have comparable proportions of vessel forms. All the sites included in this study are thought to have been occupied for at least 10 years, so differences in relative proportions are not expected to be problematic, although the possibility of nonproportional representation is considered in discussions of specific results below.

Bowls and jars also differ in the context of their use. Specifically, bowls, used for serving and eating, are used quite actively. In contrast, storage jars have a much more passive use. Bowls are expected to be seen and handled much more frequently than jars. Furthermore, if jars were stored in rear storage rooms and bowls were used for eating and serving in pit structures and front habitation rooms, it is likely that bowls would have been seen by more individuals, including those who were not members of the household, than would have jars.

Decorated white ware bowls and jars are present in both the Black Mesa and Dolores-Duckfoot samples, but the proportions, represented by sherds in the assemblages, differ over time and space. The number and proportion of decorated white ware bowl and jar sherds in the different assemblages analyzed as part of the primary database are shown in Tables 6.5 and 6.6. Three factors preclude the use of these data for determining the number of decorated white ware bowls and jars that were used at the sites: (1) bowls and jars are expected to have different breakage rates, (2) vessels of different sizes will break into different numbers of pieces, and (3) different proportions of the vessels were painted. However, the percentages shown in Tables 6.5 and 6.6 can be conservatively interpreted in terms of the relative proportion of decorated areas on jars and bowls.

The two areas are considerably different in terms of the proportions of painted bowl and jar sherds. The combined Black Mesa sites have roughly equal proportions of decorated bowl and jar sherds, whereas bowl sherds are much more common than jar sherds in the Dolores assemblage. Furthermore, the proportion of decorated bowls and jars changes over time at Dolores. Fewer than 10 percent of the

Table 6.5. Vessel Forms in the Total Assemblage of Black-on-white Sherds,
Black Mesa

Site Number	Bowls		Jars		Total	
	N	%	N	%	N	%
D:11:2023	203	55.16	165	44.84	368	100.00
D:11:2025	475	85.90	78	14.10	553	100.00
D:11:2027	214	31.06	475	68.94	689	100.00
D:11:2030	2,158	51.84	2,005	48.16	4,163	100.00
TOTAL	3,050	52.83	2,723	47.17	5,773	100.00

SOURCES: Christenson and Parry (1985:Tables H.9 and H.13); Nichols and Smiley (1984:Tables H.8 and H.11).
NOTE: All painted sherds that could be assigned to a time period with a relatively high degree of confidence are included, even when the fragments are too small to be included in the stylistic analysis.

Table 6.6. Vessel Forms in the Total Assemblage of Black-on-white Sherds, Central Mesa Verde Region

Time Period	Site	Bowls		Jars		Total	
		N	%	N	%	N	%
A.D. 800–840	Grass Mesa Village*	4	80.00	1	20.00	5	100.00
	Prince Hamlet	54	96.43	2	3.57	56	100.00
	House Creek Village	52	91.23	5	8.77	57	100.00
	Windy Wheat Hamlet	21	87.50	3	12.50	24	100.00
	Periman Hamlet	24	88.89	3	11.11	27	100.00
	TOTAL	155	91.72	14	8.28	169	100.00
A.D. 840–880	Grass Mesa Village	70	77.78	20	22.22	90	100.00
	Prince Hamlet	7	100.00	0	.00	7	100.00
	Rio Vista Village*	51	69.86	22	30.14	73	100.00
	House Creek Village	23	95.83	1	4.17	24	100.00
	Duckfoot	169	79.34	44	20.66	213	100.00
	Aldea Alfareros	182	71.09	74	28.91	256	100.00
	Pueblo de las Golondrinas*	7	30.43	16	69.57	23	100.00
	Golondrinas Oriental	0	.00	1	100.00	1	100.00
	TOTAL	509	74.09	178	25.91	687	100.00
A.D. 880–920	Grass Mesa Village	84	56.00	66	44.00	150	100.00
	Prince Hamlet	14	87.50	2	12.50	16	100.00
	Rio Vista Village	9	100.00	0	.00	9	100.00
	Weasel Pueblo*	64	59.81	43	40.19	107	100.00
	Pueblo de las Golondrinas*	44	55.70	35	44.30	79	100.00
	Golondrinas Oriental	53	72.60	20	27.40	73	100.00
	TOTAL	268	61.75	166	38.25	434	100.00

SOURCES: Data for the Dolores-area sites are from the DAP computer base at the Anasazi Heritage Center, Dolores, Colorado. The Duckfoot data are from the author's own analysis.
NOTE: All painted sherds that could be assigned to a time period with a relatively high degree of confidence are included, even when the fragments are too small to be included in the stylistic analysis. Information on the degree of confidence is not available for the Duckfoot sample, so the Duckfoot data presented here include only sherds that were used in the stylistic analysis.
*Sites with great kivas or community pit structures.

black-on-white sherds in the earliest period are jars, and the proportion increases to 38 percent in the latest period.

It is unlikely that these differences in the proportion of bowl and jar sherds can be explained in terms of differences in site-formation processes. Jars are expected to have had longer use lives than bowls. Thus, they were probably deposited less frequently in the archaeological record and are expected to be underrepresented, particularly at sites with short occupations (Mills 1989). However, many assemblages with the largest proportions of jar sherds are associated with relatively short-term occupations at the small Black Mesa sites and with contexts identified as belonging to the late Grass Mesa subphase at Dolores. Thus, the greater proportion of jar sherds in these assemblages may be indicative of greater use of painted white ware jars prehistorically.

Furthermore, differences in the percentages of jars and bowls cannot be explained as the result of temporal differences between the samples from the two areas. A small sample of early painted pottery (generally considered Basketmaker III types) is available from both areas. Of the 31 Chapin Black-on-white sherds from the Dolores sites, 29, or 94 percent, are from bowls. Conversely, 28 Lino Black-on-white sherds were found on the Black Mesa sites and only three of these, or 11 percent, are from bowls.

Comparisons among the four Black Mesa sites do not reveal any consistent patterning in the proportions of bowl to jar sherds. The largest Black Mesa site (D:11:2030), which probably was occupied the longest, has an intermediate proportion of bowls and jars. Thus, again, there is no evidence that the proportions of bowl and jar sherds are products of differences in site-formation processes.

Some differences in the proportions of bowls and jars are evident in the Dolores assemblages (Table 6.6). There is a slight tendency for sites with great kivas or community pit structures to have larger proportions of painted jar sherds. Grass Mesa Village has a great kiva that was probably in use during the early ninth century. Of all the assemblages that date to this time, that from Grass Mesa Village has the largest proportion of painted jar sherds. During the A.D. 840–880 period, community pit structures were present at Rio Vista Village, and a very large and elaborate pit structure, as well as a U-shaped roomblock and a plaza, were present at Pueblo de las Golondrinas, which is part of McPhee Village. Pueblo de las Golondrinas has the highest proportion of painted jar sherds (excluding the very small sample [$n = 1$] from Golondrinas Oriental), and Rio Vista has the next highest proportion of painted jar sherds. During the A.D. 880–920 period, the population at Grass Mesa Village apparently was highly mobile and built many relatively small, insubstantial pithouses. However, the proportion of jars at Grass Mesa Village during this period was still high. Two roomblocks at McPhee Village (Pueblo de las Golondrinas and Weasel Pueblo) had community pit structures during the A.D. 880–920 period, and both also have high proportions of decorated jars dating to this time. These results suggest that, at sites where larger social gatherings or ritual activities took place, there was a greater tendency to decorate forms (that is, jars) that were more often plain or sparsely decorated in other contexts.

Summary and Conclusions

The information and analyses presented in this chapter can be used to begin assessing the expectations for the different roles of pottery design style in the two study areas. Pottery production, distribution, and use all affect how designs are made and displayed, and therefore they have an effect on the role of those designs in social and cultural processes.

Many lines of evidence indicate that Pueblo I black-on-white pottery in both the Kayenta and Mesa Verde regions was produced on a fairly small scale at many locations. More detailed analyses of the study areas suggest that pottery was produced at most, if not all, habitation sites. Evidence of local production does not necessarily mean that all the pottery found at a site was made at that site; that is, exchange is not precluded, and it is possible that people used pottery made in some other place. However, the evidence of local production is still important for understanding the link between individuals and the design style on their pottery. If black-on-white pottery was produced by many households and/or at most sites, then individuals would have been able to exercise a fair degree of control over the designs on the pottery they used. People either made the pots themselves or at least knew, and probably had social relations with, the potters. Therefore, it is possible that designs on pottery could have been a means of expressing individual, personally designed messages.

Detailed analysis of pottery temper in both areas shows a surprising degree of homogeneity. Although temper materials were widely available, the most common materials (assorted igneous rocks in the central Mesa Verde region and sand from the Wepo Formation on northern Black Mesa) were not used. Instead, potters at locations distant from one another consistently selected the same kinds of less widely available materials, specifically, only one kind of igneous rock (in the central Mesa Verde region) and coarser sand, possibly from the Toreva Formation (in the Black Mesa area). This technological consistency has important implications for the interpretation of diversity in design style. Potters across the study areas knew how others made pots, and they all used very similar technological processes.

This suggests that if they did not paint the same designs on their pots, the design differences cannot be attributed to a lack of information or interaction. Instead, a diversity of designs is better interpreted as a deliberate effort to make different designs. In other words, potters knew what other potters were doing, and if they did things differently, it was by choice.

Various lines of evidence suggest that different kinds of social dynamics were present in the two areas during the ninth century, and it is expected that the role of style would have differed as well. Specifically, the Mesa Verde region had greater population density, more settlement aggregation, and more evidence of large-scale group activities and ceremonies than did Black Mesa and probably the whole of the Kayenta region. Social relations are expected to have been more intensive in the central Mesa Verde region and more extensive on northern Black Mesa. In the central Mesa Verde region, style is expected to have played an important role in public contexts as a means of displaying individual or group identity and marking social differences. In contrast, on northern Black Mesa, style is expected to have been used in more varied contexts as a means of expressing social solidarity and maintaining links with an extensive network.

Information on the distribution of pottery through exchange or other forms of social interaction provides some additional insight into the kinds of social dynamics that occurred in the two areas. Red wares, probably produced in specialized communities in southeastern Utah, were present on northern Black Mesa and in the central Mesa Verde region, and differences in the quantities of red ware are what would be expected given the different distances from the source. Thus, it appears that residents of both areas had similar kinds of interactions with residents of southeastern Utah. In both cases, they received goods from southeastern Utah, although what, if anything, was exchanged for the red ware is not known.

Intraregional distribution of pottery occurred in both study areas, although the amount of pottery distributed cannot be determined, because pottery made in different parts of the regions often can be detected only through detailed analysis. However, data from the central Mesa Verde region indicate that large sites with community architecture had relatively more pottery from distant parts of the region. This kind of distribution may indicate that residents of these structures participated in more exchange or that the pottery was brought to the large sites for ceremonials or public gatherings. In either case, the distribution supports the assumption that different sorts of activities took place in association with the larger-scale, or public, architecture.

Extraregional gray and white wares were found in small quantities in the assemblages from the central Mesa Verde region, but not in those from Black Mesa. These imports are most common in contexts associated with large-scale or community architecture. The small quantity of imports could be accounted for by the migration of individuals or by very small scale long-distance exchange relationships. The distribution of the imports suggests that such interaction with other regions was minimal, but what interaction occurred may have been associated with activities in community architecture that served as a central focus for exchange, as a locus for individuals who participated in long-distance exchange, or as a gathering place for immigrants.

Data on decorated vessel forms provide strong support for the expectations regarding the different roles of style in the two regions and study areas. In the central Mesa Verde region, style is expected to have been an important means of marking social identity in various kinds of interactions, including fairly large scale activities. In this region, decoration on bowls, which were used for eating and serving, is far more common than decoration on jars, most of which were probably used for storage. Thus, it appears that pottery style in the central Mesa Verde region was used to communicate with social others. Large social gatherings and contacts with socially distant people are expected to have been relatively uncommon for the residents of northern Black Mesa. In this area, style is expected to have been important in maintaining social ties rather than in emphasizing social differences. At the Black Mesa sites, decoration is roughly equally common on bowl and jar sherds, and far more decoration is present on Black Mesa jars than on jars from the central Mesa Verde region. The fact that decoration was applied to vessels not often seen by outsiders suggests that pottery style was important, not primarily to communicate with distant others, but to emphasize particularly significant information at home (see David et al. 1988).

7
The Structure of Style

This chapter presents the first part of the stylistic analysis, a study of the structure of design style. Structure is a system of organization, and design structure is the organization of designs, including layout, symmetry, and the use of elements in particular contexts or combinations.[1]

The purpose of this analysis is to describe various attributes of structure in terms of rules of design and to compare the uses of rules in different contexts.

In a general sense, structure is a means of organizing stimuli and information (such as design attributes) and thus is essential to cultural cognition and communication. According to information theory, structure limits the quantity of information that can be transmitted, but it can contribute to the quality of the information (see Campbell 1982; Moles 1966; Shannon and Weaver 1949). That is, although structure often involves redundancy and thus decreases the total amount of information in a message, it increases the chances that the information will be interpreted correctly and convey meaningful messages.

This relationship between structure and meaning has two general implications for style. First, a set of designs would appear to be random and structureless if every design were completely different and the designs exhibited no system of organization. The definition of style as "a way of doing" or, more specifically, as "a way of decorating pottery with painted designs" implies that there is some regularity to

---

1. Shepard (1965:264) considers structure to be the outlines and major divisions of the design, and her definition is widely used in ceramic analyses. The definition of structure used here is broader than Shepard's and includes the principles of organization, as well as the visible outlines.

style; that is, style involves doing something in a *particular* way. The definition also implies that structureless designs would not constitute style. Furthermore, although structureless designs could transmit information, the lack of structure suggests that the information would probably not be culturally meaningful.

Second, although structure is necessary for the meaningful transmission of information, too much structure or redundancy (in other words, no variation) would limit the amount of information that could be transmitted. In cases in which style is a matter of choice between technological alternatives, such invariant style may be of limited importance in transmitting information. Rather, invariant style would more likely be the result of a traditional way of doing things, a form of isochrestic variation (Sackett 1982). On the other hand, the redundancy inherent in highly structured style can emphasize a limited amount of information. This kind of emphasis might be present in instances in which the style involves added effort, such as in styles of decoration. In these cases, highly structured style might convey very important information, an emphatic declaration such as "I am a member of this group!" Redundant emphatic communication is also a characteristic of ritual (Rappaport 1979:175–176).

The expectations for the analysis of design style structure are limited by the database in this study, that is, the secondary database, as described in Chapter 5. To recap briefly, the database was derived from the analysis of samples of the predominant Pueblo I black-on-white types in the Kayenta and Mesa Verde regions—Kana-a and Piedra black-on-white (Figure 4.3). The two types can be distinguished on the basis of technological and other nonstructural characteristics. Only vessels and large sherds that display substantial proportions of designs are included in the analysis. Some are from tightly controlled contexts, but others have minimal provenience information. This database provides samples large enough to be examined for patterns and variation in design structure. However, most comparisons can be made only at a broad level, that is, between the Mesa Verde and Kayenta regions.

Following the expectations for the two regions developed in the previous chapters, I expect the use of style to make and mark a variety of social distinctions to have been more important in the Mesa Verde region than on Black Mesa and across the Kayenta region. If pottery design style was used in this manner, the Piedra Black-on-white designs should exhibit some regularity, indicative of a structure organizing the information, although the designs should not be so rigidly standardized that they would curtail the amount of information conveyed. In contrast, the use of style to emphasize social similarity and maintain broad networks of relationships is expected at Black Mesa and across the Kayenta region. Thus, Kana-a

Black-on-white would be expected to display relatively little variation in design structure, which is indicative of an emphatic message. Kana-a and Piedra black-on-white are different in that they have different design elements structured and combined in different ways. However, the structural analysis focuses, not on differences in the specific design content (this is the subject of the analysis presented in the following chapter), but on differences in how structural rules are manifested in the designs and the degree of structural variation.

The second expectation concerns the role of style in ritual. Because ritual is formalized and rule-bound, the structure of designs associated with ritual should also be more formalized. Thus, both Kana-a and Piedra black-on-white vessels that are found in ritual contexts (primarily burials) are expected to have more invariant design structures than are other vessels.

Analytic Approaches

To this point, the discussion of structure and communication and expectations for style structure has emphasized the presence or absence of structure and degrees of structural variation. To interpret and compare these general concepts, the various aspects of the design structure—the rules and principles by which the designs appear to be organized—must be described. This information can then be used to examine different kinds of rules and structures. Miller (1985a) similarly considers rules and variability.

Several methods of describing design structure have been used in studies of material culture. Many designs can be described in terms of a hierarchy of structural components, including the design field as a whole, methods used to divide and subdivide that field, and means of filling the various areas. Such hierarchical descriptions have a long history in the study of ceramic designs in the Southwest and elsewhere (e.g., Amsden 1936; Friedrich 1970; Hardin 1983b; Kidder and Shepard 1936). For example, Amsden (1936) describes how Hohokam pottery designs are divided and subdivided into bands or quarters, areas which are then filled with certain elements and combinations of elements. In the past, this kind of description was often used to characterize assemblages (e.g., Kidder and Shepard 1936) and was incorporated into numerous type descriptions (e.g., Beals et al. 1945). More recently, Hardin (1983b; see also Friedrich 1970) has used a hierarchical classification system in research on the relationship between design and social interaction. Jernigan (1986; see also Jernigan and Wreden 1982) has recently criticized the hierarchical approach, arguing instead for analyses based on culturally recognized design schema, which he argues can be identified on the basis of the repetitive use of schema on several vessels. Unfortunately, he does not explain how design configurations that constitute a schema can be identified in a systematic and replicative manner. As a result, his method is difficult to apply and has been criticized by several authors (Douglass and Lindauer 1988; Plog 1995).

A hierarchical description of designs often reveals clues regarding the rules by which the designs are organized, but the rules are not delineated systematically and are sometimes left implicit. In an effort to be more explicit about design rules, a number of authors have recently developed design grammars (Faris 1972; Glassie 1975; Hodder 1982a, 1982b:174–181; Holm 1965; Muller 1979; Wright 1981:115–125). These grammars describe, often through symbolic notation (for example, A-B-A-B), how the designs are organized and, ideally, also provide a means by which new designs of the same style can be generated. Grammars are used to describe particular styles (Holm 1965; Wright 1981); to characterize changes in, and differences between, architectural styles (Glassie 1975); and to draw broader conclusions about structural principles (Muller 1979).

Both hierarchical descriptions and grammars, although they can be used in some comparative studies, are generally specific to a single style or a set of closely related styles. Symmetry analysis is a more standardized method for characterizing structure (Washburn 1977:7). In symmetry analysis, the repetition of stylistic units is described using principles borrowed from crystallography. For example, in an early anthropological application of symmetry, Brainerd (1942) noted that ancestral Puebloan pottery designs were characterized by rotational, rather than reflection, symmetry (for explanations of the different kinds of finite symmetry, see the description of Variable 5 [V5] in Table 7.1). Shepard (1948) conducted an extensive study of Southwestern and other ceramics using symmetry analysis. Washburn (1977, 1983a) has recently applied the method to a variety of materials, and Washburn and Crowe (1987) explicitly describe the method of symmetry analysis. Symmetry analysis can be applied to various levels of design organization (for example, the motif or the overall layout [Washburn 1977]), and principles of symmetry can be incorporated into other analytical schemes (Crown 1981; Neily 1983).

Finally, archaeological studies that consider the covariation of attributes also provide structural information, although not always explicitly. Some descriptions of types and theoretical discussions about the nature of types emphasize attribute association (Spaulding 1982). In their analyses of style as a reflection of marriage patterns and social interaction, Deetz (1965) and Whallon (1968) considered the covariation of attributes. More recently, Plog (1990b) has addressed this issue in his analysis of how the strength of covariation changes over time and between types in the Kayenta area.

Table 7.1. Attributes Recorded During the Structural Analysis

V1 Design field (for jars only): The location—neck, shoulder, and/or body—of the design is recorded.

V2 Design layout: Three general categories of layout—bands, panels, and dividing designs—are coded for both bowls and jars. Each category is subdivided according to details of design organization.

Bands

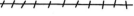
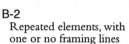

B-1
Lines only, with or without secondary elements

B-2
Repeated elements, with one or no framing lines

B-3
Repeated single elements framed above and below

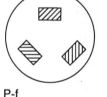

B-4
Repeated motifs (combinations of elements) framed above and below

B-5
Divided panels framed above and below

Panels

P-f
Free

P-a
Attached

P-n
Nested

Divided bowls

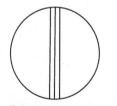

D-b
Bisected

D-q
Quartered

D-o
Offset

Divided jars

D-v
Vertical

D-s
Slant/spiral

Table 7.1. Attributes Recorded During the Structural Analysis *(continued)*

V3 Center: The presence or absence of a separate design in the center of a bowl is recorded.

V4 Relationship: How are the designs in different fields (neck, shoulder, and body of a jar; center and border of a bowl) related?

V5–V6 Symmetry: One-color design symmetry is recorded using the method developed by Washburn and Crowe (1987). Only the symmetry of the whole design, including elaborations, is recorded. Asymmetry caused by different numbers of motifs (e.g., five dots on one triangle and six dots on another) is ignored. In a few cases, symmetry is reduced because one section of an otherwise repeated design is different. If the difference appears to be the result of a space constraint (e.g., the last repetition had to be squeezed in), the recorded symmetry is not reduced, but the difference is noted. Otherwise, the design is coded as asymmetrical. One-dimensional symmetry is recorded for all horizontal bands and multiple (more than two) panels. Finite symmetry is recorded for bowls. Because no designs (with the exception of a few cases of simple checks) are repeated in more than one dimension, two-dimensional symmetry is not recorded.[a]

V5 Finite designs

c*n*

    cn (cyclic):
    Has *n*-fold rotational symmetry, but no bilateral symmetry.
    Example: $n = 2$.

d*n*

    dn (dihedral):
    Has *n* distinct mirror reflection lines.[b]
    Example: $n = 2$.

cd*n*

    cdn:
    Has both rotational and mirror symmetry.
    Example: $n = 4$.

ccdd

    The code cc, dd, or ccdd indicates a very large *n* (>6).

V6 One-dimensional designs

11
    Translation only

m1
    Horizontal reflection

12
    Half turns

mm
    Horizontal and vertical reflection with half turns

mg
    Horizontal reflection with half turns

mm/mg
    Horizontal reflection, questionable vertical reflection

Table 7.1. Attributes Recorded During the Structural Analysis *(continued)*

V7 Framing lines: The presence or absence of framing lines on the upper and lower margins of a design is recorded.

V8–V10 Multiple parallel lines: The use of sets of parallel lines (three or more) is coded in terms of three sets of possible configurations.

V8 Dead-end

R
Right angle

D
Diagonal

D
Diagonal

V9 Complex

CCr
Crisscross, right angle

CCd
Crisscross, diagonal

Sc
Spiral, circular

Sr
Spiral, right angle

Sd
Spiral, diagonal

BC2
Bend & cross, 2

BC4
Bend & cross, 4

V10 Bend

R
Right angle

D
Diagonal

C
Circular

V11–V14 Triangle use: The use of triangles is coded in terms of four sets of possible configurations. In some cases, such as the stepped-terrace pattern pictured below, a single set of triangles may be coded as belonging to more than one category.

V11 Rectangular spaces

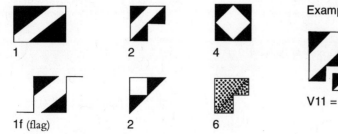

1

2

4

1f (flag)

2

6

Example of multiple coding:

V11 = 2, V13 = 1l

Table 7.1. Attributes Recorded During the Structural Analysis *(continued)*

V12 Single series

1   2   3

V13 Double series

1   1l (lightning)   1r (right triangle)   2

3   3r (right triangle)   4   5

6   7   8

V14 Other

T   F   A   B
Triangular   Flag   Alone   Bird

V = variable.

[a] Kent (1983) notes that most early (pre–A.D. 1100) textiles have one–dimensional designs, and she suggests that the use of two–dimensional designs in later periods is associated with the development of the wide loom. The same design principles may have been translated to pottery.

[b] Washburn and Crowe (1987:57) state that dihedral symmetry has both rotational and reflection symmetry. However, it is possible for a design to have reflection symmetry, but no rotational symmetry.

These methods of analyzing structure pose two problems for this analysis. First, most methods of structural analysis—with the possible exception of the analysis of covariation—tend to emphasize only well-defined rules of structure. Understandably, methods such as symmetry analysis and design grammars were developed to describe particularly elaborate or highly standardized systems of design. Asymmetrical or irregular designs are often excluded from the analysis or simply categorized as "other."

Second, several authors of ethnographic studies link design structure directly to cognitive structures, that is, to the rules employed by the artist (e.g., Hardin 1983b). In archaeological analysis, it is sometimes possible to use line overlap or other criteria to reconstruct the steps taken by the artist (e.g., Kidder and Shepard 1936; Shepard 1965). However, archaeologists' ability to interpret prehistoric cognition is severely limited.

A variety of strategies is used here to cope with these problems. The focus in this study is on interpreting the organization of the designs themselves, regardless of the artists' intentions. A combination of methods is used to discover both loose and strict *rules* of design organization. The goal is to characterize the structural variation, that is, to determine the extent to which the structure varies and to assess the regularity of that variation. To maintain the emphasis on structure and variation, the analysis focuses on only a few commonly occurring attributes.

I begin by characterizing the designs in terms of layout and symmetry, and then I examine the use of two elements—triangles and multiple parallel lines—in the designs. Eight sets of attributes, described and illustrated in Table 7.1, were recorded during analysis. The eight sets consist of Variables 1, 2, 3, 4, 5–6, 7, 8–10, and 11–14. The data are listed by case in Hegmon (1990:Appendix B).

Design Fields

A number of studies have shown that, in some cases, different designs are used on different parts of vessels. The necks and/or bodies of Zuni vessels—both jars and bowls—are clearly distinguished with lines, and the two fields are treated in different manners (Bunzel 1972:13). Similarly, in the Tarascan pottery studied by Friedrich (1970:Figure 3), certain designs were used only on the neck or the body of a vessel. However, in other cases, such as the Acoma and Hopi pottery studied by Bunzel (1972), the entire decorated area is treated as a single field.

The analysis of design attributes in this study must take into account the variation of attributes according to design field (V1 in Table 7.1).

For example, can all jar designs be treated as a group, or should neck designs be treated separately? To address this question, the covariation of design content and design field is investigated on four groups of vessels: Kana-a Black-on-white bowls, Piedra Black-on-white bowls, Kana-a Black-on-white jars, and Piedra Black-on-white jars. The purpose of these analyses of design field is to determine whether certain kinds of designs are consistently associated with certain fields, such as bowl centers or jar necks. If strong associations are found, then in further analyses the designs on these different fields must be treated separately; otherwise, designs on different fields can be combined to create larger sample sizes.

Bowls

The interiors of bowls can be seen as single circular fields, with no morphological breaks. However, it is possible that different parts of the field, specifically the center and edges, were treated differently. A number of bowls have separate designs in the center (V3) encircled by bands or panels along the rim, and in a few cases, all-over designs radiate out from a central design. Design differences associated with the different layouts are explored in the discussion of rules of design, below. The question here is whether different designs are used in different parts of the field.

No Kana-a Black-on-white bowl has a separate design in the center, so there is no need to consider a separate analysis of center designs. Twenty Piedra Black-on-white bowls have separate designs in the center. In 10 cases, the center designs are the same as, or very similar to, the designs on the edges. In the other 10 cases, the center designs consist only of simple lines (in one case the lines are fringed; in all others they are plain). These lines sometimes serve as a central point for a radiating design, or they can be interpreted as the inner frame of a very wide band. In summary, center designs are not always present, but, when present, they are incorporated into the overall design field. Thus, there is no basis for considering the centers and edges of bowls as separate fields that were subject to different design treatments. Instead, the presence or absence of a center design as part of overall bowl decoration is considered in the analysis of layout below.

Jars

Jar morphology sometimes includes abrupt changes in shape that can serve to divide the exterior of the vessel into different design fields, for example, neck, shoulder, and body. Some Kana-a and Piedra black-on-white jars have distinct designs on different parts of the vessel, most commonly one design on the neck and another on the shoulder or body (Figure 4.3c). In this section, I consider whether these different parts of jars were treated as different design fields and thus whether the fields should be analyzed separately or in combination.

On every Kana-a Black-on-white jar for which the information is available (a total of 45 vessels), all the designs are horizontal (bands or nested panels, V2 = B or P-n on Table 7.1) and thus are amenable to use in divided fields. The fields are not consistently separated with dividing lines. In 13 instances, the same or very similar designs are repeated on the neck and the shoulder and/or body (V4) (Figure 4.3a). In three of those 13 cases, the designs have different elaborations, and in four other cases, the designs are oriented in different directions. In seven instances, different designs are used in different fields. To determine whether the fields were treated differently (that is, whether certain designs or attributes were used exclusively or predominantly in certain fields), the association of designs and fields was analyzed using contingency tables.

The association of design layout (V2) and design field (V1) was analyzed for 42 Kana-a Black-on-white jars, a total of 63 design cases (designs are counted for each field in which they appear). Five different layouts are present in the three fields (Table 7.2). Expected frequencies are too small to allow statistical analysis of the table as a whole (Siegel 1956:110), and in this instance, the separate categories cannot be meaningfully combined. However, Fisher exact probability tests on sets of four cells show no significant association between layout and design field. Examination of the cells also shows that no layout is excluded from any field, and no strong association is apparent.

The association of one-dimensional symmetry (V6) and design field was analyzed for 39 Kana-a Black-on-white jars, a total of 60 cases (Table 7.3). Most symmetry classes are present in all three fields, and the empty cells have expected frequencies of zero or one. The

Table 7.2. Design Layout and Design Field on Kana-a Black-on-white Jars

Design Field (V1)	Design Layout (V2)					Total
	B-2	B-3	B-4	B-5	P-n	
Body	2(2)	2(2)	3(3)	6(7)	2(1)	15
Shoulder	4(3)	5(3)	4(5)	9(11)	2(2)	24
Neck	1(3)	2(3)	5(5)	15(11)	1(2)	24
TOTAL	7	9	12	30	5	63

NOTE: Observed (expected) frequencies. Expected frequency (rounded to the nearest whole number) is calculated by multiplying the row and column totals for a particular cell, then dividing this product by the total number of cases shown in the lower right corner. Refer to Table 7.1 for an explanation of the variable and attribute codes.

Table 7.3. One-Dimensional Design Symmetry and Design Field on Kana-a Black-on-white Jars

Design Field (V1)	DETAILED CATEGORIES						Total
	One-Dimensional Design Symmetry (V6)						
	11	m1	12	mm	mg	mm/mg	
Body	4(2)	1(1)	8(10)	1(1)	1(0)	0(1)	15
Shoulder	4(4)	1(2)	14(15)	2(2)	0(0)	3(1)	24
Neck	1(3)	2(1)	16(13)	2(2)	0(0)	0(1)	21
TOTAL	9	4	38	5	1	3	60

Design Field (V1)	COMBINED CATEGORIES		Total
	One-Dimensional Design Symmetry (V6)		
	11, 12	m1, mm, mg, mm/mg	
Body	12(12)	3(3)	15
Shoulder	18(19)	6(5)	24
Neck	17(16)	4(5)	21
TOTAL	47	13	60

NOTES: Observed (expected) frequencies. Expected frequency (rounded to the nearest whole number) is calculated by multiplying the row and column totals for a particular cell, then dividing this product by the total number of cases shown in the lower right corner. Refer to Table 7.1 for an explanation of the variable and attribute codes.
For combined categories, χ^2 = .52; df = 2; .7 < p < .8.

categories were combined for statistical analysis, and a chi-square test shows no significant association between one-dimensional symmetry and design field.

Design layout and symmetry *may* be relatively invariant attributes of a design tradition and therefore might be expected to show relatively little variation between design fields. Therefore, more detailed attributes of designs—the use of triangles (V11–V14)—were compared between design fields. The use of triangles in different fields was analyzed for 42 Kana-a Black-on-white jars, a total of 98 cases (in some instances, one set of triangles was counted as having two roles [see illustration of V11 in Table 7.1]). A large (14 × 3) contingency table shows the association (Table 7.4). Although there are a number of empty cells, the expected frequencies for these cells are either zero or one, and therefore no triangle state is definitely excluded from any field. Statistical tests of association could not be used, because the observations are not independent.

Horizontal designs are also common on Piedra Black-on-white jars: 33 of 40 vessels have some kind of horizontally oriented design or frame (Figure 4.3c). However, vertical or diagonal designs that crosscut two or more fields are also common and are present on nine vessels (some vessels have both horizontal and crosscutting designs). Thus, there appears to be no rule mandating the separation of the

Table 7.4. Triangle Use and Design Field on Kana-a Black-on-white Jars

Design Field (V1)	Rectangular Spaces (V11)				Single Series (V12)	Double Series (V13)						Other (V14)			Total
	1	2	4	6	1	1	2	4	5	7	8	T	F	A	
Body	4(7)	5(3)	1(1)	0(1)	5(4)	1(3)	5(3)	0(0)	0(1)	1(1)	1(0)	3(2)	1(2)	0(0)	27
Shoulder	10(9)	3(4)	1(2)	1(1)	5(5)	6(4)	3(4)	1(0)	1(1)	1(1)	0(0)	2(3)	2(2)	1(0)	37
Neck	11(9)	3(4)	2(1)	2(1)	3(5)	3(3)	2(3)	0(0)	1(1)	1(1)	0(0)	3(3)	3(2)	0(0)	34
TOTAL	25	11	4	3	13	10	10	1	2	3	1	8	6	1	98

NOTE: Observed (expected) frequencies. Expected frequency (rounded to the nearest whole number) is calculated by multiplying the row and column totals for a particular cell, then dividing this product by the total number of cases shown in the lower right corner. Refer to Table 7.1 for an explanation of the variable and attribute codes.

design fields for Piedra Black-on-white. In three instances, the same or very similar horizontal designs are repeated on the neck and the shoulder and/or body. In 11 instances, different designs are used in different fields. Again, contingency table analysis, described below, was used to determine whether the fields were treated differently. Designs that crosscut fields, which are present on nine vessels, were excluded from this analysis.

The association of design layout and design field was analyzed for 31 Piedra Black-on-white vessels, a total of 37 designs. Nine different layouts are present in the three fields (Table 7.5). Although there are some empty cells, the expected frequencies for these cells are zero or one. Because of the small sample size and low expected frequencies, the categories were collapsed into a 2 × 2 table, with shoulder and body designs grouped together. The Fisher exact probability test (used because not all the expected frequencies are greater than five, as is required for the use of the chi-square test [Siegel 1956:110]) shows that the distributions are not significantly different (there is a 24 percent chance that the two samples were drawn from the same pool).

The association of one-dimensional symmetry and design field was analyzed for 23 Piedra Black-on-white jars, a total of 33 designs (Table 7.6). The detailed (7 × 3) contingency table shows several empty cells, one of which has an expected frequency of three. However, when the symmetry categories are collapsed, the expected frequencies equal the observed frequencies in all cases.

Finally, the use of triangles in different design fields was analyzed for 24 Piedra Black-on-white jars, a total of 29 cases (Table 7.7). The 8 × 3 contingency table has a number of empty cells, but the expected frequencies for these cells are always zero or one, and therefore no triangle state is excluded from any field. Again, a chi-square

Table 7.5. Design Layout and Design Field on Piedra Black-on-white Jars

DETAILED CATEGORIES

Design Field (V1)	Design Layout (V2)									Total
	B-1	B-2	B-3	B-4	B-5	D-v	D-s	P-f	P-a	
Body	1(2)	3(2)	1(1)	0(0)	0(0)	1(1)	1(1)	1(1)	0(0)	8
Shoulder	4(3)	1(3)	3(2)	2(1)	2(1)	0(1)	1(2)	2(2)	1(0)	16
Neck	3(3)	4(3)	1(2)	0(1)	0(1)	2(1)	2(1)	1(1)	0(0)	13
TOTAL	8	8	5	2	2	3	4	4	1	37

COMBINED CATEGORIES

Design Field (V1)	Design Layout (V2)		Total
	Band	Divide or Panel	
Body and shoulder	17(16)	7(8)	24
Neck	8(9)	5(4)	13
TOTAL	25	12	37

NOTES: Observed (expected) frequencies. Expected frequency (rounded to the nearest whole number) is calculated by multiplying the row and column totals for a particular cell, then dividing this product by the total number of cases shown in the lower right corner. Refer to Table 7.1 for an explanation of the variable and attribute codes.
For combined categories, Fisher exact probability = .24.

Table 7.6. One-Dimensional Design Symmetry and Design Field on Piedra Black-on-white Jars

DETAILED CATEGORIES

Design Field (V1)	One-Dimensional Design Symmetry (V6)							Total
	11	m1	12	mm	mg	mm/mg	Continuous[a]	
Body	1(1)	3(2)	3(2)	0(1)	0(1)	0(0)	2(1)	9
Shoulder	2(1)	0(3)	2(3)	2(1)	4(2)	1(0)	1(2)	12
Neck	1(1)	4(3)	3(3)	1(1)	1(2)	0(0)	2(2)	12
TOTAL	4	7	8	3	5	1	5	33

COMBINED SELECTED CATEGORIES

Design Field (V1)	One-Dimensional Design Symmetry (V6)		Total
	11, 12	m1, mm, mg, mm/mg	
Body and shoulder	8(8)	10(10)	18
Neck	4(4)	6(6)	10
TOTAL	12	16	28

NOTES: Observed (expected) frequencies. Expected frequency (rounded to the nearest whole number) is calculated by multiplying the row and column totals for a particular cell, then dividing this product by the total number of cases shown in the lower right corner. Refer to Table 7.1 for an explanation of the variable and attribute codes.
For combined categories, observed = expected in all cells.
[a] Continuous designs are those (such as single or multiple parallel lines) for which one-dimensional symmetry is an irrelevant concept.

Table 7.7. Triangle Use and Design Field on Piedra Black-on-white Jars

| Design Field (V1) | Triangle Use | | | | | | | | Total |
| | Rectangular Spaces (V11) | | Single Series (V12) | | Double Series (V13) | | | Other (V14) | |
	1	4	1	2	1	2	6	Alone	
Body	0(0)	0(0)	5(4)	1(1)	0(1)	0(0)	0(0)	0(0)	6
Shoulder	1(0)	1(0)	5(7)	1(1)	2(1)	1(0)	1(0)	0(0)	12
Neck	0(0)	0(0)	8(7)	1(1)	1(1)	0(0)	0(0)	1(0)	11
TOTAL	1	1	18	3	3	1	1	1	29

NOTE: Observed (expected) frequencies. Expected frequency (rounded to the nearest whole number) is calculated by multiplying the row and column totals for a particular cell, then dividing this product by the total number of cases shown in the lower right corner. Refer to Table 7.1 for an explanation of the variable and attribute codes.

analysis could not be conducted, because the observations are not independent.

In summary, these analyses of design layout, symmetry, and triangle use on Kana-a and Piedra black-on-white jars show no distinctions between the designs used in different fields. Some designs crosscut the different fields; others are repeated in the different fields. There are cases in which different fields on the same vessel contain different designs, but there is no evidence that any attributes of design are associated with any particular fields. Two Piedra Black-on-white pitchers illustrated by Morris (1939:Plate 224*i–j*) demonstrate this clearly (Figure 7.1). The neck design on one is the body design on the other and vice versa.

As a result of these findings, the various fields of jars are not treated separately in subsequent analyses. Instead, all jar designs are treated as a group, and different layouts (for example, horizontal and divided) are considered as part of the structural analysis. Each design is treated as a separate case: If one design is repeated on a vessel, that design is treated as one case; if two different designs appear on the same vessel, each design is treated as a different case.

a   b

Figure 7.1. *Two Piedra Black-on-white pitchers that illustrate that design is independent of field (after Morris 1939:Plate 224i–j). The neck design (Case 193) on a is the body design (Case 196) on b, and the body design (Case 194) on a is the neck/shoulder design (Case 195) on b. Scale is 1:6. Case numbers here and in other figure captions refer to the case-by-case design-structure data detailed in Hegmon (1990:Appendix B).*

The Rules of Design

This section begins the actual analysis of the principles of design structure. The analysis proceeds by examining how various attributes, including layout, symmetry, and some primary forms, are used and combined. The goal of the analysis is to reveal rules about the use of those attributes in the designs and to assess variation in the application of those rules. Again, the rules do not pretend to reveal prehistoric cognition. Rather, they are used to establish an analytical basis for assessing structural variation.

Design Layout

In their description of designs on Kana-a Black-on-white pottery, Beals et al. (1945:95) conclude that "designs on all Kana-a Black-on-white pottery from the Kayenta area were built up on the framework of a line or series of lines encircling the bowl or jar horizontally." Their generalization holds up extremely well in this analysis. Layout information (V2) is available for 156 designs on both bowls and jars (including the designs illustrated by Beals et al. [1945:Figures 18–25]). Of these, 155 are continuous encircling designs, either bands or nested panels (Figure 4.3a–b). The one exception is a bowl with a dividing design that fills the entire field (Figure 7.2a). Furthermore, of the 155 continuous encircling designs, all but four have layouts that are easily classified as nested panels or one of the five forms of bands. Two exceptions are bowls that have elongated, lunate-shaped, nested designs that are classified as nested panels but might be described as nested bands; one of these is illustrated in Figure 7.2b. Another bowl clearly has a banded design, but it does not fit any of the band categories. The design consists of four sets of crosscutting parallel lines; it is classified as framed repeated motifs (V2 = B-4) but could also be interpreted as isolated panel dividers (V2 = B-5) (Figure 7.2c). One jar has bands that consist of a series of triangular motifs and therefore is classified as B-4, but the motifs could be seen as angled panels (Figure 7.2d).

In contrast to the all-encompassing description of Kana-a Black-on-white design layout offered by Beals et al. (1945), Morris's (1939:174–177) description of designs on what is now called Piedra Black-on-white involves lengthy discussion of various forms of layouts. His conclusions also hold up well in this analysis. Designs on both bowls (n = 93) and jars (n = 50) are laid out in a variety of ways. Continuous encircling designs (bands or nested panels) are common on both bowls (n = 39) and jars (n = 25), as are designs that divide or crosscut the field (V2 = D) on bowls (n = 31) and jars (n = 13). Panels that are not part of a continuous design (V2 = P-a or P-f) are

Figure 7.2. *Exceptional or difficult-to-classify Kana-a Black-on-white designs: a, Case 129, from Site D:7:134, is the only Kana-a Black-on-white vessel included in the analysis that has a dividing, rather than an encircling, design; b, Case 120, from Site D:11:2027, has elongated, bandlike nested panels; c, Case 151, from Site D:11:2030, has a banded design that was classified as framed repeated motifs (B-4) but could also be interpreted as dividers for empty panels (B-5); d, Case 38, from Site D:11:2027, is a design reconstructed from fragments of a jar on which the repeated triangular motifs (B-4) could be interpreted as angled panels. Scale is 1:3 for a–c, 1:2 for d.*

also present on both bowls ($n = 17$) and jars ($n = 5$). Bowls with bands or panels sometimes also have designs in the center (V3, $n = 18$). Finally, six bowl designs and seven jar designs cannot be classified according to this system of categorization; five of these are illustrated in Figure 7.3. In a few cases, these unclassifiable designs are irregular in many respects and lack any axis of symmetry (e.g., Figure 7.3*a*). However, most of the unclassifiable designs have regularly laid out designs that simply do not fit any of the categories. For example, the jar and bowl illustrated in Figure 7.3*b* and *c* combine portions of dividing designs and panels or bands. One bowl (Figure 7.3*d*) and one jar fragment (Figure 7.3*e*) have regular designs that are unlike any others in the sample.

Furthermore, although the majority (130 of 143) of Piedra Black-on-white designs can be classified according to the layout categories, a substantial proportion of these (11 of 130, or 8 percent) are unusual in some way or combine attributes of two categories. A few examples are shown in Figure 7.4. One bowl (Figure 7.4*a*) has a dividing design (V2 = D), but the central divider does not meet the rim and it neither bisects nor quarters the field completely. On a number of

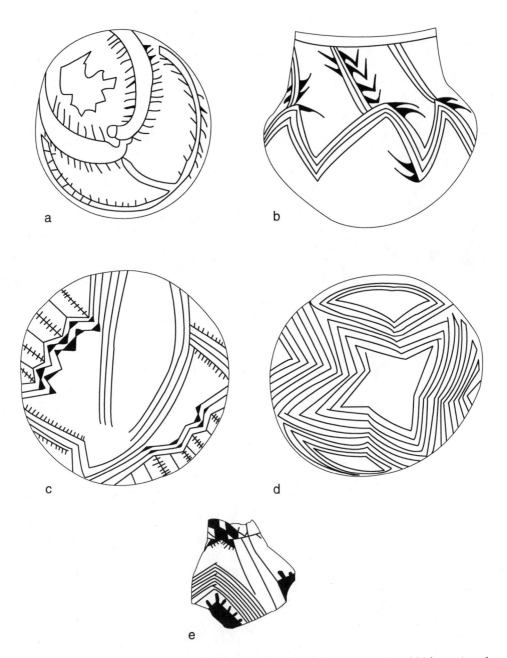

Figure 7.3. *Piedra Black-on-white vessels and sherd with unclassifiable designs:* a, *Case 230 has an irregular, asymmetrical design;* b, *Case 178 has a dividing and encircling band design;* c, *Case 244 combines a dividing design with bandlike panels;* d, *Case 256 has an all-over design with reflection symmetry;* e, *jar sherd has an unusual dividing and/or all-over design (the neck design is Case 211, the shoulder/body design is Case 212). Specimens a–d are from the La Plata district (after Morris 1939:Plates 247d, 240g, 248i, 249i); specimen e is from Pueblo de las Golondrinas. Scale is 1:4.*

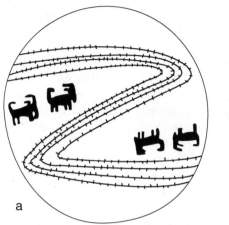
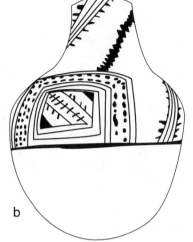
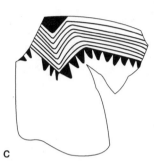

a   b   c

Figure 7.4. *Piedra Black-on-white vessels and sherd with difficult-to-classify designs: a, Case 285 has an unusual partial dividing design; b, jar has a combination of a dividing design (Case 175) and panels (Case 174); c, bowl sherd (Case 301) has a B-2 band that could also be interpreted as nested panels. Specimens a and b are from the La Plata district (after Morris 1939:Figures 481, 44); specimen c is from Weasel Pueblo. Scale is 1:4.*

vessels, including the jar illustrated in Figure 7.4*b,* attached or free panels (V2 = P-a or P-f) are combined with dividing designs. The bowl sherd illustrated in Figure 7.4*c* has a B-2 banded design, but with isolated triangles that resemble nested panels.

Rules of layout can be identified for both Kana-a and Piedra black-on-white designs. Kana-a Black-on-white designs on both jars and bowls are almost always laid out as bands or series of nested panels (V2 = B or P-n). The bands are constructed or divided in a variety of ways, but these states occur repeatedly; in addition, categories of construction and division can be identified relatively easily, and most designs fit the categories. Thus, Kana-a Black-on-white designs consist of a fairly restricted number of layout forms with relatively little mixing between the different forms. In contrast, Piedra Black-on-white design layouts are more varied. Some Piedra Black-on-white designs are laid out as bands or series of nested panels, but others consist of separate panels (V2 = P-a or P-f), designs in the centers of bowls (V3), or nonhorizontal designs that crosscut the design fields (V2 = D). Although a majority of Piedra Black-on-white designs fit one or another layout categories, some are difficult to classify and others fall outside the categories altogether. Overall, the structure of Piedra Black-on-white involves a greater variety of design layout and includes fairly continuous variation between the different layout forms, and some Piedra Black-on-white designs appear to be relatively unstructured.

These conclusions regarding differences between Piedra and Kana-a black-on-white are somewhat subjective in that they are based in large part on the inability of twentieth-century researchers to pigeon-hole ninth-century Piedra Black-on-white designs. However, the conclusions can be justified on a number of grounds. First, the layout categories were not strictly predefined but were modified as the analysis progressed. If a layout not already in the classification system had been repeated on a number of Piedra Black-on-white vessels, a new category would have been defined; however, the layouts of the unclassifiable Piedra Black-on-white designs were unlike those of any other Piedra Black-on-white design. Second, the layout categories seem to be justified because many designs, or at least portions of the designs, *did* fit the categories, even though modifications and combinations present on the Piedra Black-on-white vessels sometimes blurred the distinctions between categories. Finally, although it may be the case that twentieth-century eyes are simply blind to ninth-century regularity, I *was* able to discern regularity in the Kana-a designs, which suggests that, had such regularity been present in the Piedra designs, I would have recognized it as well.

Design Symmetry

Classification of design symmetry holds some promise for greater objectivity than does classification of design layout (although see Hodder 1991b:40–41). Symmetry classes have been defined mathematically in studies of crystal formation and other natural phenomena. However, application of these symmetry classes to pottery designs still requires some subjective judgments on the part of the researchers: What aspects of the design are to be classified? How much irregularity is allowed before the design is classified as asymmetrical? Even so, symmetry classes are finite in number and are not unique to a design style or type. Classes of finite and one-dimensional symmetry (V5 and V6) are illustrated in Figure 7.1. Design symmetry is examined to determine rules regarding what kind or kinds of symmetries are used and the association of particular kinds of symmetries with particular contexts or layouts.

Researchers have long noted (at least since Brainerd [1942]) that pottery designs in the northern Southwest tend to have rotational, rather than reflection, symmetry. This generalization holds up with both the Kana-a and Piedra black-on-white samples. A total of 121 bowls shows some form of finite symmetry (V5). Of these, all but two have some form of rotational symmetry, with or without reflection symmetry (cn or cdn). Vessels with rotational symmetry are illustrated in Figures 7.2b–c, 7.3b, and 7.4a. One Kana-a Black-on-white bowl can be rotated only 90 degrees (Figure 7.2a). One Piedra Black-on-white bowl has reflection symmetry only (Figure 7.3d).

Not all designs exhibit finite or one-dimensional symmetry. Considering only designs with clearly classifiable symmetry, I found that a small number of both Kana-a (two of 128) and Piedra black-on-white (two of 74) one-dimensional designs display no one-dimensional symmetry. These four designs consist either of bands in which different designs are used in different panels or of repeated designs that are oriented in different directions. The outlines of these designs are symmetrical, but the overall designs are not. All other Kana-a Black-on-white designs have some form of symmetry, but seven of 79 Piedra Black-on-white bowls have designs that lack any kind of symmetry (in structure or overall design) in any dimension (Figure 7.3a and c).

The use of one-dimensional symmetry in different contexts can be evaluated and compared between Kana-a and Piedra black-on-white designs. The relationship between symmetry class and layout was examined using contingency tables. To obtain as large a sample as possible, crudely executed designs and designs for which the pattern of repetition had to be inferred from fragmentary evidence were included in these analyses.

The association of layout and one-dimensional symmetry class for Kana-a Black-on-white designs (bowls and jars combined) is shown in Table 7.8. B-1 layouts (plain or elaborated lines) are not included in the portion of the table showing combined categories, because one-dimensional symmetry is an irrelevant concept for plain lines and one-dimensional symmetry options are severely limited by the nature of elaborated lines. Symmetry class is significantly associated with layout. The results appear to be the same if bowl designs and jar designs are analyzed separately. However, the separate samples are not large enough for statistical tests of association. The "Combined Selected Categories" portion of Table 7.8 shows that nested panels (V2 = P-n) have simple translation (V6 = 11) 325 percent more often than is expected (see Figure 4.3b); half turns (V6 = 12) occur over 150 percent more often than is expected in complex bands (V2 = B-4 and B-5); and vertical symmetry (m1, mm, mg, mm/mg) occurs over 150 percent more often than is expected in simple bands (V2 = B-2 and B-3). These results cannot be explained as a byproduct of layout geometry. With the exception of the simple repeated line bands (V2 = B-1), which were excluded from the chi-square analysis, all forms of symmetry are possible with any given layout. Instead, the strong association between layout and symmetry is interpreted as a rule of design, albeit a fairly loose one: Vertical symmetry is used most often in simple bands, although other forms of symmetry can also be used in simple bands; complex bands are used in configurations that have half-turn symmetry; nested panels are used in configurations that have only translational symmetry.

A similar analysis of the association between design layout and one-dimensional symmetry was conducted for all horizontally oriented Piedra Black-on-white designs, including both bands and panels on

Table 7.8. Design Layout and One-Dimensional Design Symmetry of
Kana-a Black-on-white Designs

DETAILED CATEGORIES

One-Dimensional Design Symmetry (V6)	Design Layout (V2)						Total
	B-1	B-2	B-3	B-4	B-5	P-n	
11	7(3)	12(7)	0(8)	4(6)	4(11)	13(5)	40
m1	0(1)	10(3)	1(3)	1(2)	0(4)	3(2)	15
12	1(4)	2(10)	14(13)	14(9)	28(17)	1(7)	60
mm	2(1)	0(2)	5(3)	0(2)	7(4)	0(2)	14
mg	0(0)	0(1)	5(1)	1(1)	0(2)	0(1)	6
mm/mg	0(0)	0(1)	4(1)	0(1)	0(1)	0(0)	4
TOTAL	10	24	29	20	39	17	139

COMBINED SELECTED CATEGORIES

One-Dimensional Design Symmetry (V6)	Design Layout (V2)			Total
	B-2, B-3	B-4, B-5	P-n	
11	12(14)	8(15)	13(4)	33
12	16(24)	42(27)	1(8)	59
m1, mm, mg, mm/mg	25(15)	9(17)	3(5)	37
TOTAL	53	59	17	129

NOTES: Observed (expected) frequencies. Expected frequency (rounded to the nearest whole number) is calculated by multiplying the row and column totals for a particular cell, then dividing this product by the total number of cases shown in the lower right corner. Refer to Table 7.1 for an explanation of the variable and attribute codes.
For combined categories, $\chi^2 = 52.16$; $df = 4$; $p < .001$.

bowls and jars (Table 7.9). Even when the categories are combined, the expected frequencies are too low for statistical analysis. However, examination of the distribution reveals no strong association between symmetry class and design layout. Fisher exact probability tests of sets of four cells confirm the absence of a strong association. Piedra Black-on-white designs exhibit some consistency in the use of symmetry. Of the seven possible classes of one-dimensional symmetry described by Washburn and Crowe (1987:Figure 2.26), only five are used (separately or in combination) in the Piedra Black-on-white designs and only four are common. However, there is no evidence of rules of design associating particular kinds of design symmetry with particular kinds of design layout.

In summary, designs on both Kana-a and Piedra black-on-white pottery appear to be organized according to certain rules of symmetry, although fewer rules and more variation (that is, more broken rules) are seen in the Piedra designs. Both types follow the rule, seen throughout the northern Southwest, that designs have rotational

Table 7.9. Design Layout and One-Dimensional Design Symmetry of Piedra Black-on-white Designs

DETAILED CATEGORIES

One-Dimensional Design Symmetry (V6)	Design Layout (V2)							Total
	B-1	B-2	B-3	B-4	B-5	P-n	P-a, P-f	
11	2(3)	4(5)	1(3)	1(1)	2(1)	3(1)	3(2)	16
m1	1(2)	6(3)	1(2)	0(1)	0(1)	0(1)	3(1)	11
12	2(3)	4(5)	3(2)	3(1)	0(1)	2(1)	1(2)	15
mm	0(0)	0(1)	0(0)	1(0)	1(0)	0(0)	0(0)	2
mg	5(2)	3(3)	3(2)	0(1)	0(1)	0(1)	0(1)	11
mm/mg	0(0)	0(0)	1(0)	0(0)	0(0)	0(0)	0(0)	1
TOTAL	10	17	9	5	3	5	7	56

COMBINED SELECTED CATEGORIES

One-Dimensional Design Symmetry (V6)	Design Layout (V2)			Total
	B-2, B-3	B-4, B-5	Panels	
11	5(8)	3(2)	6(4)	14
12	7(7)	3(2)	3(3)	13
m1, mm, mg, mm/mg	14(11)	2(3)	3(5)	19
TOTAL	26	8	12	46

NOTE: Observed (expected) frequencies. Expected frequency (rounded to the nearest whole number) is calculated by multiplying the row and column totals for a particular cell, then dividing this product by the total number of cases shown in the lower right corner. Refer to Table 7.1 for an explanation of the variable and attribute codes.

symmetry, with or without reflection symmetry. Both types also exhibit a limited number of forms of one-dimensional symmetry; of the seven possible forms described by Washburn and Crowe (1987: Figure 2.26), only five are used. However, although every Kana-a Black-on-white design for which information is available displays some form of symmetry (in structure, if not in overall design), some Piedra Black-on-white designs lack any kind of symmetry. Furthermore, the classes of symmetry are associated with forms of design layout in Kana-a Black-on-white, but no such association could be identified for the Piedra Black-on-white sample.

Framing Lines

Framing lines (V7) are often used to define and separate design fields and layouts. Several of the layout categories were defined in terms of the presence or absence of framing lines. However, the analysis of design layout did not take into account all possible variation in the use of framing lines. Furthermore, several authors (e.g., Conkey 1982;

Hodder 1982a) have suggested that there may be a relationship between bounded (that is, framed or separated) designs and clear-cut divisions in social organization or other cultural categories. Therefore, the use of framing lines was analyzed separately in an attempt to discern rules regarding the use of such lines in the designs. Framing lines include straight lines along the upper borders and/or rims of bowls and along the upper and lower borders of jar designs (Figures 4.3a–c, 7.1, 7.2b–c, and 7.4b). The continuous lines around nested designs (Figure 4.3b) are counted as a special case of framing lines.

Most Kana-a Black-on-white designs are framed. Upper border and/or rim frames are present on almost all Kana-a Black-on-white vessels and designs. Of the designs on jars and vessels of unknown form, upper border frames are present on all 113 cases for which information is available. The majority of bowls (41 of 44) have upper border frames. Lower border frames on jar designs are also very common, although they are not always present. Lower border frames are present on 39 banded jar designs and are absent on six, all of which are B-2 bands. In addition, five jar designs consist of nested panels. The panels are framed below, although with bent, rather than straight, lines.

The use of frames is much more variable on Piedra Black-on-white vessels. Upper and/or lower frames are present on only 57 percent of the jar designs (20 of 37 have upper frames, and 23 of 39 have lower frames). Upper frames are present on a majority of Piedra Black-on-white bowls (38 of 61), but it is not unusual for Piedra bowls to lack upper frames (see Figure 7.5a and c in the following section).

The use of frames may be associated with design layout, especially because some types of bands have frames by definition. This association was examined only on bowls. All but one of the Kana-a Black-on-white bowls have continuous horizontal designs, either bands or nested panels. The one exception, a bowl with a divided design, does have a continuous line that follows the rim, although it is not a separate framing line. Thus, 40 of the 43 (93 percent) Kana-a Black-on-white bowls with bands or nested panels have upper frames. Piedra Black-on-white designs exhibit more variability in this respect. Of the Piedra Black-on-white bowls with banded designs or nested panels, 24 (63 percent) have upper frames and 14 (37 percent) lack such frames. A majority (82 percent) of the Piedra Black-on-white bowls with other forms of design layout lack upper frames ($n = 51$).

In summary, bounded designs are present on both Kana-a Black-on-white and Piedra Black-on-white vessels, although they are much more common on the former. The association of upper frames with continuous horizontal designs may be a rule of design for both Kana-a and Piedra black-on-white. However, whereas this rule applies to almost all Kana-a Black-on-white designs, the rule is much more loosely applied to Piedra Black-on-white with continuous horizontal designs, a substantial minority of which lack upper frames. Furthermore, no rule is apparent for the use of frames with other forms of Piedra Black-on-white designs.

The Use of Design Elements

The majority of Kana-a and Piedra black-on-white designs include lines and/or triangles. The structural analysis of design elements focused on discerning rules governing how these common elements are used in the overall designs and in relation to each other. Only multiple parallel lines (V8–V10) and triangles (V11–V14) were included in the analysis.

Multiple parallel lines can be interpreted as filling various roles in the designs. In some cases, they serve as framing lines that define the layout or divide fields and panels. Some B-1 bands and divided designs consist primarily or entirely of multiple parallel lines. These lines also separate and frame other design forms, including triangles. Finally, multiple parallel lines can themselves constitute a separate design or can fill defined spaces. When one set of multiple parallel lines meets another set, the type of intersection was recorded. The three general forms of intersection noted in the assemblages are dead-end (V8), crisscross (V9 = CC), or bend-and-cross (V9 = BC).

The only form of intersection present in the Kana-a Black-on-white designs is the dead-end. Dead-ends appear in a variety of structural roles. They are most common where lines that separate and/or frame triangles meet frames and/or panel dividers; they are also present where panel dividers meet frames and in other contexts in which lines fill defined spaces.

All three types of intersection are seen in the Piedra Black-on-white designs included in the study (Figure 7.5). Dead-ends are by far the most common (present in 22 of the 32 designs that have multiple intersecting parallel lines) and are used in a variety of situations, including those in which frames or frames and fill meet, as described for Kana-a Black-on-white. Also, lines that crosscut a field and divide it into offset quarters very often dead-end on another set of lines (Figure 7.5a). Crisscross intersections (Figure 7.5b) are seen only when multiple parallel lines are used to fill an area; lines that define the structure never cross each other in this way. Finally, use of the bend-and-cross configuration is limited to designs in which lines that divide a field into regular (not offset) quarters meet (Figure 7.5b). Four of the quartered designs have multiple parallel lines, and in each case, the intersection is bend-and-cross. Twelve of the offset quartered designs have multiple parallel lines, and the intersections

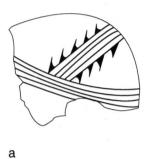

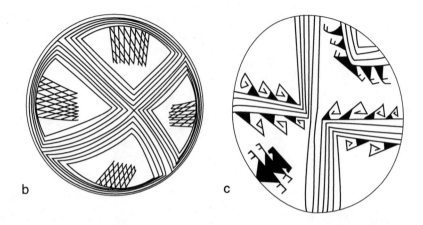

a   b   c

Figure 7.5. *The use of line intersections in Piedra Black-on-white designs: a, Case 309 has dead-end intersections between lines that divide the field into offset quarters; b, Case 241 has criss-cross intersections in the panels that are fillers for the quarter-sections and bend-and-cross intersections between the lines that divide the field; c, Case 266 has unusual combination "bend-without-crossing" intersections. Specimen a is from Golondrinas Oriental; specimens b and c are from the La Plata district (after Morris 1939:Plate 248e, Figure 47d). Scale is 1:4.*

are always dead-end, with the exception of the design on one bowl, which has barely offset quarters and a sort of bend-without-crossing intersection (Figure 7.5c). The consistent use of intersection type may represent a rule of design. However, the intersections are also probably determined by the layout form, since the bend-and-cross configuration cannot be used in offset quartered designs.

The analysis of multiple-line intersection reveals more elaborate usages in Piedra Black-on-white than in Kana-a Black-on-white designs. The only form of intersection used in Kana-a Black-on-white designs is the dead-end, and it is used in a variety of settings within the design layouts. Piedra Black-on-white has a greater variety of layouts, and more forms of intersection are noted. The different forms of intersection are regularly associated with different areas of the vessels or positions of the layout, although the association can be seen as a product of the layout and not necessarily as a rule of design.

Bent lines (V10) are used in a variety of settings in both Kana-a and Piedra black-on-white designs, as bands or panels or as frames that nest entire panels or individual elements. The association between bending angle and design layout is shown in Tables 7.10 and 7.11. In both Kana-a and Piedra black-on-white designs, there is a strong association between nested panels and right-angle bends. All nested panels have right-angle bends in their multiple parallel lines (Figure 4.3b), with or without other diagonal bends. Both diagonal and right-angle bends are present in bands and other layouts, although diagonal bends are more common. This strong association of right-angle bends with nested panels is less a rule about the use of multiple parallel lines than it is a rule about the layout of nested panels. That is, the lines are bent at right angles because all nested panels have some right angles (many are terrace-shaped).

Table 7.10. Design Layout and Bending Angle in Kana-a Black-on-white Designs

Bending Angle (V10)	Design Layout (V2)		Total
	Band	P-n	
Right	1	14	15
Diagonal	11	0	11
Right and diagonal	7	3	10
TOTAL	19	17	36

NOTE: Table entries are frequencies. Refer to Table 7.1 for an explanation of the variable and attribute codes.

Table 7.11. Design Layout and Bending Angle in Piedra Black-on-white Designs

Bending Angle (V10)	Design Layout (V2)				Total
	Band	Divided	P-a, P-f	P-n	
Right	3	0	4	3	10
Diagonal	17	8	5	0	30
Right and diagonal	0	3	2	2	7
TOTAL	20	11	11	5	47

NOTE: Table entries are frequencies. Refer to Table 7.1 for an explanation of the variable and attribute codes.

Finally, the use of triangles was analyzed and described in terms of four variables (V11–V14), each of which includes a number of possible configurations. As background for the analysis, the distribution of these categories by pottery type is shown in Table 7.12.

In Kana-a Black-on-white designs, triangles are most often incorporated into rectangular forms (V11). The association of design layout and the use of triangles in rectangular spaces is shown in Table 7.13. Some consistency in the use of triangles in rectangular forms is apparent; triangles in rectangles (V11 = 1) are more common in bands, and the most common form in nested panels is triangles in terraces (V11 = 2). This association is highly significant statistically; however, at best it is a loose rule followed in only 73 percent of the cases.

The smaller sample of Piedra Black-on-white designs containing triangles limits the analysis of this variable, especially since a majority of the Piedra cases are simple single series (V12 = 1) (Figures 4.3d and 7.5a) and these simple series are used in each layout form. Table 7.14 shows the relationship between triangle use (in double series [V13] and other contexts [V14]) and design layout. Triangles in double series tend to be associated with continuous horizontal designs (bands and nested panels), whereas other uses of triangles tend to be associated with noncontinuous panels. However, this association is

Table 7.12. Triangle Use by Pottery Type

Pottery Type	Rectangular Spaces (V11)				Single Series (V12)			Double Series (V13)					Other (V14)			Total
	1	2	4	6	1	2	3	1	2	4	6	8	T	F	B	
Kana-a Black-on-white	42	31	13	7	55	0	1	32	17	1	0	3	4	2	0	208
Piedra Black-on-white	3	1	1	64	4	1	10	4	0	0	3	0	5	2	6	104

NOTE: Table entries are frequencies. Refer to Table 7.1 for an explanation of the variable and attribute codes.

Table 7.13. Triangle Use (in Rectangular Spaces) and Design Layout in Kana-a Black-on-white Designs

DETAILED CATEGORIES

Design Layout (V2)	Triangle Use, Rectangular Spaces (V11)				Total
	1	2	4	6	
Bands	36(31)	15(22)	11(9)	4(5)	66
Panels-n	3(8)	13(6)	0(2)	2(1)	18
TOTAL	39	28	11	6	84

SELECTED CATEGORIES

Design Layout (V2)	Triangle Use, Rectangular Spaces (V11)		Total
	1	2	
Bands	36(30)	15(21)	51
Panels-n	3(9)	13(7)	16
TOTAL	39	28	67

NOTES: Expected (observed) frequencies. Expected frequency (rounded to the nearest whole number) is calculated by multiplying the row and column totals for a particular cell, then dividing this product by the total number of cases shown in the lower right corner. Refer to Table 7.1 for an explanation of the variable and attribute codes.
For combined categories, χ^2 = 12.06; df = 2; .001 < p < .01.

Table 7.14. Triangle Use (in Double Series and Other Contexts) and Design Layout in Piedra Black-on-white Designs

Design Layout (V2)	Double Series (V13)			Other (V14)			Total
	1	2	3	T	F	B	
Band	6	1	1	1	0	0	9
Panels-n	1	3	0	0	0	0	4
Panels-f and -a	1	0	1	2	2	2	8
Divided	1	0	0	0	0	4	5
TOTAL	9	4	2	3	2	6	26

NOTE: Table entries are frequencies. Refer to Table 7.1 for an explanation of the variable and attribute codes.

probably more a byproduct of structure (elongated series are used in elongated designs) than it is a rule of design. One rule of design may be evidenced by the use of triangle bird figures (V14 = B) only in divided designs (all are bisected or regular quarters) and nonnested panels, although the sample is small.

The analysis of the use of triangles and multiple parallel lines in design structure reveals fewer rules and fewer differences between Kana-a and Piedra black-on-white than do the analyses of layout and symmetry. In both pottery types, these elements are used in a variety of ways, and most uses do not appear to be restricted to any particular context. However, some less common elements (bend-and-cross intersections and bird figures) are seen only in Piedra Black-on-white designs, and the use of these elements tends to be restricted to certain contexts.

Rule Summary

The analysis of design structure reveals a number of rules or principles that describe the organization of Kana-a and Piedra black-on-white designs. To summarize this portion of the analysis, the rules and exceptions to the rules are listed below. These rules are intended to be descriptive; they do not necessarily parallel the cognitive processes of the prehistoric potter.

1. *Layout Categories:* Kana-a Black-on-white designs consist of bands or nested panels. Piedra Black-on-white designs consist of bands, panels, or dividers. *Exceptions* for both types include designs that do not fit the categories or designs that combine attributes of more than one category.

2. *Finite Symmetry:* Kana-a and Piedra black-on-white bowl designs have rotational symmetry, with or without reflection symmetry. *Exceptions* include designs with reflection symmetry only and designs with no symmetry.

3. *One-Dimensional Symmetry:* Kana-a and Piedra black-on-white horizontal designs have one-dimensional symmetry. *Exceptions* include designs in which at least one motif or panel is different.

4. *Frames:* Kana-a and Piedra black-on-white bowls with continuous horizontal designs have upper border or rim frames. *Exceptions* are bowls that lack such frames.

5. *Nested Panels:* Kana-a and Piedra black-on-white nested panels include right-angle constructions, and as a result, the multiple parallel lines associated with nested panels have right-angle bends (V10 = R). No exceptions are present in the sample.

6. *Kana-a Black-on-white One-Dimensional Symmetry and Layout:* Complex bands (B-4 and B-5) have half-turn (V6 = 12) symmetry; nested panels have simple translation (V6 = 11). *Exceptions* include complex bands or nested panels that have other forms of symmetry.

7. *Kana-a Black-on-white Triangles in Rectangular Spaces:* Triangles opposed in rectangles (V11 = 1) are used in bands, and triangles in terraces (V11 = 2) are used in nested panels. *Exceptions* include V11 = 2 in bands and V11 = 1 in nested panels.

8. *Piedra Black-on-white Triangle Birds:* Triangles in bird configurations (V14 = B) are used in divided designs and nonnested panels. No exceptions are present in the sample.

The designs can be evaluated according to whether they obey or violate these rules of design. Table 7.15 shows the number of times the rules are obeyed and violated in the Kana-a and Piedra black-on-white designs. Because the corpus of designs included in the table was also used to derive the rules, the results are not an independent test of the rules. However, the results can be used to summarize the analyses.

Five of the eight rules apply to both types (Rules 1–5). One of these (Rule 5) is followed in all cases. The other four are followed more consistently in Kana-a than in Piedra black-on-white designs. Two rules (Rules 6 and 7) apply only to Kana-a Black-on-white. These concern the relationship between layout and symmetry and the use of triangles in rectangular spaces. Rules 6 and 7 were characterized as loose rules in the above discussion, and they are followed in only 72 and 73 percent of the cases of Kana-a Black-on-white

Table 7.15. Application of the Rules of Design to Kana-a Black-on-white and Piedra Black-on-white Designs

Rule	Kana-a Black-on-white			Piedra Black-on-white		
	Number Obey	Number Violate	Percent Obey	Number Obey	Number Violate	Percent Obey
1	152	4	97.44	119	24	83.22
2	39	1	97.50	71	8	89.87
3	126	2	98.44	72	2	97.30
4	40	3	93.02	24	14	63.16
5	17	0	100.00	5	0	100.00
SUBTOTAL	374	10	97.40	291	48	85.84
6	55	21	72.37	—	—	—
7	49	18	73.13	—	—	—
8	—	—	—	6	0	100.00
TOTAL	478	49	90.70	297	48	86.09

designs. However, the Piedra Black-on-white designs did not display any regular association of these variables, and no rules could be derived. The last rule applies only to an uncommon use of triangles as bird figures, a use seen only in Piedra Black-on-white; the rule is followed in all six cases.

These rules do not describe all aspects of Kana-a and Piedra black-on-white designs. However, they do provide some basis for comparison. More aspects of Kana-a than Piedra black-on-white designs can be described in terms of rules. Furthermore, in cases in which rules can be defined, the Kana-a designs appear to conform to the rules more closely than do the Piedra designs. The implications of these differences for interpreting the potters' actions and social practices are discussed further below.

Formal Style and Ritual Contexts

Ritual involves formalized actions. Style used in ritual is expected to be more formalized than style used in other contexts, and the designs on vessels associated with ritual contexts are expected to be more rule-bound. To evaluate this expectation, vessels from ritual and nonritual contexts were compared with respect to the eight rules of design. Ritual contexts include burials and pit structure floors (some pit structures had burials on their floors and may have been deliberately destroyed). Nonritual contexts include trash deposits, storage areas, and surface habitation rooms. Vessels with poor provenience information or for which no provenience information was available were excluded from this analysis. Designs were classified according to whether they violated one or more rules or whether they obeyed all the applicable rules.

The association of contexts and incidences of rule violation are shown for the two types in Tables 7.16 and 7.17. The Fisher exact probability test is used instead of the chi-square test in Table 7.17 because one of the expected frequencies is less than five (see Siegel 1956:110). There is no significant association of rule violations with either ritual or nonritual contexts. Therefore, the expectation linking formalized designs with formal contexts is not supported.

Interpreting Style Structure

The analysis of the structure of style combined traditional techniques for describing designs and classifying types with recent concepts about the nature of style. The sample used in the analysis included designs identified according to traditional typological categories (Kana-a

Table 7.16. Design Rule Violation and Context, Kana-a Black-on-white

Context	Obey Rules	Violate Rules	Total
Domestic	37(35)	11(13)	48
Ritual	14(16)	7(5)	21
TOTAL	51	18	69

NOTES: Observed (expected) frequencies. Expected frequency (rounded to the nearest whole number) is calculated by multiplying the row and column totals for a particular cell, then dividing this product by the total number of cases shown in the lower right corner.
$\chi^2 = 1.47$; $df = 1$; $.2 < p < .3$.

Table 7.17. Design Rule Violation and Context, Piedra Black-on-white

Context	Obey Rules	Violate Rules	Total
Domestic	39(40)	21(20)	60
Ritual	7(6)	2(3)	9
TOTAL	46	23	69

NOTES: Observed (expected) frequencies. Expected frequency (rounded to the nearest whole number) is calculated by multiplying the row and column totals for a particular cell, then dividing this product by the total number of cases shown in the lower right corner.
Fisher exact probability = .24.

Black-on-white and Piedra Black-on-white). Although the criteria for classifying the vessels emphasized characteristics other than design structure, it is possible that the results were influenced by differences in how the two types were defined. Several potential biases may have influenced the samples. Kana-a Black-on-white is easily identified on the basis of line brushwork and technological characteristics; almost no other design criteria were used to distinguish this pottery type. In contrast, Piedra Black-on-white is less easily distinguished on the basis of technological characteristics, and designs with non-Piedra forms (for example, the basketstitch design typical of Basketmaker III types or the scrolls typical of Cortez Black-on-white) were excluded from the analysis. Kana-a Black-on-white also represents a longer span of time than does Piedra Black-on-white, and a late transitional form of Kana-a (sometimes called Wepo Black-on-white) was included in the Kana-a Black-on-white sample. These biases may have increased the variability in the Kana-a Black-on-white sample. Therefore, the conclusion of this analysis—that the structure of Piedra Black-on-white is more variable than that of Kana-a Black-on-white—cannot be explained as a result of sample bias.

Much of the analysis involved classifying design attributes and deriving rules, including loose rules, that described design regularities. The methods used necessarily involved some degree of subjectivity, particularly regarding decisions about what constituted a rule of design.

However, the methods were described in detail, and the analysis should be replicable; therefore, problems resulting from analytic subjectivity should be minimal.

The structural analyses revealed a number of differences between Kana-a and Piedra black-on-white designs. Most significantly, although both types exhibited some degree of structural regularity, the Piedra Black-on-white designs exhibited more variability in several respects, including the number of attribute states, the discreteness of the states, and the "violation" of apparent structural rules. These differences between the two types can be interpreted from a number of perspectives. Typologically, Kana-a Black-on-white is much easier for twentieth-century researchers to characterize and define, as comparisons between type descriptions by Beals et al. (1945:95) and Morris (1939:174–177) demonstrate. The comparison is problematic for the development of archaeological systematics. However, the differences between the two types may provide important clues as to the different roles played by style in the two areas.

Morris (1939:179) explains the variability in Piedra Black-on-white designs as being a result of individual expression by the Pueblo I artists. He contrasts such individual expression with more uniform (and possibly less expressive) types of design, which might include those on the Kana-a Black-on-white analyzed here. However, he does not discuss the role that such expression might have had in cultural processes. Recent research on style has shown that individual expression in designs can communicate important information about individual and social identities (Weissner 1984, 1989).

The two types of design can also be interpreted from the perspective of information theory. Information is directly related to diversity and variability; however, some degree of structure and redundancy is necessary to communicate that information in a meaningful way. Kana-a Black-on-white exhibits a high degree of structure and limited variability. In contrast, Piedra Black-on-white exhibits some structure but much more variability. Thus, Piedra Black-on-white designs would be able to communicate more kinds of information, whereas the Kana-a Black-on-white designs might emphasize one or a few important messages.

Finally, the differences between the types can also be interpreted in terms of structure and agency or practice. The design regularities identified in this analysis suggest that there are structural regularities to both Piedra and Kana-a black-on-white, even if the rules derived here were not the rules consciously applied by the prehistoric potters. However, the greater variability of the Piedra designs suggests that this design tradition involved more individual expression. In part, this variability may have been a reflection of the overall structure, in that the rules provided for several options. In part, this variability may

have been a result of practice—by individual potters—that deviated
from the structure. In either case, the greater variability suggests that
Piedra Black-on-white conveyed different kinds of information than
did Kana-a Black-on-white. Specifically, the variation—in both rules
and practice—in the Piedra Black-on-white designs suggests that the
designs may have conveyed more information relating to individual
identity and changing social relations. In contrast, the invariance of
Kana-a Black-on-white designs suggests that the designs conveyed
more information about relatively stable group identity.

These results conform to the expectations of the role of design
style in the Kayenta and Mesa Verde regions. The intensive occupation of the central Mesa Verde region and evidence of architectural
boundaries and community definition both suggest that the use of
style to express social distinctions would have been more important
in this area. The variable designs on Piedra Black-on-white, whether
interpreted from the perspective of artistic expression or information
theory, provide a medium for such communication. The more invariant
designs on Kana-a Black-on-white are better interpreted as an expression of social similarity used to maintain extensive ties and minimize differences.

8

Style as Difference

Differences and contrasts are basic components of style and its role in cultural processes. Style can be defined in a general sense as "a way of doing," and the style that is the subject of this study is defined as "a way of decorating pottery with painted designs." This understanding of style implies that there are many possible ways of doing (or painting) and that style involves a choice between those alternatives. If there were no possibility of choice, then there would be no differences and thus no stylistic variation. By the same token, difference is essential if style is to convey information because, if there is no potential for difference, the information content is zero. The use of style to display or express contrasts is argued to be one of style's most important qualities (see Weissner 1984), and the meaning of style (for example, us vs. them) is often an expression of those contrasts.

In this chapter, differences in pottery design style within and between assemblages are assessed and considered in relation to the social and cultural context. Difference is assessed in two general ways. Assemblages are compared, and the similarity or difference between them is assessed. The diversity or homogeneity of an individual assemblage—that is, the amount of difference present within that assemblage—is also measured.

Style can play an important role in many settings, from reinforcing cultural values in an intimate private situation ("every day at mealtimes" [David et al. 1988:379]) to fostering group competition at public gatherings (e.g., Strathern and Strathern 1971). However, the use of style, particularly the use of stylistic differences, to make and mark social distinctions is expected to be particularly important in interactions between people who do not know each other well (who are socially distant). In these situations, individuals can use visible style to express their identity and position at the onset and thus establish a basis for further interaction. These expectations, developed in Chapters 2–4, have several important implications for interpreting the role of stylistic differences in the ninth-century northern Southwest.

First, the central Mesa Verde region had a greater population density, more aggregated settlements, and more evidence of large-scale social gatherings than did Black Mesa. Residents of the area, including those at Duckfoot and Dolores, would likely have had more interactions with socially distant people. Therefore, the use of style to make and mark social distinctions is expected to have been greater in the central Mesa Verde region than on northern Black Mesa. The analysis of vessel form (Chapter 6) established that painted designs at Dolores and Duckfoot, but not at Black Mesa, are strongly associated with the more visible vessels (bowls rather than jars) that *could have been* used to express social differences. Assuming that the pottery designs *were* used to express social distinctions, then a greater diversity of design style is expected in the Dolores and Duckfoot assemblages than in the Black Mesa assemblages.

Second, the occupation of northern Black Mesa was less socially intensive than that of the central Mesa Verde region. Population density was much lower, settlements were smaller, and mobility was greater on northern Black Mesa. Therefore, the expression of social differences—through stylistic or other means—is expected to have been limited on Black Mesa. Instead, style might have been used as a means of expressing similarity in order to maintain extensive contacts. Architecturally, there is little evidence of social group differentiation, and the analysis of design structure showed limited variation in Kana-a Black-on-white designs from Black Mesa and across the Kayenta region. Therefore, social differences are not expected to have been strongly expressed in design style, although it is possible that the style may have been used for other kinds of expression (for example, at an individual level). This second expectation, like the first, predicts a greater degree of stylistic diversity in the central Mesa Verde region than on northern Black Mesa. However, the two expectations emphasize different social processes—that is, the use of style to express social distinctions in the central Mesa Verde region and the use of style to maintain extensive networks on Black Mesa.

Third, architectural and settlement evidence suggests that well-defined social groups may have been present at Dolores and possibly across the central Mesa Verde region by the early ninth century A.D. The repeated use of unit-pueblo architecture, including private storage areas attached to habitation rooms, indicates that the basic social units were well defined. On a larger scale, aggregated settlements and clusters of small sites surrounding the large settlements suggest the existence of spatially discrete communities. Many of the larger settlements had relatively formalized architecture, including community pit structures. Furthermore, these community pit structures were associated with particular roomblocks, which suggests that they were controlled by localized groups. These social groups are expected to have been defined stylistically, and such stylistic definition of groups would be manifested as (1) heightened diversity when the area as a whole is considered (high diversity is also predicted by the first implication) and (2) stylistic differences between communities.

Fourth, throughout the ninth century, some sites at Dolores and in other parts of the Mesa Verde region had great kivas or community pit structures that are interpreted as settings for large-scale rituals or other gatherings. These activities would have brought together many socially distant people, and there is some evidence (Blinman 1989) that participants brought pottery to activities in community pit structures. Although more formalized style was expected in ritual contexts, the analyses presented in Chapter 7 showed no differences in design formality when pottery from ritual and nonritual contexts was compared. However, even if the same kinds of pottery were being used in ritual and other activities, assemblages associated with large-scale social activities might be distinctive in another way. That is, because many groups and individuals would have participated, stylistic differences between those groups or individuals would result in diverse assemblages.

Finally, social and economic conditions changed during the course of the ninth century at Dolores. Before about A.D. 860–880, climatic conditions were favorable for agriculture, and people moved into the valley, with the population peaking at around A.D. 860–880 (Petersen 1988; Schlanger 1988). Some large, aggregated settlements were founded during the A.D. 800–840 period; during the A.D. 840–880 period, the settlement pattern was dominated by large, aggregated settlements. Agriculture was probably intensified during the A.D. 840–880 period, and models of agricultural strategies predict that much of the arable land would have been in use by the end of the period (Kohler et al. 1986). Climatic conditions deteriorated after about A.D. 880, the occupation in the northern part of the valley became increasingly mobile, and reliance on wild resources increased. People began leaving the valley, and the area was mostly abandoned by A.D. 910 or 920.

It is difficult to relate these changing conditions at Dolores directly to style and stylistic differentiation. For various reasons, high levels of diversity might be expected to have occurred at certain times during the ninth century. It is expected that stylistic differentiation would have increased in the first few decades of the ninth century, when people moved into Dolores and established aggregated communities, and also during the A.D. 840–880 period, as aggregated communities became more established and competition for resources may have increased. Given this situation, style is best interpreted, not in terms of a list of a priori expectations, but in light of patterns of variation in the social context.

In this chapter, I evaluate these expectations and consider the role of style as difference with data from the central Mesa Verde region and northern Black Mesa. The following three sections review the analytical methods, including the measurement of diversity and the coding system. Differences in design style are then analyzed as diversity within, and similarity between, assemblages, including comparisons between the areas and modeling periods and variation within areas.

The Measurement of Difference

Differences are manifest as diversity within, or dissimilarity between, groups or assemblages. Diversity and dissimilarity are closely related and can be functions of the same data at different scales of analyses. This interrelationship can be explained by considering three assemblages, each consisting of five kinds of things in equal proportions. Assemblage 1 contains A, B, C, D, and E; Assemblage 2 contains B, C, D, E, and F; and Assemblage 3 contains F, G, H, I, and J. Intuitively, all three assemblages are equally diverse. Assemblages 1 and 2 are very similar, Assemblages 2 and 3 are highly dissimilar, and Assemblages 1 and 3 are completely dissimilar. A combination of the two similar assemblages (1 and 2) produces an assemblage only slightly more diverse than the separate assemblages, whereas a combination of two dissimilar assemblages (1 and 3, or 2 and 3) produces a much more diverse assemblage.

The assessment of diversity and dissimilarity is fairly straightforward and intuitively obvious as long as each kind of thing is present in equal amounts and each assemblage is the same size. More complicated situations require more detailed and quantifiable measures of diversity and similarity. As background for the analysis presented here, some of these measures and their archaeological applications are reviewed below.

Similarity

Similarity between two assemblages can be assessed with some form of distance measure—often called a similarity coefficient—that compares the composition of the assemblages and determines the graphic distance between them. Similarity coefficients can be used to determine pairs of assemblages that are relatively close or distant, and matrices of coefficients are used as the basis for more complex orderings such as seriation.

Similarity coefficients have often been used in archaeological stylistic analyses, particularly in the early ceramic sociology studies.
Cronin (1962) used similarity coefficients to compare assemblages
within and between sites (see discussion in Plog 1978). A number of
authors used multivariate analysis of matrices of similarity measures
to identify relatively homogeneous groups of assemblages, both within
and between sites (e.g., Freeman and Brown 1964; Hill 1970;
Kintigh 1985; Longacre 1970; Tuggle 1970). In most of these studies,
stylistic similarity is interpreted as an indication of shared learning, a
result of certain patterns of postmarital residence, as well as of a
general sharing of ideas. Kintigh (1985) also discusses the role of
symbolism in stylistic similarity.

Similarity can be measured in various ways, including the Pearson r
correlation coefficient (e.g., Plog 1976; though see Cowgill 1990)
and specific indices developed for the particular situation (Kintigh
1985). The Brainerd-Robinson coefficient (Brainerd 1951; Robinson
1951), developed especially for use in archaeological chronologies,
has proven to be particularly useful in archaeological applications.
Although the Brainerd-Robinson seriation method has been criticized
(Doran and Hodson 1975:272), the coefficient remains a useful measure of similarity (Cowgill 1990). The Brainerd-Robinson coefficient
is based on a comparison of frequencies and percentages, rather than
on continuous measurements, and therefore is easily applied to archaeological assemblages.

Diversity

The diversity of an assemblage is a function of (1) richness, or the
number of different categories present, and (2) evenness, or the relative proportions of the categories. Archaeologists have recently devoted considerable attention to developing techniques for measuring
and interpreting diversity (e.g., Leonard and Jones 1989).

Two kinds of methods are used in the archaeological study of
diversity. Some methods focus on richness and measure assemblage
diversity in terms of the number of different categories of things (for
example, types and design attributes) present (e.g., DeBoer and Moore
1982; Jones et al. 1983; Kintigh 1984; Lindauer 1989). Other methods
assess overall diversity by using indices (including the Shannon and
Weaver information statistic, also called the H-statistic) that quantify
both richness and evenness (e.g., Braun 1985; Conkey 1980; Hegmon 1986; Pollock 1983a). Some researchers, especially in the last
few years, have used not only indices of overall diversity, but also
separate measures of richness—and sometimes evenness—in their
analyses (Leonard et al. 1989; Rice 1981, 1989).

Various indices of diversity have been developed by ecologists studying the distribution of species in ecological communities. One set of indices, including the Simpson index (which is used by Grayson [1984:Chapter 5]), is dependent primarily on the relative quantities of the most abundant species, whereas a second set of indices, including the *H*-statistic, is more sensitive to rarer species (Peet 1974:304). Pielou (1975:10) argues that *H* should be used for samples from an infinitely large community and the related Brillouin's index should be used for a fully censused community. Peet (1974:293) argues that Brillouin's index is strongly and unpredictably affected by sample size and therefore not a good indicator of overall diversity.

The *H*-statistic was developed in communication theory by Shannon (Shannon and Weaver 1949) as a measure of entropy or choice. In this context, *H* is a measure of the amount of information that can be conveyed by a message. Thus, the *H*-statistic is appealing to analysts of style because it offers a means of measuring the amount of information that *could* be conveyed stylistically. However, the statistic says nothing about the meaning of that information—that is, whether it conveys culturally meaningful messages (Abramson 1963:2; Shannon and Weaver 1949:100). *H* is based on the proportion of items in each category:

$$H = -\sum p_i \log(p_i),$$

where p_i is the fraction of the items in the ith category. *H* actually measures the amount of information conveyed by one item (Shannon and Weaver 1949:28); the amount of information conveyed by *n* items would be $n \times H$. *H* is at a minimum (there is no diversity) if all the items are in the same category. *H* is at a maximum when all the items are evenly distributed among the *n* categories (Pielou 1975:15):

$$H_{\max} = n\left(\frac{1}{n}\right) \times \log\left(\frac{1}{n}\right)$$
$$= \log n.$$

An index of evenness, or *J*, is calculated as the ratio of observed to maximum *H* (Pielou 1975:15):

$$J = \frac{H}{H_{\max}},$$

and 1-*J* is used as a measure of redundancy (Moles 1966).

Both richness and diversity indices can be used advantageously in archaeological studies of diversity. In some cases, the two can produce similar conclusions (Conkey 1980; Kintigh 1984, 1989b). However, because they have different properties, the two indices may be best suited to different kinds of situations. Consideration of two simple assemblages illustrates the differences. Each assemblage consists of 100 artifacts of four types (A, B, C, and D):

Assemblage 1: 25A 25B 25C 25D
Assemblage 2: 97A 1B 1C 1D

The two assemblages are equally rich (each contains four types), but Assemblage 1 has more variety since no one type is dominant. The H-statistic reflects this greater variety: $H_1 = .60$, whereas $H_2 = .01$. Thus, with assemblages that are large in relation to the number of types, such that each assemblage contains at least a small proportion of each type, the H-statistic is more useful than richness as a measure of diversity (see Toll [1985] for an example of this kind of situation).

Richness measures are more sensitive to the presence of rare types. If one item of type E is added to Assemblage 1, richness = 5, an increase of 25 percent, whereas $H = .62$, an increase of only 3 percent. Richness measures would be more strongly distorted by the presence of a few rare types, although the effect may be lessened with proper control of sample size, as is discussed below. Whether greater sensitivity is advantageous or disadvantageous depends on the situation.

For the sake of example in stylistic analysis, I assume that every social group has a distinctive style. In the analysis of an aggregation site—that is, a site where a number of social groups periodically gather for short periods—an index that is highly sensitive to richness is probably advantageous. The analysis of Magdalenian aggregation sites exemplifies this situation (Conkey 1980, 1989; Kintigh 1984, 1989b). Each group would be expected to leave only a few artifacts at the aggregation site; therefore the presence of each style, regardless of proportion, would be significant, and richness would be an appropriate measure. Conversely, analyses of horizontal social complexity are concerned with the interaction of social groups (Pollock 1983a). In this situation, both the presence and proportion of styles would be significant in interpretations of the integration of social groups; any style present in only a very small proportion might represent a peripheral group and should have less weight in the stylistic analysis. Therefore the H-statistic or another diversity index would be a more appropriate measure.

Archaeologists have analyzed and interpreted stylistic diversity in research on a variety of subjects. Whallon (1968) interprets an increase in homogeneity to mean an increase in endogamy (less movement of women potters) during the Iroquois Confederacy. Conkey (1980) argues that a high degree of stylistic diversity in carved bone indicates the presence of hunter–gatherer aggregation sites. DeBoer and Moore (1982) and Lindauer (1989) relate stylistic diversity to the use of pottery vessels for public display and/or for transmitting messages.

Sample Size and Diversity Measures

Diversity, whether measured as richness or with an overall index, is partly a function of the number of things present and therefore may be affected by sample size. Recent research has developed the means to derive important information about assemblage formation from the relationship between diversity and sample size (Shott 1989). A fairly extensive body of literature exists on methods to control for the effect of sample size on diversity or richness measures (e.g., Jones et al. 1983; Kintigh 1984; Leonard and Jones 1989; Plog and Hegmon 1993; Rhode 1988). Plog and I (Plog and Hegmon 1993) have recently argued that the effect of sample size should not automatically be removed in all cases, because differences in sample size may be related to significant real differences in prehistoric behaviors, such as the length of site occupation. However, when differences in sample size are due to differences in archaeological methods, as is the case in much of this research, the effect of sample size must be accounted for. In this research, pottery samples were selected in a manner that afforded maximum control of context and temporal placement. Such control was relatively easy to achieve for small, single-occupation sites (such as Duckfoot) but much more difficult for large sites occupied for nearly a century (such as Grass Mesa Village). As a result, assemblages from small sites are often as large as or larger than those from large sites.

Richness is a measure of the number of categories present in a given assemblage. Thus, the effect of sample size on richness is fairly straightforward: The larger the assemblage, the greater the chance that more categories will be represented. Two methods of controlling the effect of sample size in studies of assemblage richness have been proposed recently. Both predict what the richness should be for a given sample size and then compare the predicted and observed values to determine if a given sample is richer or less rich than expected. The methods differ in how they determine expected richness. Jones et al. (1983) use regression to derive a curve of expected values, whereas Kintigh (1984) uses a simulation that draws multiple samples of different sizes. Both methods are useful and appropriate in different situations (Rhode [1988] compares the two). Kintigh's sampling approach requires detailed information about the underlying population from which the samples are drawn, and it assumes that all the assemblages are derived from the same population. The regression approach makes fewer assumptions, but it requires a large number of assemblages so that very rich or very poor assemblages can emerge as outliers (Jones et al. 1983:69), and it often yields only very general results that contribute little to explaining differences between assemblages.

The effect of sample size on the H-statistic is less straightforward. Because H is a measure of the amount of information conveyed by one item, H should be independent of the number of items. Unfortunately, theoretical independence is the case only with very large samples that are fully representative of the underlying community (Pielou 1975:12). Such samples must be much larger than the number of categories and have little variation in richness, criteria which are rarely met in archaeology. Shott (1989) demonstrates the strong positive relationship between diversity and sample size with several sets of archaeological and ethnoarchaeological data.

The relationship between diversity indices and sample size can be assessed by comparing samples of different sizes drawn from the same baseline population. Computer simulation is used to draw repeated samples of various sizes from an infinitely large baseline population that contains five categories present in the proportions 1:2:3:4:5 (the simulation code is given in Hegmon [1990:Appendix C]). The H-statistic is calculated for each sample, using Kintigh's (1989a) DIVMEAS program, and the mean H-statistics for 20 samples of each size are shown in Table 8.1. With relatively small samples, H increases as sample size increases, but as sample size continues to become larger, increases in H level off and H_{300} is equal to H_{1000}.

Researchers using the H-statistic as a measure of diversity in archaeological research have used various methods to control for the effects of sample size. Conkey (1980:618) showed that sample size could not account for all differences in H, because samples of different sizes had the same H values. Using correlation coefficients, I have previously shown that sample size and H are not strongly related (Hegmon 1989c). Phagan and Hruby (1988) examined regression curves when H was plotted against sample size. However, none of these methods is completely satisfactory. It is not always possible to demonstrate an overall lack of association between H and sample size, and the method does not facilitate the assessment of a particular sample. Phagan and Hruby's method is probably the most systematic, but it requires a large number of data points and can only be used to detect relatively extreme outliers.

To control more rigorously the effects of sample size on H or on other diversity indices, simulation (partly modeled after Kintigh's [1984, 1989a, 1989b] work on sample size and richness) is used to determine expected diversity values for different sample sizes. The technique provides a method both for controlling the effect of sample size and for considering the significance of differences in diversity scores.[1] The simulation draws multiple samples of different

Table 8.1. Diversity Measures for Samples of Different Sizes Drawn from the Same Baseline Population

Sample Size	Mean H-statistic[a]	Mean Richness[a]
20	.59	4.60
30	.63	4.90
40	.61	4.85
50	.62	5.00
60	.63	4.95
70	.64	5.00
80	.64	5.00
90	.64	5.00
100	.64	5.00
150	.64	5.00
200	.64	5.00
250	.64	5.00
300	.65	5.00
400	.65	5.00
500	.65	5.00
1,000	.65	5.00

[a] Over 20 samples of given size.

---

1. One of the few methods proposed to evaluate the significance of differences in diversity scores (Hutcheson 1970) does not control for the effect of sample size.

sizes from an infinitely large baseline assemblage. The mean diversity index and its standard deviation for each sample size can then be calculated and compared with observed values. A critical factor in this approach, as in Kintigh's, is the composition of the baseline assemblage. I suggest that when the underlying population structure is not known or when all the assemblages cannot be assumed to derive from the same population, the baseline assemblage can be modeled on the assemblage with the highest diversity index. Then, for each observed assemblage, the question can be asked: Is this more or less diverse than would be expected if a sample of this size were drawn from the most diverse assemblage?

The extent to which the observed diversity index differs from the simulated value can generally be assessed by comparing the observed value with the simulated mean. The difference can be more rigorously evaluated by taking into account the simulated standard deviation and determining the standardized Z-score:

$$Z = \frac{observed - mean}{SD}$$

The Z-score can then be used to determine the probability that the observed value falls outside the expected range for the mean. The Z-scores can also be used to compare differences in diversity between assemblages of different sizes.

To demonstrate, I use Conkey's (1980) data on design elements carved in bone at Altamira and four other Magdalenian sites in Cantabria, Spain. Conkey suggests that Altamira and (possibly) Cueto de la Mina were prehistoric aggregation sites, an interpretation based partly on studies of design-element diversity that used the H-statistic. Her conclusions are supported by Kintigh's (1984) analysis of richness using the sampling approach, and these data have been used in other research on the effect of sample size and diversity, including Rhode's (1988) and Kintigh's (1989a) diversity programs (see also Conkey 1989).

The simulated baseline assemblage is modeled after that of Altamira, which has the largest and most diverse assemblage of the five sites. The H-statistic values for simulated samples of different sizes are shown in Table 8.2 and compared with the observed values for the five sites in Table 8.3 and Figure 8.1. The observed H for Altamira is larger than that predicted by the simulation, and the Z-score of 1.82 is significant, with a probability of .03. The observed H-statistic for Cueto de la Mina is nearly identical to the simulated value, and the observed H-statistics for the other three sites are significantly less than the simulated values. Thus, the assemblages from Altamira—and probably also Cueto de la Mina—are more diverse than the assemblages from the other sites, and Conkey's (1980) conclusions are supported.

Table 8.2. Simulated H-statistics for Different Sample Sizes, Using Altamira as a Baseline

Sample Size	H-statistic[a]	
	Mean	SD
20	1.06	.060
30	1.18	.060
40	1.22	.056
50	1.25	.052
60	1.28	.042
80	1.30	.044
100	1.33	.034
120	1.35	.029
140	1.36	.031
160	1.36	.029

SD = standard deviation.
[a] Over 50 samples of given size.

Table 8.3. Observed and Simulated *H*-statistics for the Cantabrian Sites

| Site | Sample Size | Observed *H*-statistic[a] | Simulated *H*-statistic | | Z-score |
			Mean[b]	SD	
La Paloma	23	1.01	1.11	.059	−1.69*
El Cierro	35	1.08	1.20	.058	−2.07*
El Juyo	53	1.08	1.25	.054	−3.15***
Cueto de la Mina	69	1.28	1.29	.042	−.24
Altamira	152	1.42	1.36	.033	1.82*

SD = standard deviation.

[a] Observed *H*-values differ from those given by Conkey (1980:Table 4) because she uses the natural logarithm, whereas these calculations use base 10.

[b] Over 50 samples, of the same size as observed, drawn from the baseline assemblage.

*$p \leq .05$.

***$p \leq .001$.

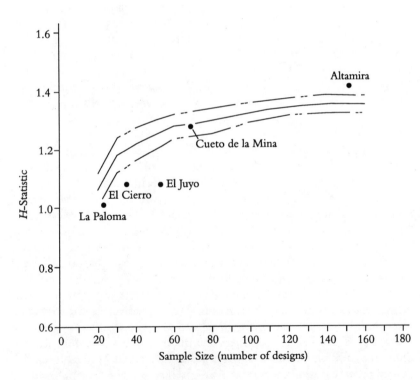

Figure 8.1. *Observed and simulated* H-*statistics for the Cantabrian sites listed in Table 8.3, calculated on the basis of Conkey's (1980) data. The points are the observed* H-*statistics for the five sites; the solid line shows the simulated mean* H-*statistic with different sample sizes; and the broken lines are the simulated mean plus and minus one standard deviation.*

Background for Analysis

The goal of the analysis in this chapter is to characterize differences in design style within and between assemblages. The history of pottery design style analysis in the last 25 years demonstrates the importance of understanding the many factors that can affect stylistic differences. The importance of considering the effect of sample size in the study of diversity was discussed above.

The early ceramic sociology studies were concerned, in large part, with patterns of similarity and difference, and several of these studies, particularly those of Hill (1966, 1970) and Longacre (1964a, 1970), have undergone more than two decades of evaluation and criticism. Although some of the particular conclusions of these studies can no longer be substantiated, the vast amount of research and debate they have inspired (including later work by J. Hill [1985] and Longacre [1981, ed. 1991]) demonstrates the importance of their contributions.

Hill (1966, 1970) and Longacre (1964a, 1970) used designs on pottery to make interpretations about social relations between the potters (what came to be called "learning-interaction theory"). They argued that women learn pottery making from their mothers, and thus spatially distinct clusters of stylistically similar pottery could be interpreted as evidence of matrilocal groups. This approach has been criticized by those who argue that potters learn from many people, not just their matrilineal relatives (Stanislawski 1973; Stanislawski and Stanislawski 1978).

Interpretations based on learning-interaction theory emphasize relations between the *producers* of pottery and often assume that pottery was made, used, and deposited in the same place. However, much research has shown that movement and exchange of pottery was common throughout the Southwest, and interpretations of the distribution of pottery style must take exchange into account (Plog 1980a). Related research demonstrates the importance of accounting for temporal differences, vessel form, and site-formation processes in stylistic analyses (Plog 1978, 1980a; Schiffer 1989; Skibo et al. 1989).

The intense scrutiny applied to many stylistic analyses makes clear the importance of using replicable criteria of design classification in stylistic analyses (Douglass and Lindauer 1988; Plog 1995). Replicable criteria help to increase the objectivity of the analysis, and they facilitate evaluation, reinterpretation, and expansion of the original analysis.

Several recent studies emphasize the importance of considering how different kinds and levels of design attributes should be analyzed and compared (Plog 1980a; Redman 1978). These studies use hierarchical systems of design classification that allow the separate consideration of different kinds of attributes, such as the shape of primary forms (for example, triangles or terraces) and the composition of filled areas (for example, solid or hatched). The separation of different kinds of attributes is particularly important because measures of similarity and diversity consider the number of items present in alternative categories.

Finally, recent work has demonstrated the importance of considering sherd size and conjoinability. Larger sherds are expected to have a greater diversity of design attributes. Sherds from the same vessel are obviously very similar, and several researchers (e.g., Schiffer 1989; Skibo et al. 1989) have demonstrated the problems that can be caused by drawing conclusions about clusters of similar sherds without determining if the sherds were originally parts of the same vessel.

The Database and Background Analyses

The analyses of style as difference use the primary database as described in Chapter 5. This database includes information recorded for both sherds and vessels from sites on northern Black Mesa and in the central Mesa Verde region. The pottery is from relatively unmixed, fairly well dated, excavated contexts. This database provides a means of controlling for, and assessing changes over time in, pottery style. The data are listed, by sherd or vessel, in Hegmon (1990:Appendix D).

Before the stylistic analysis, the pottery was analyzed according to several technological criteria, discussed in Chapter 6. First, the sherds were examined to see if any fit with other sherds, so that each vessel would be counted only once. Second, vessel form (V20 in the coding system, discussed in the following section) was recorded for each sherd or vessel and thus could be controlled for in the stylistic analysis. Rim diameter (V99) was also measured, and these data were used in the analysis of vessel form discussed in Chapter 6. Finally, the paint (V16), finish (V14, V15), and temper (V17) were analyzed, using a binocular microscope, to gain information applicable to studies of production and exchange. These techniques allow separation of pottery made in different regions and thus provide a means of controlling for long-distance exchange. Extraregional imports were excluded from the analysis of stylistic difference. However, this fairly gross scale of analysis provides little information on intraregional exchange. Thus, intraregional exchange cannot be strictly controlled for in the analysis. Instead, intraregional exchange is taken into account in interpretations of the results (see Crown 1981:364). That is, the focus is on how pottery style is used, regardless of where the pottery was made. In addition, some of the expectations consider that some assemblages (for example, those associated with large-scale activities) might include pottery from a large area.

The Coding System

The analysis of stylistic differences requires a replicable method that facilitates comparisons between alternative attribute states. Furthermore, because the database is dominated by sherds and includes relatively few whole vessels, the analytical system had to be applicable to the partial designs present on sherds.

The coding system used in this analysis is based on a hierarchy of design attributes. The system was designed specifically for ninth-century pottery, and it involves making observations about attributes emphasized in some of the classic type definitions and pottery studies (especially Beals et al. 1945; Breternitz et al. 1974; Colton and Hargrave 1937; Morris 1939). Traditional type designations (V19) were also recorded for each sherd or vessel. The method of analysis was modeled in part on that used by Black Mesa researchers (Plog and Hantman 1986). Some of the attributes of structure that could be considered on sherds were also included in the analysis. The coding system is described in Table 8.4.

Although the coding system was first used to record a large number of design attributes, the analysis focused on six sets of attributes that were present frequently enough to permit comparisons. Each set of attributes represents hierarchically equivalent alternatives that appear to fill the same roles in designs. This assumption of hierarchical equivalence is an analytical technique—it does not pretend to replicate the cognitive structures of the prehistoric artists. The sets of attributes are summarized in Figure 8.2.

Primary forms (V21, V36, V38, V46, V48, V51, V52, V54, V55, V62, V63, V66, V67, V68) are discrete shapes that stand alone as the basic units of designs. *Secondary forms,* or fringe (V50, V69), are attached to the primary forms. *Extensions on triangles* (V34, V42) are a special case of the secondary forms. *Composition* (V52, V53, V87, V88, V89) refers to the fill of an area or a primary form. Unframed lines are considered both as primary forms—because they constitute basic units of design—and as composition—because they are a kind of fill for certain areas. *Line width* (V82, V83) is a detail of design that is often used to distinguish between types and appears to be particularly sensitive to spatial and temporal differences (Hantman et al. 1984; Plog and Hantman 1986). In cases in which two line width modes were present, both were recorded, but the larger mode (V83) was used in the analysis of diversity. *Triangle use* (V24, V25, V26, V27, V28, V29) is an attribute of structure that was considered in Chapter 7. It is included here to provide some means of comparing the two analyses and different databases.

The sherds and vessels are highly variable in terms of the size and proportion of the design that they represent. Therefore, in the analysis that follows, the basic unit is not the sherd or the vessel, but the design attribute. For example, in comparing designs between two sites, the analysis considers how many cases of triangles and terraces are present on the two sites, regardless of whether the triangles and terraces are present on the same or different sherds (each attribute is

Table 8.4. Explanation of the Attribute Coding System

V1 Case

V2 Site number

V3 FS number (DAP sites); PD number (CCAC sites); bag number (BMAP sites)

V4 Catalog number (DAP sites); FS number (CCAC sites)

V5 PL number (DAP and CCAC sites)

V6 Whole or reconstructible vessel number. A two-digit number is a BMAP final number (fn) or a DAP or CCAC reconstructible vessel number (rc). A four-digit number beginning with 10 (e.g., 1004) denotes a vessel (or sherds from more than one provenience) reconstructed as part of this research.

V7 Modeling period number (DAP and CCAC sites)

V12 Wholeness
   1 whole/almost whole vessel
   2 partial vessel (more than $1/8$ but less than $3/4$ present)
   3 sherd

V13 Sherd size (cm^2)

V14 Polish
   1 unpolished, rough
   2 smoothed
   3 polished

V15 Slip
   1 unslipped
   2 wash
   3 clear slip

V16 Paint type
   1 glaze
   3 mineral
   4 organic

V17 Temper (see Table 6.1)
   3, 12 crushed andesite/diorite
   4 crushed sherd and andesite/diorite
   6 sand
   9 crushed sherd and quartz sand
   11 crushed trachyte basalt
   13, 16, 18 crushed sedimentary rock
   50 crushed andesite/diorite and sand
   52 quartz sand in Tusayan White Ware from Black Mesa

V19 Type
   1 San Juan White Ware, cannot determine type
   2 Chapin Black-on-white
   3 Piedra Black-on-white

   4 Cortez Black-on-white
   5 Mancos Black-on-white
   12 Red Mesa Black-on-white
   21 Lino Black-on-white
   22 Kana-a Black-on-white
   23 Black Mesa Black-on-white
   24 Sosi Black-on-white
   25 Dogoszhi Black-on-white
   26 Tusayan White Ware, cannot determine type
   27 Mesa Verde Black-on-white
   28 Black Mesa or Sosi black-on-white
   29 Wepo Black-on-white
   30 early Tusayan White Ware (Kana-a or Wepo black-on-white)

V20 Vessel form
   1, 2 bowl
   5 jar

V21 Triangles *(primary forms)*
   1 present

V24 Triangles in a line *(triangle use)*
   1 present

V25 Triangle checkerboard *(triangle use)*
   1, 2, 3, 4 present

V26 Triangles attached to scrolls *(triangle use)*
   1, 2, 3 present

V27 Triangles in rectangular spaces *(triangle use)*
   1, 2, 3, 4, 5, 6, 7 present

V28 Triangles in corners of diagonal lines *(triangle use)*
   1 present

V29 Triangles on flags *(triangle use)*
   1, 2, 3 present

V34 Triangle extensions *(triangle extensions)*
   1 plain
   2 flag
   3 single, indeterminate form (i.e., plain or flag)
   4 multiple tails

V36 Scrolls *(primary forms)*
   1 present

V38 Spirals *(primary forms)*
   1 present

V42 Scrolls are triangle extensions *(triangle extensions)*
   1 yes, present

V46 Checks *(primary forms)*
   1 4-sided, right angles
   2 4-sided, oblique
   3 4-sided, miscellaneous
   4 triangular (see V25)

Table 8.4. Explanation of the Attribute Coding System *(continued)*

V48	Terraces *(primary forms)*		V67	Curved lines
	1 present			1 curved only with contour of vessel
V50	Fringe on solids *(secondary forms)*			3 basic design is curvilinear *(primary forms)*
	1 serrated			2, 4 only small part of design is curvilinear
	2 ticks		V68	Squiggle/rickrack lines *(primary forms)*
	3 attached dots			1 squiggle
	4 ticks and/or dots (both or cannot distinguish)			2 rickrack
	5 hooks			3 squiggle and/or rickrack
V51	Flags present in any form (see V29) *(primary forms)*		V69	Fringe on lines *(secondary forms)*
				1 railroad tracks
	1 present			2 ticks
V52	Dots			3 dots
	1 free *(primary forms)*			4 ticks and/or dots (both or cannot distinguish)
	3 filler *(composition)*			5 hooks
	4 free dots in a line *(primary forms)*			6 ticks and railroad tracks
	7 present, cannot determine role		V80	Line width mode *(line width)*
V53	Z's and/or basketstitch *(composition)*			1 more than one mode of line width present (see Figure 5.1e)
	1, 2, 3 present		V82	Average line width of smaller mode (mm) *(line width)*
V54	Framed cross *(primary forms)*			
	1 present		V83	Average line width of larger mode (mm) *(line width)*
V55	T-figure *(primary forms)*			
	1 present		V87	Solid *(composition)*
V62	Circle *(primary forms)*			1 present
	1 present, miscellaneous		V88	Hatch *(composition)*
	2 single			1, 2, 3 present
	3 concentric		V89	Multiple lines *(composition)*
V63	Rectangular solids *(primary forms)*			1 present
	1, 2 present		V99	Rim diameter (cm)
V66	Straight lines *(primary forms)*		V100	Rim arc (degrees)
	1 present			

NOTE: This table lists all the variables used in this portion of the research. The variable numbering is not continuous, because some variables were added or eliminated as the coding system was finalized. Words in italics refer to attribute sets explained in text, this chapter, and shown in Figure 8.2. During analysis, numeric codes (as listed in the table) were entered for the categorical variables, and measurements were entered for the analytic variables. In addition, the following entries were made to indicate absence, inapplicability, or lack of data:

    0 = no data or not applicable, categorical variable

    − 0.0 = no data or not applicable, analytical variable

    8 = absent as far as can be determined (i.e., on sherd)

    9 = definitely absent

V = variable; FS = field specimen; PD = provenience designation; DAP = Dolores Archaeological Program; CCAC = Crow Canyon Archaeological Center; BMAP = Black Mesa Archaeological Project.

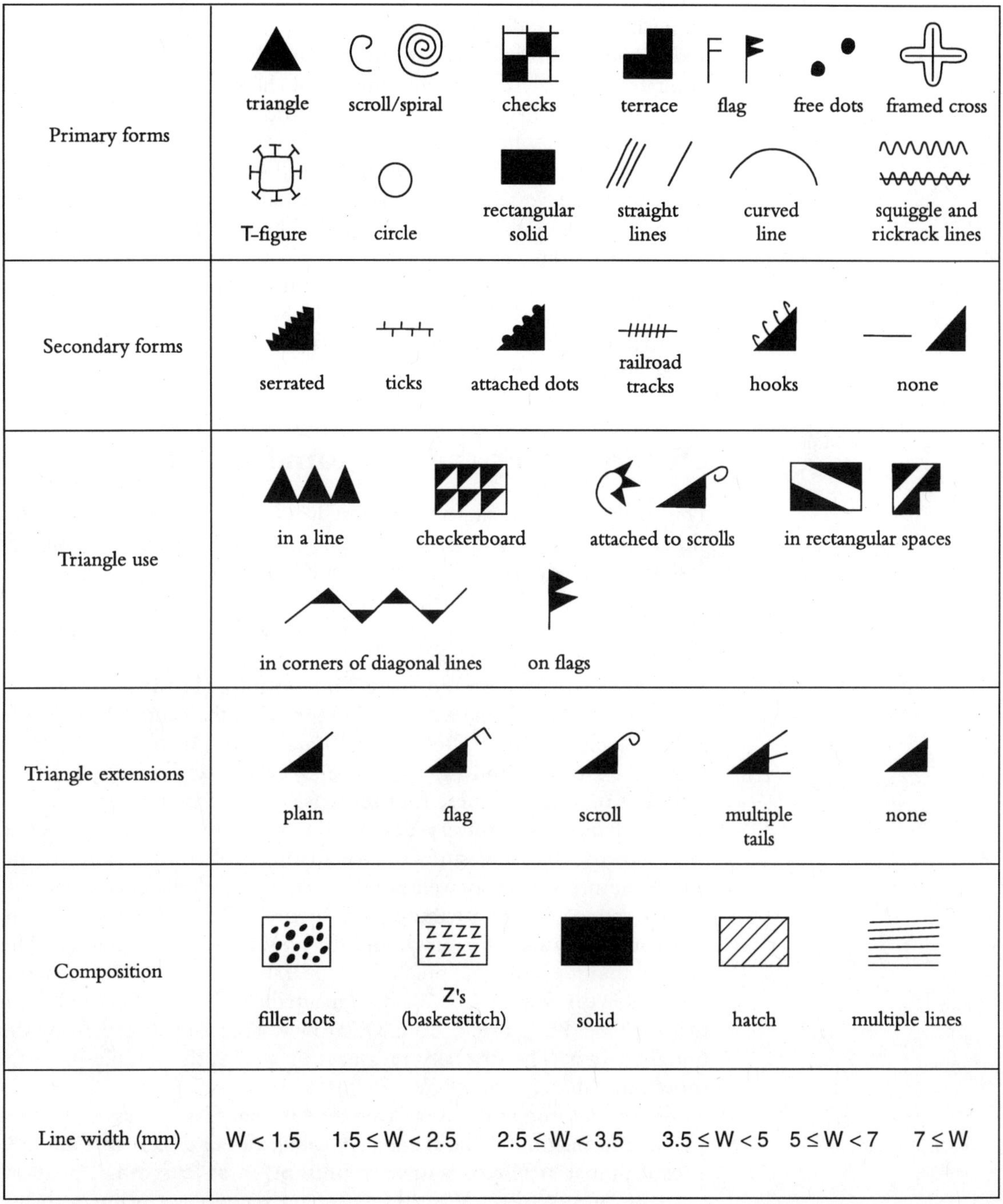

Primary forms	triangle	scroll/spiral	checks	terrace	flag free dots framed cross
	T-figure	circle	rectangular solid	straight lines	curved line squiggle and rickrack lines
Secondary forms	serrated	ticks	attached dots	railroad tracks	hooks none
Triangle use	in a line	checkerboard	attached to scrolls	in rectangular spaces	
	in corners of diagonal lines	on flags			
Triangle extensions	plain	flag	scroll	multiple tails	none
Composition	filler dots	Z's (basketstitch)	solid	hatch	multiple lines
Line width (mm)	W < 1.5 1.5 ≤ W < 2.5 2.5 ≤ W < 3.5 3.5 ≤ W < 5 5 ≤ W < 7 7 ≤ W				

Figure 8.2. *Sets of design attributes that were used in the analysis of difference. Refer to Table 8.4 for a complete explanation of the attribute coding system.*

counted only once for each sherd on which it appears). This technique has been used in previous analyses (Hegmon 1986). Although it does not permit detailed study of the covariation of attributes, it facilitates the analysis of large numbers of sherds. Attribute covariation was considered in the more detailed study of design structure on large sherds and whole vessels in Chapter 7.

The coding system outlined in Table 8.4 was used to describe all the sherds and vessels in the primary database (after refitting), with the exception of those from D:7:134. These data are listed case by case in Hegmon (1990:Appendix D). A sample from D:7:134 was added after the initial analysis was completed, and an abbreviated coding system was used for this sample. Specifically, only the six sets of attributes described above, and illustrated in Figure 8.2, were coded for this sample.

Difference at the Regional Level

The analysis begins at the broadest level, with comparisons of regions and time periods. In this section, I consider the diversity of design style within and between time periods and regions. This analysis provides an important baseline for more detailed site-based analyses in subsequent sections. The more detailed analyses also provide insight into the broader patterns.

These broad analyses compare four settings: (1) the A.D. 800–840 period at Dolores; (2) the A.D. 840–880 period in the central Mesa Verde region (including both Dolores and Duckfoot); (3) the A.D. 880–920 period at Dolores; and (4) the A.D. 840–880 period on Black Mesa. The sites included in these four settings are listed in Table 8.5.

The diversity of pottery designs was measured for each of these four settings. Two measures of overall diversity (the *H*-statistic and the Brillouin index), as well as richness, were calculated for each of the six sets of design attributes (see Figure 8.2). The measures were calculated separately for bowls and for bowls and jars combined. The limited number of jars precluded separate analysis of jar designs. Samples with fewer than 20 design attributes were excluded from the analysis. The sample from D:7:134 was also excluded from the initial analysis. The diversity measures, as well as the sample sizes, are shown in Tables 8.6 and 8.7.

These data suggest several avenues for analysis. First, sample sizes are large in relation to the number of categories of design attributes. As a result, most attribute states are present, in at least small proportions, in most settings. With the possible exception of primary forms, there are only small differences in richness between the settings. Therefore, in this case, richness is not very useful as a basis of comparison.

Table 8.5. Sites Used in the Comparisons of Time Periods and Regions

Context	Site Name or Number
Dolores A.D. 800–840 MP 3	Grass Mesa Village Prince Hamlet House Creek Village Windy Wheat Hamlet Periman Hamlet
Dolores and Duckfoot A.D. 840–880 MP 4	Grass Mesa Village Prince Hamlet Rio Vista Village House Creek Village Duckfoot Aldea Alfareros Pueblo de las Golondrinas
Dolores A.D. 880–920 MP 5	Grass Mesa Village Prince Hamlet Rio Vista Village Weasel Pueblo Pueblo de las Golondrinas Golondrinas Oriental
Black Mesa ca. A.D. 840–880 BM	D:11:2023 D:11:2025 D:11:2027 D:11:2030

MP = modeling period; BM = Black Mesa.

Second, there are large differences in sample size among the four settings. The sample from Black Mesa is as much as 11 times larger than the early sample from the central Mesa Verde region. This difference in sample size does not reflect any real difference in prehistoric behavior, because the Black Mesa sites tend to be smaller than the Dolores sites and were occupied for shorter periods. Rather, the difference is due to the multiple occupations and/or the more complex stratigraphy at the Dolores sites, which limit the size of an assemblage for which good contextual information is available. Thus, sample size should be controlled for when comparing these two areas (Plog and Hegmon 1993). In cases in which the diversity measures for the central Mesa Verde region during the A.D. 800–840 period are larger than those for Black Mesa, the difference can be interpreted as a real difference in diversity (that is, not determined by sample size). However, in cases in which the diversity measures for the Black Mesa sample are larger, the difference is not necessarily meaningful unless the effect of sample size is taken into account.

Thus, comparison of the four settings focuses on the two measures of overall diversity, and the simulation technique is used to account

Table 8.6. Design Style Diversity, Bowls

Design Attribute	Context[a]	Sample Size	Diversity Measures		
			Richness	H-statistic	Brillouin Index
Primary forms	MP 3	84	7	.52	.48
	MP 4	336	10	.34	.33
	MP 5	154	9	.47	.44
	BM	504	7	.33	.33
Secondary forms	MP 3	74	2	.07	.07
	MP 4	336	5	.22	.21
	MP 5	138	4	.24	.22
	BM	466	5	.37	.36
Triangle extensions	MP 3	17	—	—	—
	MP 4	45	4	.43	.38
	MP 5	26	2	.30	.27
	BM	133	4	.17	.15
Line width	MP 3	52	6	.64	.58
	MP 4	258	6	.56	.54
	MP 5	102	5	.57	.54
	BM	321	6	.41	.40
Composition	MP 3	89	4	.40	.38
	MP 4	359	5	.30	.29
	MP 5	142	4	.29	.27
	BM	553	3	.30	.30
Triangle use	MP 3	13	—	—	—
	MP 4	54	5	.30	.26
	MP 5	29	5	.36	.29
	BM	140	4	.42	.40

NOTE: Dashes indicate that diversity measures were not calculated, because the sample size was less than 20.

[a] Refer to Table 8.5 for a list of the sites that make up each context (MP = modeling period, central Mesa Verde region; BM = Black Mesa). The date ranges for each context are as follows: MP 3 = A.D. 800–840, MP 4 = A.D. 840–880, MP 5 = A.D. 880–920, BM = ca. A.D. 840–880.

for differences in sample size. For each of the six sets of design attributes, simulation is used to determine the expected diversity for samples of various sizes drawn from a population with the same composition as the most diverse assemblage (judged according to the H-statistic). Z-scores are then used to compare the expected mean and observed values, and the Z-scores for each set of design attributes are ranked. These results are reported in Tables 8.8–8.11.

For example, consider primary forms on bowls. The greatest diversity ($H = .52$) is present in the A.D. 800–840 assemblage from Dolores (Table 8.6). Thus, the baseline for the simulation of primary form

Table 8.7. Design Style Diversity, Bowls and Jars Combined

Design Attribute	Context[a]	Sample Size	Diversity Measures		
			Richness	H-statistic	Brillouin Index
Primary forms	MP 3	86	7	.52	.48
	MP 4	441	10	.35	.33
	MP 5	219	10	.47	.44
	BM	998	10	.37	.33
Secondary forms	MP 3	76	2	.07	.06
	MP 4	438	6	.23	.22
	MP 5	198	4	.21	.20
	BM	931	5	.36	.35
Triangle extensions	MP 3	17	—	—	—
	MP 4	67	5	.47	.43
	MP 5	40	4	.41	.37
	BM	228	4	.19	.18
Line width	MP 3	53	6	.64	.57
	MP 4	334	6	.58	.56
	MP 5	142	5	.58	.55
	BM	639	6	.42	.41
Composition	MP 3	91	4	.40	.37
	MP 4	469	5	.30	.29
	MP 5	203	4	.29	.28
	BM	1,106	4	.31	.31
Triangle use	MP 3	13	—	—	—
	MP 4	75	5	.37	.33
	MP 5	46	5	.36	.31
	BM	245	5	.44	.43

NOTE: Dashes indicate that diversity measures were not calculated, because the sample size was less than 20.

[a] Refer to Table 8.5 for a list of the sites that make up each context (MP = modeling period, central Mesa Verde region; BM = Black Mesa). The date ranges for each context are as follows: MP 3 = A.D. 800–840, MP 4 = A.D. 840–880, MP 5 = A.D. 880–920, BM = ca. A.D. 840–880.

diversity on bowls is an infinitely large assemblage with the same composition as the A.D. 800–840 assemblage. The four assemblages have sample sizes of 84, 336, 154, and 504. The simulation draws 50 samples of each size from the baseline assemblage. The diversity of each sample is calculated, and the mean and standard deviation across the 50 samples are recorded in Tables 8.8 and 8.9.

Several patterns are apparent in these results. First, the relative diversity of the four assemblages (as indicated by the observed diversity measures for samples of different sizes) and the Z-scores (which correct for sample size) correspond fairly closely. In all cases, the assemblage that has the largest observed diversity measure also has

Table 8.8. Observed and Simulated Brillouin Indices, Bowls

Design Attribute	Context[a]	Observed Brillouin Index	Simulated Brillouin Index		Z-score	
			Mean[b]	SD	Value	Rank
Primary forms	MP 3	.48	.46	.043	.47	1
	MP 4	.33	.51	.025	−7.20***	3
	MP 5	.44	.49	.035	−1.43	2
	BM	.33	.51	.018	−10.00***	4
Secondary forms	MP 3	.07	.33	.041	−6.34***	3
	MP 4	.21	.37	.022	−7.27***	4
	MP 5	.22	.35	.037	−3.51***	2
	BM	.36	.36	.020	.00	1
Triangle extensions	MP 4	.38	.37	.045	.22	1
	MP 5	.27	.34	.047	−1.49	2
	BM	.15	.41	.020	−13.00***	3
Line width	MP 3	.58	.56	.039	.51	1
	MP 4	.54	.62	.019	−4.21***	3
	MP 5	.54	.60	.030	−2.00*	2
	BM	.40	.62	.016	−13.75***	4
Composition	MP 3	.38	.37	.034	.29	1
	MP 4	.29	.39	.018	−5.56***	3
	MP 5	.27	.38	.030	−3.67***	2
	BM	.30	.40	.016	−6.25***	4
Triangle use	MP 4	.26	.37	.034	−3.24***	3
	MP 5	.29	.36	.043	−1.63	2
	BM	.40	.40	.020	.00	1

SD = standard deviation.
[a] Refer to Table 8.5 for a list of the sites that make up each context (MP = modeling period, central Mesa Verde region; BM = Black Mesa). The date ranges for each context are as follows: MP 3 = A.D. 800–840, MP 4 = A.D. 840–880, MP 5 = A.D. 880–920, BM = ca. A.D. 840–880.
[b] Over 50 samples, of the same size as observed, drawn from the baseline assemblage.
*$p \leq .05$.
***$p \leq .001$.

the largest Z-score. Thus, size has a limited effect on the diversity measures, at least in these cases.

Second, the Z-score ranks are very similar in all four tables (Tables 8.8–8.11). With one exception—H-statistics for secondary forms on bowls and jars in the A.D. 800–840 and 840–880 periods in the central Mesa Verde region—all the ranks are exactly the same.

Table 8.9. Observed and Simulated *H*-statistics, Bowls

Design Attribute	Context[a]	Observed *H*-statistic	Simulated *H*-statistic		*Z*-score	
			Mean[b]	SD	Value	Rank
Primary forms	MP 3	.52	.50	.047	.43	1
	MP 4	.34	.52	.025	−7.20***	3
	MP 5	.47	.51	.036	−1.11	2
	BM	.33	.52	.018	−10.56***	4
Secondary forms	MP 3	.07	.36	.043	−6.74***	3
	MP 4	.22	.38	.022	−7.27***	4
	MP 5	.24	.37	.038	−3.42***	2
	BM	.37	.37	.021	.00	1
Triangle extensions	MP 4	.43	.41	.051	.39	1
	MP 5	.30	.39	.059	−1.53	2
	BM	.17	.43	.021	−12.38***	3
Line width	MP 3	.64	.63	.044	.23	1
	MP 4	.56	.64	.019	−4.21***	3
	MP 5	.57	.64	.032	−2.19*	2
	BM	.41	.64	.017	−13.53***	4
Composition	MP 3	.40	.40	.036	.00	1
	MP 4	.30	.40	.018	−5.56***	3
	MP 5	.29	.40	.031	−3.67***	2
	BM	.30	.40	.016	−6.25***	4
Triangle use	MP 4	.30	.40	.037	−2.70**	3
	MP 5	.36	.41	.049	−1.02	2
	BM	.42	.42	.021	.00	1

SD = standard deviation.

[a] Refer to Table 8.5 for a list of the sites that make up each context (MP = modeling period, central Mesa Verde region; BM = Black Mesa). The date ranges for each context are as follows: MP 3 = A.D. 800–840, MP 4 = A.D. 840–880, MP 5 = A.D. 880–920, BM = ca. A.D. 840–880.

[b] Over 50 samples, of the same size as observed, drawn from the baseline assemblage.

*p ≤ .05.
**p ≤ .01.
***p ≤ .001.

This suggests that there is little difference between the vessel forms and that the two diversity indices achieve similar results, at least in this analysis. Therefore, subsequent analyses focus on the *H*-statistic and on combined samples of bowls and jars.

Third, the different sets of design attributes evidence very different results when diversity is compared between the regions and time

Table 8.10. Observed and Simulated Brillouin Indices, Bowls and Jars

Design Attribute	Context[a]	Observed Brillouin Index	Simulated Brillouin Index		Z-score	
			Mean[b]	SD	Value	Rank
Primary forms	MP 3	.48	.46	.043	.47	1
	MP 4	.33	.51	.025	−7.20***	3
	MP 5	.44	.49	.035	−1.43	2
	BM	.33	.51	.018	−10.00***	4
Secondary forms	MP 3	.06	.31	.038	−6.58***	4
	MP 4	.22	.35	.020	−6.50***	3
	MP 5	.20	.34	.032	−4.38***	2
	BM	.35	.36	.013	−.77	1
Triangle extensions	MP 4	.43	.42	.043	.23	1
	MP 5	.37	.40	.048	−.63	2
	BM	.18	.45	.022	−12.27***	3
Line width	MP 3	.57	.56	.036	.28	1
	MP 4	.56	.62	.018	−3.33***	3
	MP 5	.55	.60	.029	−1.72*	2
	BM	.41	.63	.011	−20.00***	4
Composition	MP 3	.37	.38	.038	−.26	1
	MP 4	.29	.39	.016	−6.25***	3
	MP 5	.28	.38	.023	−4.35***	2
	BM	.31	.40	.012	−7.50***	4
Triangle use	MP 4	.33	.40	.030	−2.33**	3
	MP 5	.31	.39	.042	−1.90*	2
	BM	.43	.43	.022	.00	1

SD = standard deviation.

[a] Refer to Table 8.5 for a list of the sites that make up each context (MP = modeling period, central Mesa Verde region; BM = Black Mesa). The date ranges for each context are as follows: MP 3 = A.D. 800–840, MP 4 = A.D. 840–880, MP 5 = A.D. 880–920, BM = ca. A.D. 840–880.

[b] Over 50 samples, of the same size as observed, drawn from the baseline assemblage.

*$p \leq .05$.

**$p \leq .01$.

***$p \leq .001$.

periods. Black Mesa has the greatest diversity of secondary forms and triangle use but the least diversity for the other four sets of attributes. A high level of design diversity in the Black Mesa sample was not expected. However, it may be significant that Black Mesa diversity is high only for relatively subtle or detailed attributes of design (that is, there was little diversity in the forms present, but those forms were elaborated or used in a variety of ways).

Table 8.11. Observed and Simulated *H*-statistics, Bowls and Jars

Design Attribute	Context[a]	Observed *H*-statistic	Simulated *H*-statistic		*Z*-score	
			Mean[b]	SD	Value	Rank
Primary forms	MP 3	.52	.49	.046	.65	1
	MP 4	.35	.51	.021	−7.62***	3
	MP 5	.47	.52	.029	−1.72*	2
	BM	.37	.51	.014	−10.00***	4
Secondary forms	MP 3	.07	.34	.040	−6.75***	4
	MP 4	.23	.36	.020	−6.50***	3
	MP 5	.21	.36	.033	−4.55***	2
	BM	.36	.36	.013	.00	1
Triangle extensions	MP 4	.47	.46	.048	.21	1
	MP 5	.41	.45	.056	−.71	2
	BM	.19	.47	.023	−12.17***	3
Line width	MP 3	.64	.62	.041	.49	1
	MP 4	.58	.64	.018	−3.33***	3
	MP 5	.58	.63	.030	−1.67*	2
	BM	.42	.64	.011	−20.00***	4
Composition	MP 3	.40	.40	.039	.00	1
	MP 4	.30	.40	.016	−6.25***	3
	MP 5	.29	.39	.023	−4.35***	2
	BM	.31	.40	.012	−7.50***	4
Triangle use	MP 4	.37	.43	.033	−1.82*	3
	MP 5	.36	.43	.048	−1.46	2
	BM	.44	.44	.023	.00	1

SD = standard deviation.

[a] Refer to Table 8.5 for a list of the sites that make up each context (MP = modeling period, central Mesa Verde region; BM = Black Mesa). The date ranges for each context are as follows: MP 3 = A.D. 800–840, MP 4 = A.D. 840–880, MP 5 = A.D. 880–920, BM = ca. A.D. 840–880.

[b] Over 50 samples, of the same size as observed, drawn from the baseline assemblage.

*p ≤ .05.

***p ≤ .001.

The results can be summarized and compared across the four assemblages by summing the *Z*-scores and calculating their mean (Table 8.12). The diversity of designs from Black Mesa is much less than that for any of the time periods in the central Mesa Verde region. Of the three periods, the A.D. 840–880 period has the least diverse designs, and the designs from the latest period are slightly less diverse than those from the earliest. The greater diversity of the designs on pottery from the central Mesa Verde region conforms to the expectations developed above.

Table 8.12. Mean Z-scores of Design Style Diversity, Bowls and Jars

Context[a]	Mean Z-score[b]			
	Bowls		Bowls and Jars	
	Brillioun Index	H-statistic	Brillioun Index	H-statistic
MP 3	−1.27	−1.52	−1.52	−1.40
MP 4	−4.54	−4.43	−4.23	−4.22
MP 5	−2.29	−2.16	−2.40	−2.41
BM	−7.17	−7.12	−8.42	−8.28

[a] Refer to Table 8.5 for a list of the sites that make up each context (MP = modeling period, central Mesa Verde region; BM = Black Mesa). The date ranges for each context are as follows: MP 3 = A.D. 800–840, MP 4 = A.D. 840–880, MP 5 = A.D. 880–920, BM = ca. A.D. 840–880.
[b] Mean across four or six sets of design style attributes, compiled from Tables 8.8–8.11.

The diversity analysis focused on stylistic differences within a given context. Here, differences between contexts are evaluated using similarity measures. The Brainerd-Robinson similarity coefficient is used to assess the similarity of the four contexts (Black Mesa and the three time periods in the central Mesa Verde region) for the six sets of design attributes and the mean coefficients, including both bowls and jars. The similarity matrices are shown in Table 8.13.

The three assemblages from the central Mesa Verde region are more similar to each other than they are to the Black Mesa assemblage, both overall and for each individual set of attributes except primary forms. The regional difference is greatest for line width and also appears to be very large for triangle use and extensions, although the small samples from the A.D. 800–840 occupation of the central Mesa Verde region limit the comparisons. Line width and possibly also secondary forms appear to be temporally sensitive, since the A.D. 800–840 and 880–920 assemblages from the central Mesa Verde region are more similar to the A.D. 840–880 assemblage than they are to each other. No strong pattern is apparent in the matrix of similarity coefficients for primary forms. Only 17 points separate the highest (180) and lowest (163) coefficients (the smallest spread of any in the sets of similarity coefficients), and there is no suggestion of regional differentiation.

These data indicate that there were regional differences in the style of painted designs during the Pueblo I period. Although the same basic attributes (the primary forms) are present in pottery from both the Mesa Verde and Kayenta regions, these forms are used, filled, and elaborated in different ways in the two regions. Furthermore, the data confirm the findings of other researchers (e.g., Plog and Hantman 1986) that line width is a particularly sensitive indicator of differences over time and between regions.

Table 8.13. Brainerd-Robinson Similarity Coefficients, by Context

Primary Forms

Context[a]	MP 3	MP 4	MP 5	BM
MP 3	—	163	176	168
MP 4	163	—	176	172
MP 5	176	176	—	180
BM	168	172	180	—

Secondary Forms

Context	MP 3	MP 4	MP 5	BM
MP 3	—	183	182	161
MP 4	183	—	194	175
MP 5	182	194	—	178
BM	161	175	178	—

Triangle Extensions

Context	MP 4	MP 5	BM
MP 4	—	189	111
MP 5	189	—	115
BM	111	115	—

Line Width

Context	MP 3	MP 4	MP 5	BM
MP 3	—	172	164	100
MP 4	172	—	175	107
MP 5	164	175	—	82
BM	100	107	82	—

Composition

Context	MP 3	MP 4	MP 5	BM
MP 3	—	181	181	168
MP 4	181	—	196	167
MP 5	181	196	—	172
BM	168	167	172	—

Triangle Use

Context	MP 4	MP 5	BM
MP 4	—	191	152
MP 5	191	—	159
BM	152	159	—

Average Brainerd-Robinson Similarity Coefficients

Context	MP 3	MP 4	MP 5	BM
MP 3	—	175	176	149
MP 4	175	—	187	147
MP 5	176	187	—	148
BM	149	147	148	—

[a] Refer to Table 8.5 for a list of the sites that make up each context (MP = modeling period, central Mesa Verde region; BM = Black Mesa). The date ranges for each context are as follows: MP 3 = A.D. 800–840, MP 4 = A.D. 840–880, MP 5 = A.D. 880–920, BM = ca. A.D. 840–880.

The comparison of regions and time periods provides a broad understanding of stylistic differences during the ninth century A.D. In the following sections, I attempt to provide a more detailed understanding of the differences by investigating differences within and between sites and communities.

Style, Settlement, and Temporal Change on Black Mesa

The above analyses indicate that pottery style on northern Black Mesa was much less diverse than that in the central Mesa Verde region. The limited stylistic diversity apparent in the Black Mesa assemblage was not unexpected. To better understand the apparent homogeneity, the data from northern Black Mesa are examined in more detail.

Of the four sites included in the analyses described above, three (D:11:2023, D:11:2025, and D:11:2027) are small habitation sites that were occupied, probably sequentially, between about A.D. 850 and 880. The fourth site, D:11:2030, is the largest ninth-century site known in the Black Mesa study area. It is located near the three smaller sites and was probably occupied before and during the occupation of the three sites.

These sites were included in the analysis because they provide samples of pottery from well-documented and adequately dated sites. Unfortunately, using these sites also poses some potential problems. Given their proximity, it is possible that they represent a single community. Thus, the difference between the Black Mesa sites and Dolores-Duckfoot might be a result of comparing one community to many (David Braun, personal communication 1991). A sample from Site D:7:134 was added to the analysis in order to consider this possibility. Site D:7:134 is approximately 16 km north of the other sites, and it was occupied in the late ninth and early tenth centuries (from about A.D. 850 to 950). It was not included in the initial analysis, because most of the pottery from the site can be dated only generally to this 100-year period. However, the sample from D:7:134 is ideal for assessing the source of the stylistic homogeneity at the group of other sites. That is, if the D:7:134 sample is equally homogeneous, it would strongly suggest that the homogeneity is characteristic of the Pueblo I occupation of northern Black Mesa as a whole and is not an artifact of the restricted sample.

To compare design style diversity at D:7:134 and the other Black Mesa sites, the diversity measures were calculated for the sample from D:7:134 and the assemblage from all the Black Mesa sites combined (Table 8.14). These results indicate that the assemblage

Table 8.14. The Effect of the D:7:134 Assemblage on Measures of
Black Mesa Design Style Diversity

Design Attribute	Site(s)	Sample Size	H-statistic
Primary forms	D:7:134	331	.31
	D:11:2023, 2025, 2027, 2030	998	.33
	all	1,329	.35
Secondary forms	D:7:134	101	.48
	D:11:2023, 2025, 2027, 2030	931	.35
	all	1,032	.37
Triangle extensions	D:7:134	84	.10
	D:11:2023, 2025, 2027, 2030	228	.18
	all	312	.18
Line width	D:7:134	214	.39
	D:11:2023, 2025, 2027, 2030	639	.42
	all	853	.42
Composition	D:7:134	372	.31
	D:11:2023, 2025, 2027, 2030	1,106	.31
	all	1,478	.31
Triangle use	D:7:134	85	.39
	D:11:2023, 2025, 2027, 2030	245	.43
	all	330	.43

from D:7:134 is no more diverse than the assemblages from the other sites. Furthermore, with the exception of the measure for secondary forms, inclusion of the sample from D:7:134 with the samples from the other sites *lowers* the diversity measures. Because it does not appear that restricting the analysis to only the four nearby sites (D:11:2023, D:11:2025, D:11:2027, and D:11:2030) artificially lowers design style variation, the subsequent analyses continue to include only the well-controlled assemblages from the four well-dated sites.

Site D:11:2030 is much larger than Sites D:11:2023, D:11:2025, and D:11:2027, and it was occupied for a longer period. Thus, the D:11:2030 pottery assemblage might be expected to exhibit more diverse design style. Diversity measures for the four sites are shown in Table 8.15. Although the sample size for D:11:2030 is larger than that for the other sites, the sample itself is not consistently more diverse. No site is consistently more or less diverse than the others across the different sets of attributes. Therefore, even without the simulation to control for sample size, the suggestion that the largest site has the most diverse pottery can be rejected.

The three small sites provide an opportunity to examine two suggestions about the effect of time and social groups on stylistic

Table 8.15. Design Style Diversity, Black Mesa Sites

Design Attribute	Site	Sample Size	H-statistic
Primary forms	D:11:2023	181	.34
	D:11:2025	149	.35
	D:11:2027	250	.39
	D:11:2030	418	.35
Secondary forms	D:11:2023	127	.38
	D:11:2025	113	.35
	D:11:2027	165	.38
	D:11:2030	307	.31
Line width	D:11:2023	129	.37
	D:11:2025	97	.40
	D:11:2027	137	.42
	D:11:2030	276	.42
Composition	D:11:2023	206	.28
	D:11:2025	160	.31
	D:11:2027	268	.31
	D:11:2030	472	.32
Triangle use	D:11:2023	33	.31
	D:11:2025	30	.43
	D:11:2027	77	.51
	D:11:2030	105	.38

differences. First, given the architectural similarity of the three sites and their sequential occupation, it is likely that they were occupied by the same small group of people (perhaps an extended family) who may have been part of a larger community that included the occupants of D:11:2030. If the occupants of the small sites employed a distinctive pottery style that distinguished them as a group within the larger community, then the pottery assemblages from the three sites should be more similar to each other than to the assemblage from D:11:2030. Second, if pottery style changed during the approximately 30-year period that the three small sites were occupied, then the pottery from the sites that are closer in time should be more similar stylistically. These possibilities are examined using matrices of similarity coefficients (Table 8.16). These results support the suggestion that pottery style changed noticeably over a period of 30 years. On the basis of tree-ring dating, Sites D:11:2023, D:11:2025, and D:11:2027 are argued to have been occupied sequentially. Considering either the mean or the five coefficients separately, D:11:2023 is more similar to D:11:2025 than to D:11:2027, and D:11:2027 is more similar to D:11:2025 than to D:11:2023. However, the three sites are not more similar to each other than they are to the large

Table 8.16. Brainerd–Robinson Similarity Coefficients, Black Mesa Sites

Primary Forms

Site	D:11:2023	D:11:2025	D:11:2027	D:11:2030
D:11:2023	—	188	174	185
D:11:2025	188	—	183	195
D:11:2027	174	183	—	183
D:11:2030	185	195	183	—

Secondary Forms

Site	D:11:2023	D:11:2025	D:11:2027	D:11:2030
D:11:2023	—	181	176	179
D:11:2025	181	—	182	190
D:11:2027	176	182	—	183
D:11:2030	179	190	183	—

Line Width

Site	D:11:2023	D:11:2025	D:11:2027	D:11:2030
D:11:2023	—	176	174	172
D:11:2025	176	—	194	149
D:11:2027	174	194	—	148
D:11:2030	172	149	148	—

Composition

Site	D:11:2023	D:11:2025	D:11:2027	D:11:2030
D:11:2023	—	193	181	188
D:11:2025	193	—	187	194
D:11:2027	181	187	—	192
D:11:2030	188	194	192	—

Triangle Use

Site	D:11:2023	D:11:2025	D:11:2027	D:11:2030
D:11:2023	—	175	158	150
D:11:2025	175	—	181	153
D:11:2027	158	181	—	162
D:11:2030	150	153	162	—

Average Brainerd–Robinson Similarity Coefficients

Site	D:11:2023	D:11:2025	D:11:2027	D:11:2030
D:11:2023	—	183	173	175
D:11:2025	183	—	185	176
D:11:2027	173	185	—	174
D:11:2030	175	176	174	—

site, D:11:2030. Thus, if the three small sites were occupied by a distinct social group, that group did not distinguish itself stylistically.

Stylistic Differences at Dolores and Duckfoot

The results of the previous broad-scale analysis indicate that there was greater diversity in pottery design style in the central Mesa Verde region than on northern Black Mesa and a relatively low level of diversity during the A.D. 840–880 period in the central Mesa Verde region. Here, the central Mesa Verde region data are examined in more detail in an attempt to better understand the nature of the diversity.

The sample from the central Mesa Verde region consists of pottery from 10 sites in the Dolores River valley and from the Duckfoot site, located approximately 24 km from the valley. The Dolores sites are divided into three periods (A.D. 800–840, 840–880, and 880–920), and the Duckfoot site assemblage is included in the A.D. 840–880 group. Although it is possible that the inclusion of the Duckfoot pottery in the A.D. 840–880 samples inflated the diversity indicated for this period, the fact that diversity is lower during the A.D. 840–880 period than during the preceding or following periods (Table 8.12) suggests that such inflation is unlikely. Nevertheless, to assess how the inclusion of the Duckfoot sample affected the diversity indices, the *H*-statistic was recalculated using only the Dolores A.D. 840–880 assemblages (Table 8.17). Line-width diversity decreases slightly, primary form diversity increases slightly, and the diversity of the other attributes remains unchanged when Duckfoot is excluded. Simulation is used to account for the effect of sample size. Using as a baseline the entire A.D. 840–880 assemblage, the simulation assesses the diversity of samples that match the Dolores samples in size. These data, also listed in Table 8.17, show that the inclusion or exclusion of Duckfoot has no significant effect on the stylistic diversity (that is, no *Z*-scores are statistically significant). These results suggest that there is relatively little stylistic differentiation between Duckfoot and the Dolores sites.

Possible stylistic differences between Duckfoot and Dolores are further examined using the similarity coefficient. The A.D. 840–880 assemblage is divided into three parts: Grass Mesa community (Grass Mesa Village and Prince Hamlet), the Duckfoot site, and McPhee Village (Aldea Alfareros and Pueblo de las Golondrinas). The samples from Rio Vista and House Creek villages are not included, because they were not part of either Dolores community, and the other McPhee sites are not included because their assemblages date to a later period. The matrices of similarity coefficients among the three

Table 8.17. The Effect of the Duckfoot Site Assemblage on A.D. 840–880 Design Style Diversity in the Central Mesa Verde Region

Design Attribute	Including Duckfoot	Excluding Duckfoot				
	Total A.D. 840–880 H-statistic[a]	Sample Size	Observed H-statistic	Simulated H-statistic		Z-score
				Mean	SD	
Primary forms	.35	183	.38	.34	.036	1.11
Secondary forms	.23	180	.23	.22	.035	.29
Line width	.58	137	.55	.56	.026	−.38
Composition	.30	190	.30	.30	.020	.00

SD = standard deviation.
[a]From Table 8.7.

samples and the mean values are shown in Table 8.18. These results show that Grass Mesa and McPhee are not more similar to each other than they are to Duckfoot. In fact, McPhee Village is slightly more similar to Duckfoot than it is to Grass Mesa. Thus, there is no evidence of stylistic differentiation between Duckfoot and Dolores, and there is little evidence of stylistic differentiation between the Dolores communities.

Stylistic Differences and Social Change at Dolores

During the early to mid-ninth century, people moved into the Dolores River valley. This trend was reversed in the last two decades of the century, and by A.D. 920 the valley was virtually abandoned. During the period of decline, the use of formalized architecture continued at some communities (for example, McPhee) but was replaced by a much more variable and mobile occupation at others (for example, Grass Mesa). Some, but not all, sites had special structures that were probably used for large-scale integrative activities. The variation in settlement patterns and social processes may have been associated with variation in the role of style, and possible dimensions of variation are examined below.

Style and Large-Scale Integrative Structures

Several Dolores sites have community pit structures that probably housed community-wide or intercommunity rituals and other integrative activities. Style is argued to have an important role in the exchange of information among socially distant people and thus would have been particularly important in large-scale integrative

Table 8.18. Brainerd-Robinson Similarity Coefficients for Assemblages from
the Central Mesa Verde Region, A.D. 840–880

Primary Forms

Site or Community[a]	Grass Mesa Community	Duckfoot Site	McPhee Village
Grass Mesa community	—	188	189
Duckfoot site	188	—	191
McPhee Village	189	191	—

Secondary Forms

Site or Community	Grass Mesa Community	Duckfoot Site	McPhee Village
Grass Mesa community	—	189	186
Duckfoot site	189	—	194
McPhee Village	186	194	—

Line Width

Site or Community	Grass Mesa Community	Duckfoot Site	McPhee Village
Grass Mesa community	—	156	158
Duckfoot site	156	—	184
McPhee Village	158	184	—

Composition

Site or Community	Grass Mesa Community	Duckfoot Site	McPhee Village
Grass Mesa community	—	180	180
Duckfoot site	180	—	196
McPhee Village	180	196	—

Average Brainerd-Robinson Similarity Coefficients

Site or Community	Grass Mesa Community	Duckfoot Site	McPhee Village
Grass Mesa community	—	178	178
Duckfoot site	178	—	191
McPhee Village	178	191	—

[a] Grass Mesa community consists of data from Grass Mesa Village and Prince Hamlet; McPhee Village consists of data from Aldea Alfareros and Pueblo de las Golondrinas.

activities. Furthermore, if there were any stylistic differences between social groups, the different styles would have been represented when members of different groups came together for activities in the community pit structures. Therefore, pottery associated with the community pit structures is expected to have a greater diversity of designs than pottery at sites without a community pit structure. Results of a previous analysis (Hegmon 1989c), which served as a pilot study for this work, suggested that this was indeed the case. This finding is examined in more detail here.

Table 8.19. Design Style Diversity at Sites With and Without Community Pit Structures,
Central Mesa Verde Region

Modeling Period	Design Attribute	Community Pit Structure[a]	Sample Size	Observed H-statistic	Simulated H-statistic		Z-score
					Mean	SD	
MP 4	primary forms	present	32	.32	.29	.065	.46
A.D. 840–880		absent	409	.35	—	—	—
	secondary forms	present	33	.34	—	—	—
		absent	405	.22	.33	.025	−4.40***
	line width	present	22	.64	—	—	—
		absent	312	.57	.63	.016	−3.75***
	composition	present	33	.28	.29	.052	−.19
		absent	436	.30	—	—	—
MP 5	primary forms	present	115	.47	—	—	—
A.D. 880–920		absent	104	.45	.43	.042	.48
	secondary forms	present	104	.20	.22	.031	−.65
		absent	94	.22	—	—	—
	line width	present	73	.59	—	—	—
		absent	69	.56	.57	.030	−.33
	composition	present	107	.30	—	—	—
		absent	96	.27	.30	.030	−1.00

NOTE: The simulated H-statistic was calculated only for the less-diverse assemblage in each pair to determine whether its lack of diversity could be accounted for by its sample size.

[a] Modeling Period 4 sites with community pit structures are Rio Vista Village and Pueblo de las Golondrinas; those without are Grass Mesa Village, Prince Hamlet, House Creek Village, Duckfoot, and Aldea Alfareros. Modeling Period 5 sites with community pit structures are Weasel Pueblo and Pueblo de las Golondrinas; those without are Grass Mesa Village, Prince Hamlet, Rio Vista Village, and Golondrinas Oriental.

***$p \leq .001$.

Of the Dolores sites included in the analysis, three have community pit structures. These are Rio Vista during the A.D. 840–880 period and Pueblo de las Golondrinas and Weasel Pueblo (both part of McPhee Village) during the A.D. 840–920 and A.D. 880–920 periods, respectively.[2] Diversity measures were calculated for the groups of sites with and without community pit structures for each of the time periods, for a total of eight sets of comparisons (Table 8.19, Observed H-statistic column). In five comparisons, the sites with community pit structures have greater diversity; in three comparisons, the sites that lack community pit structures have greater diversity.

To judge the significance of these differences, expected diversity measures are simulated for the different sample sizes. For each

2. Grass Mesa Village had a great kiva in the early ninth century, but the pottery sample associated with this use of the site is too small for separate analysis.

comparison (one attribute at sites with and without community pit structures during one period), the baseline for the simulation is modeled on the assemblage with the higher diversity index, and samples of the same size as the assemblage with the lower diversity index are simulated. These results are used to determine if the assemblage with the lower diversity measure is significantly less diverse than would be expected for a sample of that size drawn from a population with the same composition as the assemblage with the higher diversity measure. The simulated and observed diversity indices are compared with Z-scores (Table 8.19, Z-score column).

The results show that, for the A.D. 840–880 period, sites with community pit structures have a greater diversity of pottery designs. Sites that lack community pit structures have significantly less diversity of secondary forms and line widths. Furthermore, the diversity of primary forms at sites with community pit structures is greater than would be expected for an assemblage of that size, although not significantly so. There are no significant differences in the A.D. 880–920 comparisons.

These results confirm earlier findings that a greater diversity of pottery designs is associated with sites with community pit structures, at least during the mid-ninth century. This relatively high diversity is expected to be associated with large-scale integrative activities at these structures for two reasons. First, many socially distant people would have come together for these activities, and stylistic information is expected to have been particularly important in such contexts. Second, because many individuals and social groups would have brought pottery to these activities, stylistic differences between them would have resulted in a more diverse assemblage.

Style and Changing Adaptations

In the last part of the ninth century, after A.D. 880, the occupation of Dolores underwent some major changes before the valley was abandoned early in the tenth century. Agricultural conditions worsened, and subsistence strategies may have emphasized more reliance on wild resources. The mid-century pattern of settlement in complex aggregated sites continued into the last decades of the century in the central part of the area, including at McPhee Village. However, in the northern part of the study area around Grass Mesa Village, where arable land was more limited, settlement patterns changed dramatically as the large roomblocks and community pit structures were replaced by a scattering of small pithouses, possibly with one large community pit structure. This change is interpreted as indicating an increase in mobility. Overall stylistic diversity increased between the A.D. 840–880 and 880–920 periods (Table 8.12). Here, the possible sources of that increase are examined.

The pottery assemblage associated with the more mobile occupation (called the Grass Mesa subphase) was examined to determine if it is significantly more or less diverse than the assemblage associated with the contemporaneous but less mobile occupation (the later part of the Periman subphase). In the analysis, the Grass Mesa subphase assemblages are from Grass Mesa Village and Rio Vista Village; the A.D. 880–920 Periman assemblages are from the McPhee Village sites. Diversity indices comparing the two contexts are shown in Table 8.20. Although the Periman subphase sample is much larger, the Grass Mesa subphase sample is slightly more diverse for two of the four sets of attributes (primary and secondary forms). The simulation and Z-scores are used to account for sample size. Although the Z-scores are not significant at a .05 level, a trend is consistent across all four sets of attributes. Specifically, in the two cases in which the observed H-statistics are greater for the Grass Mesa subphase samples (primary and secondary forms), the simulation is used to calculate diversity measures for samples the size of the Periman subphase samples. In both cases, the simulated values are equal to or greater than the observed values for the Periman samples, suggesting that the observed greater diversity of the Grass Mesa values indicates a real difference between the samples that cannot be accounted for by differences in sample size. In the two cases (line width and composition)

Table 8.20. Design Style Diversity, Grass Mesa and Periman Subphases, A.D. 880–910

Design Attribute	Subphase[a]	Sample Size	Observed H-statistic	Simulated H-statistic		Z-score
				Mean	SD	
Primary forms	Grass Mesa	71	.46	—	—	—
	Periman	142	.45	.45	.034	.00
Secondary forms	Grass Mesa	61	.23	—	—	—
	Periman	132	.20	.22	.032	−.63
Line width	Grass Mesa	46	.57	.56	.047	.21
	Periman	93	.58	—	—	—
Composition	Grass Mesa	63	.29	.28	.033	.30
	Periman	134	.29	—	—	—

NOTE: The simulated H-statistic was calculated only for the less-diverse assemblage in each pair to determine whether its lack of diversity could be accounted for by its sample size.

SD = standard deviation.

[a] Grass Mesa Subphase (A.D. 870–910) sites are Grass Mesa Village and Rio Vista Village; Periman Subphase (A.D. 840–910) sites are Weasel Pueblo, Pueblo de las Golondrinas, and Golondrinas Oriental.

for which the observed Grass Mesa subphase *H*-statistics are *not* greater than the observed Periman *H*-statistics, the simulation is used to calculate measures for samples the size of the Periman subphase samples. In these cases, the simulated mean *H*-statistics for samples the size of the Grass Mesa subphase sample are less than the observed values, indicating that the observed values are more diverse than would be expected for samples of those sizes. Thus, there is a slight suggestion that stylistic diversity was greater during the relatively ephemeral Grass Mesa subphase occupation than it was during the larger-scale Periman subphase occupation.

Increasing competition for resources may have been associated with the worsening climatic conditions and may also have contributed to the gradual abandonment of the Dolores River valley at the end of the ninth century (Kohler et al. 1986; Petersen 1988; Schlanger 1988). If this is true, stylistic differentiation between communities might have increased during the last decades of the century. To examine this possibility, similarity coefficients between Grass Mesa community and McPhee Village are compared for the A.D. 840–880 and 880–920 periods (Table 8.21).

These results show that similarity between Grass Mesa community and McPhee Village increases for line width and composition but decreases for primary forms and is unchanged for secondary forms. Overall, there is no strong change in stylistic similarity between the two groups of sites. The inclusion of factors that could not be controlled for in this analysis may have contributed to the inconclusiveness of the results. Specifically, settlement at Grass Mesa community changed and mobility increased after A.D. 880. Therefore, differences between Grass Mesa community and McPhee Village over the two time periods might have involved changing relations between the two groups of sites, or changes within Grass Mesa community, or both.

Table 8.21. Design Style Similarity, McPhee Village and Grass Mesa Community, A.D. 840–880 and A.D. 880–920

Design Attribute	Brainerd-Robinson Similarity Coefficients	
	A.D. 840–880	A.D. 880–920
Primary forms	189	180
Secondary forms	186	186
Line width	158	172
Composition	180	196

NOTE: McPhee Village sites are Aldea Alfareros, Weasel Pueblo, Pueblo de las Golondrinas, and Golondrinas Oriental. Grass Mesa Community sites are Grass Mesa Village and Prince Hamlet.

Interpreting Style as Difference

Much of what style is involves difference. If style is a way of doing (in general) or a way of decorating pottery with painted designs (the particular aspect of style that is the focus here), then there must be many ways of doing and therefore choice between alternatives. Differences are essential to what style is and to the capacity of style to make and mark contrasts and thus express personal and social identity.

Several implications regarding the potential role of stylistic differences in design style in the ninth-century northern Southwest were outlined at the beginning of this chapter. The first two implications concern the overall contrast between northern Black Mesa and the central Mesa Verde region. Residents of Dolores and Duckfoot would have had more contact with socially distant people as a result of the greater population density, as well as the existence of aggregated settlements and large-scale social gatherings. Thus, style is expected to have had a more important role in making and marking social distinctions in the central Mesa Verde region than on Black Mesa. Analyses of stylistic differences in this chapter and of design structure and vessel form (in Chapters 6 and 7) suggest that pottery design style filled this role. Painted designs are strongly associated with socially visible vessels (that is, bowls) in the central Mesa Verde region but not on northern Black Mesa, which suggests that the designs *could* have been used to express social differences. Analysis reveals a much higher level of diversity and structural variability in the designs on pottery from Dolores and Duckfoot and across the Mesa Verde region than in the designs on pottery from Black Mesa and across the Kayenta region. This diversity is interpreted as an expression of social differences, a necessary means of maintaining one's identity within the relatively intense social milieu of the central Mesa Verde region. In contrast, the design homogeneity in the Black Mesa pottery is more likely an expression of social similarity, a means of maintaining an expansive network.

The design homogeneity seen in pottery from northern Black Mesa is not uniform across all kinds of design attributes. For two sets of attributes—secondary forms and triangle use—the Black Mesa assemblage is *more* diverse (see Tables 8.8–8.11). These two kinds of attributes involve relatively subtle aspects of design. In particular, secondary form diversity is based on the presence of fringe on a primary form and whether that fringe consists of dots, ticks, or a combination of dots and ticks (Figure 8.3). It may be that this variation is the result of an additional level of communication. That is, the overall homogeneity of design structure and many design forms can be interpreted as a means of expressing social similarity. At the same time, small-scale differences, perhaps involving the individual

Figure 8.3. *Pottery from northern Black Mesa, illustrating attributes that were considered in the analysis of secondary forms: a, early Tusayan White Ware with no secondary form (V69 = 9); b, Kana-a Black-on-white with ticks (V69 = 2); c, Kana-a Black-on-white with dots (V69 = 3); d, Kana-a Black-on-white with ticks and/or dots (V69 = 4). V69 is explained in Table 8.4. Scale is 1:2.*

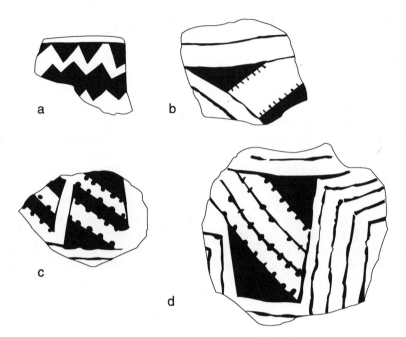

identities of the people who made and used the pots, may be expressed at a more subtle level. If women were the primary producers of pottery (as is generally the case when production is fairly small scale and wheels are not used [Murdock and Provost 1973; see also Wright 1991]), then the subtle variation may be the result of a dialogue among women, possibly paralleling the situation Hodder (1982b:68–73) notes with the gourds that women decorate and use in the Baringo district.

The third implication concerns the definition of social groups. Architectural and settlement evidence, including unit-pueblo architecture, private storage, aggregated settlements, and community pit structures, suggests that social groups were more clearly defined and distinguished in the central Mesa Verde region than on northern Black Mesa. Stylistic parallels to these architectural boundaries are not clear-cut, however, and the style can be interpreted on several levels. Stylistic differences between the Mesa Verde and Kayenta regions, manifest in both the structural analysis and the analysis of design elements, suggest that there was some social differentiation at the regional level. Similarly, differences between Piedra Black-on-white in southwestern Colorado and White Mesa Black-on-white in southeastern Utah indicate intraregional differences across the whole of the Mesa Verde region. At a smaller scale, that is, between communities at Dolores or between Dolores and Duckfoot, there is no evidence of stylistic differentiation. However, the high level of stylistic diversity within this area as a whole suggests that stylistically differentiated groups (such as descent groups or sodalities) may have cross-cut settlements.

The fourth implication with regard to the role of stylistic differences concerns the use of certain sites or structures for more than the usual type and degree of interaction among socially distant people. A greater degree of stylistic diversity is expected in these situations. Community pit structures in the Dolores area are argued to have been used for community and intercommunity rituals and other large-scale gatherings. A greater diversity of design is present in assemblages from sites that had community pit structures during the A.D. 840–880 period, although there are no significant differences during the subsequent period. These results may indicate that stylistic information exchange was more important at these structures and that special pottery was made for, and/or brought to, activities in these structures. The results may also indicate that more social units were bringing pottery to activities in these structures. The absence of a difference in stylistic diversity between sites with and without community pit structures during the later period may be a product of an overall increase in diversity that is masking any differences between sites.

No structures comparable to community pit structures were found on Black Mesa. The only possible architectural difference between sites is a matter of size; one habitation site is much larger than the others. However, comparison of pottery designs from the large and smaller sites also shows no difference in design style diversity.

Finally, changes in stylistic diversity can be interpreted in the context of the conditions that existed during the ninth century at Dolores. Because the changes have various implications for social organization and the use of style to express social differences, specific expectations for changes in the role of style were not developed. Instead, changes in stylistic differences can be used to make interpretations about social relations. This use of stylistic information is justified by the fairly close fit between patterns of stylistic variation and the other expectations developed throughout this volume. Specifics are discussed below.

Stylistic diversity in the central Mesa Verde region was greatest during the A.D. 800–840 period. There were relatively few people living in the Dolores area during the first two decades of this period, but the population began increasing and some large aggregated settlements were founded by A.D. 840. The high level of diversity in the pottery assemblage thus appears to have been associated with immigration and the establishment of new settlements, and the different styles may be indicative of different social groups coming together. Hence, the high diversity can be interpreted as an indication that the residents of Dolores were maintaining separate identities during the first stages of larger-scale settlement.

During the A.D. 840–880 period, stylistic diversity at Dolores and Duckfoot declined. This is the period in which population levels peaked, many large aggregated settlements were present, agriculture was intensified, and there may have been competition for land and resources. The lower level of diversity suggests that fewer stylistic distinctions were made, and at least two interpretations of these results are possible. The decrease in diversity could indicate an overall decrease in social distinctions, suggesting more area-wide cooperation. Conversely, the overall decrease in diversity could indicate that style was being used to emphasize a few important distinctions, such as those between competing groups. Given the architectural evidence of discrete social units and evidence of economic competition, the second interpretation is more likely.

Stylistic diversity increased again during the A.D. 880–920 period, although the diversity measures for this period are not as large as those associated with the A.D. 800–840 period. Climatic conditions at Dolores deteriorated during the last decades of the ninth century, the occupation in the northern part of the valley became increasingly mobile, and reliance on wild resources increased. People began leaving the valley, and the area was mostly abandoned by A.D. 910 or 920. The high levels of diversity during this time can tentatively be interpreted as indicating a return to the social conditions present before A.D. 840. That is, social units may have become increasingly atomized and may have once again expressed their differences stylistically.

The association of minimum diversity with a time of maximum population density (the A.D. 840–880 period) is also important for methodological reasons. Most ninth-century pottery was made by small-scale producers, possibly with one potter per household or at least one potter per site. High levels of diversity could be interpreted simply as a result of more potters making more pots. If this interpretation were correct, it would mean that the differences observed in the comparisons between the central Mesa Verde region and northern Black Mesa are simply a result of the differences in the quantity of production and not necessarily related to the role of design style or any kind of stylistic information. However, data from Dolores clearly indicate that this interpretation is not correct, since the lowest levels of diversity are associated with the period of greatest population density.

The analyses presented in this and the previous two chapters clearly indicate that patterns of stylistic variation were very different in the Kayenta and Mesa Verde regions during the ninth century. Furthermore, both inter- and intraregional analyses indicate that the differences in stylistic patterning parallel differences in social processes and thus suggest that style can be interpreted in terms of its roles in those social processes. The last chapter considers the implications of these results for understanding not only developments in the Southwest, but also the anthropological study of style.

9

Conclusions

This work was motivated by a desire to better understand why we humans devote so much time and energy to the elaboration of our material culture. Such a question presupposes that there is a reason behind the practice and that this reason goes beyond the human desire for beauty or individual artistic expression. The research presented here was based on the assumption that material culture is meaningfully constituted and that it plays a role in society and social relations. I have drawn on the concept of style—broadly defined as "a way of doing"—to explore material culture from this perspective. The research described in this report has considered style and patterns of stylistic variation in both social and cultural contexts in an attempt to understand stylistic differences in terms of the different contexts.

Specifically, the focus in this study has been on black-on-white painted pottery made during the ninth century A.D. in the northern Southwest. The style of interest was defined as "a way of decorating pottery with painted designs." The research involved comparisons of two areas that appear to have been quite different in terms of social organization and scale. An understanding of the kinds of roles style can play was used to make predictions regarding the roles of pottery design style in those areas. Observed patterns of stylistic variation were then interpreted from this perspective.

Summary: Pottery Design Style

The Ninth-Century Northern Southwest

The ninth century A.D., the latter part of the Pueblo I period, was a time of change and regional differentiation in the northern Southwest. In many areas, the earliest widespread evidence of year-round sedentism is dated to the ninth century. In some areas, fairly large, aggregated communities—the first villages—developed at this time. Associated with many of these large communities is what appears to be fairly elaborate community architecture, including oversize pit structures, plazas, and great kivas. In some instances, population density increased during the ninth century, and there is some evidence of subsistence intensification. Changes in pottery design style appear to have been associated with these cultural developments.

Painted pottery was made in the northern Southwest beginning by around A.D. 700. However, by the ninth century, both the quantity and elaboration of the painted pottery had increased substantially. New designs were developed; these new designs were applied to more kinds of vessels; and the designs covered larger areas of the vessels than they had before. The pots themselves were also more finely made, with whiter clay and slips and finer temper. In addition, pottery designs that were very similar across the northern Southwest in earlier times gave way to regional design traditions by the ninth century. These trends continued after the ninth century, as the quantity of painted pottery continued to increase and localized style zones developed.

These general observations suggest that pottery design style took on new and possibly increasingly important roles as settlement and social organization changed during the ninth century. In the next section, the role of style is considered more specifically in terms of developments in two parts of the northern Southwest.

Comparing the Kayenta and Mesa Verde Regions

Much of this research involved comparisons between the Kayenta and Mesa Verde regions, with a particular focus on northern Black Mesa in northeastern Arizona and the central Mesa Verde region (including the Dolores area) in southwestern Colorado. The two areas experienced very different occupational histories in terms of demography, architecture, exchange, and other factors (Chapter 4). However, analyses of pottery production, considering both pottery-making equipment and pottery composition, reveal no differences in the organization of production in the two regions (Chapter 6). In both areas, pottery-making equipment was found at almost all sites. Furthermore, the overall compositional heterogeneity of the pottery and the compositional differences between sites and areas suggest that pottery, including decorated white wares, was made at a small scale during the ninth century. It is likely that at least one member of most communities, if not most households, made pottery. Thus, differences in the pottery found in the two regions cannot be explained in terms of differences in the organization of production. Furthermore, the small scale of production suggests that people who used the pottery could have had some influence on, or control over, the pottery designs.

The distribution of pottery decoration is quite different in the Kayenta and Mesa Verde regions (Chapter 6). Although painted pottery is common in both areas, it is more abundant on northern Black Mesa. That is, assemblages from the Black Mesa sites have much larger proportions of painted pottery than do assemblages from the central Mesa Verde region. In both areas, bowls are commonly painted, and in the central Mesa Verde region, bowls account for a large majority of the painted pottery. On northern Black Mesa, jars as well as bowls are commonly painted, and although there are some differences between the sites, the proportion of painted jars and bowls is much more similar. This difference in vessel form is significant because bowls—used to prepare, serve, and eat food—would have been actively used in face-to-face social interactions, in contrast to jars, which were often used for storage.

Several levels of analysis indicate that patterns of design style variation are quite different in the two areas. Traditional typologies provide some baseline evidence. On northern Black Mesa and across the Kayenta area, most painted white ware dating to the ninth century can be classified as Kana-a Black-on-white, and researchers have long noted that the designs on Kana-a Black-on-white appear to be highly regular and are amenable to classification (e.g., Beals et al. 1945). In the Mesa Verde region, ninth-century white ware includes much more typological variability. In the central and western parts of the region, Piedra Black-on-white is the most abundant white ware, but earlier (Chapin Black-on-white) and later (Cortez Black-on-white) types also occasionally appear in ninth-century assemblages. In addition, in the western portion of the region, Piedra Black-on-white is rare, but another type, called White Mesa Black-on-white, is present. Typologies are at least in part a product of archaeologists' perceptions, and typologies do not describe design variation in much detail. Still, the typological descriptions strongly suggest that patterns of design variation were different in the two areas. Analyses conducted as part of this research were developed to better describe and understand these different patterns of variation.

Design structure was investigated by comparing designs on Kana-a Black-on-white in the Kayenta region and Piedra Black-on-white in the central and eastern Mesa Verde regions (Chapter 7). *Structure* is defined as a system of organization, and attributes of design structure include layout and symmetry, as well as the use of design forms in certain contexts or combinations. Designs on the two types are structured differently. However, the difference is not simply a matter of difference in content. Rather, the two pottery types evidence different kinds and degrees of organization. Specifically, whereas some structural "rules" apply to both types, Kana-a Black-on-white designs appear to be much more rigidly structured and rule-bound than do the Piedra Black-on-white designs. Within each type, no structural differences are apparent when vessels from ritual (primarily burial) and domestic contexts are compared. This suggests that vessels used in these ritual contexts were not distinguished from other vessels, at least in terms of design style.

Analyses of various design attributes on pottery from northern Black Mesa and the central Mesa Verde region also demonstrate major differences between the regions (Chapter 8). Again, the differences go beyond differences in content. Although many of the same design attributes are present on pottery from both areas, the attributes are used in different ways. Design style in the central Mesa Verde region is much more diverse than design style on northern Black Mesa. Furthermore, a greater degree of diversity is associated with community pit structures that may have housed large-scale activities at Dolores than is associated with sites that lack community pit structures. A high degree of design diversity is apparent in the Black Mesa assemblages only when fairly subtle aspects of design—such as the use of secondary elements—are considered.

These results indicate that pottery design style played different roles in the two areas. The emphasis on bowl designs (or the relative lack of jar designs) in the Mesa Verde pottery suggests that the designs were particularly important in face-to-face interactions and other active contexts. The greater degree of structural variation apparent in Piedra Black-on-white suggests that it might have conveyed different kinds of messages than did the more rule-bound Kana-a Black-on-white. A similar difference between the pottery designs from the two regions is suggested by the diversity of designs in the central Mesa Verde region in contrast to the homogeneity of designs on northern Black Mesa.

Sequences of Stylistic Variation

The analyses summarized above concern synchronic comparisons between two areas and regions. The stylistic differences suggest that style played different roles in the two areas. A broader perspective is possible if change over time—in both patterns of design style variation and other cultural processes—is considered, using information obtained from the analyses presented here in combination with other sources that deal with other areas and later time periods.

Pottery associated with the ninth-century occupation of northern Black Mesa exhibits relatively little design diversity. However, designs on pottery from post–A.D. 1000 occupations of northern Black Mesa appear to be very different. Plog (1990b) reports that designs on the later types (Black Mesa and Sosi black-on-white) are more diverse and less consistently organized than are those on Kana-a Black-on-white (design attributes on the later types showed less covariation). Furthermore, my earlier work (Hegmon 1986), using an analytical method similar to that used in Chapter 8, demonstrates that designs on black-on-white pottery from Black Mesa were most diverse during the period from A.D. 1050 to 1075, when population was at its peak (Hegmon 1986; see also Hantman 1983:260; Plog 1986:Chapter 10).

At Dolores, in the central Mesa Verde region, the degree of design diversity changed over the course of the ninth century. Diversity is greatest in assemblages dating to the first four decades, a time when many sites were relatively small and dispersed, although at least one aggregated site with a great kiva was present. The lowest levels of diversity are noted for assemblages dating to the A.D. 840–880 period, when population density and aggregation were greatest and there was some evidence of increased organizational scale. Diversity increases again to a moderate level in assemblages dating to the last part of the century, when climatic conditions worsened and some aggregated settlements were replaced by more mobile and ephemeral occupations.

The occupation of Dolores ended by A.D. 910 or 920, and design style diversity increased in the A.D. 880–920 period, just before abandonment. There is even some evidence that a greater degree of diversity was associated with an increase in settlement mobility during the Grass Mesa subphase. In the Kayenta area, Black Mesa was abandoned by A.D. 1150, but after reaching a maximum in the A.D. 1050–1075 period, design style diversity decreased just before abandonment.

This comparison of the ninth- through twelfth-century occupational history of northern Black Mesa with the ninth-century occupational history of the Dolores area suggests that apparently similar processes are associated with very different patterns of design style diversity. An increase in population is associated with an increase in diversity in one area (Black Mesa) and a decrease in diversity in the other (Dolores). The period of highest population density at Dolores (the mid-ninth-century Periman subphase) is characterized by aggregated settlements with large-scale ritual facilities. No such aggregation is seen on Black Mesa, and the only known ritual facilities are regular-size pit structures and kivas. Diversity increases just before abandonment at Dolores, but not at Black Mesa. These contrasting sequences further support the argument that pottery designs played different roles in the different regions of the northern Southwest.

The Role of Style

Style encompasses a broad range of meanings and can convey a variety of information (Chapter 2). It can be used to reinforce basic cultural values or reproduce important structural relations. In conveying this sort of information, style may contribute to group solidarity. At the same time, style may be used to make and mark social distinctions, both at individual and group levels. Style clearly can have many meanings, and it must be interpreted at multiple levels.

The production and use of style are complex, but not random, processes. Style is not simply a characteristic of a time and place—it is a means of expression and communication used by the people who lived at that time and place. Given sufficient understanding of the social and cultural situation at a given time and place, it should be possible to predict the role of style in that context. However, although the roles filled by style may be predictable, the specific manifestations of style (that is, particular designs on certain kinds of material culture) are much more difficult to predict. Furthermore, many stylistic media are perishable and will not survive in the archaeological record. So, although the role of style should be predictable, in many cases it may not be possible to use archaeological data to systematically evaluate predictions regarding style. Instead, the predictions can be used as a framework for interpreting observed distributions of style and patterns of stylistic variation.

In this study, differences in the occupational histories of northern Black Mesa and the central Mesa Verde region led to the expectation that style played different roles in these two areas during the ninth century. Differences in the apparent structural "rules" and levels of design diversity in pottery were interpreted in light of those expectations and predictions. Specifically, more stylistic expression of differences was expected in the central Mesa Verde region, and the high levels of diversity, particularly at sites with evidence of large-scale gatherings, are viewed as evidence of that stylistic expression. In contrast, the more homogeneous style observed on Black Mesa is understood as a manifestation of the expression of social similarity and perhaps solidarity.

More detailed interpretations consider the use of style to express group or individual identity at multiple levels. During the Pueblo I period, pottery styles appear to have distinguished regions at a broad level. Within the Mesa Verde region, the distribution of types (for example, White Mesa Black-on-white in southeastern Utah and Piedra Black-on-white in southwestern Colorado) suggests that there were some large-scale intraregional differences. At the level of communities within an area or region, no stylistic differences are evident either on northern Black Mesa or in the central Mesa Verde region.

These broad style zones with limited intercommunity differences could have facilitated some sort of extensive cooperation. Weissner (1983) argues that groups that share or pool risk are often delineated stylistically. Although it is unlikely that ninth-century populations pooled resources at the scale of style zones, there is some evidence of distribution across areas that shared the same basic styles (for example, Black Mesa and the Apache-Sitgreaves area [Hantman and Plog 1982]). Furthermore, the high degree of settlement mobility on Black Mesa and the large-scale population movements in southwestern Colorado (Schlanger 1988) suggest that extensive social networks would have been an important means of facilitating the movement of people as a risk-reduction strategy.

At an even smaller scale, at the level of social units within spatially distinct communities, architectural evidence suggests that small social units were clearly defined in the central Mesa Verde region, but not on northern Black Mesa. I argue that the high level of design style diversity observed in pottery from the central Mesa Verde region may be a result of the stylistic definition of those small-scale units. Such units could have included both family/household groups and organizations such as sodalities, age-grades, and religious societies that crosscut kinship and residence lines. Such units are defined or distinguished stylistically in societies known ethnographically (e.g., Graves 1981, 1985; Larick 1985). Consideration of horticultural societies in Chapter 3 strongly suggested that limitations on the distribution of resources are an essential component of a horticultural mode of production, especially when subsistence practices are intensified. Thus, the stylistic definition of small-scale units may be an important factor in organizing the distribution of produce and other resources. The increase in stylistic diversity associated with post–A.D. 1000 occupations of Black Mesa, particularly during the time when population density was greatest, may indicate that the expression of social group differences became more important at this time.

The observation that design style diversity at Dolores was lowest during the period (A.D. 840–880) when population was greatest, when many communities were aggregated, and when subsistence strategies intensified is somewhat problematic to this argument. It may be that the mid-century developments reflected an increase in the scale of organization, perhaps as a response to competition for good land and resources. Thus, the decrease in stylistic diversity could be related to a decrease in horizontal differentiation.

The overall homogeneity of design style on northern Black Mesa suggests that social differences were less prevalent or at least were not emphasized in material culture. However, the high levels of diversity apparent in relatively subtle aspects of design in the Black Mesa assemblages indicate that style was not expressing social unity at all levels. Instead, the subtle diversity suggests that style may have been used as a means of expressing individual identities or differences, while at the same time reinforcing overall social unity.

Conclusions: Understanding Style

At a number of points in this work, I have argued for interpretations based on multiple levels of meaning or analysis. Very often the answer to a theoretical or methodological debate is "all of the above." I believe that much of the significance of this work derives from syntheses and compromises of various levels of analysis. To conclude this work and summarize its methodological and theoretical implications, I focus on these compromises.

This research included analyses of style at various levels, from the presence and state of particular attributes (for example, triangles or rectangles and the width of lines) on sherds to aspects of overall design structure (for example, layout and symmetry) on whole vessels. Thus, I follow the fairly recent trend of considering several kinds of stylistic variation and avoid debate about which one analytical technique is best (see summary in Hegmon 1992a). I gain what information I can from the material available, including sherds from carefully controlled, well-dated contexts and whole vessels with less-than-ideal provenience information.

The information derived from the analysis of particular forms both overlaps and complements that derived from the analysis of design structure. Both sets of analyses demonstrate that designs in the Mesa Verde region are much more variable than those in the Kayenta region. The structural information provides detail on the nature of that variability, specifically, differences in the application of design rules. The attribute analysis provides detail on smaller-scale differences over time and space and demonstrates the feasibility of using attribute-based analyses in fine-scale chronological studies.

Not only can style be analyzed at various levels, it can also convey various levels of meaning, from the aesthetic to the iconographic. Furthermore, style plays various roles in social relations and is used to express concepts ranging from individual identity to group solidarity. Ethnographic cases can be found to demonstrate these various meanings and roles. The problem is how to interpret them archaeologically.

I suggest that the answer to this problem of interpretation involves consideration of both specific context and general processes. That is, the particular meaning of a specific attribute of style often cannot be determined. However, the general range of meanings conveyed by a set of attributes can be interpreted by considering the dimensions of variation of those attributes and the contexts in which that variation is observed.

To illustrate, I return to the consideration of design style diversity in ninth-century black-on-white pottery. Black Mesa pottery exhibits relatively low levels of diversity in comparison with pottery from the central Mesa Verde region. Assemblages from the A.D. 840–880 period at Dolores also show relatively little diversity when compared with Dolores assemblages from the preceding and subsequent periods. Design structure and social context are used to interpret these low levels of diversity in very different ways.

The Black Mesa designs are argued to have been important in maintaining an extensive social network. An extensive occupation is suggested by the settlement pattern, which was characterized by low population density and small sites dispersed across the landscape. The designs appear to have been part of a relatively highly structured tradition (Kana-a Black-on-white). The lack of diversity in both content and structure in the Black Mesa pottery designs would have limited the quantity of information that could have been conveyed, but the redundancy would have emphasized whatever information was conveyed.

In contrast, I argue that the relatively low diversity observed in the mid-century assemblages at Dolores is related to a decrease in horizontal differentiation. The designs were part of a relatively flexible design tradition (Piedra Black-on-white) that could have conveyed a wide variety of information. High levels of stylistic diversity in the preceding and subsequent periods suggest that style could have conveyed a variety of information that might have emphasized small-scale social differences. In the A.D. 840–880 period, those differences might have been deemphasized and replaced by a larger scale of organization.

In both cases, low levels of stylistic diversity are argued to have been associated with a relative lack of social differentiation. However, on Black Mesa, the homogeneity was associated with what appeared to be an extensive social network. At Dolores, the homogeneity was associated with intensive social relations and what appeared to be an increase in organizational scale. Thus, homogeneous pottery design style is not necessarily associated with a particular kind of social organization and does not necessarily convey one particular kind of message. Rather, the style can be interpreted through a combination of detailed analysis of various dimensions of variation and consideration of the social and cultural context. Highly standardized design styles prevalent later in the Southwest (such as Dogoszhi Black-on-white and Mesa Verde Black-on-white) can perhaps be understood in this way. This kind of perspective can help us to understand both the phenomenon of style and material culture elaboration and the processes of prehistory.

References

Abel, L. J.
  1955   *Pottery Types of the Southwest: Wares 5A, 10A, 10B, 12A, San Juan Red Ware, Mesa Verde Gray, and White Ware, San Juan White Ware.* Ceramic Series, no. 3B. Museum of Northern Arizona, Flagstaff.

Abramson, N.
  1963   *Information Theory and Coding.* McGraw-Hill, New York.

Adams, E. C. (compiler)
  1989   The Homol'ovi Research Program: Investigations Into the Prehistory of the Middle Colorado River Valley. *Kiva* 54(3):173–329.

Adams, E. C., and K. A. Hays
  1991   *Homol'ovi II: Archaeology of an Ancestral Hopi Village, Arizona.* Anthropological Papers, no. 55. University of Arizona Press, Tucson.

Adams, M. J.
  1973   Structural Aspects of a Village Art. *American Anthropologist* 75:265–279.

Adler, M. A.
  1989a   Agrarian Strategies and the Development of Prehistoric Aggregated Settlements on the Northern Colorado Plateau. Paper presented at the 88th Annual Meeting of the American Anthropological Association, Washington, D.C.
  1989b   Ritual Facilities and Social Integration in Nonranked Societies. In *The Architecture of Social Integration in Prehistoric Pueblos,* edited by W. D. Lipe and M. Hegmon, pp. 35–52. Occasional Papers, no. 1. Crow Canyon Archaeological Center, Cortez, Colorado.
  1990   *Communities of Soil and Stone: An Archaeological Investigation of Population Aggregation Among the Mesa Verde Region Anasazi, A.D. 900–1300.* Ph.D. dissertation, University of Michigan. University Microfilms, Ann Arbor.

Adler, M. A., and M. Metcalf
  1991   *Draft Report on Archaeological Survey of Lower East Rock and Sand Canyons, Montezuma County, Colorado.* Crow Canyon Archaeological Center, Cortez, Colorado. Report submitted to the Bureau of Land Management, San Juan Resource Area Office, Durango, Colorado.

Adler, M. A., and R. H. Wilshusen
  1990   Large-Scale Integrative Facilities in Tribal Societies: Cross-Cultural and Southwestern US Examples. *World Archaeology* 22:133–145.

Ahlstrom, R. V. N.
  1985   *The Interpretation of Archaeological Tree-Ring Dates.* Unpublished Ph.D. dissertation, Department of Anthropology, University of Arizona, Tucson.

Ambler, J. R.
  1983   Kayenta Craft Specialization and Social Differentiation. In *Proceedings of the Anasazi Symposium, 1981,* edited by J. E. Smith, pp. 75–82. Mesa Verde Museum Association, Mesa Verde National Park, Colorado.
  1987   *AZ D-11-9, a Locus for Pueblo II Grimy Activities on Central Black Mesa, Northeastern Arizona.* Archaeological Series, no. 2. Northern Arizona University, Flagstaff.

Amsden, C. A.
  1936   *An Analysis of Hohokam Pottery Design.* Medallion Papers, no. 23. Gila Pueblo, Globe, Arizona.

Anderson, J. K.
  1978   D:11:338. In *Excavation on Black Mesa, 1977: A Preliminary Report,* edited by A. L. Klesert, pp. 93–98. Center for Archaeological Investigations Research Paper, no. 1. Southern Illinois University, Carbondale.

Appadurai, A. (editor)
  1986   *The Social Life of Things.* Cambridge University Press, Cambridge.

Arnold, D. E.
  1983   Design Structure and Community Organization in Quinua, Peru. In *Structure and Cognition in Art,* edited by D. K. Washburn, pp. 56–73. Cambridge University Press, Cambridge.
  1985   *Ceramic Theory and Cultural Process.* Cambridge University Press, Cambridge.

Bannister, B., J. S. Dean, and W. J. Robinson
  1969   *Tree-Ring Dates from Utah S-W: Southern Utah Area.* Laboratory of Tree-Ring Research, University of Arizona, Tucson.

Bateson, G.
  1972   *Steps to an Ecology of Mind.* Ballantine, New York.

Beals, R. L., G. W. Brainerd, and W. Smith
  1945   *Archaeological Studies in Northeast Arizona: A Report on the Archaeological Work of the Rainbow Bridge–Monument Valley Expedition.* Publications in American Archaeology and Ethnology, vol. 44, no. 1. University of California, Berkeley.

Beaumont, E. C., and G. H. Dixon
  1965   *Geology of the Kayenta and Chilchinbito Quad-*

rangles, Navajo County, Arizona. Bulletin, no. 1202-A. Geological Survey, Washington, D.C.

Bender, B.
1975   Emergent Tribal Formations in the American Midcontinent. *American Antiquity* 50:52–62.
1978   Gatherer-Hunter to Farmer: A Social Perspective. *World Archaeology* 10:204–222.
1990   The Dynamics of Nonhierarchical Societies. In *The Evolution of Political Systems: Sociopolitics in Small-Scale Sedentary Societies,* edited by S. Upham, pp. 247–263. Cambridge University Press, Cambridge.

Berreman, G. D.
1978   Scale and Social Relations. *Current Anthropology* 19:225–245.

Binford, L. R.
1965   Archaeological Systematics and the Study of Culture Process. *American Antiquity* 31:203–210.
1972   Archaeology as Anthropology. In *An Archaeological Perspective,* authored by L. R. Binford, pp. 20–32. Reprinted. Seminar Press, New York. Originally published 1962, *American Antiquity* 28:217–225.
1980   Willow Smoke and Dogs' Tails: Hunter-Gatherer Settlement Systems and Archaeological Site Formation. *American Antiquity* 45:4–20.
1989a   *Debating Archaeology.* Academic Press, New York.
1989b   Styles of Style. *Journal of Anthropological Archaeology* 8:51–67.

Binford, L. R., and S. R. Binford
1966   A Preliminary Analysis of Functional Variability in the Mousterian of Levallois Facies. In Recent Studies in Paleoanthropology, edited by J. D. Clarke and F. C. Howell, pp. 238–295. *American Anthropologist* 68(2), part 2.

Bishop, R. L., V. Canouts, S. P. DeAtley, A. Qöyawayma, and C. W. Aikins
1988   The Formation of Ceramic Analytical Groups: Hopi Pottery Production and Exchange, A.D. 1300–1600. *Journal of Field Archaeology* 15:317–337.

Blinman, E.
1986a   Additive Technologies Group Final Report. In *Dolores Archaeological Program: Final Synthetic Report,* compiled by D. A. Breternitz, C. K. Robinson, and G. T. Gross, pp. 53–101. Bureau of Reclamation, Engineering and Research Center, Denver.
1986b   Exchange and Interaction in the Dolores Area. In *Dolores Archaeological Program: Final Synthetic Report,* compiled by D. A. Breternitz, C. K. Robinson, and G. T. Gross, pp. 663–701. Bureau of Reclamation, Engineering and Research Center, Denver.
1986c   Technology: Ceramic Containers. In *Dolores*

Archaeological Program: Final Synthetic Report, compiled by D. A. Breternitz, C. K. Robinson, and G. T. Gross, pp. 595–609. Bureau of Reclamation, Engineering and Research Center, Denver.
1987   Letter Report: Interim Results, Sand Canyon and Green Lizard Ceramic Study. Ms. on file, Crow Canyon Archaeological Center, Cortez, Colorado.
1988a   Ceramic Vessels and Vessel Assemblages in Dolores Archaeological Program Collections. In *Dolores Archaeological Program: Supporting Studies: Additive and Reductive Technologies,* compiled by E. Blinman, C. J. Phagan, and R. H. Wilshusen, pp. 449–482. Bureau of Reclamation, Engineering and Research Center, Denver.
1988b   *The Interpretation of Ceramic Variability: A Case Study from the Dolores Anasazi.* Unpublished Ph.D. dissertation, Department of Anthropology, Washington State University, Pullman.
1988c   Justification and Procedures for Ceramic Dating. In *Dolores Archaeological Program: Supporting Studies: Additive and Reductive Technologies,* compiled by E. Blinman, C. J. Phagan, and R. H. Wilshusen, pp. 501–544. Bureau of Reclamation, Engineering and Research Center, Denver.
1989   Potluck in the Protokiva: Ceramics and Ceremonialism in Pueblo I Villages. In *The Architecture of Social Integration in Prehistoric Pueblos,* edited by W. D. Lipe and M. Hegmon, pp. 113–124. Occasional Papers, no. 1. Crow Canyon Archaeological Center, Cortez, Colorado.

Blinman, E., and C. D. Wilson
1986   Ceramic Data and Interpretations: The Middle Canyon Sites. In *Dolores Archaeological Program: Anasazi Communities at Dolores: Middle Canyon Area,* compiled by A. E. Kane and C. K. Robinson, pp. 1088–1119. Bureau of Reclamation, Engineering and Research Center, Denver.
1988a   Ceramic Data and Interpretations. In *Dolores Archaeological Program: Anasazi Communities at Dolores: Grass Mesa Village,* compiled by W. D. Lipe, J. N. Morris, and T. A. Kohler, pp. 989–1024. Bureau of Reclamation, Engineering and Research Center, Denver.
1988b   Ceramic Data and Interpretations: The McPhee Community Cluster. In *Dolores Archaeological Program: Anasazi Communities at Dolores: McPhee Village,* compiled by A. E. Kane and C. K. Robinson, pp. 1294–1341. Bureau of Reclamation, Engineering and Research Center, Denver.
1992   Ceramic Production and Exchange in the Northern San Juan Region. In *Ceramic Production and Distribution: An Integrated Approach,* edited by

G. J. Bey III and C. A. Pool, pp. 155–173. Westview Press, Boulder, Colorado.

Blinman, E., C. D. Wilson, R. M. R. Waterworth, M. P. Errickson, and L. P. Hart
1984   *Additive Technologies Group Laboratory Manual.* Dolores Archaeological Program Technical Reports, DAP-149. Report submitted to the Bureau of Reclamation, Upper Colorado Region, Salt Lake City.

Boas, F.
1955   *Primitive Art.* Reprinted. Dover Publications, New York. Originally published 1927, Harvard University Press, Cambridge.

Bogatyrev, P.
1936   Costume as Sign (The Functional and Structural Concept in Ethnography). In *Semiotics of Art,* edited by L. Matejka and I. R. Titunik, pp. 13–19. Translated by Y. Lockwood. Massachusetts Institute of Technology Press, Cambridge.

Bogucki, P.
1988   *Forest Farmers and Stockherders: Early Agriculture and its Consequences in North-Central Europe.* Cambridge University Press, Cambridge.

Bourdieu, P.
1973   The Berber House. In *Rules and Meaning,* edited by M. Douglas, pp. 98–110. Penguin, Middlesex, England.
1977   *Outline of a Theory of Practice.* Translated by R. Nice. Cambridge University Press, Cambridge.

Boyd, R., and P. J. Richerson
1985   *Culture and the Evolutionary Process.* University of Chicago Press, Chicago.
1987   The Evolution of Ethnic Markers. *Cultural Anthropology* 2:65–79.

Bradley, B. A.
1992   Excavations at Sand Canyon Pueblo. In *The Sand Canyon Archaeological Project: A Progress Report,* edited by W. D. Lipe, pp. 79–97. Occasional Papers, no. 2. Crow Canyon Archaeological Center, Cortez, Colorado.

Brainerd, G. W.
1942   Symmetry in Primitive Conventional Design. *American Antiquity* 8:164–166.
1951   The Place of Chronological Ordering in Archaeological Analysis. *American Antiquity* 16:301–313.

Braithwaite, M.
1982   Decoration as Ritual Symbol: A Theoretical Proposal and an Ethnographic Study in Southern Sudan. In *Symbolic and Structural Archaeology,* edited by I. Hodder, pp. 80–88. Cambridge University Press, Cambridge.

Brandt, S. A., and J. D. Clark (editors)
1984   *From Hunters to Farmers: The Causes and Consequences of Food Production in Africa.* University of California Press, Berkeley.

Braun, D. P.
1980   Experimental Interpretation of Ceramic Vessel Use on the Basis of Rim and Neck Formal Attributes. In *The Navajo Project,* authored by D. C. Fiero, R. W. Munson, M. T. McClain, S. M. Wilson, and A. H. Zier, pp. 171–231. Research Paper, no. 11. Museum of Northern Arizona, Flagstaff.
1985   Ceramic Decorative Diversity and Illinois Woodland Regional Integration. In *Decoding Prehistoric Ceramics,* edited by B. A. Nelson, pp. 129–153. Southern Illinois University Press, Carbondale.
1991a   Are There Cross-Cultural Regularities in Tribal Social Practices? In *Between Bands and States,* edited by S. A. Gregg, pp. 423–444. Center for Archaeological Investigations Occasional Paper, no. 9. Southern Illinois University, Carbondale.
1991b   Why Decorate a Pot? Midwestern Household Pottery, 200 B.C.–A.D. 600. *Journal of Anthropological Archaeology* 10:360–397.
1995   Style, Selection, and Historicity. In *Style, Society, and Person,* edited by C. Carr and J. Neitzel, pp. 123–141. Plenum Press, New York.

Braun, D. P., and S. Plog
1982   Evolution of "Tribal" Social Networks: Theory and Prehistoric North American Evidence. *American Antiquity* 47:504–525.

Breternitz, D. A., C. K. Robinson, and G. T. Gross (compilers)
1986   *Dolores Archaeological Program: Final Synthetic Report.* Bureau of Reclamation, Engineering and Research Center, Denver.

Breternitz, D. A., A. H. Rohn, Jr., and E. A. Morris (compilers)
1974   *Prehistoric Ceramics of the Mesa Verde Region.* 2nd ed. Ceramic Series, no. 5. Museum of Northern Arizona, Flagstaff.

Brew, J. O.
1946   *Archaeology of Alkali Ridge, Southeastern Utah.* Papers of the Peabody Museum of American Archaeology and Ethnology, vol. 21. Harvard University, Cambridge.

Brisbin, J. M.
1986   Excavations at Windy Wheat Hamlet (Site 5MT4644), a Pueblo I Habitation. In *Dolores Archaeological Program: Anasazi Communities at Dolores: Early Anasazi Sites in the Sagehen Flats Area,* compiled by A. E. Kane and G. T. Gross, pp. 638–864.

Bureau of Reclamation, Engineering and Research Center, Denver.

1988   Excavations at Pueblo de Las Golondrinas (Site 5MT5107), a Multiple-Occupation Pueblo I Site. In *Dolores Archaeological Program: Anasazi Communities at Dolores: McPhee Village,* compiled by A. E. Kane and C. K. Robinson, pp. 790–905. Bureau of Reclamation, Engineering and Research Center, Denver.

Bromfield, C. S.

1967   *Geology of the Mount Wilson Quadrangle, Western San Juan Mountains, Colorado.* Bulletin, no. 1227. Geological Survey, Washington, D.C.

Bronitsky, G.

1986   The Use of Materials Science Techniques in the Study of Pottery Construction and Use. In *Advances in Archaeological Method and Theory,* vol. 9, edited by M. B. Schiffer, pp. 209–276. Academic Press, New York.

Bullard, W. R., Jr.

1962   *The Cerro Colorado Site and Pithouse Architecture in the Southwestern United States Prior to A.D. 900.* Papers of the Peabody Museum of Archaeology and Ethnology, vol. 44, no. 2. Harvard University, Cambridge.

Bunzel, R.

1972   *The Pueblo Potter: A Study of Creative Imagination in Primitive Art.* Reprinted. Dover Publications, New York. Originally published 1929, Contributions to Anthropology, no. 8, Columbia University, New York.

Burns, B. T.

1983   *Simulated Anasazi Storage Behavior Using Crop Yields Reconstructed from Tree Rings: A.D. 652–1968.* Ph.D. dissertation, University of Arizona. University Microfilms, Ann Arbor.

Burridge, K. O. L.

1975   The Melanesian Manager. In *Studies in Social Anthropology: Essays in Memory of E. E. Evans-Pritchard by His Former Oxford Colleagues,* edited by J. H. M. Beattie and R. G. Lienhardt, pp. 86–104. Claredon Press, Oxford.

Campbell, J.

1982   *Grammatical Man.* Simon and Schuster, New York.

Carlson, R. L.

1970   *White Mountain Redware: A Pottery Tradition of East-Central Arizona and Western New Mexico.* Anthropological Papers, no. 19. University of Arizona, Tucson.

Carneiro, R. L.

1967   On the Relationship Between Size of Popula-

tion and Complexity of Social Organization. *Southwestern Journal of Anthropology* 23:234–243.

Carr, C.

1990   Advances in Ceramic Radiography and Analysis: Applications and Potentials. *Journal of Archaeological Science* 17:13–34.

Cashdan, E. A.

1985   Coping with Risk: Reciprocity Among the Basarwa of Northern Botswana. *Man* 20:454–474.

Catlin, M.

1986   Intersite Diversity and the Role of Limited-Activity Sites in Subsistence-Settlement Systems on Black Mesa. In *Spatial Organization and Exchange: Archaeological Survey on Northern Black Mesa,* edited by S. Plog, pp. 169–186. Southern Illinois University Press, Carbondale.

Chapman, R.

1981   The Emergence of Formal Disposal Areas and the "Problem" of Megalithic Tombs in Prehistoric Europe. In *The Archaeology of Death,* edited by R. Chapman, I. Kinnes, and K. Randsborg, pp. 71–81. Cambridge University Press, Cambridge.

Chase, P. G.

1991   Symbols and Paleolithic Artifacts: Style, Standardization, and the Imposition of Arbitrary Form. *Journal of Anthropological Archaeology* 10:193–214.

Christenson, A. L., and W. J. Parry (editors)

1985   *Excavations on Black Mesa, 1983: A Descriptive Report.* Center for Archaeological Investigations Research Paper, no. 46. Southern Illinois University, Carbondale.

Clemen, R. T.

1976   Aspects of Prehistoric Social Organization on Black Mesa. In *Papers on the Archaeology of Black Mesa, Arizona,* edited by G. J. Gumerman and R. C. Euler, pp. 113–135. Southern Illinois University Press, Carbondale.

Cohen, M. N.

1989   *Health and the Rise of Civilization.* Yale University Press, New Haven.

Colton, H. S.

1939   *Prehistoric Culture Units and Their Relationships in Northern Arizona.* Bulletin, no. 17. Museum of Northern Arizona, Flagstaff.

1953   *Potsherds: An Introduction to the Study of Prehistoric Southwestern Ceramics and Their Use in Historic Reconstruction.* Bulletin, no. 25. Museum of Northern Arizona, Flagstaff.

Colton, H. S., and L. L. Hargrave

1937   *Handbook of Northern Arizona Pottery Wares.*

Bulletin, no. 11. Museum of Northern Arizona, Flagstaff.

Conkey, M. W.

1980 The Identification of Prehistoric Hunter-Gatherer Aggregation Sites: The Case of Altamira. *Current Anthropology* 21:609–630.

1982 Boundedness in Art and Society. In *Symbolic and Structural Archaeology,* edited by I. Hodder, pp. 115–128. Cambridge University Press, Cambridge.

1989 The Use of Diversity in Stylistic Analysis. In *Quantifying Diversity in Archaeology,* edited by R. D. Leonard and G. T. Jones, pp. 118–129. Cambridge University Press, Cambridge.

1990 Experimenting with Style in Archaeology: Some Historical and Theoretical Issues. In *Uses of Style in Archaeology,* edited by M. W. Conkey and C. A. Hastorf, pp. 5–17. Cambridge University Press, Cambridge.

Conkey, M. W., and C. A. Hastorf (editors)

1990 *Uses of Style in Archaeology.* Cambridge University Press, Cambridge.

Connelly, J. C.

1979 Hopi Social Organization. In *Southwest,* edited by A. Ortiz, pp. 539–553. Handbook of North American Indians, vol. 9. Smithsonian Institution, Washington, D.C.

Cordell, L. S., and G. J. Gumerman (editors)

1989 *Dynamics of Southwest Prehistory.* Smithsonian Institution Press, Washington, D.C.

Cordell, L. S., and F. Plog

1979 Escaping the Confines of Normative Thought: A Reevaluation of Puebloan Prehistory. *American Antiquity* 44:405–429.

Costin, C. L.

1991 Craft Specialization: Issues in Defining, Documenting, and Explaining the Organization of Production. In *Archaeological Method and Theory,* vol. 3, edited by M. B. Schiffer, pp. 1–56. University of Arizona Press, Tucson.

Cowgill, G. L.

1990 Why Pearson's *r* is Not a Good Similarity Coefficient for Comparing Collections. *American Antiquity* 55:512–521.

Cronin, C.

1962 An Analysis of Pottery Design Elements, Indicating Possible Relationships Between Three Decorated Types. In *Chapters in the Prehistory of Eastern Arizona, I,* authored by P. S. Martin, J. B. Rinaldo, W. A. Longacre, C. Cronin, L. G. Freeman, Jr., and J. Schoenwetter, pp. 105–114. Fieldiana: Anthropology, vol. 53. Chicago Natural History Museum, Chicago.

Crotty, H. K.

1983 *Honoring the Dead: Anasazi Ceramics from the Rainbow Bridge–Monument Valley Expedition.* University of California, Los Angeles.

Crown, P. L.

1981 *Variability in Ceramic Manufacture at the Chodistaas Site, East-Central Arizona.* Ph.D. dissertation, University of Arizona. University Microfilms, Ann Arbor.

1990 Converging Traditions: Salado Polychrome Ceramics in Southwestern Prehistory. Paper presented at the 55th Annual Meeting of the Society for American Archaeology, Las Vegas.

Cushing, F. H.

1974 *Zuni Breadstuff.* Indian Notes and Monographs, no. 8. Reprinted. Museum of the American Indian, Heye Foundation, New York. Originally published 1920, Museum of the American Indian, New York.

Daifuku, H.

1961 *Jeddito 264: A Report on the Excavation of a Basketmaker III–Pueblo I Site in Northeastern Arizona with a Review of Some Current Theories in Southwestern Archaeology.* Papers of the Peabody Museum of American Archaeology and Ethnology, vol. 33, no. 1. Harvard University, Cambridge.

Davenport, W.

1959 Nonunilinear Descent and Descent Groups. *American Anthropologist* 61:557–572.

David, N., J. Sterner, and K. Gavua

1988 Why Pots Are Decorated. *Current Anthropology* 29:365–389.

Davis, W. A.

1985 *Anasazi Subsistence and Settlement on White Mesa, San Juan County, Utah.* University Press of America, Lanham, Maryland.

Dean, J. S.

1970 Aspects of Tsegi Phase Social Organization: A Trial Reconstruction. In *Reconstructing Prehistoric Pueblo Societies,* edited by W. A. Longacre, pp. 140–174. University of New Mexico Press, Albuquerque.

1982 Dendroclimatic Variability on Black Mesa, A.D. 385 to 1970. Paper presented at the 47th Annual Meeting of the Society for American Archaeology, Minneapolis.

1988 Dendrochronology and Paleoenvironmental Reconstruction on the Colorado Plateaus. In *The Anasazi in a Changing Environment,* edited by G. J. Gumerman, pp. 119–167. Cambridge University Press, Cambridge.

Dean, J. S., R. C. Euler, G. J. Gumerman, F. Plog, R. H. Hevly, and T. N. V. Karlstrom
    1985   Human Behavior, Demography, and Paleoenvironment on the Colorado Plateaus. *American Antiquity* 50:537–554.

Dean, J. S., A. J. Lindsay, Jr., and W. J. Robinson
    1978   Prehistoric Settlement in Long House Valley, Northeastern Arizona. In *Investigations of the Southwestern Anthropological Research Group,* edited by R. C. Euler and G. J. Gumerman, pp. 25–44. Museum of Northern Arizona, Flagstaff.

DeBoer, W. R.
    1990   Interaction, Imitation, and Communication as Expressed in Style: The Ucayali Experience. In *Uses of Style in Archaeology,* edited by M. W. Conkey and C. A. Hastorf, pp. 82–104. Cambridge University Press, Cambridge.
    1991   The Decorative Burden: Design, Medium and Change. In *Ceramic Ethnoarchaeology,* edited by W. A. Longacre, pp. 144–161. University of Arizona Press, Tucson.

DeBoer, W. R., and J. A. Moore
    1982   The Measurement and Meaning of Stylistic Diversity. *Nawpa Pacha* 20:147–162.

DeCorse, C. R.
    1989   Material Aspects of Limba, Yalunka and Kuranko Ethnicity: Archaeological Research in Northeastern Sierra Leone. In *Archaeological Approaches to Cultural Identity,* edited by S. J. Shennan, pp. 125–140. Unwin Hyman, London.

Deetz, J.
    1965   *The Dynamics of Stylistic Change in Arikara Ceramics.* Illinois Studies in Anthropology, no. 4. University of Illinois Press, Urbana.

Deutchman, H. L.
    1980   Chemical Evidence of Ceramic Exchange on Black Mesa. In *Models and Methods in Regional Exchange,* edited by R. E. Fry, pp. 119–133. SAA Papers, no. 1. Society for American Archaeology, Washington, D.C.

Dietler, M., and I. Herbich
    1989   Tich Matek: The Technology of Luo Pottery Production and the Definition of Ceramic Style. *World Archaeology* 21:148–164.

Dittert, A. E., Jr., F. W. Eddy, and B. L. Dickey
    1963   Evidences of Early Ceramic Phases in the Navajo Reservoir District. *El Palacio* 70(1–2):5–12.

Dittert, A. E., Jr., and F. Plog
    1987   *Generations in Clay: Pueblo Pottery in the American Southwest.* Northland Press, Flagstaff.

Dondis, D. A.
    1973   *A Primer of Visual Literacy.* Massachusetts Institute of Technology Press, Cambridge.

Doran, J. E., and F. R. Hodson
    1975   *Mathematics and Computers in Archaeology.* Harvard University Press, Cambridge.

Douglas, M., and B. Isherwood
    1979   *The World of Goods.* Basic Books, New York.

Douglass, A. A., and O. Lindauer
    1988   Hierarchical and Nonhierarchical Approaches to Ceramic Design Analysis: A Response to Jernigan. *American Antiquity* 53:620–626.

Doyel, D. E.
    1991   Hohokam Exchange and Interaction. In *Chaco and Hohokam: Prehistoric Regional Systems in the American Southwest,* edited by P. L. Crown and W. J. Judge, pp. 225–252. School of American Research Press, Santa Fe.

Drennan, R. D.
    1976   Religion and Social Evolution in Formative Mesoamerica. In *The Early Mesoamerican Village,* edited by K. V. Flannery, pp. 345–368. Academic Press, New York.
    1983   Ritual and Ceremonial Development at the Early Village Level. In *The Cloud People: Divergent Evolution of the Zapotec and Mixtec Civilizations,* edited by K. V. Flannery and J. Marcus, pp. 46–50. Academic Press, New York.
    1987   Regional Demography in Chiefdoms. In *Archaeological Reconstructions and Chiefdoms in the Americas,* edited by R. D. Drennan and C. A. Uribe, pp. 307–324. University Press of America, New York.

Dunnell, R. C.
    1978   Style and Function: A Fundamental Dichotomy. *American Antiquity* 43:192–202.

Durkheim, E.
    1968   *The Elementary Forms of the Religious Life.* Translated by J. W. Swain. Reprinted. The Free Press, New York. Originally published 1915, George Allen and Unwin.

Earle, T. K.
    1990   Style and Iconography as Legitimation in Complex Chiefdoms. In *Uses of Style in Archaeology,* edited by M. W. Conkey and C. A. Hastorf, pp. 73–81. Cambridge University Press, Cambridge.

Earle, T. K., and R. W. Preucel
    1987   Processual Archaeology and the Radical Critique. *Current Anthropology* 28:501–538.

Eckel, E. B., J. S. Williams, F. W. Galbraith, and others
    1949   *Geology and Ore Deposits of the La Plata District,*

Colorado. Professional Paper, no. 219. Geological Survey, Washington, D.C.

Eddy, F. W.
1966 *Prehistory in the Navajo Reservoir District, Northwestern New Mexico.* Papers in Anthropology, no. 15, parts 1 and 2. Museum of New Mexico, Santa Fe.

Eddy, F. W., A. E. Kane, and P. R. Nickens
1984 *Southwest Colorado Prehistoric Context: Archaeological Background and Research Directions.* Office of Archaeology and Historic Preservation, Colorado Historical Society, Denver.

Eder, J. F.
1984 The Impact of Subsistence Change on Mobility and Settlement Pattern in a Tropical Forest Foraging Economy: Some Implications for Archaeology. *American Anthropologist* 86:837–853.

Eggan, F.
1950 *Social Organization of the Western Pueblos.* University of Chicago Press, Chicago.
1955 Social Anthropology: Methods and Results. In *Social Anthropology of North American Tribes,* edited by F. Eggan, pp. 485–551. University of Chicago Press, Chicago.

Ekren, E. B., and F. N. Houser
1965 *Geology and Petrology of the Ute Mountains Area, Colorado.* Professional Paper, no. 481. Geological Survey, Washington, D.C.

Eriksen, T. H.
1991 The Cultural Contexts of Ethnic Differences. *Man* 26:127–144.

Etzkorn, M. C.
1986 Excavations at Hamlet de la Olla (Site 5MT2181), a Multiple-Occupation Anasazi Site. In *Dolores Archaeological Program: Anasazi Communities at Dolores: Early Small Settlements in the Dolores River Canyon and Western Sagehen Flats Area,* compiled by T. A. Kohler, W. D. Lipe, and A. E. Kane, pp. 498–557. Bureau of Reclamation, Engineering and Research Center, Denver.
1993a Other Pottery Tools. In *The Duckfoot Site, Volume 1: Descriptive Archaeology,* edited by R. R. Lightfoot and M. C. Etzkorn, pp. 147–152. Occasional Papers, no. 3. Crow Canyon Archaeological Center, Cortez, Colorado.
1993b Sherds. In *The Duckfoot Site, Volume 1: Descriptive Archaeology,* edited by R. R. Lightfoot and M. C. Etzkorn, pp. 131–135. Occasional Papers, no. 3. Crow Canyon Archaeological Center, Cortez, Colorado.
1993c Stone and Mineral Artifacts. In *The Duckfoot Site, Volume 1: Descriptive Archaeology,* edited by R. R. Lightfoot and M. C. Etzkorn, pp. 157–182. Oc-

casional Papers, no. 3. Crow Canyon Archaeological Center, Cortez, Colorado.

Evans-Pritchard, E. E.
1940 *The Nuer.* Oxford University Press, New York.

Faris, J. C.
1972 *Nuba Personal Art.* Duckworth, London.

Feinman, G., and J. Neitzel
1984 Too Many Types: An Overview of Sedentary Prestate Societies in the Americas. In *Advances in Archaeological Method and Theory,* vol. 7, edited by M. B. Schiffer, pp. 39–102. Academic Press, New York.

Fetterman, J., and L. Honeycutt
1986 *The Mockingbird Mesa Survey, Southwestern Colorado.* Woods Canyon Archaeological Associates. Report submitted to the Bureau of Land Management, Montrose District Office, Montrose, Colorado.

Fewkes, J. W.
1898 Archaeological Expedition Into Arizona in 1895. In *Seventeenth Annual Report of the Bureau of American Ethnology, 1895–1896,* part 2, pp. 519–742. Smithsonian Institution, Washington, D.C.
1904 Two Summers' Work in Pueblo Ruins. In *Twenty-Second Annual Report of the Bureau of American Ethnology, 1900–1901,* part 1, pp. 3–195. Smithsonian Institution, Washington, D.C.

Fish, P. R.
1978 Consistency in Archaeological Measurement and Classification: A Pilot Study. *American Antiquity* 43:86–89.

Flannery, K. V.
1968 The Olmec and the Valley of Oaxaca: A Model for Inter-regional Interaction in Formative Times. In *Dumbarton Oaks Conference on the Olmec,* edited by E. P. Benson, pp. 79–110. Dumbarton Oaks, Washington, D.C.
1972 The Origins of the Village as a Settlement Type in Mesoamerica and the Near East: A Comparative Study. In *Man, Settlement and Urbanism,* edited by P. J. Ucko, R. Tringham, and G. W. Dimbleby, pp. 23–53. Duckworth, London.
1976 Analysis of Stylistic Variation Within and Between Communities. In *The Early Mesoamerican Village,* edited by K. V. Flannery, pp. 251–254. Academic Press, New York.

Flannery, K. V. (editor)
1986 *Gila Naquitz: Archaic Foraging and Early Agriculture in Oaxaca, Mexico.* Academic Press, New York.

Fletcher, R.
1989 The Messages of Material Behavior: A Preliminary Discussion of Non-verbal Meaning. In

The Meaning of Things: Material Culture and Symbolic Expression, edited by I. Hodder, pp. 33–40. Unwin Hyman, London.

Ford, R. I.
1972   An Ecological Perspective on the Eastern Pueblos. In *New Perspectives on the Pueblos,* edited by A. Ortiz, pp. 1–18. University of New Mexico Press, Albuquerque.

Forde, C. D.
1931   Hopi Agriculture and Land Ownership. *Journal of the Royal Anthropological Institute of Great Britain and Ireland* 61:357–406.

Forge, A.
1973   Introduction. In *Primitive Art and Society,* edited by A. Forge, pp. xiii–xx. Oxford University Press, London.

Foster, G. M.
1960   Life-Expectancy of Utilitarian Pottery in Tzintzuntzan, Michoacán, Mexico. *American Antiquity* 25:606–609.

Franczyk, K. J.
1988   *Stratigraphic Revision and Depositional Environments of the Upper Cretaceous Toreva Formation in the Northern Black Mesa Area, Navajo and Apache Counties, Arizona.* Bulletin, no. 1685. Geological Survey, Washington, D.C.

Franklin, N. R.
1986   Stochastic vs. Emblemic: An Archaeologically Useful Method for the Analysis of Style in Australian Rock Art. *Rock Art Research* 3:121–124.
1989   Research with Style: A Case Study from Australian Rock Art. In *Archaeological Approaches to Cultural Identity,* edited by S. J. Shennan, pp. 278–290. Unwin Hyman, London.

Freeman, L. G., Jr., and J. A. Brown
1964   Statistical Analysis of Carter Ranch Pottery. In *Chapters in the Prehistory of Eastern Arizona, II,* authored by P. S. Martin, J. B. Rinaldo, W. A. Longacre, L. G. Freeman, Jr., J. A. Brown, R. H. Hevly, and M. E. Cooley, pp. 126–154. Fieldiana: Anthropology, vol. 55. Chicago Natural History Museum, Chicago.

Fried, M.
1975a   The Myth of Tribe. *Natural History* 84:12–20.
1975b   *The Notion of Tribe.* Cummings, Menlo Park, California.

Friedrich, M. H.
1970   Design Structure and Social Interaction: Archaeological Implications. *American Antiquity* 35:332–343.

Fritz, J. M.
1987   Chaco Canyon and Vijayanagara: Proposing Spatial Meaning in Two Societies. In *Mirror and Metaphor: Material and Social Constructions of Reality,* edited by D. W. Ingersoll, Jr., and G. Bronitsky, pp. 313–349. University Press of America, Lanham, Maryland.

Fuller, S. L.
1984   *Late Anasazi Pottery Kilns in the Yellowjacket District, Southwestern Colorado.* CASA Papers, no. 4. Complete Archaeological Service Associates, Cortez, Colorado.

Garrett, E. M.
1986   A Petrographic Analysis of Black Mesa Ceramics. In *Spatial Organization and Exchange: Archaeological Survey on Northern Black Mesa,* edited by S. Plog, pp. 114–142. Southern Illinois University Press, Carbondale.
1990   Petrographic Analysis of Selected Ceramics from the Northern Southwest. Ms. on file, Department of Sociology and Anthropology, New Mexico State University, Las Cruces.

Gebauer, A. B.
1987   Stylistic Analysis: A Critical Review of Concepts, Models, and Applications. *Journal of Danish Archaeology* 6:223–229.

Gebauer, A. B., and T. D. Price (editors)
1992   *Transitions to Agriculture in Prehistory.* Prehistory Press, Madison, Wisconsin.

Gebhart-Sayer, A.
1985   The Geometric Designs of the Shipibo-Conibo in Ritual Context. *Journal of Latin American Lore* 11:143–175.

Geertz, C.
1983   *Local Knowledge.* Basic Books, New York.

Gibbs, L.
1987   Identifying Gender Representations in the Archaeological Record: A Contextual Study. In *The Archaeology of Contextual Meaning,* edited by I. Hodder, pp. 79–89. Cambridge University Press, Cambridge.

Giddens, A.
1984   *The Constitution of Society: Outline of the Theory of Structuration.* University of California Press, Berkeley.

Gieb, P. R., and M. M. Callahan
1988   Clay Residue on Polishing Stones. *The Kiva* 53:357–362.

Gifford, E. W.
1928   Pottery-Making in the Southwest. *University*

of California Publications in American Archaeology and Ethnology 23:352–373.

Gillespie, W. B.

1976 Culture Change at the Ute Canyon Site: A Study of the Pithouse-Kiva Transition in the Mesa Verde Region. Unpublished Master's thesis, Department of Anthropology, University of Colorado, Boulder.

Gilman, P. A.

1987 Architecture as Artifact: Pit Structures and Pueblos in the American Southwest. American Antiquity 52:538–564.

Gladwin, H. S.

1945 The Chaco Branch: Excavations at White Mound and in the Red Mesa Valley. Medallion Papers, no. 33. Gila Pueblo, Globe, Arizona.

Gladwin, W., and H. S. Gladwin

1934 A Method for Designation of Cultures and Their Variations. Medallion Papers, no. 15. Gila Pueblo, Globe, Arizona.

Glassie, H.

1975 Folk Housing in Middle Virginia: A Structural Analysis of Historic Artifacts. University of Tennessee Press, Knoxville.

Godelier, M.

1978 Perspectives in Marxist Anthropology. Translated by R. Brain. Cambridge University Press, Cambridge.

Goffman, E.

1974 Frame Analysis: An Essay on the Organization of Experience. Harper and Row, New York.

Gombrich, E.

1979 The Use of Art for the Study of Symbols. In Psychology and the Visual Arts, edited by J. Hogg, pp. 149–170. Penguin Books, Harmondsworth, England.

Goody, J.

1982 Cooking, Cuisine and Class. Cambridge University Press, Cambridge.

Gorman, F. J. E., and S. T. Childs

1981 Is Prudden's Unit Type of Anasazi Settlement Valid and Reliable? North American Archaeologist 2(3):153–192.

Gosselain, O. P.

1992 Technology and Style: Potters and Pottery Among Bafia of Cameroon. Man 27:559–586.

Gould, R.

1982 The Mustoe Site: The Application of Neutron Activation Analysis in the Interpretation of a Multi-component Archaeological Site. Ph.D. dissertation, University of Texas. University Microfilms, Ann Arbor.

Gould, R. A.

1967 Notes on Hunting, Butchering, and Sharing

of Game Among the Ngatatjara and Their Neighbors in the West Australian Desert. Kroeber Anthropological Society Papers 36:41–66.

Graves, M. W.

1981 Ethnoarchaeology of Kalinga Ceramic Design. Ph.D. dissertation, University of Arizona. University Microfilms, Ann Arbor.

1985 Ceramic Design Variation Within a Kalinga Village: Temporal and Spatial Processes. In Decoding Prehistoric Ceramics, edited by B. A. Nelson, pp. 5–34. Southern Illinois University Press, Carbondale.

Grayson, D. K.

1984 Quantitative Zooarchaeology. Academic Press, New York.

Green, M.

1985 Chipped Stone Raw Materials and the Study of Interaction on Black Mesa, Arizona. Center for Archaeological Investigations Occasional Paper, no. 11. Southern Illinois University, Carbondale.

1986 The Distribution of Chipped Stone Raw Materials at Functionally Nonequivalent Sites. In Spatial Organization and Exchange: Archaeological Survey on Northern Black Mesa, edited by S. Plog, pp. 143–168. Southern Illinois University Press, Carbondale.

Green, M., K. Jacobi, B. Boeke, H. L. O'Brien, E. S. Word, R. L. Boston, H. B. Trigg, G. D. Glennie, and M. Gould

1985 Arizona D:11:2030. In Excavations on Black Mesa, 1983: A Descriptive Report, edited by A. L. Christenson and W. J. Parry, pp. 223–259. Center for Archaeological Investigations Research Paper, no. 46. Southern Illinois University, Carbondale.

Gregg, S. A. (editor)

1991 Between Bands and States. Center for Archaeological Investigations Occasional Paper, no. 9. Southern Illinois University, Carbondale.

Gross, D. R.

1979 A New Approach to Central Brazilian Social Organization. In Brazil: Anthropological Perspectives: Essays in Honor of Charles Wagley, edited by M. L. Margolis and W. E. Carter, pp. 321–343. Columbia University Press, New York.

Gross, G. T.

1986a The Grass Mesa Locality Testing Program, 1979–1980. In Dolores Archaeological Program: Anasazi Communities at Dolores: Early Small Settlements in the Dolores River Canyon and Western Sagehen Flats Area, compiled by T. A. Kohler, W. D. Lipe, and A. E. Kane, pp. 45–153. Bureau of Reclamation, Engineering and Research Center, Denver.

1986b Technology: Facilities. In Dolores Archaeological Program: Final Synthetic Report, compiled by

D. A. Breternitz, C. K. Robinson, and G. T. Gross, pp. 611–632. Bureau of Reclamation, Engineering and Research Center, Denver.

Guernsey, S. J.
1931 *Explorations in Northeastern Arizona.* Papers of the Peabody Museum of American Archaeology and Ethnology, vol. 12, no. 1. Harvard University, Cambridge.

Guernsey, S. J., and A. V. Kidder
1921 *Basket-Maker Caves of Northern Arizona: Report on the Explorations, 1916–1917.* Papers of the Peabody Museum of American Archaeology and Ethnology, vol. 8, no. 2. Harvard University, Cambridge.

Gumerman, G. J.
1991 Trends in Western Anasazi Archaeology: From Fewkes to the Future. *Kiva* 56:99–122.

Gumerman, G. J. (editor)
1988a *The Anasazi in a Changing Environment.* Cambridge University Press, Cambridge.
1988b *The Archaeology of the Hopi Buttes District, Arizona.* Southern Illinois University Press, Carbondale.

Gumerman, G. J., and J. S. Dean
1989 Prehistoric Cooperation and Competition in the Western Anasazi Area. In *Dynamics of Southwest Prehistory,* edited by L. S. Cordell and G. J. Gumerman, pp. 99–148. Smithsonian Institution Press, Washington, D.C.

Gumerman, G. J., and S. A. Skinner
1968 A Synthesis of the Prehistory of the Central Little Colorado Valley, Arizona. *American Antiquity* 33:185–199.

Gumerman, G. J., D. Westfall, and C. S. Weed
1972 *Archaeological Investigations on Black Mesa: The 1969–1970 Seasons.* Studies in Anthropology, no. 4. Prescott College, Prescott, Arizona.

Guthe, C. E.
1925 *Pueblo Pottery Making: A Study at the Village of San Ildefonso.* Papers of the Phillips Academy Southwestern Expedition, no. 2. Yale University Press, New Haven.

Haas, J., and W. Creamer
1993 *Stress and Warfare Among the Kayenta Anasazi of the Thirteenth Century A.D.* Fieldiana: Anthropology, New Series, no. 21. Field Museum of Natural History, Chicago.

Hack, J. T.
1942 *The Changing Physical Environment of the Hopi Indians of Arizona.* Papers of the Peabody Museum of American Archaeology and Ethnology, vol. 35, no. 1. Harvard University, Cambridge.

Haggett, P.
1965 *Locational Analysis in Human Geography.* Edward Arnold, London.

Hallasi, J. A.
1979 Archeological Excavation at the Escalante Site, Dolores, Colorado, 1975 and 1976. In *The Archeology and Stabilization of the Dominguez and Escalante Ruins,* authored by A. D. Reed, J. A. Hallasi, A. S. White, and D. A. Breternitz, pp. 197–425. Cultural Resource Series, no. 7. Bureau of Land Management, Colorado State Office, Denver.

Hally, D. J.
1986 The Identification of Vessel Function: A Case Study from Northwest Georgia. *American Antiquity* 51:267–295.

Hantman, J. L.
1983 *Social Networks and Stylistic Distributions in the Prehistoric Plateau Southwest.* Ph.D. dissertation, Arizona State University. University Microfilms, Ann Arbor.

Hantman, J. L., K. G. Lightfoot, S. Upham, F. Plog, S. Plog, and B. Donaldson
1984 Cibola Whitewares: A Regional Perspective. In *Regional Analysis of Prehistoric Ceramic Variation: Contemporary Studies of the Cibola Whitewares,* edited by A. P. Sullivan and J. L. Hantman, pp. 17–35. Anthropological Research Papers, no. 31. Arizona State University, Tempe.

Hantman, J. L., and S. Plog
1982 The Relationship of Stylistic Similarity to Patterns of Material Exchange. In *Contexts for Prehistoric Exchange,* edited by T. K. Earle and J. E. Ericson, pp. 237–261. Academic Press, New York.

Hardin, M. A.
1983a *Gifts of Mother Earth: Ceramics in the Zuni Tradition.* Heard Museum, Phoenix.
1983b The Structure of Tarascan Pottery Painting. In *Structure and Cognition in Art,* edited by D. K. Washburn, pp. 8–24. Cambridge University Press, Cambridge.
1991 Sources of Ceramic Variability at Zuni Pueblo. In *Ceramic Ethnoarchaeology,* edited by W. A. Longacre, pp. 40–47. University of Arizona Press, Tucson.

Hargrave, L. L.
1935 *Report on Archaeological Reconnaissance in the Rainbow Plateau Area of Northern Arizona and Southern Utah.* University of California Press, Berkeley.

Harris, L.
1983 Forces and Relations of Production. In *A Dictionary of Marxist Thought,* edited by T. Bottomore, L. Harris, V. G. Kiernan, and R. Miliband, pp. 178–180. Harvard University Press, Cambridge.

Hathaway, J. H.
1988 Archaeomagnetic Dating Results. In *Dolores Archaeological Program: Supporting Studies: Additive and Reductive Technologies,* compiled by E. Blinman, C. J. Phagan, and R. H. Wilshusen, pp. 545–591. Bureau of Reclamation, Engineering and Research Center, Denver.

Haury, E. W.
1962 The Greater American Southwest. In *Courses Toward Urban Life,* edited by R. J. Braidwood and G. R. Willey, pp. 106–131. Aldine, Chicago.
1976 *The Hohokam, Desert Farmers and Craftsmen: Excavations at Snaketown, 1964–1965.* University of Arizona Press, Tucson.

Hawley, F. M.
1936 *Field Manual of Prehistoric Southwestern Pottery Types.* Bulletin, no. 291. University of New Mexico, Albuquerque.

Hayden, B.
1990 Nimrods, Piscators, Pluckers and Planters: The Emergence of Food Production. *Journal of Anthropological Archaeology* 9:31–69.
1992 Models of Domestication. In *Transitions to Agriculture in Prehistory,* edited by A. B. Gebauer and T. D. Price, pp. 11–19. Monographs in World Archaeology, no. 4. Prehistory Press, Madison, Wisconsin.

Hayden, B., and A. Cannon
1982 The Corporate Group as an Archaeological Unit. *Journal of Anthropological Archaeology* 1:132–158.

Hayes, A. C.
1964 *The Archeological Survey of Wetherill Mesa, Mesa Verde National Park, Colorado.* Archeological Research Series, no. 7-A. National Park Service, Washington, D.C.

Hayes, A. C., D. M. Brugge, and W. J. Judge (editors)
1981 *Archeological Surveys of Chaco Canyon.* Publications in Archeology, no. 18A. National Park Service, Washington, D.C.

Hayes, A. C., and J. A. Lancaster
1975 *Badger House Community, Mesa Verde National Park.* Publications in Archeology, no. 7E. National Park Service, Washington, D.C.

Haynes, D. D., and R. J. Hackman (compilers)
1978 *Geology, Structure, and Uranium Deposits of the Marble Canyon 1° × 2° Quadrangle, Arizona.* Geological Survey, Washington, D.C.

Haynes, D. D., J. D. Vogel, and D. G. Wyant (compilers)
1972 *Geology, Structure, and Uranium Deposits of the Cortez Quadrangle, Colorado and Utah.* Miscellaneous Geology Inventory Map I-629. United States Geologic Service, Washington, D.C.

Hays, K. A.
1989 Katsina Depictions on Homol'ovi Ceramics: Toward a Fourteenth-Century Pueblo Iconography. *Kiva* 54:297–311.
1991 Social Contexts of Style and Information in a Seventh-Century Basketmaker Community. Paper presented at the 56th Annual Meeting of the Society for American Archaeology, New Orleans.
1992 *Anasazi Ceramics as Text and Tool: Toward a Theory of Ceramic Design "Messaging."* Unpublished Ph.D. dissertation, Department of Anthropology, University of Arizona, Tucson.

Hegmon, M.
1986 Information Exchange and Integration on Black Mesa, Arizona, A.D. 931–1150. In *Spatial Organization and Exchange: Archaeological Survey on Northern Black Mesa,* edited by S. Plog, pp. 256–281. Southern Illinois University Press, Carbondale.
1989a Risk Reduction and Variation in Agricultural Economies: A Computer Simulation of Hopi Agriculture. In *Research in Economic Anthropology,* vol. 11, edited by B. Isaac, pp. 89–121. JAI Press, Greenwich, Connecticut.
1989b Social Integration and Architecture. In *The Architecture of Social Integration in Prehistoric Pueblos,* edited by W. D. Lipe and M. Hegmon, pp. 5–14. Occasional Papers, no. 1. Crow Canyon Archaeological Center, Cortez, Colorado.
1989c The Styles of Integration: Ceramic Style and Pueblo I Integrative Architecture in Southwestern Colorado. In *The Architecture of Social Integration in Prehistoric Pueblos,* edited by W. D. Lipe and M. Hegmon, pp. 125–141. Occasional Papers, no. 1. Crow Canyon Archaeological Center, Cortez, Colorado.
1990 *Style as a Social Strategy: Dimensions of Ceramic Stylistic Variation in the Ninth Century Northern Southwest.* Unpublished Ph.D. dissertation, Department of Anthropology, University of Michigan, Ann Arbor.
1991a Report on Post-Doctoral Fellowship in Materials Research. Ms. on file, Conservation Analytical Laboratory, Smithsonian Institution, Washington, D.C.
1991b The Risks of Sharing and Sharing as Risk Reduction: Interhousehold Food Sharing in Egalitarian Societies. In *Between Bands and States,* edited by S. Gregg, pp. 309–329. Southern Illinois University Press, Carbondale.
1992a Archaeological Research on Style. *Annual Review of Anthropology* 21:517–536.

1992b Variability in Food Production, Strategies of Storage and Sharing, and the Pit House to Pueblo Transition in the Northern Southwest. Paper presented at the Santa Fe Institute Workshop on Resource Stress, Economic Uncertainty, and Human Responses in the Prehistoric Southwest, February 1992, Santa Fe.

1993 Analyses of Production and Stylistic Information. In *The Duckfoot Site, Volume 1: Descriptive Archaeology,* edited by R. R. Lightfoot and M. C. Etzkorn, pp. 152–156. Occasional Papers, no. 3. Crow Canyon Archaeological Center, Cortez, Colorado.

1995 Pueblo I Ceramic Production in Southwest Colorado: Analyses of Igneous Rock Temper. *Kiva* 60:371–390.

Hegmon, M., and J. R. Allison

1990 The Local Economy and Regional Exchange: Early Red Ware Production and Distribution in the Northern Southwest. Proposal approved for Neutron Activation Analysis at the University of Missouri Research Reactor, Columbia. Ms. on file, University of Missouri, Columbia.

Hegmon, M., W. Hurst, and J. R. Allison

1994 The Local Economy and Regional Exchange: Early Red Ware Production and Distribution in the Northern Southwest. In *The Organization of Ceramic Production in the American Southwest,* edited by B. J. Mills and P. L. Crown. University of Arizona Press, Tucson, in press.

Heinen, H. D., and K. Ruddle

1974 Ecology, Ritual, and Economic Organization in the Distribution of Palm Starch Among the Warao of the Orinoco Delta. *Journal of Anthropological Research* 30:116–138.

Helm, C.

1973 The Kiln Site. In *Highway U-95 Archaeology: Comb Wash to Grand Flat,* edited by G. Dalley, pp. 209–219. University of Utah Department of Anthropology, Salt Lake City.

Helms, M. W.

1987 Art Styles as Interaction Spheres in Central America and the Caribbean: Polished Black Wood in the Greater Antilles. In *Chiefdoms in the Americas,* edited by R. D. Drennan and C. A. Uribe, pp. 67–84. University Press of America, Lanham, Maryland.

Henrickson, E. F., and M. M. A. McDonald

1983 Ceramic Form and Function: An Ethnographic Search and an Archeological Application. *American Anthropologist* 85:630–643.

Herbich, I.

1987 Learning Patterns, Potter Interaction and Ceramic Style Among the Luo of Kenya. *The African Archaeological Review* 5:193–204.

Hill, D. V.

1985 Pottery Making at the Ewing Site (5MT927). *Southwestern Lore* 51(1):19–31.

Hill, J. N.

1966 A Prehistoric Community in Eastern Arizona. *Southwestern Journal of Anthropology* 22:9–30.

1970 *Broken K Pueblo: Prehistoric Social Organization in the American Southwest.* Anthropological Papers, no. 18. University of Arizona, Tucson.

1985 Style: A Conceptual Evolutionary Framework. In *Decoding Prehistoric Ceramics,* edited by B. A. Nelson, pp. 362–385. Southern Illinois University Press, Carbondale.

Himmelweit, S.

1983 Mode of Production. In *A Dictionary of Marxist Thought,* edited by T. Bottomore, L. Harris, V. G. Kiernan, and R. Miliband, pp. 335–337. Harvard University Press, Cambridge.

Hitchcock, R. K.

1982 Patterns of Sedentism Among the Basarwa of Eastern Botswana. In *Politics and History in Band Societies,* edited by E. Leacock and R. Lee, pp. 223–267. Cambridge University Press, Cambridge.

Hodder, I.

1979 Economic and Social Stress and Material Culture Patterning. *American Antiquity* 44:446–454.

1982a Sequences of Structural Change in the Dutch Neolithic. In *Symbolic and Structural Archaeology,* edited by I. Hodder, pp. 162–177. Cambridge University Press, Cambridge.

1982b *Symbols in Action.* Cambridge University Press, Cambridge.

1982c Theoretical Archaeology: A Reactionary View. In *Symbolic and Structural Archaeology,* edited by I. Hodder, pp. 1–10. Cambridge University Press, Cambridge.

1987 Comment on "Processual Archaeology and the Radical Critique" by Timothy K. Earle and Robert W. Preucel. *Current Anthropology* 28:516–517.

1989 Post-modernism, Post-structuralism and Postprocessual Archaeology. In *The Meaning of Things,* edited by I. Hodder, pp. 64–78. Unwin Hyman, London.

1990 Style as Historical Quality. In *Uses of Style in Archaeology,* edited by M. W. Conkey and C. A. Hastorf, pp. 44–51. Cambridge University Press, Cambridge.

1991a The Decoration of Containers: An Ethnographic and Historical Study. In *Ceramic Ethnoar-*

chaeology, edited by W. A. Longacre, pp. 71–94. University of Arizona Press, Tucson.

1991b   Reading the Past. 2nd ed. Cambridge University Press, Cambridge.

Hogan, P.
1986   Excavations at LeMoc Shelter (Site 5MT2151), a Multiple-Occupation Anasazi Site. In Dolores Archaeological Program: Anasazi Communities at Dolores: Early Small Settlements in the Dolores River Canyon and Western Sagehen Flats Area, compiled by T. A. Kohler, W. D. Lipe, and A. E. Kane, pp. 155–329. Bureau of Reclamation, Engineering and Research Center, Denver.

Holm, B.
1965   Northwest Coast Indian Art: An Analysis of Form. University of Washington Press, Seattle.

Holm, B., and B. Reid
1975   Form and Freedom. Institute of the Arts, Rice University, Houston.

Holmes, W. H.
1878   Report on the Ancient Ruins of Southwestern Colorado, Examined During the Summers of 1875 and 1876. In Tenth Annual Report of the U.S. Geological and Geographical Survey of the Territories for 1876, pp. 383–408. Geological Survey, Washington, D.C.

1903   Aboriginal Pottery of the Eastern United States. In Twentieth Annual Report of the Bureau of American Ethnology, 1898–1899, pp. 1–201. Smithsonian Institution, Washington, D.C.

Hostetler, J.
1964   The Amish Use of Symbols and Their Function in Bounding the Community. Journal of the Royal Anthropological Institute of Great Britain and Ireland 94:11–22.

Hough, W.
1897   The Hopi in Relation to Their Plant Environment. American Anthropologist 10:33–44.

Hurst, W.
1983   The Prehistoric Peoples of San Juan County, Utah. In San Juan County, Utah, edited by A. K. Powell, pp. 17–44. Utah State Historical Society, Salt Lake City.

Hurst, W., M. Bond, and S. E. E. Schwindt
1985   Piedra Black-on-white, White Mesa Variety: Formal Description of a Western Mesa Verde Anasazi Pueblo I White Ware Type. Pottery Southwest 12(3):1–7.

Hutcheson, K.
1970   A Test for Comparing Diversities Based on the Shannon Formula. Journal of Theoretical Biology 29:151–154.

Ingold, T.
1983   The Significance of Storage in Hunting Societies. Man 18:553–571.

1986   The Appropriation of Nature: Essays on Human Ecology and Social Relations. Manchester University Press, Manchester, England.

1988   Notes on the Foraging Mode of Production. In Hunters and Gatherers 1: History, Evolution, and Social Change, edited by T. Ingold, D. Riches, and J. Woodburn, pp. 269–285. Berg, Oxford.

Irwin, G. J.
1978   Pots and Entrepots: A Study of Settlement, Trade, and the Development of Economic Specialization on Papuan Prehistory. World Archaeology 9:299–319.

Jennings, J. D.
1966   Glen Canyon: A Summary. Anthropological Papers, no. 81. University of Utah, Salt Lake City.

Jernigan, E. W.
1986   A Non-hierarchical Approach to Ceramic Decoration Analysis: A Southwestern Example. American Antiquity 51:3–20.

Jernigan, E. W., and K. B. Wreden
1982   The White Mound–Kiatuthlanna–Red Mesa Stylistic Tradition. In Cholla Project Archaeology, Volume 5: Ceramic Studies, edited by J. J. Reid, pp. 39–427. Archaeological Series, no. 161. Arizona State Museum, Tucson.

Johnson, A. W., and T. Earle
1987   The Evolution of Human Societies: From Foraging Group to Agrarian State. Stanford University Press, Stanford.

Johnson, G. A.
1982   Organizational Structure and Scalar Stress. In Theory and Explanation in Archaeology: The Southampton Conference, edited by C. Renfrew, M. J. Rowlands, and B. A. Segraves, pp. 389–421. Academic Press, New York.

Jones, G. T., D. K. Grayson, and C. Beck
1983   Artifact Class Richness and Sample Size in Archaeological Surface Assemblages. In Lulu Linear Punctated: Essays in Honor of George Irving Quimby, edited by R. C. Dunnell and D. Grayson, pp. 55–73. Anthropological Papers, no. 72. Museum of Anthropology, University of Michigan, Ann Arbor.

Jones, K., and M. Hegmon
1991   The Medium and the Message: A Survey of Information Conveyed by Material Culture in Middle Range Societies. Paper presented at the 56th Annual Meeting of the Society for American Archaeology, New Orleans.

Jopling, C. F. (editor)
1971   Art and Aesthetics in Primitive Societies. E. P. Dutton, New York.

Kabo, V.
1985   The Origins of the Food-Producing Economy. Current Anthropology 26:601–614.

Kamilli, D. C.
1983   Petrographic Analysis of Selected Potsherds and Rock Samples from the Dolores Archaeological Program, Southern Colorado. Ms. on file, Anasazi Heritage Center, Dolores, Colorado.

Kane, A. E.
1986a   Prehistory of the Dolores River Valley. In Dolores Archaeological Program: Final Synthetic Report, compiled by D. A. Breternitz, C. K. Robinson, and G. T. Gross, pp. 353–435. Bureau of Reclamation, Engineering and Research Center, Denver.
1986b   Social Organization and Cultural Process in Dolores Anasazi Communities, A.D. 600–900. In Dolores Archaeological Program: Final Synthetic Report, compiled by D. A. Breternitz, C. K. Robinson, and G. T. Gross, pp. 633–661. Bureau of Reclamation, Engineering and Research Center, Denver.
1988   McPhee Community Cluster Introduction. In Dolores Archaeological Program: Anasazi Communities at Dolores: McPhee Village, compiled by A. E. Kane and C. K. Robinson, pp. 2–59. Bureau of Reclamation, Engineering and Research Center, Denver.
1989   Did the Sheep Look Up? Sociopolitical Complexity in Ninth Century Dolores Society. In The Sociopolitical Structure of Prehistoric Southwestern Societies, edited by S. Upham, K. G. Lightfoot, and R. A. Jewett, pp. 307–361. Westview Press, Boulder, Colorado.

Kane, A. E., and C. K. Robinson (compilers)
1986   Dolores Archaeological Program: Anasazi Communities at Dolores: Middle Canyon Area. Bureau of Reclamation, Engineering and Research Center, Denver.
1988   Dolores Archaeological Program: Anasazi Communities at Dolores: McPhee Village. Bureau of Reclamation, Engineering and Research Center, Denver.

Karlstrom, T. N. V.
1988   Alluvial Chronology and Hydrologic Change of Black Mesa and Nearby Regions. In The Anasazi in a Changing Environment, edited by G. J. Gumerman, pp. 45–91. Cambridge University Press, Cambridge.

Keane, S. P., and V. L. Clay
1987   Geological Sources of Unusual Minerals and Rocks of the Dolores Project Area. In Dolores Archaeological Program: Supporting Studies: Settlement and Environment, compiled by K. L. Petersen and J. D. Orcutt, pp. 506–546. Bureau of Reclamation, Engineering and Research Center, Denver.

Kelly, R. L.
1991   Sedentism, Sociopolitical Inequality, and Resource Fluctuations. In Between Bands and States, edited by S. A. Gregg, pp. 135–158. Center for Archaeological Investigations Occasional Paper, no. 9. Southern Illinois University, Carbondale.
1992   Mobility/Sedentism: Concepts, Archaeological Measures, and Effects. Annual Review of Anthropology 21:43–66.

Kent, K. P.
1983   Temporal Shifts in the Structure of Traditional Southwestern Textile Design. In Structure and Cognition in Art, edited by D. K. Washburn, pp. 113–137. Cambridge University Press, Cambridge.

Kent, S.
1991   Excavations at a Small Mesa Verde Pueblo II Anasazi Site in Southwestern Colorado. Kiva 57:55–75.

Kidder, A. V.
1924   An Introduction to the Study of Southwestern Archaeology with a Preliminary Account of the Excavations at Pecos. Yale University Press, New Haven.

Kidder, A. V., and S. J. Guernsey
1919   Archaeological Investigations in Northeastern Arizona. Bureau of American Ethnology Bulletin, no. 65. Smithsonian Institution, Washington, D.C.

Kidder, A. V., and A. O. Shepard
1936   The Pottery of Pecos, Volume 2. Papers of the Phillips Academy Southwestern Expedition, no. 7. Yale University Press, New Haven.

Kimmelman, M.
1989   Unnerving Art. New York Times Magazine. 20 August: 41–42.

Kintigh, K. W.
1984   Measuring Archaeological Diversity by Comparison with Simulated Assemblages. American Antiquity 49:44–54.
1985   Social Structure, the Structure of Style, and Stylistic Patterns in Cibola Pottery. In Decoding Prehistoric Ceramics, edited by B. A. Nelson, pp. 35–74. Southern Illinois University Press, Carbondale.
1989a   The Archaeologist's Analytical Toolkit: Diversity Module. Ms. and computer programs in possession of author, Department of Anthropology, Arizona State University, Tempe.
1989b   Sample Size, Significance, and Measures of Diversity. In Quantifying Diversity in Archaeology, edited by R. D. Leonard and G. T. Jones, pp. 25–36. Cambridge University Press, Cambridge.

Kleidon, J. H.
1988 Excavations at Aldea Alfareros (Site 5MT4479), a Pueblo I Habitation Site. In *Dolores Archaeological Program: Anasazi Communities at Dolores: McPhee Village,* compiled by A. E. Kane and C. K. Robinson, pp. 559–661. Bureau of Reclamation, Engineering and Research Center, Denver.

Klesert, A. L.
1977 *An Analysis of Intra-site Ceramic Design Variability.* Unpublished M.A. Thesis, Department of Anthropology, Southern Illinois University, Carbondale.
1983 *Anasazi Settlement and Adaptation on the North Rim of Black Mesa, Arizona.* Center for Archaeological Investigations Research Paper, no. 34. Southern Illinois University, Carbondale.

Kohler, T. A.
1988 The Probability Sample at Grass Mesa Village. In *Dolores Archaeological Program: Anasazi Communities at Dolores: Grass Mesa Village,* compiled by W. D. Lipe, J. N. Morris, and T. A. Kohler, pp. 51–74. Bureau of Reclamation, Engineering and Research Center, Denver.
1992 Field Houses, Villages, and the Tragedy of the Commons in the Early Northern Anasazi Southwest. *American Antiquity* 57:617–635.

Kohler, T. A., and M. H. Matthews
1988 Long-Term Anasazi Land Use and Forest Reduction: A Case Study from Southwest Colorado. *American Antiquity* 53:537–564.

Kohler, T. A., J. D. Orcutt, E. Blinman, and K. L. Petersen
1986 Anasazi Spreadsheets: The Cost of Doing Agricultural Business in Prehistoric Dolores. In *Dolores Archaeological Program: Final Synthetic Report,* compiled by D. A. Breternitz, C. K. Robinson, and G. T. Gross, pp. 525–538. Bureau of Reclamation, Engineering and Research Center, Denver.

Kohler, T. A., and C. R. Van West
1992 The Calculus of Self Interest in the Development of Cooperation: Sociopolitical Development and Risk Among the Northern Anasazi. Paper presented at the Santa Fe Institute Workshop on Resource Stress, Economic Uncertainty, and Human Responses in the Prehistoric Southwest, February 1992, Santa Fe.

Kojo, Y.
1989 Autonomous Ceramic Production in the Northern Southwest. Paper presented at the 54th Annual Meeting of the Society for American Archaeology, Atlanta.

Kosse, K.
1992 Middle Range Societies from a Scalar Per-

spective. Paper presented at the Third Southwest Symposium, Tucson.

Kramer, C.
1985 Ceramic Ethnoarchaeology. *Annual Review of Anthropology* 14:77–120.

Kubler, G.
1962 *The Shape of Time: Remarks on the History of Things.* Yale University Press, New Haven.

Kuckelman, K. A.
1986 Excavations at Aldea Sierritas (Site 5MT2854), a Basketmaker III/Pueblo I Habitation. In *Dolores Archaeological Program: Anasazi Communities at Dolores: Early Anasazi Sites in the Sagehen Flats Area,* compiled by A. E. Kane and G. T. Gross, pp. 284–417. Bureau of Reclamation, Engineering and Research Center, Denver.
1988 Excavations at Golondrinas Oriental (Site 5MT5108), a Pueblo I Hamlet. In *Dolores Archaeological Program: Anasazi Communities at Dolores: McPhee Village,* compiled by A. E. Kane and C. K. Robinson, pp. 907–985. Bureau of Reclamation, Engineering and Research Center, Denver.

Kuckelman, K. A., and R. G. Harriman
1988 Excavations at Rabbitbrush Pueblo (Site 5MT4480), a Pueblo I Habitation. In *Dolores Archaeological Program: Anasazi Communities at Dolores: McPhee Village,* compiled by A. E. Kane and C. K. Robinson, pp. 989–1056. Bureau of Reclamation, Engineering and Research Center, Denver.

Lange, F., N. Mahaney, J. B. Wheat, and M. L. Chenault
1986 *Yellow Jacket: A Four Corners Anasazi Ceremonial Center.* Johnson Books, Boulder, Colorado.

Larick, R.
1985 Spears, Style and Time Among Maa-Speaking Pastoralists. *Journal of Anthropological Archaeology* 4:206–220.
1991 Warriors and Blacksmiths: Mediating Ethnicity in East African Spears. *Journal of Anthropological Archaeology* 10:299–331.

Larson, E. S., and W. Cross
1956 *Geology and Petrology of the San Juan Region, Southwestern Colorado.* Professional Paper, no. 258. Geological Survey, Washington, D.C.

Layhe, R. W.
1981 *A Locational Model for Demographic and Settlement System Change: An Example from the American Southwest.* Ph.D. dissertation, Southern Illinois University. University Microfilms, Ann Arbor.
1984 Arizona D:7:134. In *Excavations on Black Mesa, 1971–1976: A Descriptive Report,* edited by S. Powell, pp. 121–130. Center for Archaeological In-

vestigations Research Paper, no. 48. Southern Illinois University, Carbondale.

Layhe, R. W., S. Sessions, C. Miksicek, and S. Plog (editors)
1976　*The Black Mesa Archaeological Project: A Preliminary Report for the 1975 Season.* University Museum Archaeological Service Report, no. 48. Southern Illinois University, Carbondale.

Layton, R.
1981　*The Anthropology of Art.* Columbia University Press, New York.

Leacock, E.
1983　Primitive Communism. In *A Dictionary of Marxist Thought,* edited by T. Bottomore, pp. 394–395. Harvard University Press, Cambridge.

Leacock, E., and R. Lee
1982　Introduction. In *Politics and History in Band Societies,* edited by E. Leacock and R. Lee, pp. 1–20. Cambridge University Press, Cambridge.

Leacock, E., and R. Lee (editors)
1982　*Politics and History in Band Societies.* Cambridge University Press, Cambridge.

LeBlanc, S. A.
1989　Cibola: Shifting Cultural Boundaries. In *Dynamics of Southwest Prehistory,* edited by L. S. Cordell and G. J. Gumerman, pp. 337–369. Smithsonian Institution Press, Washington, D.C.

Lee, R.
1969　Eating Christmas in the Kalahari. *Natural History* 78(10):14–22, 60–63.
1979　*The !Kung San: Men, Women and Work in a Foraging Society.* Cambridge University Press, Cambridge.
1988　Reflections on Primitive Communism. In *Hunters and Gatherers 1: History, Evolution, and Social Change,* edited by T. Ingold, D. Riches, and J. Woodburn, pp. 252–268. Berg, Oxford.

Lee, R., and I. DeVore
1968　*Man the Hunter.* Aldine, Chicago.

Lekson, S. H.
1986　*Great Pueblo Architecture of Chaco Canyon, New Mexico.* Reprinted. University of New Mexico Press, Albuquerque. Originally published 1984, National Park Service, Albuquerque.

Leonard, R. D.
1989　*Anasazi Faunal Exploitation: Prehistoric Subsistence on Northern Black Mesa, Arizona.* Center for Archaeological Investigations Occasional Paper, no. 13. Southern Illinois University, Carbondale.

Leonard, R. D., and G. T. Jones (editors)
1989　*Quantifying Diversity in Archaeology.* Cambridge University Press, Cambridge.

Leonard, R. D., F. E. Smiley, and C. M. Cameron
1989　Changing Strategies of Anasazi Lithic Procurement on Black Mesa, Arizona. In *Quantifying Diversity in Archaeology,* edited by R. D. Leonard and G. T. Jones, pp. 100–108. Cambridge University Press, Cambridge.

Leonhardy, F. C., and V. L. Clay
1985　Bedrock Geology, Quaternary Stratigraphy, and Geomorphology. In *Dolores Archaeological Program: Studies in Environmental Archaeology,* compiled by K. L. Petersen, V. L. Clay, M. H. Matthews, and S. W. Neusius, pp. 131–138. Bureau of Reclamation, Engineering and Research Center, Denver.

Levi-Strauss, C.
1963　*Structural Anthropology.* Basic Books, New York.

Lightfoot, R. R.
1992a　*Archaeology of the House and Household: A Case Study of Assemblage Formation and Household Organization in the American Southwest.* Unpublished Ph.D. dissertation, Department of Anthropology, Washington State University, Pullman.
1992b　Architecture and Tree-Ring Dating at the Duckfoot Site in Southwestern Colorado. *Kiva* 57:213–236.
1994　*The Duckfoot Site, Volume 2: Archaeology of the House and Household.* Occasional Papers, no. 3. Crow Canyon Archaeological Center, Cortez, Colorado.

Lightfoot, R. R., and M. C. Etzkorn (editors)
1993　*The Duckfoot Site, Volume 1: Descriptive Archaeology.* Occasional Papers, no. 3. Crow Canyon Archaeological Center, Cortez, Colorado.

Lindauer, O.
1989　Understanding Stylistic Diversity of Painted Ceramic Designs: An Investigation of Hohokam Red-on-buff Vessels. Paper presented at the 54th Annual Meeting of the Society for American Archaeology, Atlanta.

Lindsay, A. J., Jr., J. R. Ambler, M. A. Stein, and P. M. Hobler
1968　*Survey and Excavation North and East of Navajo Mountain, Utah, 1959–1962.* Bulletin, no. 45. Museum of Northern Arizona, Flagstaff.

Linford, L. D. (editor)
1983　*Kayenta Anasazi Archaeology on Central Black Mesa, Northeastern Arizona: The Pinon Project.* Navajo Nation Papers in Anthropology, no. 10. Navajo Nation Cultural Resource Management Program, Window Rock, Arizona.

Lipe, W. D.
1970   Anasazi Communities in the Red Rock Pla-
       teau, Southeastern Utah. In *Reconstructing Prehistoric
       Pueblo Societies*, edited by W. A. Longacre, pp. 84–
       139. University of New Mexico Press, Albuquerque.
1978   The Southwest. In *Ancient Native Americans*,
       edited by J. D. Jennings, pp. 327–401. W. H. Free-
       man, San Francisco.
1989   Social Scale of Mesa Verde Anasazi Kivas. In
       *The Architecture of Social Integration in Prehistoric
       Pueblos*, edited by W. D. Lipe and M. Hegmon, pp.
       53–71. Occasional Papers, no. 1. Crow Canyon Ar-
       chaeological Center, Cortez, Colorado.

Lipe, W. D. (editor)
1992   *The Sand Canyon Archaeological Project: A Pro-
       gress Report*. Occasional Papers, no. 2. Crow Canyon
       Archaeological Center, Cortez, Colorado.

Lipe, W. D., and C. D. Breternitz
1980   Approaches to Analyzing Variability Among
       Dolores Area Structures, A.D. 600–950. *Contract Ab-
       stracts and CRM Archeology* 1(2):21–28.

Lipe, W. D., and M. Hegmon
1989   Historical and Analytical Perspectives on Ar-
       chitecture and Social Integration in the Prehistoric
       Pueblos. In *The Architecture of Social Integration in
       Prehistoric Pueblos*, edited by W. D. Lipe and M.
       Hegmon, pp. 15–34. Occasional Papers, no. 1. Crow
       Canyon Archaeological Center, Cortez, Colorado.

Lipe, W. D., J. N. Morris, and T. A. Kohler (compilers)
1988   *Dolores Archaeological Program: Anasazi Commu-
       nities at Dolores: Grass Mesa Village*. Bureau of Rec-
       lamation, Engineering and Research Center, Denver.

Lister, R. H.
1965   *Contributions to Mesa Verde Archaeology, II: Site
       875, Mesa Verde National Park, Colorado*. University
       of Colorado Studies Series in Anthropology, no. 9.
       University of Colorado Press, Boulder.

Lister, R. H., and F. C. Lister
1969   *The Earl H. Morris Memorial Pottery Collection*.
       University of Colorado Studies Series in Anthro-
       pology, no. 16. University of Colorado Press, Boulder.
1978   *Ten Centuries of Prehistoric Ceramic Art in the
       Four Corners Country of the Southwestern United
       States as Illustrated by the Earl H. Morris Memorial
       Pottery Collection in the University of Colorado Mu-
       seum*. Maxwell Museum of Anthropology and Uni-
       versity of New Mexico Press, Albuquerque.

Longacre, W. A.
1964a Archaeology as Anthropology: A Case Study.
       Science 144:1454–1455.
1964b The Ceramic Analysis. In *Chapters in the Pre-
       history of Eastern Arizona, II*, authored by P. S. Mar-

tin, J. B. Rinaldo, W. A. Longacre, L. G. Freeman, Jr.,
J. A. Brown, R. H. Hevly, and M. E. Cooley, pp.
110–125. Fieldiana: Anthropology, vol. 55. Chicago
Natural History Museum, Chicago.
1970   *Archaeology as Anthropology: A Case Study*. An-
       thropological Papers, no. 17. University of Arizona,
       Tucson.
1981   Kalinga Pottery: An Ethnoarchaeological
       Study. In *Patterns of the Past: Studies in Honour of
       David Clarke*, edited by I. Hodder, G. Isaacs, and N.
       Hammond, pp. 49–66. Cambridge University Press,
       Cambridge.
1991a Ceramic Ethnoarchaeology: An Introduction.
       In *Ceramic Ethnoarchaeology*, edited by W. A. Long-
       acre, pp. 1–10. University of Arizona Press, Tucson.
1991b Sources of Ceramic Variability Among the
       Kalinga of Northern Luzon. In *Ceramic Ethnoar-
       chaeology*, edited by W. A. Longacre, pp. 95–111.
       University of Arizona Press, Tucson.

Longacre, W. A. (editor)
1991   *Ceramic Ethnoarchaeology*. University of Ari-
       zona Press, Tucson.

Lucius, W. A.
1984   The Ceramic Data Base. In *Dolores Archaeo-
       logical Program: Synthetic Report, 1978–1981*, pre-
       pared under the supervision of D. A. Breternitz, pp.
       215–223. Bureau of Reclamation, Engineering and
       Research Center, Denver.

Lucius, W. A., and D. A. Breternitz
1981   The Current Status of Red Wares in the Mesa
       Verde Region. In *Collected Papers in Honor of Erik
       Kellerman Reed*, edited by A. H. Schroeder, pp. 99–
       111. Papers, no. 6. Archaeological Society of New
       Mexico, Albuquerque.

Macdonald, W. K.
1990   Investigating Style: An Exploratory Analysis of
       Some Plains Burials. In *Uses of Style in Archaeology*,
       edited by M. W. Conkey and C. A. Hastorf, pp.
       52–60. Cambridge University Press, Cambridge.

Martin, P. S.
1936   *Lowry Ruin in Southwestern Colorado*. Anthro-
       pological Series, vol. 23, no. 1. Field Museum of
       Natural History, Chicago.
1938   *Archaeological Work in the Ackmen-Lowry Area,
       Southwestern Colorado, 1937*. Anthropological Series,
       vol. 23, no. 2. Field Museum of Natural History,
       Chicago.
1939   *Modified Basket Maker Sites: Ackmen-Lowry
       Area, Southwestern Colorado, 1938*. Anthropological
       Series, vol. 23, no. 3. Field Museum of Natural
       History, Chicago.

Martin, P. S., and E. S. Willis
1940   *Anasazi Painted Pottery in Field Museum of Natural History.* Anthropology Memoirs, vol. 5. Field Museum of Natural History, Chicago.

Matson, R. G.
1991   *The Origins of Southwestern Agriculture.* University of Arizona Press, Tucson.

Matson, R. G., W. D. Lipe, and W. R. Haase IV
1988   Adaptational Continuities and Occupational Discontinuities: The Cedar Mesa Anasazi. *Journal of Field Archaeology* 15:245–264.

McCracken, G. D.
1988   *Culture and Consumption: New Approaches to the Symbolic Character of Consumer Goods and Activities.* Indiana University Press, Bloomington.

McNitt, F.
1957   *Richard Wetherill: Anasazi.* University of New Mexico Press, Albuquerque.

Mead, H. M.
1990   Tribal Art as Symbols of Identity. In *Art and Identity in Oceania,* edited by A. Hanson and L. Hanson, pp. 269–281. University of Hawaii Press, Honolulu.

Meillassoux, C.
1972   From Reproduction to Production. *Economy and Society* 1:93–105.
1973   On the Mode of Production of the Hunting Band. In *French Perspectives in African Studies,* edited by P. Alexandre, pp. 187–203. Oxford University Press, London.

Meltzer, D. J.
1981   A Study of Style and Function in a Class of Tools. *Journal of Field Archaeology* 8:313–326.

Middleton, J., and D. Tait (editors)
1958   *Tribes Without Rulers: Studies in African Segmentary Systems.* Routledge & Kegan Paul, London.

Miller, D.
1982   Structures and Strategies: An Aspect of the Relationship Between Social Hierarchy and Culture Change. In *Symbolic and Structural Archaeology,* edited by I. Hodder, pp. 89–98. Cambridge University Press, Cambridge.
1985a   *Artefacts as Categories.* Cambridge University Press, Cambridge.
1985b   Ideology and the Harappan Civilization. *Journal of Anthropological Archaeology* 4:34–71.

Mills, B. J.
1989   Integrating Functional Analysis of Vessels and Sherds Through Models of Ceramic Assemblage Formation. *World Archaeology* 21:133–147.

Mills, B. J., and P. L. Crown (editors)
1994   *The Organization of Ceramic Production in the American Southwest.* University of Arizona Press, Tucson, in press.

Milner, C. M.
1991   Localization in Small-Scale Societies: Late Prehistoric Social Organization in the Western Great Lakes. In *Between Bands and States,* edited by S. A. Gregg, pp. 35–57. Center for Archaeological Investigations Occasional Paper, no. 9. Southern Illinois University, Carbondale.

Moles, A.
1966   *Information Theory and Esthetic Perception.* Translated by J. E. Cohen. University of Illinois Press, Urbana.

Morris, E. A.
1980   *Basketmaker Caves in the Prayer Rock District, Northeastern Arizona.* Anthropological Papers, no. 35. University of Arizona, Tucson.

Morris, E. H.
1927   *The Beginnings of Pottery Making in the San Juan Area: Unfired Prototypes and Wares of the Earliest Ceramic Period.* Anthropological Papers, vol. 28, part 2. American Museum of Natural History, New York.
1939   *Archaeological Studies in the La Plata District, Southwestern Colorado and Northwestern New Mexico.* Publication, no. 519. Carnegie Institution of Washington, Washington, D.C.

Morris, J. N.
1986   *Monitoring and Excavation at Aulston Pueblo (Site 5MT2433), a Pueblo II Habitation Site.* Four Corners Archaeological Project Report, no. 6. Complete Archaeological Service Associates, Cortez, Colorado.
1988   Excavations at Weasel Pueblo (Site 5MT5106), a Pueblo I–Pueblo III Multiple-Occupation Site. In *Dolores Archaeological Program: Anasazi Communities at Dolores: McPhee Village,* compiled by A. E. Kane and C. K. Robinson, pp. 664–787. Bureau of Reclamation, Engineering and Research Center, Denver.
1991   *Archaeological Excavations on the Hovenweep Laterals.* Four Corners Archaeological Project Report, no. 16. Complete Archaeological Service Associates, Cortez, Colorado.

Muller, J. D.
1979   Structural Studies of Art Styles. In *The Visual Arts,* edited by J. M. Cordwell, pp. 139–211. Mouton, The Hague.

Munn, N. D.
1986   *Walbiri Iconography: Graphic Representation and*

Cultural Symbolism in a Central Australian Society. 2nd ed. University of Chicago Press, Chicago.

Murdock, G. P., and C. Provost
1973 Factors in the Division of Labor by Sex: A Cross-Cultural Analysis. *Ethnology* 12:203–225.

Naroll, R.
1956 A Preliminary Index of Social Development. *American Anthropologist* 56:687–715.

Neff, H.
1989 The Effect of Interregional Distribution on Plumbate Pottery Production. In *Ancient Trade and Tribute,* edited by B. Voorhies, pp. 249–267. University of Utah Press, Salt Lake City.

Neff, H. (editor)
1992 *Chemical Characterizations of Ceramic Pastes in Archaeology.* Monographs in World Archaeology, no. 7. Prehistory Press, Madison, Wisconsin.

Neff, H., and M. D. Glascock
1992 The Local Economy and Regional Exchange: Early Red Ware Production in the Northern Southwest. Report on Archaeological Neutron Activation Analysis. Ms. on file, Research Reactor Facility, University of Missouri, Columbia.

Neily, R. B.
1983 *The Prehistoric Community on the Colorado Plateau: An Approach to the Study of Change and Survival in the Northern San Juan Area of the American Southwest.* Ph.D. dissertation, Southern Illinois University. University Microfilms, Ann Arbor.

Nelson, G. C., and A. E. Kane
1986 Excavations at Singing Shelter (Site 5MT4683), a Multicomponent Site. In *Dolores Archaeological Program: Anasazi Communities at Dolores: Middle Canyon Area,* compiled by A. E. Kane and C. K. Robinson, pp. 858–1047. Bureau of Reclamation, Engineering and Research Center, Denver.

Nelson, S. M.
1990 Diversity of the Upper Paleolithic "Venus" Figurines and Archaeological Mythology. In *Powers of Observation: Alternative Views in Archaeology,* edited by S. M. Nelson and A. B. Kehoe. Anthropological Papers, no. 2. American Anthropological Association, Washington, D.C.

Neusius, P. D.
1988 Functional Analysis of Selected Flaked Lithic Assemblages from the Dolores River Valley: A Low-Power Microwear Approach. In *Dolores Archaeological Program: Supporting Studies: Additive and Reductive Technologies,* compiled by E. Blinman, C. J. Phagan, and R. H. Wilshusen, pp. 209–282. Bureau of Reclamation, Engineering and Research Center, Denver.

Nichols, D. L., and S. Powell
1987 Demographic Reconstructions in the American Southwest: Alternative Behavioral Means to the Same Archaeological Ends. *The Kiva* 52:193–207.

Nichols, D. L., and F. E. Smiley (editors)
1984 *Excavations on Black Mesa, 1982: A Descriptive Report.* Center for Archaeological Investigations Research Paper, no. 39. Southern Illinois University, Carbondale.

Nordenskiöld, G.
1979 *The Cliff Dwellers of the Mesa Verde, Southwestern Colorado: Their Pottery and Implements.* Translated by D. L. Morgan. Reprinted. Rio Grande Press, Glorieta, New Mexico. Originally published 1893, P. A. Norstedt and Söner, Stockholm.

Olsson, G.
1970 Explanation, Prediction, and Meaning Variance: An Assessment of Distance Interaction Models. *Economic Geography* 46:223–233.

Olszewski, D. I.
1984 Arizona D:11:2023. In *Excavations on Black Mesa, 1982: A Descriptive Report,* edited by D. L. Nichols and F. E. Smiley, pp. 183–192. Center for Archaeological Investigations Research Paper, no. 39. Southern Illinois University, Carbondale.

Olszewski, D. I., M. C. Trachte, and R. M. Kohl
1984 Arizona D:11:2027. In *Excavations on Black Mesa, 1982: A Descriptive Report,* edited by D. L. Nichols and F. E. Smiley, pp. 209–222. Center for Archaeological Investigations Research Paper, no. 39. Southern Illinois University, Carbondale.

Orcutt, J. D.
1986 Settlement Behavior Modeling Synthesis. In *Dolores Archaeological Program: Final Synthetic Report,* compiled by D. A. Breternitz, C. K. Robinson, and G. T. Gross, pp. 539–576. Bureau of Reclamation, Engineering and Research Center, Denver.

Orcutt, J. D., and E. Blinman
1987 Leadership and the Development of Social Complexity: A Case Study from the Dolores Area of the American Southwest. Ms. in possession of authors.

Orcutt, J. D., E. Blinman, and T. A. Kohler
1990 Explanations of Population Aggregation in the Mesa Verde Region Prior to A.D. 900. In *Perspectives on Southwestern Prehistory,* edited by P. E. Minnis and C. L. Redman, pp. 196–212. Westview Press, Boulder, Colorado.

Ortner, S. B.
1978 *Sherpas Through Their Rituals.* Cambridge University Press, Cambridge.
1984 Theory in Anthropology Since the Sixties.

Comparative Studies in Society and History 14:126–166.

Osborn, A.
1989   Multiculturalism in the Eastern Andes. In *Archaeological Approaches to Cultural Identity*, edited by S. J. Shennan, pp. 141–156. Unwin Hyman, London.

O'Shea, J. M.
1981   Coping with Scarcity: Exchange and Social Storage. In *Economic Archaeology: Towards an Integration of Ecological and Social Approaches*, edited by A. Sheridan and G. N. Baily, pp. 167–183. International Series, no. 96. British Archaeological Reports, Oxford.

Parry, W. J., and A. L. Christenson
1987   *Prehistoric Stone Technology on Northern Black Mesa, Arizona*. Center for Archaeological Investigations Occasional Paper, no. 12. Southern Illinois University, Carbondale.

Peacock, D. P. S.
1981   Archaeology, Ethnology and Ceramic Production. In *Production and Distribution: A Ceramic Viewpoint*, edited by H. Howard and E. Morris, pp. 187–194. International Series, no. 120. British Archaeological Reports, Oxford.
1982   *Pottery in the Roman World: An Ethnoarchaeological Approach*. Longmans, London.

Peet, R. K.
1974   The Measurement of Species Diversity. *Annual Review of Ecology and Systematics* 5:285–307.

Perlman, I., and F. Asaro
1969   Pottery Analysis by Neutron Activation. *Archaeometry* 11:21–52.

Petersen, K. L.
1986   Resource Studies. In *Dolores Archaeological Program: Final Synthetic Report*, compiled by D. A. Breternitz, C. K. Robinson, and G. T. Gross, pp. 469–491. Bureau of Reclamation, Engineering and Research Center, Denver.
1987   Summer Warmth: A Critical Factor for the Dolores Anasazi. In *Dolores Archaeological Program: Supporting Studies: Settlement and Environment*, compiled by K. L. Petersen and J. D. Orcutt, pp. 60–71. Bureau of Reclamation, Engineering and Research Center, Denver.
1988   *Climate and the Dolores River Anasazi: A Paleoenvironmental Reconstruction from a 10,000-Year Pollen Record, La Plata Mountains, Southwestern Colorado*. Anthropological Papers, no. 113. University of Utah, Salt Lake City.

Petersen, K. L., M. H. Matthews, and S. W. Neusius
1986   Environmental Archaeology. In *Dolores Archaeological Program: Final Synthetic Report*, compiled

by D. A. Breternitz, C. K. Robinson, and G. T. Gross, pp. 149–349. Bureau of Reclamation, Engineering and Research Center, Denver.

Petersen, K. L., and J. D. Orcutt (compilers)
1987   *Dolores Archaeological Program: Supporting Studies: Settlement and Environment*. Bureau of Reclamation, Engineering and Research Center, Denver.

Phagan, C. J.
1986   Technology: Lithic Tools. In *Dolores Archaeological Program: Final Synthetic Report*, compiled by D. A. Breternitz, C. K. Robinson, and G. T. Gross, pp. 578–594. Bureau of Reclamation, Engineering and Research Center, Denver.

Phagan, C. J., and T. H. Hruby
1988   Reductive Technologies at McPhee Village. In *Dolores Archaeological Program: Anasazi Communities at Dolores: McPhee Village*, compiled by A. E. Kane and C. K. Robinson, pp. 1345–1390. Bureau of Reclamation, Engineering and Research Center, Denver.

Pielou, E. C.
1975   *Ecological Diversity*. John Wiley and Sons, New York.

Plog, F.
1974   *The Study of Prehistoric Change*. Academic Press, New York.
1983   Political and Economic Alliances on the Colorado Plateaus, A.D. 400–1450. In *Advances in World Archaeology*, vol. 2, edited by F. Wendorf and A. Close, pp. 289–330. Academic Press, New York.

Plog, S.
1976   Measurement of Prehistoric Interaction Between Communities. In *The Early Mesoamerican Village*, edited by K. V. Flannery, pp. 255–272. Academic Press, New York.
1978   Social Interaction and Stylistic Similarity: A Reanalysis. In *Advances in Archaeological Method and Theory*, vol. 1, edited by M. B. Schiffer, pp. 143–182. Academic Press, New York.
1980a   *Stylistic Variation in Prehistoric Ceramics: Design Analysis in the American Southwest*. Cambridge University Press, Cambridge.
1980b   Village Autonomy in the American Southwest: An Evaluation of the Evidence. In *Models and Methods of Regional Exchange*, edited by R. E. Fry, pp. 135–146. SAA Papers, no. 1. Society for American Archaeology, Washington, D.C.
1982   Settlement Types, Sedentism, and Culture Change on Northern Black Mesa. Paper presented at the Advanced Seminar on Black Mesa, Arizona, School of American Research, Santa Fe.

1983 Analysis of Style in Artifacts. *Annual Review of Anthropology* 12:125–142.

1989a Ritual, Exchange, and the Development of Regional Systems. In *The Architecture of Social Integration in Prehistoric Pueblos,* edited by W. D. Lipe and M. Hegmon, pp. 143–154. Occasional Papers, no. 1. Crow Canyon Archaeological Center, Cortez, Colorado.

1989b The Sociopolitics of Exchange (and Archaeological Research) in the Northern Southwest. In *The Sociopolitical Structure of Prehistoric Southwestern Societies,* edited by S. Upham, K. G. Lightfoot, and R. A. Jewett, pp. 129–148. Westview Press, Boulder, Colorado.

1990a Agriculture, Sedentism, and Environment in the Evolution of Political Systems. In *The Evolution of Political Systems: Sociopolitics in Small-Scale Sedentary Societies,* edited by S. Upham, pp. 177–199. Cambridge University Press, Cambridge.

1990b Sociopolitical Implications of Stylistic Variation in the American Southwest. In *Uses of Style in Archaeology,* edited by M. W. Conkey and C. A. Hastorf, pp. 61–72. Cambridge University Press, Cambridge.

1995 Approaches to Style: Complements and Contrasts. In *Style, Society, and Person,* edited by C. Carr and J. Neitzel, pp. 369–387. Plenum Press, New York.

Plog, S. (editor)
1986 *Spatial Organization and Exchange: Archaeological Survey on Northern Black Mesa.* Southern Illinois University Press, Carbondale.

Plog, S., and J. L. Hantman
1986 Multiple Regression Analysis as a Dating Method in the American Southwest. In *Spatial Organization and Exchange: Archaeological Survey on Northern Black Mesa,* edited by S. Plog, pp. 87–113. Southern Illinois University Press, Carbondale.

Plog, S., and M. Hegmon
1993 The Sample Size–Richness Relationship: The Relevance of Research Questions, Sampling Strategies, and Behavioral Variation. *American Antiquity,* in press.

Pollock, S.
1983a Style and Information: An Analysis of Susiana Ceramics. *Journal of Anthropological Archaeology* 2:354–390.

1983b *The Symbolism of Prestige: An Archaeological Example from the Royal Cemetery of Ur.* Ph.D. dissertation, University of Michigan. University Microfilms, Ann Arbor.

Powell, S. L.
1983 *Mobility and Adaptation: The Anasazi of Black Mesa, Arizona.* Southern Illinois University Press, Carbondale.

Powell, S. L. (editor)
1984 *Excavations on Black Mesa, 1971–1976: A Descriptive Report.* Center for Archaeological Investigations Research Paper, no. 48. Southern Illinois University, Carbondale.

Powell, S. L., P. P. Andrews, D. L. Nichols, and F. E. Smiley
1983 Fifteen Years on the Rock: Archaeological Research, Administration, and Compliance on Black Mesa, Arizona. *American Antiquity* 48:228–252.

Poyer, L.
1991 Maintaining Egalitarianism: Social Equality on a Micronesian Atoll. In *Between Bands and States,* edited by S. A. Gregg, pp. 359–375. Center for Archaeological Investigations Occasional Paper, no. 9. Southern Illinois University, Carbondale.

Preucel, R. W.
1988 *Seasonal Agricultural Circulation and Residential Mobility: A Prehistoric Example from the Pajarito Plateau, New Mexico.* Unpublished Ph.D. dissertation, Department of Anthropology, University of California, Los Angeles.

Preucel, R. W. (editor)
1991 *Processual and Postprocessual Archaeologies: Multiple Ways of Knowing the Past.* Center for Archaeological Investigations Occasional Paper, no. 10. Southern Illinois University, Carbondale.

Prudden, T. M.
1903 The Prehistoric Ruins of the San Juan Watershed in Utah, Arizona, Colorado, and New Mexico. *American Anthropologist* 5:224–288.

1918 *A Further Study of Prehistoric Small House Ruins in the San Juan Watershed.* Memoirs, vol. 5, no. 1. American Anthropological Association, Lancaster, Pennsylvania.

Rafferty, J. E.
1985 The Archaeological Record on Sedentariness: Recognition, Development, and Implications. In *Advances in Archaeological Method and Theory,* vol. 8, edited by M. B. Schiffer, pp. 113–156. Academic Press, New York.

Rapoport, A.
1982 *The Meaning of the Built Environment: A Nonverbal Communication Approach.* Sage Publications, Beverly Hills.

Rappaport, R. A.
1971a Ritual, Sanctity, and Cybernetics. *American Anthropologist* 73:59–76.

1971b The Sacred in Human Evolution. *Annual Review of Anthropology* 2:23–44.

1979 *Ecology, Meaning, and Religion.* North Atlantic Books, Richmond, California.

1984 *Pigs for the Ancestors: Ritual in the Ecology of a New Guinea People.* 2nd ed. Yale University Press, New Haven.

Redman, C. L.
1978 Multivariate Artifact Analysis: A Basis for Multidimensional Interpretations. In *Social Archaeology: Beyond Subsistence and Dating,* edited by C. L. Redman, M. J. Berman, E. V. Curtin, W. T. Langhorne, Jr., N. M. Versaggi, and J. C. Wanser, pp. 349–372. Academic Press, New York.

Reed, A. D.
1979 The Dominguez Ruin: A McElmo Phase Pueblo in Southwestern Colorado. In *The Archeology and Stabilization of the Dominguez and Escalante Ruins,* authored by A. D. Reed, J. A. Hallasi, A. S. White, and D. A. Breternitz, pp. i–196. Cultural Resource Series, no. 7. Bureau of Land Management, Colorado State Office, Denver.

Reed, A. D., W. K. Howell, P. R. Nickens, and J. C. Horn
1985 *Archaeological Investigations on the Johnson Canyon Road Project, Ute Mountain Ute Tribal Lands, Colorado.* Nickens and Associates, Montrose, Colorado. Report submitted to the Bureau of Indian Affairs, Albuquerque Area Office, Albuquerque.

Reed, E. K.
1958 *Excavations in Mancos Canyon, Colorado.* Anthropological Papers, no. 35. University of Utah, Salt Lake City.

Reina, R., and J. Hill
1978 *The Traditional Pottery of Guatemala.* University of Texas Press, Austin.

Rhode, D.
1988 Measurement of Archaeological Diversity and the Sample-Size Effect. *American Antiquity* 53:708–716.

Rice, P. M.
1981 Evolution of Specialized Pottery Production: A Trial Model. *Current Anthropology* 22:219–240.

1987 *Pottery Analysis: A Sourcebook.* University of Chicago Press, Chicago.

1989 Ceramic Diversity, Production, and Use. In *Quantifying Diversity in Archaeology,* edited by R. D. Leonard and G. T. Jones, pp. 109–117. Cambridge University Press, Cambridge.

Roberts, F. H. H., Jr.
1929 *Shabik'eshchee Village: A Late Basket Maker Site in the Chaco Canyon, New Mexico.* Bureau of American Ethnology Bulletin, no. 92. Smithsonian Institution, Washington, D.C.

1930 *Early Pueblo Ruins in the Piedra District, Southwestern Colorado.* Bureau of American Ethnology Bulletin, no. 96. Smithsonian Institution, Washington, D.C.

1931 *The Ruins at Kiatuthlanna.* Bureau of American Ethnology Bulletin, no. 100. Smithsonian Institution, Washington, D.C.

1939 The Development of a Unit-Type Dwelling. In *So Live the Works of Man,* edited by D. D. Brand and F. E. Harvey, pp. 311–323. University of New Mexico Press, Albuquerque.

Robinson, C. K., and J. M. Brisbin
1986 Excavations at House Creek Village (Site 5MT2320), a Pueblo I Habitation. In *Dolores Archaeological Program: Anasazi Communities at Dolores: Middle Canyon Area,* compiled by A. E. Kane and C. K. Robinson, pp. 661–855. Bureau of Reclamation, Engineering and Research Center, Denver.

Robinson, C. K., G. T. Gross, and D. A. Breternitz
1986 Overview of the Dolores Archaeological Program. In *Dolores Archaeological Program: Final Synthetic Report,* compiled by D. A. Breternitz, C. K. Robinson, and G. T. Gross, pp. 3–50. Bureau of Reclamation, Engineering and Research Center, Denver.

Robinson, W. S.
1951 A Method for Chronological Ordering of Archaeological Deposits. *American Antiquity* 16:293–301.

Rohn, A. H.
1971 *Mug House, Mesa Verde National Park, Colorado.* Archeological Research Series, no. 7-D. National Park Service, Washington, D.C.

1977 *Cultural Change and Continuity on Chapin Mesa.* Regents Press of Kansas, Lawrence.

1989 Northern San Juan Prehistory. In *Dynamics of Southwest Prehistory,* edited by L. S. Cordell and G. J. Gumerman, pp. 149–177. Smithsonian Institution Press, Washington, D.C.

Rye, O. S.
1976 Keeping Your Temper Under Control: Materials and the Manufacture of Papuan Pottery. *Archaeology and Physical Anthropology in Oceania* 11:106–137.

1981 *Pottery Technology: Principles and Reconstruction.* Manuals on Archaeology, 4. Taraxacum, Washington, D.C.

Sackett, J. R.
1973 Style, Function and Artifact Variability in Palaeolithic Assemblages. In *The Explanation of Cul-*

ture Change, edited by C. Renfrew, pp. 317–328. Duckworth, London.

1977 The Meaning of Style in Archaeology: A General Model. *American Antiquity* 42:369–380.

1982 Approaches to Style in Lithic Archaeology. *Journal of Anthropological Archaeology* 1:59–112.

1985 Style and Ethnicity in the Kalahari: A Reply to Weissner. *American Antiquity* 50:154–159.

1986 Isochrestism and Style: A Clarification. *Journal of Anthropological Archaeology* 5:266–277.

1990 Style and Ethnicity in Archaeology: The Case for Isochrestism. In *Uses of Style in Archaeology,* edited by M. W. Conkey and C. A. Hastorf, pp. 32–43. Cambridge University Press, Cambridge.

Sahlins, M. D.
1968 *Tribesmen.* Prentice-Hall, Englewood Cliffs, New Jersey.

1972 *Stone Age Economics.* Aldine, Chicago.

Sampson, C. G.
1988 *Stylistic Boundaries Among Mobile Hunter-Foragers.* Smithsonian Institution Press, Washington, D.C.

Schiffer, M. B.
1989 Formation Processes of Broken K Pueblo: Some Hypotheses. In *Quantifying Diversity in Archaeology,* edited by R. D. Leonard and G. T. Jones, pp. 37–58. Cambridge University Press, Cambridge.

Schiffer, M. B., and J. M. Skibo
1987 Theory and Experiment in the Study of Technological Change. *Current Anthropology* 28:595–622.

Schlanger, S. H.
1986 Population Studies. In *Dolores Archaeological Program: Final Synthetic Report,* compiled by D. A. Breternitz, C. K. Robinson, and G. T. Gross, pp. 493–524. Bureau of Reclamation, Engineering and Research Center, Denver.

1987 Population Measurement, Size, and Change, A.D. 600–1175. In *Dolores Archaeological Program: Supporting Studies: Settlement and Environment,* compiled by K. L. Petersen and J. D. Orcutt, pp. 568–613. Bureau of Reclamation, Engineering and Research Center, Denver.

1988 Patterns of Population Movement and Long-Term Population Growth in Southwestern Colorado. *American Antiquity* 53:773–793.

1992 Places for the Living, Places for the Dead: Mortuary Variability in the Northern Southwest. Ms. on file, Office of Archaeological Studies, Museum of New Mexico, Santa Fe.

Schlanger, S. H., and R. H. Wilshusen
1993 Local Abandonments and Regional Conditions in the North American Southwest. In *Abandonment of Settlements and Regions: Ethnoarchaeological and Archaeological Approaches,* edited by C. M. Cameron and S. A. Tomka, pp. 85–98. Cambridge University Press, Cambridge.

Schortman, E. M.
1989 Interregional Interaction in Prehistory: The Need for a New Perspective. *American Antiquity* 54:52–65.

Sebastian, L.
1985 *Archaeological Investigations Along the Turquoise Trail: The Mitigation Program,* vol. II. Office of Contract Archaeology, University of New Mexico, Albuquerque.

1986 Excavations at Prince Hamlet (Site 5MT2161), a Pueblo I Habitation Site. In *Dolores Archaeological Program: Anasazi Communities at Dolores: Early Small Settlements in the Dolores River Canyon and Western Sagehen Flats Area,* compiled by T. A. Kohler, W. D. Lipe, and A. E. Kane, pp. 333–496. Bureau of Reclamation, Engineering and Research Center, Denver.

Service, E. R.
1971 *Primitive Social Organization: An Evolutionary Perspective.* 2nd ed. Random House, New York.

Shanks, M., and C. Tilley
1987a *Reconstructing Archaeology: Theory and Practice.* Cambridge University Press, Cambridge.

1987b *Social Theory and Archaeology.* Polity Press, England.

Shannon, C. E., and W. E. Weaver
1949 *The Mathematical Theory of Communication.* University of Illinois Press, Urbana.

Shapiro, M.
1953 Style. In *Anthropology Today,* edited by A. L. Kroeber, pp. 287–312. Aldine, Chicago.

Shennan, S. J. (editor)
1989 *Archaeological Approaches to Cultural Identity.* Unwin Hyman, London, England.

Shepard, A. O.
1939 Technology of La Plata Pottery. In *Archaeological Studies in the La Plata District: Southwestern Colorado and Northwestern New Mexico,* authored by E. H. Morris, pp. 249–287. Publication, no. 519. Carnegie Institution of Washington, Washington, D.C.

1942 *Rio Grande Glaze Paint Ware.* Contributions to American Anthropology and History, vol. 7, no. 39. Carnegie Institution of Washington, Washington, D.C.

1948   *The Symmetry of Abstract Design with Special Reference to Ceramic Decoration.* Publication, no. 574. Carnegie Institution of Washington, Washington, D.C.

1965   *Ceramics for the Archaeologist.* Publication, no. 609. Carnegie Institution of Washington, Washington, D.C.

Shott, M. J.
1989   Diversity, Organization, and Behavior in the Material Record. *Current Anthropology* 30:283–315.

Siegel, S.
1956   *Nonparametric Statistics for the Behavioral Sciences.* McGraw-Hill, New York.

Silberbauer, G.
1982   Political Process in G\wi Bands. In *Politics and History in Band Society,* edited by E. Leacock and R. Lee, pp. 23–35. Cambridge University Press, Cambridge.

Sinopoli, C. M.
1991   *Approaches to Archaeological Ceramics.* Plenum Press, New York.

Skibo, J. M., M. B. Schiffer, and N. Kowalski
1989   Ceramic Style Analysis in Archaeology and Ethnoarchaeology: Bridging the Analytical Gap. *Journal of Anthropological Archaeology* 8:388–409.

Smiley, F. E., and R. V. N. Ahlstrom
1994   *Archaeological Chronometry: Radiocarbon and Tree-Ring Models and Applications from Black Mesa.* Center for Archaeological Investigations Occasional Paper, no. 16. Southern Illinois University, Carbondale, in press.

Smiley, F. E., D. L. Nichols, and P. P. Andrews (editors)
1983   *Excavations on Black Mesa, 1981: A Descriptive Report.* Center for Archaeological Investigations Research Paper, no. 36. Southern Illinois University, Carbondale.

Smith, M. F., Jr.
1985   Toward an Economic Interpretation of Ceramics: Relating Vessel Size and Shape to Use. In *Decoding Prehistoric Ceramics,* edited by B. A. Nelson, pp. 254–309. Southern Illinois University Press, Carbondale.

Smith, W.
1962   Schools, Pots, and Potters. *American Anthropologist* 64:1165–1178.

Spaulding, A. C.
1982   Structure in Archaeological Data: Nominal Variables. In *Essays on Archaeological Typology,* edited by R. Whallon and J. A. Brown, pp. 1–20. Center for American Archaeology Press, Evanston, Illinois.

Stanislawski, M. B.
1973   Review of *Archaeology as Anthropology: A Case Study,* by W. A. Longacre. *American Antiquity* 38:117–121.

Stanislawski, M. B., and B. B. Stanislawski
1978   Hopi and Hopi-Tewa Ceramic Tradition Networks. In *The Spatial Organization of Culture,* edited by I. Hodder, pp. 61–76. University of Pittsburgh Press, Pittsburgh.

Stark, B.
1981   The Rise of Sedentary Life. In *Supplement to the Handbook of Middle American Indians,* edited by J. A. Sabloff, pp. 345–373. University of Texas Press, Austin.

1985   Archaeological Identification of Pottery-Production Locations: Ethnoarchaeological and Archaeological Data in Mesoamerica. In *Decoding Prehistoric Ceramics,* edited by B. A. Nelson, pp. 158–194. Southern Illinois University Press, Carbondale.

Stark, M. T., and W. A. Longacre
1993   Kalinga Ceramics and New Technologies: Social and Cultural Contexts of Ceramic Change. In *The Social and Cultural Contexts of New Ceramic Technologies,* edited by W. D. Kingery, pp. 1–32. The American Ceramic Society, Westerville, Ohio.

Steen, C. R.
1966   *Excavations at Tse-Ta'a, Canyon de Chelly National Monument, Arizona.* Archaeology Research Series, no. 9. National Park Service, Washington, D.C.

Sterner, J.
1989   Who is Signalling Whom? Ceramic Style, Ethnicity and Taphonomy Among the Sirak Bulahay. *Antiquity* 63:451–459.

Stevenson, M. C.
1904   The Zuñi Indians: Their Mythology, Esoteric Fraternities, and Ceremonies. In *Twenty-Third Annual Report of the Bureau of American Ethnology, 1901–1902,* pp. 3–634. Smithsonian Institution, Washington, D.C.

Stodder, A. W.
1987   The Physical Anthropology and Mortuary Practice of the Dolores Anasazi: An Early Pueblo Population in Local and Regional Context. In *Dolores Archaeological Program: Supporting Studies: Settlement and Environment,* compiled by K. L. Petersen and J. D. Orcutt, pp. 336–504. Bureau of Reclamation, Engineering and Research Center, Denver.

Stone, G. D.
1984   Arizona D:11:2025. In *Excavations on Black Mesa, 1982: A Descriptive Report,* edited by D. L. Nichols and F. E. Smiley, pp. 193–208. Center for

Archaeological Investigations Research Paper, no. 39. Southern Illinois University, Carbondale.

Strathern, A.
1971 *The Rope of Moka.* Cambridge University Press, Cambridge.

Strathern, A., and M. Strathern
1971 *Self-Decoration in Mount Hagen.* University of Toronto Press, Toronto.

Sullivan, A. P.
1988 Prehistoric Southwestern Ceramic Manufacture: The Limitations of Current Evidence. *American Antiquity* 53:23–35.

Sullivan, A. P., and J. L. Hantman (editors)
1984 *Regional Analysis of Prehistoric Ceramic Variation: Contemporary Studies of the Cibola Whitewares.* Anthropological Research Papers, no. 31. Arizona State University, Tempe.

Swedlund, A. C., and S. E. Sessions
1976 A Developmental Model of Prehistoric Population Growth on Black Mesa, Northeastern Arizona. In *Papers on the Archaeology of Black Mesa, Arizona,* edited by G. J. Gumerman and R. C. Euler, pp. 136–148. Southern Illinois University Press, Carbondale.

Swink, C.
1993 Limited Oxidation Firing of Organic Painted Pottery in Anasazi-Style Trench Kilns. *Pottery Southwest* 20(1–4):1–5.

Tajfel, H. (editor)
1978 *Differentiation Between Social Groups.* Academic Press, New York.

Thompson, C., J. R. Allison, S. A. Baker, J. C. Janetski, B. Loosle, and J. D. Wilde
1988 *The Nancy Patterson Village Archaeological Research Project: Field Year 1986—Preliminary Report No. 4.* Technical Series, no. 87-24. Brigham Young University Museum of Peoples and Cultures, Provo, Utah.

Thompson, R. F.
1974 *African Art in Motion.* University of California Press, Berkeley.

Tilley, C.
1982 Social Formation, Social Structures, and Social Change. In *Symbolic and Structural Archaeology,* edited by I. Hodder, pp. 26–38. Cambridge University Press, Cambridge.

Toll, H. W.
1981 Ceramic Comparisons Concerning Redistribution in Chaco Canyon, New Mexico. In *Production and Distribution: A Ceramic Viewpoint,* edited by H. Howard and E. L. Morris, pp. 83–121. Interna-

tional Series, no. 120. British Archaeological Reports, Oxford.
1985 *Pottery, Production, Public Architecture, and the Chaco System.* Unpublished Ph.D. dissertation, Department of Anthropology, University of Colorado, Boulder.
1991 Material Distributions and Exchange in the Chaco System. In *Chaco and Hohokam: Prehistoric Regional Systems in the American Southwest,* edited by P. L. Crown and W. J. Judge, pp. 77–107. School of American Research Press, Santa Fe.

Toll, H. W., T. C. Windes, and P. J. McKenna
1980 Late Ceramic Patterns in Chaco Canyon: The Pragmatics of Modeling Ceramic Exchange. In *Models and Methods in Regional Exchange,* edited by R. E. Fry, pp. 98–117. SAA Papers, no. 1. Society for American Archaeology, Washington, D.C.

Travis, S. E.
1984 Modeling Levels of Socioeconomic Interaction Within the Dolores River Valley: A Tentative Assessment. In *Dolores Archaeological Program: Synthetic Report, 1978–1981,* prepared under the supervision of D. A. Breternitz, pp. 105–128. Bureau of Reclamation, Engineering and Research Center, Denver.

Trigger, B. G.
1989 *A History of Archaeological Thought.* Cambridge University Press, Cambridge.
1990a Maintaining Economic Equality in Opposition to Complexity: An Iroquoian Case Study. In *The Evolution of Political Systems: Sociopolitics in Small-Scale Sedentary Societies,* edited by S. Upham, pp. 119–145. Cambridge University Press, Cambridge.
1990b Monumental Architecture: A Thermodynamic Explanation of Symbolic Behavior. *World Archaeology* 22:119–132.

Tuggle, H. D.
1970 *Prehistoric Community Relations in East-Central Arizona.* Ph.D. dissertation, University of Arizona. University Microfilms, Ann Arbor.

Turner, C. G., II, and L. Lofgren
1966 Household Size of Prehistoric Western Pueblo Indians. *Southwestern Journal of Anthropology* 22:117–132.

Turner, V.
1969 *The Ritual Process.* Aldine, Chicago.

Tweto, O.
1979 Geologic map of Colorado. United States Geologic Service, Washington, D.C.

Upham, S.
1982 *Polities and Power: An Economic and Political*

History of the Western Pueblo. Academic Press, New York.

1987 A Theoretical Consideration of Middle Range Societies. In *Archaeological Reconstructions and Chiefdoms in the Americas,* edited by R. Drennan and C. Uribe, pp. 345–368. University Press of America, New York.

1990 Analog or Digital?: Toward a Generic Framework for Explaining the Development of Emergent Political Systems. In *The Evolution of Political Systems: Sociopolitics in Small-Scale Sedentary Societies,* edited by S. Upham, pp. 87–115. Cambridge University Press, Cambridge.

van der Leeuw, S. E.
1977 Towards a Study of the Economics of Pottery Making. *Ex Horreo* 4:68–76.
1984 Pottery Manufacture: Some Complications for the Study of Trade. In *Pots and Potters: Current Approaches in Ceramic Archaeology,* edited by P. M. Rice, pp. 55–69. Monograph, no. 24. UCLA Institute of Archaeology, Los Angeles.

Vansina, J.
1978 *The Children of Woot: A History of the Kuba Peoples.* University of Wisconsin Press, Madison.

Van West, C. R.
1990 *Modeling Prehistoric Climatic Variability and Agricultural Production in Southwestern Colorado: A GIS Approach.* Unpublished Ph.D. dissertation, Department of Anthropology, Washington State University, Pullman.

Van West, C. R., and W. D. Lipe
1992 Modeling Prehistoric Climate and Agriculture in Southwestern Colorado. In *The Sand Canyon Archaeological Project: A Progress Report,* edited by W. D. Lipe, pp. 105–119. Occasional Papers, no. 2. Crow Canyon Archaeological Center, Cortez, Colorado.

Veblen, T.
1953 *The Theory of the Leisure Class: An Economic Study of Institutions.* Reprinted. New American Library, New York. Originally published 1899, MacMillan.

Vivian, G., and P. Reiter
1965 *The Great Kivas of Chaco Canyon and Their Relationships.* University of New Mexico Press, Albuquerque.

Vivian, R. G.
1990 *The Chacoan Prehistory of the San Juan Basin.* Academic Press, New York.

Voss, J. A.
1980 *Tribal Emergence During the Neolithic of North-*

western Europe. Ph.D. dissertation, University of Michigan. University Microfilms, Ann Arbor.

Wallace, A. F. C.
1966 *Religion: An Anthropological View.* Random House, New York.

Washburn, D. K.
1977 *A Symmetry Analysis of Upper Gila Area Ceramic Design.* Papers of the Peabody Museum of American Archaeology and Ethnology, vol. 68. Harvard University, Cambridge.
1983a Symmetry Analysis of Ceramic Design: Two Tests of the Method on Neolithic Material from Greece and Spain. In *Structure and Cognition in Art,* edited by D. K. Washburn, pp. 138–164. Cambridge University Press, Cambridge.
1983b Toward a Theory of Structural Style in Art. In *Structure and Cognition in Art,* edited by D. K. Washburn, pp. 1–7. Cambridge University Press, Cambridge.
1989 The Property of Symmetry and the Concept of Ethnic Style. In *Archaeological Approaches to Cultural Identity,* edited by S. J. Shennan, pp. 157–173. Unwin Hyman, London.

Washburn, D. K., and D. Crowe
1987 *Symmetries of Culture: Theory and Practice of Plane Pattern Analysis.* University of Washington Press, Seattle.

Wasley, W. W.
1959 *Cultural Implications of Style Trends in Southwestern Prehistoric Pottery.* Ph.D. dissertation, University of Arizona. University Microfilms, Ann Arbor.

Waterworth, R. M. R., and E. Blinman
1986 Modified Sherds, Unidirectional Abrasion, and Pottery Scrapers. *Pottery Southwest* 13(2):4–7.

Watson, P. J.
1986 Archaeological Interpretation, 1985. In *American Archaeology Past and Future: A Celebration of the Society for American Archaeology, 1935–1985,* edited by D. J. Meltzer, D. D. Fowler, and J. A. Sabloff, pp. 439–457. Smithsonian Institution Press, Washington, D.C.

Weissner, P.
1982a Beyond Willow Smoke and Dogs' Tails: A Comment on Binford's Analysis of Hunter-Gatherer Settlement Systems. *American Antiquity* 47:171–178.
1982b Risk, Reciprocity, and Social Influence on !Kung San Economics. In *Politics and History in Band Societies,* edited by E. Leacock and R. Lee, pp. 61–84. Cambridge University Press, Cambridge.
1983 Style and Social Information in Kalahari San Projectile Points. *American Antiquity* 48:253–276.

1984 Reconsidering the Behavioral Basis of Style: A Case Study Among the Kalahari San. *Journal of Anthropological Archaeology* 3:190–234.
1985 Style or Isochrestic Variation? A Reply to Sackett. *American Antiquity* 50:160–166.
1989 Style and Changing Relations Between the Individual and Society. In *The Meaning of Things: Material Culture and Symbolic Expression,* edited by I. Hodder, pp. 56–63. Unwin Hyman, London.
1990 Is There a Unity to Style? In *Uses of Style in Archaeology,* edited by M. W. Conkey and C. A. Hastorf, pp. 105–112. Cambridge University Press, Cambridge.

Welbourn, A.
1984 Endo Ceramics and Power Strategies. In *Ideology, Power and Prehistory,* edited by D. Miller and C. Tilley, pp. 17–24. Cambridge University Press, Cambridge.

Whallon, R.
1968 Investigations of Late Prehistoric Social Organization in New York State. In *New Perspectives in Archaeology,* edited by S. R. Binford and L. R. Binford, pp. 223–244. Aldine, Chicago.

Wheat, J. B.
1955 MT-1, a Basketmaker III Site Near Yellow Jacket, Colorado (A Progress Report). *Southwestern Lore* 21:18–26.

Whiteley, P. M.
1985a Unpacking Hopi "Clans": Another Vintage Model Out of Africa? *Journal of Anthropological Research* 41:359–374.
1985b Unpacking Hopi "Clans" II: Further Questions About Hopi Descent Groups. *Journal of Anthropological Research* 42:9–79.
1988 *Deliberate Acts.* University of Arizona Press, Tucson.

Wills, W. H.
1991 Organizational Strategies and the Emergence of Prehistoric Villages in the American Southwest. In *Between Bands and States,* edited by S. A. Gregg, pp. 161–180. Center for Archaeological Investigations Occasional Paper, no. 9. Southern Illinois University, Carbondale.
1992 Foraging Systems and Plant Cultivation During the Emergence of Agricultural Economies in the Prehistoric American Southwest. In *Transitions to Agriculture in Prehistory,* edited by A. B. Gebauer and T. D. Price, pp. 153–176. Prehistory Press, Madison, Wisconsin.

Wills, W. H., and T. C. Windes
1989 Evidence for Population Aggregation and Dispersal During the Basketmaker III Period in Chaco Canyon, New Mexico. *American Antiquity* 54:347–369.

Wilshusen, R. H.
1985 *Sipapus, Ceremonial Vaults, and Foot Drums (Or, a Resounding Argument for Protokivas).* Dolores Archaeological Program Technical Reports, DAP-278. Final report submitted to the Bureau of Reclamation, Upper Colorado Region, Salt Lake City.
1986a Excavations at Periman Hamlet (Site 5MT4671), Area 1, a Pueblo I Habitation. In *Dolores Archaeological Program: Anasazi Communities at Dolores: Middle Canyon Area,* compiled by A. E. Kane and C. K. Robinson, pp. 24–208. Bureau of Reclamation, Engineering and Research Center, Denver.
1986b The Relationship Between Abandonment Mode and Ritual Use in Pueblo I Anasazi Protokivas. *Journal of Field Archaeology* 13:245–254.
1988a The Pitstructure to Pueblo Transition: An Alternative to McGuire and Schiffer's Explanation. In *Dolores Archaeological Program: Supporting Studies: Additive and Reductive Technologies,* compiled by E. Blinman, C. J. Phagan, and R. H. Wilshusen, pp. 703–708. Bureau of Reclamation, Engineering and Research Center, Denver.
1988b Sipapus, Ceremonial Vaults, and Foot Drums (Or, a Resounding Argument for Protokivas). In *Dolores Archaeological Program: Supporting Studies: Additive and Reductive Technologies,* compiled by E. Blinman, C. J. Phagan, and R. H. Wilshusen, pp. 649–671. Bureau of Reclamation, Engineering and Research Center, Denver.
1989 Unstuffing the Estufa: Ritual Floor Features in Anasazi Pit Structures and Pueblo Kivas. In *The Architecture of Social Integration in Prehistoric Pueblos,* edited by W. D. Lipe and M. Hegmon, pp. 89–111. Occasional Papers, no. 1. Crow Canyon Archaeological Center, Cortez, Colorado.
1991 *Early Villages in the American Southwest: Cross-Cultural and Archaeological Perspectives.* Ph.D. dissertation, University of Colorado. University Microfilms, Ann Arbor.

Wilshusen, R. H. (compiler)
1986 Excavations at Rio Vista Village (Site 5MT2182), a Multicomponent Pueblo I Village. In *Dolores Archaeological Program: Anasazi Communities at Dolores: Middle Canyon Area,* compiled by A. E. Kane and C. K. Robinson, pp. 210–658. Bureau of Reclamation, Engineering and Research Center, Denver.

Wilshusen, R. H., and E. Blinman
1992 Pueblo I Village Formation: A Reevaluation

of Sites Recorded by Earl Morris on Ute Mountain Ute Tribal Lands. *Kiva* 57:251–269.

Wilson, A. L.
1978   Elemental Analysis of Pottery in the Study of Its Provenance: A Review. *Journal of Archaeological Science* 5:219–236.

Wilson, C. D.
1993   The People Between: Ceramic Patterns and Interpretations of the Mogollon-Anasazi Frontier. Paper presented at the meeting of the Arizona Archaeological Council, Flagstaff, May 1993.

Wilson, C. D., and E. Blinman
1988   Identification of Non–Mesa Verde Ceramics in Dolores Archaeological Program Collections. In *Dolores Archaeological Program: Supporting Studies: Additive and Reductive Technologies,* compiled by E. Blinman, C. J. Phagan, and R. H. Wilshusen, pp. 363–374. Bureau of Reclamation, Engineering and Research Center, Denver.
1991a   Ceramic Types of the Mesa Verde Region. Handout prepared for the Colorado Council of Professional Archaeologists Ceramic Workshop, Boulder. Ms. on file, Office for Archaeological Studies, Museum of New Mexico, Santa Fe.
1991b   Changing Specialization of White Ware Manufacture in the Northern San Juan Region. Paper presented at the 56th Annual Meeting of the Society for American Archaeology, New Orleans.

Wilson, C. D., V. L. Clay, and E. Blinman
1988   Clay Resources and Resource Use. In *Dolores Archaeological Program: Supporting Studies: Additive and Reductive Technologies,* compiled by E. Blinman, C. J. Phagan, and R. H. Wilshusen, pp. 375–394. Bureau of Reclamation, Engineering and Research Center, Denver.

Wilson, P. J.
1988   *The Domestication of the Human Species.* Yale University Press, New Haven.

Winter, J. C.
1977   *Hovenweep 1976.* Archaeological Report, no. 3. San Jose State University, San Jose.

Winterhalder, B.
1990   Open Field, Common Pot: Harvest Variability and Risk Avoidance in Agricultural and Foraging Societies. In *Risk and Uncertainty in Tribal and Peasant Economies,* edited by E. Cashdan, pp. 67–87. Westview Press, Boulder, Colorado.

Wobst, H. M.
1977   Stylistic Behavior and Information Exchange. In *Papers for the Director: Research Essays in Honor of James B. Griffin,* edited by C. E. Cleland, pp. 317–342. Anthropological Papers, no. 67. Museum of Anthropology, University of Michigan, Ann Arbor.

Wolf, E. R.
1990   Distinguished Lecture: Facing Power—Old Insights, New Questions. *American Anthropologist* 92:586–596.

Woodburn, J.
1982   Egalitarian Societies. *Man* 17:431–451.

Wright, H. T. (editor)
1981   *An Early Town on the Deh Luran Plain: Excavations at Tepe Farukhabad.* Memoirs of the Museum of Anthropology, no. 13. University of Michigan, Ann Arbor.

Wright, R. P.
1986   The Boundaries of Technology and Stylistic Change. In *Ceramics and Civilization,* vol. 2, edited by W. D. Kingery, pp. 1–20. The American Ceramic Society, Columbus, Ohio.
1991   Women's Labor and Pottery Production in Prehistory. In *Engendering Archaeology: Women and Prehistory,* edited by J. M. Gero and M. W. Conkey, pp. 194–223. Basil Blackwell, Oxford.

Wyckoff, L. L.
1990   *Designs and Factions: Politics, Religion, and Ceramics on the Hopi Third Mesa.* University of New Mexico Press, Albuquerque.

Wylie, M. A.
1982   Epistemological Issues Raised by a Structuralist Archaeology. In *Symbolic and Structural Archaeology,* edited by I. Hodder, pp. 39–46. Cambridge University Press, Cambridge.